D0305417

GODS, MONGRELS
&
DEMONS

BY THE SAME AUTHOR

HISTORY

The People's War: Britain 1939–45

Revolutionary Empire: The Rise of the English-Speaking Empires from the Fifteenth Century to the 1780s

The Myth of the Blitz

Disasters and Heroes: War, Memory and Representation

EDITED

Speak for Yourself: A Mass Observation Anthology (with Dorothy Sheridan)

Time to Kill: The Soldier's Experience of World War II in the West (with Paul Addison)

LITERARY CRITICISM

Russia Discovered: Nineteenth-Century Fiction from Pushkin to Chekhov

T. S. Eliot

Byron

ESSAYS

Revolving Culture: Notes from the Scottish Republic

Scotlands of the Mind

VERSE

Waking in Waikato

Horace in Tolcross

Colours of Grief

Dipa's Bowl

ANGUS CALDER

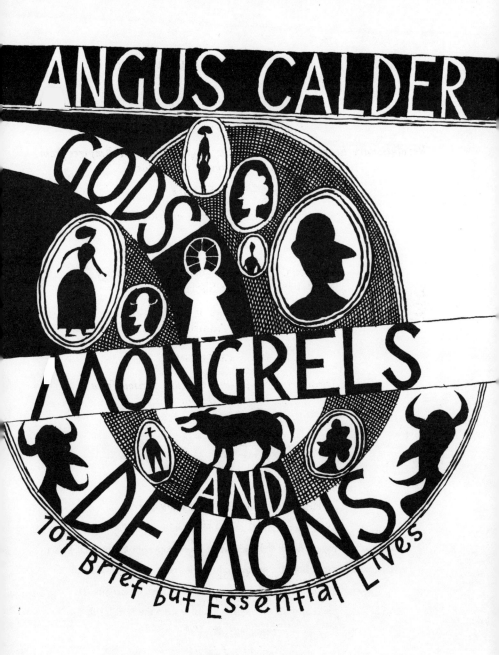

GODS MONGRELS AND DEMONS

101 Brief but Essential Lives

BLOOMSBURY

First published in Great Britain in 2003

Bloomsbury Publishing Plc, 38 Soho Square, London W1D 3HB

A CIP catalogue record for this book is available from the British Library

ISBN 0 7475 6050 1

10 9 8 7 6 5 4 3 2 1

Typeset by Palimpsest Book Production, Polmont, Stirlingshire

Printed in Great Britain by Clays Limited, St Ives plc

For Douglas William Peter Calder, *b.*1989 and
Hugh Rowell Duffield, *b.*2003
May their lives be enjoyably alternative

World is crazier and more of it than we think,
Incorrigibly plural. I peel and portion
A tangerine and spit the pips and feel
The drunkenness of things being various.

Louis MacNeice, 'Snow', January 1935

INTRODUCTION

At a late stage of my work on this odd book, my friend Sally Evans, who with her husband Ian King ran till lately the bookshop on the corner of my street, drew my attention to a recent acquisition which she thought might interest me. I duly purchased and surveyed *A Clutch of Curious Characters*, selected and introduced by Richard Glyn Jones for Xanadu in 1984. It proved to be a collection of twenty-one biographical essays on unusual people, by various hands, the longest and most distinguished being Lytton Strachey's analysis of Florence Nightingale. Glyn Jones briefly expounds his own conception of 'character'. It involves not mere eccentricity, but acting from some irresistible inner impulse – 'the term denotes something of strength as well as strangeness'. This minds me to explore the word further.

The notion of 'character' manipulated by Glyn Jones can be traced back some distance through literature in English. Applied to personages in fiction the term is, of course, completely neutral. Applied ethically, as in the terms 'character-building' and 'of good character', it has headmasterly and preachy overtones. But *OED* gives as a 'colloquial' usage, from 1773, 'an odd or eccentric person'.

Now, I don't see most of the people in this book as 'characters' in that limiting sense – rather, as creatures who have extended my sense of the potentialities, both comic and tragic, of human nature.

Gods are here to provide an overarching conception of potentialities. The trickster Anancy, the generous Ganesh, ferocious yet maternal Kali, immensely versatile Ogun, while superhuman, are, in their myriad emanations, very human. Since races do not exist – though racism, damnably, does – mongrelism is our common lot. It may be a bitter one, as in the case of Merle Oberon, not altogether benign in such an instance as Queen Victoria, or fecund, as in that of Pushkin, but whether we want to accept it or not, we are all mongrels. (I recall my late friend Jim Stewart, an Anglo-South African, describing how when he was a young Trotskyite opposed to apartheid he was hauled up before an Afrikaner minister of the government. As the man's anger deepened, so did the pigmentation of his visage, till one saw clearly some Khoikhoi, or 'Hottentot', forebear.) As for Demons – the diverse daemons which drove Wittgenstein and Xenakis, Billie Holiday and Mother Jones, to name but four, were creatures inured to struggle and ferocious in achievement.

Hazlitt wrote of Scott's Waverley Novels that they provided 'a new edition of human nature'. On my own puny scale I make hints towards something like that, and do so with definite ethical purpose. I want to help undermine notions of 'normality' which have contributed, over the last couple of hundred years, to appalling horrors. The idea of a 'career' has been ideologically hegemonic in the west over that period. At its most exalted – and dangerous – it took shape in the myth of Napoleon which so fascinated Stendhal's Julien and myriad other young men. The military career requires wars for fulfilment. More prosaically, biographies and memoirs describe to us how British politicians progress from apprenticeship in local government to Westminster benches, ministerial office and finally (once proved counter-productive) to the House of Lords. Just so, academics rise by publications till at last they can turn with relief to administration, conductors and string quartets augment their imperial sway over standard repertoire, civil servants ascend by steps to positions where they can inflict maximum damage before they receive their knighthoods. Patterns of incremental achievement on given paths are presented as normative. Those who shy at one fence or another are pitied for failure. Those who retreat from what others would see as fulfilment, as Glenn Gould did from the concert platform, disturb normal people greatly till after they die, upon which they can be regarded as 'geniuses'.

But my father, Peter Ritchie Calder, had no 'career' to show me as I was growing up. The youngest of four children of a juteworker in Forfar, by Dundee, he left school at fifteen, spurning the chance of university which his evident brightness gave him, to become a journalist. He was a star on Fleet Street by his early twenties. (Incidentally, it was he, not Dustin Hoffman, who tracked Agatha Christie down in a hotel in Harrogate after she went missing so that her cheating husband would be accused of her murder.) As a feature, sometimes 'stunt', writer he was sent to interview Rutherford after he had split the atom. The great man despised the press. Dad charmed him into explaining what had been done so that he in turn could explain it to his mass readership. He became a 'science writer', informing himself through friendship with leading scientists of his own generation. But war against Hitler flung him into frontline reporting of the London Blitz (see my entry here on Flora Solomon.) His fierce attacks on official and Governmental handling of the aftermath of air raids greatly annoyed Churchill's War Cabinet. It was decided to hijack this turbulent talent, so Dad was put in charge of Political Warfare – 'White Propaganda' at Bush House. After the war he returned to Fleet Street as Science Editor of the *News Chronicle*, but also undertook globe-trotting, fact-finding missions on behalf of the new United Nations Organisation. These eventually provided basis for his lectures from the Montague Burton Chair of International Relations at Edinburgh University – which, since he had no degree, awarded him an honorary MA to make him legitimate. Meanwhile he was one of the founders (vice-chairman) of the Campaign for Nuclear Disarmament, which did not dissuade his old Labour Party comrade Harold Wilson from awarding him a Life Peerage as Lord Ritchie-Calder of Balmashannar in the Royal Burgh of Forfar. He helped that extraordinary historian the late John Erickson set up the Edinburgh Conversations, bringing US and Soviet bigwigs and top brass together as the Cold War raged on, and paradoxically was both President of the Scottish–Soviet Friendship Society and an Honorary Citizen of Jerusalem. I could go on and on – to mention, for instance, his role as adviser on science when *Encyclopaedia Britannica* was restructured as *Macropaedia* and *Micropaedia*. Not long before he died he was saying that the work he was proudest of had been helping Jennie Lee, the coalminer's daughter from Fife, set up the Open University.

My father's exuberant non-career left me unconvinced by the notion that worthwhile people must follow persistent steady paths (though of course some have done so). Committed careerists may in fact be very dangerous. Look what such components of society – military men, politicians, bureaucrats, businessmen – following their chosen trajectories, have achieved in the era of the mature Nation State: monstrous world wars which murdered tens of millions, mass starvation in a world of plenty, and the crass consumerist conventions which provide tacky new motor vehicles in senseless profusion rather than building sturdy cars to last a lifetime.

It seems clear to me that every child should be encouraged to deviate as far as possible from careerist norms. I hope that this book provides excellent examples for the young to follow (as well as several that they'd better not).

2

Academic seminars are not always dour occasions. For more than thirty years, Edinburgh University History Department has let me attend Wednesday afternoon papers by local and visiting scholars which have provided, beside much sound instruction, not infrequent fallabout hilarity. There was a period when Edinburgh was internationally recognised as a prime centre for the study of the Black Diaspora and Pan-Africanism, and their many attendant Gods, Mongrels and Demons. I have sensed at my elbow while compiling this book the spirits of Professor George ('Sam') Shepperson and the sadly late Professor Paul Edwards. Helping Paul's penultimate PhD student, Polly Rewt, prepare an exhibition on the history of black people in Scotland took me into many byways and back-alleys of mongrelism.

I confidently assign the genesis of this dictionary to a paper given in the early nineties by Clare Anderson, then a research student, on Indian convicts on Mauritius in the early nineteenth century, through which I met Sheik Adam, who suitably opens this book. I set my notes on Clare's talk prominently aside, hoping to do something with them some day. Meanwhile, tackling various Scottish writers and sportspersons for the *New Dictionary of National Biography* gave me an affection for the Brief Life genre. Then, four or five years ago, my resolve to produce such a dictionary as this one was suddenly cemented by the arrival at the History Seminar of Cassandra Pybus, from the University of Tasmania, who gave a paper on Esca Daykin. Her story of the White Rajahs and the wanderings of Esca recalled the richness of novels by Dickens, but happened to be true.

As my project took shape I received suggestions and assistance from many people. I have tried to acknowledge these in my references, but some names had escaped me before I put my tales together – to their owners, many apologies. Some very good tips came from my publisher, Bill Swainson of Bloomsbury. I must give special thanks to Moira Elias, who, amongst other vital assistance, for a period showered me with cuttings of obituaries from her daily *Independent*. Also to the Society of Authors for assistance from the Francis Head Bequest and the Royal Literary Fund for a very generous grant – these have kept me in power-cards, and my household deity Ogun has taken due note.

As always, my thanks go to the staff of the National Library of Scotland. In lists of books referred to, place of publication is London, unless it is otherwise stated.

All mistakes here are my own. Readers with specialist knowledge will notice omissions as well as errors. I am left tantalised by questions which I have had neither time nor space to follow up . . .

Edinburgh, June 2003

Sheik Adam (India, Tasmania) *fl.* 1834–1850s

From 1814 the British Government had the problem of administering Mauritius. This volcanic island had been uninhabited by humans when the roving Dutch took it over in 1598 and named it after the *stadtholder* Maurice of Nassau. A huge and comically ugly flightless pigeon, the dodo, toddled around there guilelessly with no predators to fear, until the Dutch came, and the pigs which they brought with them. By 1681, all the dodos had been eaten. The Dutch cleared out in 1710. Five years later, the French took the island over, calling it Île de France. In their hands, it became a significant producer of sugar, with slave labour imported from East Africa. So its conquest by Britain in 1810 seemed a thoroughly good idea. Four years later the Treaty of Paris confirmed Britain in possession. It was a nuisance that the British Parliament had highmindedly outlawed the slave trade in 1807. How could British Governors develop the island?

So far as public works went, the answer seemed to be convict labour from British India. Two shiploads of convicts from Bengal arrived in December 1815. Many more followed. In 1826, Bombay replaced Bengal as supplier.

Bullshit was uttered about how delinquent subcontinentals would be reformed by strict discipline and surveillance. In practice, convicts mixed freely with the local population, cohabited with local women, and dealt in stolen goods. Importation of more convicts was stopped in 1839 after slavery (not just the trade) had been abolished throughout the British Empire – indentured labour from India was destined to replace slave labour, and it was feared that convicts would corrupt their fellow countrymen. Just before this, Sheik Adam had exposed the complete inefficacity of British 'surveillance'.

It is not clear what crime this notable man had committed within the East India Company's Bombay Presidency. He arrived in Mauritius in 1834 and soon escaped. He returned to convict HQ after a month, and hung around for another six months. Recaptured after absconding again at the end of 1837, he was put in chains. When he next escaped, he was wearing a chain attached to neck and leg. He was at large for about two months, and was spotted sea-fishing in a canoe. In June 1838 he was found working as a servant for a French planter. In October, he escaped again. Recaptured, he made off again in January 1839. Grabbed, he absconded once more, and was arrested at the end of February carrying a bundle of stolen linen. His last escape, in June 1840, revealed how much he had learnt from previous experience on the loose.

A herb called 'devil's flower' (*datura stramonium*) lurked in the Mauritian countryside. It was known to certain criminals in India who were called 'daturias'. Sheik Adam baked cakes of wheat flour and sugar which he spiked with this herb, also sometimes with seeds of a tree, *deces arbustes*, 'thorn apple'. Cases of robbery with 'poisoning' soon came to the attention of the police.

His first sting began when on 9 June a person whom witnesses thought was Portuguese arrived with four Indians at the hut of Zamor Catatum in Trou aux Biches, a small village on the north coast. They asked for light for their pipes, saying they were on their way to Grand Bay to buy some fish. Next day, they returned with some rice and a bottle of gin. Zamor had with him a couple of former African or Creole slaves. They accepted their guests' largesse, and some of Sheik Adam's cakes. Then they conked out. Next day at 2 p.m. the local carpenter Lubin Germain met Zamor on the beach. He was delirious and was eating sand. Back in his hut, Pedre and Alexis were found naked and comatose. As well as their clothes, the gang had made off with linen, fourteen piastres in various currencies, several cooking pots and all Zamor's chickens. After Zamor died a few days later, an autopsy put mortality down to either cannabis or devil's flower. But perhaps his seizure was not caused by the cakes.

On 17 June, on the Pamplemousses road in Flacq, Pierre Louis saw an Indian and two Creoles sitting on a tree trunk. He joined them, and was offered a cake. He thought it tasted nasty and couldn't finish it. The Indian sympathetically gave him wine. All four walked on, till Pierre Louis fell down unconscious. He awoke in police custody, picked up as a drunk. He had lost all his linen and two piastres. In Sheik Adam's last reported sting, on 17 July, he fell in with Marcellin and Theodore, on the road to Flacq. They stopped to carouse at a liquor shop, after which the Indian took out a cake and split it in half. Theodore wanted to keep his share for his child, but the pleasant stranger at once whipped out another cake and persuaded him to eat that himself. Feeling dizzy as they went on, the black men left the road to drink at a stream, whereupon the Indian took off in his wagon with their meagre belongings.

This was too good, or bad, to last. An accomplice in the robbing of Zamor was spotted wearing the dead man's shoes and trousers. He offered to lead the police to the true culprit and with his help Sheik Adam was found. He had rented a hut in Port Louis, calling himself Abdoul Cader. His landlady said that he had cooked himself an early breakfast then left 'to work' for most of the day.

A court found him guilty of 'poisoning', but the authorities, who might have been expected to welcome a pretext for hanging Sheik Adam, decided simply to pass the problem on. He was retransported to Van Diemen's Land, grimmest of the Australian convict colonies. The authorities there registered the arrival in April 1841 of 'Adam Shiek'. He was 5' 4¾" tall, with a copper complexion, 'small pock' marks, pointed nose and large chin.

Here, with bizarre irony, he was employed as a cook by Francis Henslowe, a police magistrate in Campbell Town. One would say that he kept out of trouble, except that in 1849, as 'John Adams', he married a servant, Sarah Swift, a prostitute who had been transported from

Liverpool confessing that she had stabbed 'with intent Elizabeth – with a pair of scissors (I was drunk at the time).' While 'Adams' quiescently applied his herbal skills without outrage, his wife was frequently disciplined, for petty theft, drunkenness, disturbing the peace – and talking in chapel.

Clare Anderson, Convicts in the Indian Ocean: Transportation from South Asia to Mauritius, 1815–1853, *2000; thanks to Clare Anderson*

Mary Adams (England) 1898–1984

It is not beyond belief that a top-class academic scientist should become one of the first producers in the world's first television service, should move on to give invaluable advice to the British government during times of desperate danger in 1940–41, and return to TV to supervise amongst many other things the development of a puppet for children so unforgettable that he was revived in the new millennium after a quarter of a century's gap. But it is extraordinary that this person was a woman.

Mary Adams' father was a farmer, Edward Campin, who died of tuberculosis in 1910. Her mother moved to Penarth in Wales and brought Mary and two brothers up in conditions of severe hardship. But Mary battled through with a scholarship to Godolphin School, Salisbury, and a place at the University of Wales, Cardiff, where she graduated in 1921 with first-class honours in botany. She went on to do research at Newnham College, Cambridge, producing learned papers on cytology, the branch of biology which deals with cells. In 1925 she married Vyvyan Adams, son of an Anglican clergyman. She found further work in Cambridge in extramural studies, and established her lifelong interest in popular education. In 1928 she made a successful series of broadcasts on heredity. Excited by the potential of this new medium for mass instruction, she joined the BBC as adult education officer. In 1936 she became the first woman television producer. In charge of education, political material, talks and culture, she had a miniscule budget but made up for this with the breadth of her contacts in academia and public life.

One child, a daughter, had been born in 1935, but her marriage was not an easy one. Vyvyan had entered Parliament as Conservative MP for West Leeds (1931–45). He was on the reforming wing of his party and an early and outspoken anti-Nazi, a very serious politician who would probably have made cabinet rank had he not drowned in an accident on the eve of a parliamentary comeback in 1951. Mary's sympathies were all with the left – she was a socialist, even a 'romantic communist' (*DNB*). One of her collection of bolshie friends was Tom Harrisson, thirteen years her junior, a self-proclaimed anthropologist with no degree who lived for months in the New Hebrides as a lone white man among people he said were cannibals. He was delighted with the company of a tiny, vivacious, brainy blonde with bright blue eyes who always dressed very elegantly. She was very happy to produce him on TV, talking about his 'cannibals'.

It was a momentous friendship, in so far as Tom went on to co-found Mass-Observation, a pioneering social survey, and Mary moved after the outbreak of war into the Ministry of Information, as director of intelligence. She pushed successfully for the use of social surveys – still a dubious novelty – to monitor public opinion. M-O was in danger of collapsing – Mary's use of it during her time at MoI preserved it to accomplish now-famous work in the Blitz and in wartime factories. On the basis of what she learnt from Harrisson and from the Government's own new Wartime Social Survey, she was able to give calming and constructive advice to the War Cabinet in days of widespread panic. In 1941, Mary moved back to broadcasting, with the North American Service.

When BBC TV resumed in 1946, Mary was back fizzing with ideas. She promoted Muffin the Mule for children (1946–55), then Andy Pandy and his friends motheaten Teddy and raggedy rag-doll Looby Loo (1950–69, 1970–76, revived 2002). But as Head of TV Talks from 1948 to 1954 and then Assistant to the Controller of TV Programmes until she retired in 1958, her great interest was in pushing science, especially medicine, on to the screen.

Before the war she had discussed with the famous zoologist Julian Huxley the idea of a Consumers Association to protect the public from shoddy goods and services. In 1957 this was set up, and next year she became its Deputy Chairman. She induced its magazine, *Which?*, to publish the first comparative tests of contraceptives and the BBC, which she still advised, to overcome its squeamishness about advertising and to broadcast brand ratings in the first consumer programmes. She sat for five years on the Independent Television Authority regulating the BBC's rivals, and agitated for a range of good causes – from Anglo-Chinese understanding to unmarried mothers, from railway design to women's groups (and more). On public platforms she exuded confidence. She loved stirring things up, not least by putting a feminist spin on them.

But at home she was indecisive. '. . . A streak within her compelled her to dread, then court, loneliness . . . She could not live in harmony with herself . . .' (*DNB*). I glimpsed this private woman when my own interest in Mass-Observation drew me to interview her in her London flat not long before she died.

Dictionary of National Biography; *Judith M. Heimann*, The Most Offending Soul Alive: Tom Harrisson and His Remarkable Life, *(Honolulu) 1999; Ian McLaine*, Ministry of Morale: Home Front Morale and the Ministry of Information in World War II, *1979*

Prince Albert John Frederick Charles Alfred George of Schleswig-Holstein (Britain/Germany) 1869–1931

Queen Victoria (q.v.) had her eye on her fifth child and second daughter, the good-natured Helena, 'Lenchen', as the one who would help her, and not get married and go away. But her Consort, Albert, thought otherwise and his early death left his grief-stricken widow completely unable to contest his hallowed judgement. Luckily, she could have her cake and eat it . . .

In the 1860s the longstanding 'Schleswig-Holstein Question' overboiled. The two duchies in question, on the boundary of Denmark and Prussia, were the personal heritage of the Duke of Augustenberg. The historical and legal intricacies of the 'question' were such that Prime Minister Lord Palmerston declared that he had known only three people who had understood it: the Prince Consort, who was dead, a certain German professor, who had gone mad, and himself – but he had forgotten the answer. It became a cause of war between the two countries, then in 1864 a Treaty was signed in Vienna by which the King of Denmark renounced his rights in favour of the emperor of Austria and the king of Prussia. This made the Duke's younger brother Prince Christian even more unemployed than before. Of amiable disposition, he was underrated by the remark that he was interested only in smoking, eating and shooting birds. Christian was perfectly happy to marry Lenchen, fifteen years his junior, and live in Windsor Great Park with her. Indeed, he was given the title of Ranger of the park and from 1872 the home of the 'Schleswig-Holsteins' was Cumberland Lodge, traditionally occupied by the Ranger, where he and Lenchen and scores of servants and grooms raised four children. The youngest of these, Marie-Louse, would write loyally that he had a 'profound knowledge of forestry' and 'loved poetry and literature' (Marie-Louise, 23). However, shooting was certainly a passion. When they were out together just after Christmas 1891, his royal brother-in-law the Duke of Connaught removed one of his eyes with an errant shot. Thereafter Prince Christian acquired no fewer than five glass eyes, so that he could always match the state of his active organ – thus, one was 'artfully bloodshot' for use on the morning after the night before (Packard, 265).

His boys were the first members of the royal family ever to be sent to 'public' boarding schools for education. A footman at the Lodge, one Rayworth, had instructed them in the sport of cricket, which they had taken up with zeal. Prince Christian Jr captained Wellington at it and his younger brother Albert captained Charterhouse. But Albert was much less proficient than Christian, who also captained the Sandhurst team when he went there to train as an army officer, and who hobnobbed with the great Dr W. G. Grace, the man whose astonishing feats with bat and ball had made watching cricket a favourite pastime among the Victorian masses.

In 1900, while *aide-de-camp* to Lord Roberts during the Boer War, Christian scored a century in a match in Pretoria, then died suddenly of enteric fever. But the Great Park cricket team (1861–1924) played on at Cumberland Lodge and here, in 1911, Albert ('Abbie') organised a rather spectacular match between his old school Charterhouse, and a Veteran's XI for which W. G. Grace agreed to play. The big-bearded doctor was now sixty-three and this would be his last significant game. Sadly, he scored no runs and took no wickets.

Albert was now heir to the titles of his childless uncle the Duke of Augustenberg and to large family estates in Silesia. He emigrated to look after these and acquired German citizenship. When war broke out in 1914 he felt compelled to volunteer his services (in his mid forties) to his cousin Kaiser Wilhelm, but made the condition that he must not be engaged on the Western Front, where other cousins might be involved on the British side. So he was given work on the defences of Berlin. Anti-German feeling in Britain meant that he was execrated there. He inherited the title of Schleswig-Holstein in 1921. He died in Berlin ten years later, still unmarried, and it seemed that the line of Augustenberg/ Schleswig-Holstein perished with him.

His lively sister Marie-Louise had fallen in love at a ball in Berlin in 1889 with a tall, dishy cavalry officer, Prince Aribert of Anhalt Dessau. Marie-Louise had her way and married Aribert. Unfortunately he was homosexual. Finding her marriage to be sham, she eventually skedaddled to North America, ostensibly for her health, and was called back to receive the news that Aribert had persuaded his father to dissolve their union, by decree, under surviving feudal law, on the caddish grounds that she had refused to consummate it.

Poor Helena, Princess Christian, an opium addict in later life, died believing that fate had denied her grandchildren. Not so. Abbie had confided in his sisters that he had an illegitimate daughter, born in 1900. He would not tell them or anyone else who the mother was. The child, Valerie, was fostered in an obscure town in Hungary by a Jewish couple named Schwab. She married an Austrian lawyer named Wagner in 1935, but soon decided to transfer to the Duke of Arenberg. The Nazi Government would not permit their union if, as was believed, she was Jewish, so her aunts had to write testifying that she wasn't and that their late brother had expressed regrets about fostering her with people of another race (Chomet, 67). She married her Duke, acquired the title of Serene Highness, but committed suicide in France in 1953. So ended the last spasm of the 'Schleswig-Holstein Question'.

S. Chomet, Helena: Princess Reclaimed, *(New York) 1999;* DNB *('Marie-Louise' – no 'Albert'); Helen Hudson*, Cumberland Lodge: A House Through History, *(Chichester) 1989; Princess Marie-Louise*, My Memories of Six Reigns, *1956; Jerome M. Packard*, Victoria's Daughters, *(Stroud) 1999*

Anancy (Spider – Ghana/West Indies)

After the English conquered from the Spaniards the almost-empty island of Jamaica in the 1650s, its slowly developing planter economy drew black labour preponderantly from the Gold Coast of West Africa. 'Coromantee' slaves from this area were, rather perversely, prized as big strong workers and feared as rebels. Independent 'Maroon' communities of runaway slaves, formed in tracts of unplanted country, evolved under the dominance of 'Coromantees' speaking the allied Twi and Asante languages of their Akan peoples, which provided structures and words for the evolving Jamaican-English creole tongue. Into the twentieth century, descendants of Maroons still used Twi on occasion (Alleyne, 123–25; Cassidy and Le Page, xli). And over the whole island their spider-god Anancy (Anansi, Ananse) ruled wherever folk tales were shared among agricultural labourers or told to children, including genteel children. Even tales originating in Europe were 'Nancy Stories'.

A common story explained how a spider had come to take charge of all stories. In the jungle, Tiger is king of the beasts. The lowliest, weakest beast is Anancy. One day Anancy persuades Tiger to challenge him. If Spider will bring Tiger a gourd full of honey bees and can capture Snake and produce him alive, Tiger will renounce his suzerainty over stories. Anancy quite easily fools 154 honey bees into flying into an open gourd which he then seals. Snake is harder. At last Anancy plays on Snake's vanity. Is he as long as that tall bamboo tree? Anancy cuts the bamboo down and, as Snake strains himself to match its length, ties him to it, then bears him in triumph to Tiger (Sherlock, 1966).

Anancy is extremely wily, though sometimes – too clever by half – his schemes bring him near to disaster. As Rex Nettleford has put it, he 'supposedly expresses much of the Jamaican spirit in his ostentatious professions of love, in his wrong and strong, brave but cowardly postures of bluff, in his love for leisure and corresponding dislike for work, and in his lovable rascality' (quoted in Barrett, 34). He talks with a distinctive lisp – 'push' for 'put', 'lickle' for 'little'. His relations with his wife Crooky and his neighbours Tiger, Goat, Peafowl, Kissander the Cat, and others, replicate those of human villagers. He is either a spider who can change into a man or a human who turns into a spider and whisks himself up to the roof when danger threatens, to hang in his web of 'Anancy ropes', so called in Jamaican creole. He is a trickster who can 'play fool to ketch wise'.

But Anancy is also a trickster-deity. An amused Victorian, in 1868, commented that 'Anansay . . . is the Jove, the Thor, the Bramah of Negro mythology. His great strength is in his cunning, and in his metamorphic versatility; he out-Proteuses Proteus' (Cassidy and Le Page, 'Anancy, Annancy'). In Jamaica his name might be given to a very beautiful local spider with yellow stripes, but in the Gold Coast one of the names of Onyeame, the creator of all things, has been Anansi Kokuroka, 'the Great Spider'. In a poem, 'Ananse', Kamau Brathwaite presents him as the god who inspired slave revolt, who still sits in the ceilings of the poor beyond the reach of their brooms.

Mervyn C. Alleyne, Roots of Jamaican Culture, *1988; Leonard E. Barrett*, The Sun and the Drum: African Roots in Jamaican Folk Tradition, *(Kingston) 1976; F. G. Cassidy and R. Le Page*, Dictionary of Jamaican English, *2nd edn, (Cambridge) 1980; Philip Sherlock*, Anansi the Spider Man: Jamaican Folk Tales, *1956; Philip Sherlock*, West Indian Folk Tales, *(Oxford) 1966*

Archie Angel (Orkney) *fl.* 1760

There is a large body of myths involving Spaniards from the Armada of 1588 wrecked on various remote parts of the British and Irish coasts. Any person combining dark hair and eyes with a somewhat sallow complexion who hails ancestrally from such parts is likely to be given in her or his presumed genealogy a hidalgo settled thus in the area. It is a much retold – and reprinted – myth about Fair Isle, that especially remote, but inhabited, island about equidistant between the Orkneys and Shetland, that certain distinctive patterns in its world-famous knitting derive from the sock-mending, if not the sweater-making, talents attributed to Spanish seamen. It is nearly certain that they came from Norse tradition (Thom, 84). However, one motif does suggest the griffon, that legendary beast with an eagle's head and a lion's body.

And it is certain that in September 1588 *El Gran Grifon* crashed into Fair Isle. It was not a galleon, but an *urca* – 'hulk'. It was originally from Rostock, that Hanseatic port in the Baltic, and had been either chartered or forcibly requisitioned for Philip II's great assault on England. It was big for the day – 650 tons – as befitted the vessel of **Admiral Juan Gomez de Medina** (q.v.), who commanded twenty-three transports, hulks and store ships in the eighth division of the Armada. It carried some three hundred men, crew and soldiers.

Fair Isle was a scrap of land, just six square miles. There were maybe 115 residents, in seventeen households. They subsisted mainly on fish, fresh and cured, and bannocks of barley or oatmeal. They kept cattle for milk, pigs for meat and sheep for wool. Don Juan was a very brave gentleman, and also a humane one. His armed men could easily have dominated the islanders, less than half their number. But they paid in *ryals* for the food they consumed. Unfortunately this soon amounted to nearly all the comestibles available. Noticing this, the islanders hid their remaining stock, and started (it is said) to chuck stray Spaniards into the sea. Because of continuing bad weather, it was seven weeks before Don Juan could get word across the waters to the tacksman who leased the island from the Stewart Earl of Shetland. Meanwhile, some fifty Spaniards died. At last relief appeared, and finally the survivors were shipped to Shetland. There eventually a vessel was found to take them further. They arrived at Anstruther in Fife, where Don Juan went ashore to seek further succour. The local minister of religion, James Melvill, kept a diary, which is vivid concerning the day of Gomez's apparition. He harangued the Spaniard in person on the superiority of the Reformed religion, and pointed out that Protestants washed up thus in Spain could expect pretty savage treatment. Gomez indicated that he had done favours to Scots traders in Cadiz and more might be expected. The laird, summoned, decided that the Papists could land. Melvill noted that 260 men who came ashore were for 'the maist part young, berdless, sillie, trauchled and houngered' (beardless, innocent, weary and hungry). They were fed kale, 'pottage' and fish. The good minister rejoiced that Protestants were able to show their superior humanity towards these folk. The valiant Gomez eventually got most of his unlucky lads back to Spain. He found a ship from Anstruther 'arrested' in Cadiz when he returned there and good as his word displayed 'grait kyndnes' in sorting out its problems with the authorities (Tudor, 429–44; Ker, *passim*; Hunter, 123; Melvill).

Some time in the 1730s, another ship was wrecked off Aikerness in Westray, at night. The locals did not save any of the crew, but next dawn they combed the beach. We are told that they stripped battered corpses of clothes and valuables and then left them to the seabirds. Accounts of a key episode vary. They agree that there was one survivor, a boy child, who was tied to a dead woman, or, alternatively, to a dog. He may have been an infant or as old as ten. If the former, he could give no account of himself. If the latter, he spoke a language which no local could make out. But a piece of wood washed up and attributed to the shattered vessel bore the legend 'Archangel'. If this denoted Russian origins, and the child was able to speak, there would indeed have been no way of understanding him. All accounts agree that the boy was brought up by a local family, and named 'Archie Angel'. It is clear that in about 1760 he married Jean Drever of Aikerness. Their first child was born in 1763. By 1774 there were four more. Descendants of Archie multiplied to the point where the 1841 census found fifteen Westray residents named Angel. The surname, in Orkney at least, seems effectively to have died out by the end of the nineteenth century, and the last known descendant of Archie to have borne it, a Mrs Mason, passed away in 1938. However, Archie remains in the genealogical record. There is no doubt whatsoever that someone of that name existed.

If Archie's story were told out of oral tradition in a part of the world recently preliterate, one would accept the basic tale and attribute deviations between accounts to diverging interests of different lineages reciting it over nearly three centuries. But Scotland was well into written records, which were vitally important to its legal system. Orkney, furthermore, has produced scholars far out of proportion to its small population. So I find here a subconscious, perhaps in some cases part-conscious, determination to assert a minor myth.

Some questions . . . There was undoubtedly much commerce between Russia and Britain at this time, just after the death of Peter the Great. But would a ship from Archangel, that remote port in Arctic waters which certainly played a part in the trade, have carried its name in Roman or Cyrillic script? I think it more likely that a ship so named would have been British. If it was engaged in smuggling, that might explain why no stories are told of owners making enquiries. In any case, no research into the matter seems to have been done, nor, suspiciously, is the date of the wreck clear. A recent comprehensive survey of wrecks on Scottish coastlines reports a ship registered in Archangel going down on Westray in '1730' (Whittaker, 59). This appears to be merely an echo of the Westray folk story. Secondly, the islanders had, fairly or unfairly, the reputation of 'wreckers'. All around the ruggeder coastlines of the British Isles, there are tales of ships deliberately lured on to rocks by false displays of lights. Let us concede that the Westraymen were not in this instance guilty – they still seem to have made no effort to save people on the putative *Archangel*. The touching tale of Archie's origins might transfigure with glamour an act of collective amnesia. It might also, alternatively, have served to cover up the inconvenient reality that a bairn had been born who was the unacceptable, illegitimate byblow of some important person, quietly fostered out to a kind family.

Yet when all is said and done, the tale, with or without that dog, is hauntingly beautiful. As the islands' great recent poet, George Mackay Brown, observed, '. . . Orkney lay athwart a great sea-way from Viking times onward . . . The shores are strewn with wrack, jetsam, occasional treasure.' This was in the preface to Mackay Brown's volume of 1989, called *The Wreck of the Archangel* after its title poem.

> A man listens. This can't be! – One thin cry
> Between wavecrash and circling wolves of wind
> And there, in the lantern pool
> A child's face, a dwindling, in seaweed tassels . . .

The sea's harp plays on. Mackay Brown thinks of the saved and sea-changed child enduring on Westray the full biblical span:

> The seventy ploughtimes, creeltimes,
> Harvests of fish and corn,
> His feet in thrall always
> To the bounteous terrible harp.

And that, for my money, *is* Archie.

George Mackay Brown, The Wreck of the Archangel and Other Poems, *1989; Anne Cormack*, *'Ah Didna Ken Thoo Wir an Angel'*, The Orkney View, *Feb/Mar 1997; Colin Elliott*, Discovering Armada Britain, *1987; J. R. Hunter*, Fair Isle:

The Archaeology of an Island Community, *(Edinburgh) 1996; W. P. Ker, 'The Spanish Story of the Armada'*, Scottish Historical Review, *vol. XVII, 1920; Ernest Walter Marwick*, An Orkney Anthology, *vol. 1. (Edinburgh) 1991;* Mr James Melvill's Diary, *(Edinburgh) 1829; David Scott, 'The Angels of Westray'*, Orcadian, *18 February 1971; Valerie M. Thom*, Fair Isle: An Island Saga, *(Edinburgh) 1989; John R. Tudor*, The Orkneys and Shetland, *1883; Ian G. Whittaker*, Off Scotland: A Comprehensive Record of Maritime and Aviation Losses in Scottish Waters, *(Edinburgh) 1998; thanks to Kirkwall Library*

George Antheil (USA) 1900–59

Antheil grew up in Trenton, PA, where his indulgent father owned a small shoe shop. At first he was very lucky. With superior musical training, he found a rich patron, Mrs Edward (Marie Louise Curtis) Bok, whose fortune would eventually support the Curtis Institute of Music in Philadelphia. He bounced into Europe as a precocious pianist, playing his own avant-garde compositions at concerts in Budapest, Vienna, Munich, Berlin, and so forth, where they provoked mild enthusiasm, and also riots – he took to quelling his audiences by having all doors locked and keeping a pistol on top of the piano. He arrived in Paris in June 1923.

Antheil's was precisely the genius which the Parisian avant-garde, considering itself to be more *avant* than any other, was waiting to hail. He lodged above Sylvia Beach's famous bookshop, Shakespeare and Company. When he made his Paris debut at the Théâtre des Champs-Elysées, sitting in one box were Erik Satie, composer notorious for Goon-like wit, Darius Milhaud, notorious for his adorable failure to imitate jazz in his ballet *Le Boeuf sur le Toit*, the painter Fernand Léger, addicted to machines, and the madly anti-Semitic poet Ezra Pound. James Joyce, ever the loner, sat in another box. They were gratified by the greatest music riot since the first performance of Stravinsky's *Rite of Spring* eleven years before. After the first movement of a sonata by Antheil himself, no one could hear another note he played.

Antheil's reputation, just for now, in the city of nascent Surrealism, was stellar. The likes of Pablo Picasso acknowledged it. His *Ballet Mécanique*, originally conceived as the score for a film by Léger, was a *succès fou* as concert piece in 1926 – scored for pianola with amplifier, two pianos, three xylophones, small and large wooden aircraft propellers, metal propeller, tam-tam, three bass drums and fire siren. The work, as Antheil rescored it in 1952, now seems to possess an almost pastoral charm. But in the mid twenties it was drastic enough to delight extreme modernists.

Then Antheil's reputation went pear-shaped. He took his masterpiece to New York. There were now to be ten pianos (an admirer, **Aaron Copland** [q.v.] played one of them) and also a mechanical piano. The Ballet's performance under the baton of Eugene Goossens in Carnegie Hall was foolishly hyped as a circus-type event sure to provoke a riot. But New Yorkers either left the hall, or laughed, as the wind driving a propeller, misdirected, hit the audience, and the fire siren, cranked up too late for its cue, wouldn't thereafter stop when it was meant to. 'Expected Riots Peter Out . . . Sensation Fails to Materialise' read one headline. Even the ever-patient Mrs Bok was disgusted, so much so that she refused to stump up more sponsorship, though she kept up Antheil's regular allowance.

Back in Paris, Antheil found himself out of fashion. A book about him by Pound, praising his music extravagantly and badmouthing everyone else's, had done him nothing but harm, and to compound this evil (please forgive the pun), Ezra now denounced the new turn which Antheil's work had taken, following his master Stravinsky into neo-classicism. After a spell when he had some success, in Weimar Germany, with an opera, *Transatlantic*, about a US presidential election, and collaborated usefully with W. B. Yeats, producing background music for *Fighting the Waves* at the Abbey Theatre, he returned to the USA, but for Bok, broke, in 1933.

He turned his hand to various ways of making money. With his wife, he wrote a lonely-hearts column. He had made a hobby of endocrinology, the study of ductless glands. In the thirties, this was fad science. Antheil now contributed articles about glands to *Esquire*. It is clearly a cheap slur to suggest that the sex-goddess film-star **Hedy Lamarr** (q.v.) was drawn to contact him by fears about what her glands might be doing to her famous figure . . .

The truth was that they met at a party. Antheil had very sensibly taken himself off to Hollywood in 1936. He would live in California for the rest of his life, producing altogether thirty-three film scores. In 1940, he published a work of prophecy, *Shape of War to Come*. So he was at once intrigued by an idea which Hedy had suggested to her first husband, the odious arms manufacturer Mandl, of a radio-controlled torpedo. Getting to work together on it (this was all very serious, there is no hint of a sexual affair) they encountered the problem that it might be jammed. 'They hit on the idea of changing the frequency at random intervals synchronised between the transmitter and receiver. Because of Antheil's background [in 'mechanical music'] . . . they used player-piano rolls to synchronise the signals. This is also why the number of frequencies used – 88 – matches the number of keys on the piano' (Burgess). They patented their idea in 1942. The actual torpedo never materialised, but their principle of 'spread spectrum' or 'frequency hopping' today has various uses in computer modems, satellite transmissions, mobile phones and so forth. In 1997, the US authorities revealed at last that the Lamarr–Antheil device was the basis for their secure military communications (Katz).

Serious contemporary musicians had always respected Antheil, and his reputation spread after his Fourth Symphony (1944), using American 'folk' elements, was premiered under the baton of the great Stokowski (recently seen shaking hands with Mickey Mouse in Disney's *Fantasia*). A survey in 1947 found him to be one of the most performed US composers. Ironically, while his acclaim as a tuneful though 'contemporary' composer subsided after his death from a heart attack, his once-scandalous *Ballet* survived as his sole acknowledged masterpiece.

Mark Burgess, Letter, The Times, *29 January 2000; Ephraim Katz, ed.,* The Macmillan International Film Encyclopaedia, *rev. edn 1998; Stanley Sadie, ed.,* New Grove Dictionary of Music and Musicians, *vol. 1, 2001; Linda Whitesitt,* The Life and Music of George Antheil, *(Epping) 1983*

Aztec Children (Mexico?) *fl.* 1853

In the year 1853, there were brought over to this country [Britain] from America two diminutive children, a boy and a girl, said to be aged respectively 17 and 11, and who were represented as descendants of the ancient Aztecs. The height of each was under 3 feet. Their figure was slender and not ill-proportioned; that which was chiefly remarkable being their features. While the forehead and chin receded, the nose was so singularly prominent as to suggest the idea of the face of a bird. Yet, with dark lively eyes, an olive complexion, and glossy long black hair, and a great fund of good nature, they were far from unpleasing. They spoke no intelligible language, but understood a few words of English, and seemed to have a taste for music. Shewn to the public as curiosities, they were usually exhibited on a large table, on which they ran about amusing themselves. Their exhibitor told a very incredible story of how they had been obtained from the ancient city of Iximaga, where they were reverenced as gods. A certain Señor Velasquez, accompanied by a Canadian and an American, penetrated into this ancient city of Central America, where they made the acquaintance of one of the guardian priests of these undersized deities, who was so charmed with the accounts of the outer world, that he resolved to steal the gods of his people and escape with the strangers. One after the other – the Canadian, the American, and the priest – were overtaken by disaster and Velasquez alone was left to tell the wondrous tale, with no attestation but such as the children themselves furnished. Professor Owen considered them mere dwarfs, and other authorities held a similar opinion. Belonging probably to some Indian tribe, they were doubtless monstrosities, and this becoming apparent, interest in them ceased.

(Chambers, 593)

'Professor Owen' was presumably Richard Owen (1804–92), who had the Hunterian Chair in London's Royal College of Surgeons. But it would have taken a combination of Professor Challenger and Indiana Jones to get to the bottom of this particular story.

Chambers's Encyclopaedia, *rev. edn, vol. I, 1879*

James Miranda Barry (Ireland) 1799–1865

Elizabeth Garrett Anderson obtained a licence to practise as an apothecary in 1865, and next year took charge of St Mary's dispensary in London, set up to serve poor women. This eventually became the Elizabeth Garrett Anderson Hospital. Anderson herself acquired an MD from Paris in 1870. But by then it was generally believed that she had been long anticipated as a qualified, practising woman doctor: that James Barry, who had retired from the second-highest rank in the Army Medical Service – Inspector General – in 1859, had successfully disguised her gender through forty-six years in uniform, despite having, at some point, given birth to a child.

This wonderful story, which at once made the newspapers after Barry's death, has been elaborated in numerous biographies, novels and plays. Documented information begins with obscurity and ends with dubiety.

Entering Edinburgh University in 1809, Barry declared a birth date of 1799. Ten years of age was young to matriculate, but this was not unprecedented. However, when Barry applied to join the Army in 1813, year of birth was registered as 1795 (minimum age for entry was fourteen). What seems clear is that Mrs Mary Ann Bulkely arrived in London from Ireland in 1805 with a daughter aged nearly fifteen and another child considerably younger. Her husband, after suffering bankruptcy, had kicked her out. She now sought help from her brother James Barry, a famous 'history' painter, who had mixed in the high-flying intellectual circles dominated by Dr Johnson. He was now elderly, infirm, and plagued by poverty and paranoid depression. But luckily for Mrs Bulkely, he retained some distinguished friends.

General Francesco Miranda (*c.*1754–1816), whose name the younger James Barry would assume, was a South American revolutionary. He had served with the French army on the rebels' side in the American War of Independence and had taken up the idea that Spain's New World colonies should likewise free themselves from European rule, with an Inca Emperor heading a mighty new nation from Patagonia to the Mississippi. He roamed Europe seeking support. In England, he got it from the brilliant though impotent Whig opposition. Learned and charming, he 'was the first South American of culture Europe had known; many doors were open to him . . . He glittered' (Naipaul, 138). In 1805, he turned up off Venezuela with an American ship and two hundred men, but his proclaimed 'Colombian' state was bloodily aborted. Meanwhile, he had left his mistress in London under the painter Barry's protection . . .

The painter died in February 1806 and was interred in Westminster Abbey beside Joshua Reynolds. Another friend had arranged financial help which he had not lived to receive. This was David Steuart Erskine, the 11th Earl of Buchan (1742–1829). Buchan was a fussy, boring, extremely vain man who was obsessed with the antiquities of his native Scotland and stood forth as connoisseur of the arts. He came from a family renowned for its liberal views and was a pioneer advocate, in print (1791), of education for women. A plausible story would have it that Miranda, back in London, was impressed by the interest which Mary Anne Bulkely's precocious younger child took in his own fine library, and that he and the protofeminist Earl cooked up the scheme to matriculate this 'girl', renamed 'James Miranda', at Edinburgh University, then the world's greatest centre of medical education. When Barry showed up there, the General and the Earl were his sponsors.

With paternity obfuscated, Barry moved after swift graduation in

1811 to Guy's Hospital in London. Meanwhile, Miranda had returned to lead rebellion in South America, then to die in a Spanish prison.

Barry was gazetted Hospital Assistant in the Army in July, 1813. Lord Charles Somerset, governor at the Cape of Good Hope, which had been seized from Holland, was a widower. From the moment of his arrival, Barry became his personal physician. Lord Charles, not kindly viewed by historians, was a lofty aristocrat on a hiding to nothing. In the Cape Colony, Europeans from various parts who spoke a form of Dutch had enslaved the indigenous Khoikhoi ('Hottentots') and their Roman Law, still in place, gave Somerset autocratic powers. When settlers from Britain arrived in 1820, they thought him arrogant and unsympathetic, and had to fight him to maintain a freely critical press. His friend Barry cut a curious figure – under 5' tall, almost dwarfed by his own uniform sword, red-headed, quarrelsome, with a high-pitched, shrill voice. He was a vegetarian, and eventually became a teetotaller. There were strict orders that no one should enter Barry's bedroom, where the doctor slept with the first of a series of poodles, always called Psyche. But Barry was a good dancer and talked like a 'ladies' man'. He fought a duel with the Governor's aide de camp, Cloete, who called him out when he made disparaging remarks about a woman who had called to visit Somerset.

Apart from this, Barry was an outstanding doctor and a pioneer in hospital and sickroom hygiene. European medicine could not cure more than a couple of diseases until nearly the middle of the twentieth century, but hygiene helped check them. Barry also, sensibly, encouraged sea bathing. Snappy with people in authority, Barry was gentle and kind with patients and he took up cudgels for the unfortunate – alleviating conditions for lepers, lunatics and sick prisoners. Barry fell foul of vested interests when, given the post of Colonial Medical Inspector in 1822, he sought to regulate unqualified medical practitioners and outlaw useless and dangerous drugs. Meanwhile, Somerset had gone home, returning in 1821 with a new wife, who became Barry's long-term friend. A two-man Commission of Inquiry set up to report on government in former Dutch and French colonies arrived in the Cape to be bombarded with complaints about Somerset. A scurrilous imputation of an unnatural sexual relationship between the Governor and his doctor (reputed by some to be his own son) got as far as the Westminster House of Commons. Somerset returned to Britain to face his critics there in 1826. In his absence, Barry was promoted to Staff Surgeon and, in 1828, transferred to Mauritius. Barry stayed just ten quarrelsome months there before leaving for England to nurse Somerset through a serious illness. To scant avail – back on his feet for a while, Somerset succumbed to a seizure in 1831. The little doctor attended that great friend's funeral. Lord Charles's brother, Fitzroy Somerset (later, as Lord Raglan, held responsible for the dismal inefficiency of British military organisation in the Crimea), lived on, Barry's staunch protector at the top of the army.

Barry, usually in hot water, needed one. The rest of his career took him mostly to very unhealthy places, with one more salubrious sojourn in Corfu. Thence Barry dashed on a dramatic visit to the Crimea, where Florence Nightingale – whose record, sadly, showed that her understanding of hygiene did not match Barry's – was denounced by the little doctor, seated on horseback, in front of a crowd of soldiers, servants and camp followers. She wrote after Barry's death, 'I should say that she was the most hardened creature I ever met throughout the army' (Rose, p. 220). Barry went on to Canada, where he fell ill. He returned home exhausted in 1859, and retired.

Everywhere, Barry's behaviour was similar. He sympathised with slaves, prisoners, mad people, paupers and common soldiers. In St Helena, he impudently put a competent black woman in charge of the civil section of the hospital. He was court-martialled for protesting directly to the Secretary at War in Whitehall over the failings of the Commissariat – but fully and honourably acquitted. Those closest to Barry were always the latest poodle and the current dignified, discreet black manservant.

Barry was lodging in a dentist's house in Marylebone, London, when 'summer diarrhoea' struck mortally in 1865. A charwoman, Sophia Bishop, called upon to lay out the corpse, reported to the doctor who had certified the death, Major McKinnon, that the body was 'that of a perfect female' and showed signs – 'stretch marks' – of having had a child when young.

Stretch marks can have other causes than previous pregnancy, and the latest medically informed writers on Barry support the common-sense view that 'he' was a hermaphrodite. 'A true hermaphrodite is defined as an individual where both ovarian and testicular tissue is present . . . Testicular tissue in true hermaphrodites at puberty is atrophic and unlikely to function. At puberty, ovarian tissue achieves considerable development while the testicular tissue regresses, resulting in the dominance of feminine secondary sexual characteristics . . .' (Kubba, 355).

It would not have been clear when Barry arrived at the Cape that 'his' voice was never going to break and he may have been uncertain for some time about his own sexual character. It must have taken Barry great fortitude to come to terms with physical abnormality. The story of a brilliant person condemned by abnormal physique to a deeply lonely life without physical intimacy, who nevertheless fought stubbornly, as a great reforming physician and surgeon, to rescue and improve the lives of other unfortunates, is truly moving to contemplate. Unfortunately, the image of a sharp-featured, clever, warm-hearted eccentric capitulates before that of the brave pioneering female who madly risks all in a passionate teenage romance with a great aristocrat. Our culture has decided that Barry must remain a woman.

'David Erskine', Dictionary of National Biography; *A. K. Kubba and M. Young, 'The Life Work and Gender of Dr James Barry MD, 1795–1865', in* Proceedings of the Royal College of Physicians of Edinburgh, *vol. 31, 2001; V. S. Naipaul,* The Loss of El Dorado, *1969; William L. Pressly,* James Barry The Artist as Hero, *1983; June Rose,* The Perfect Gentleman, *1977; thanks to Norman Kreitman and David McKail*

Matsuo Bashō (Japan) 1644–94

In a book published in 1998, it was suggested that there might be as many as five million active practitioners of *haiku* in Japan (Shirane, 1). That would amount to about one poet for every twenty-five persons – surely a uniquely high ratio. But then, haiku is an exceptional poetic form. Because an unrhymed poem of seventeen syllables might seem feasible for any person able to count to seventeen, the form attracts dabblers. In Japan, sharing haikus through haiku clubs is a social, recreational activity. Myriad Westerners now adopt the form.

One infers that haiku is seen as 'undemanding'. I think the vast preponderance of Western haikutasters would shrink from following the example of the acknowledged all-time master of haiku, Matsuo Bashō, for whom production of verses was eventually related to austere spirituality. Towards the end of his life, he is said to have had more than 2,000 disciples. He got fed up with people visiting him in his house in Edo. 'Whenever people come, there is useless talk', he declared in the autumn of 1693, and as the last New Year of his life arrived, his verse response was

Year after year
on the monkey's face
the monkey's mask.
(Ueda, 32–34, 170)

The man finally known as Bashō was born in 1644 at or near Ueno, about 200 miles west of the city of Edo, now Tokyo, where the shogun ruled. He was one of six children of a low-ranking samurai reduced to farming. As a child he was called Kinsaku. He entered the service of Todo Yoshitada, a young relative of a local feudal ruler. Yoshitada liked *haikai* writing. His servant, primarily his study-mate, joined him in this pursuit, assuming the pen name Sobo. In 1664 two poems of his – along with one by Yoshitada, who wrote as Sengin – were published in a verse anthology produced in Kyoto, thirty miles to the south-east, site of the Emperor's court.

Haiku was 'a verse form evolved for the ordinary man, in contrast with most other Japanese poetry, which is aristocratic in form and tradition' (Tsunoda, 450). Bashō and his young lord got together at a moment, under the Tokugawa shogunate which had brought peace to Japan at the end of the sixteenth century CE, when the voice of commoners was finding literary expression, much as happened at exactly the same time with theatre and the novel in Britain. Previously, books had been handwritten manuscripts possessed by an aristocratic elite, members of which might use Chinese as their Western counterparts employed Latin, in homage to a senior tradition. Meanwhile travelling minstrels had chanted military epics to illiterate peasants. Few samurai, craftsmen or farmers had been literate. But by the mid seventeenth century CE, samurai had been transformed into bureaucrats, merchants were calling tunes in expanding urban centres, and the *haikai* linked verse practised in earlier centuries among the elite had become popular reading, second only to Buddhist texts. Six hundred and fifty separate *haikai* books were were published in Kyoto in the second half of the century. In the consciousness of Basho's literate contemporaries a strong 'vertical' sense of a cultural past including both the classical tradition and popular legend intersected with the 'horizontal' level of 'urban common life and a new social order' (Shirane, 3–9).

The history of the evolution of *haikai* from *waka*, a thirty-one-syllable form dating back to the eighth century, involves aristocratic pleasure in linked verse, *renga*, where two or more poets met to compose a sequence collectively under strict aesthetic rules, and cheap and cheeerful, even crude, linked sequences composed orally by illiterate villagers. The term *haikai*, which can be translated as 'light-hearted', was used to contrast with serious, formal, and usually melancholy, aristocratic *waka* and linked verse. The opening verse of a linked verse series consisted of seventeen syllables and was known as the *hokku*. Bashō became famous as a master of both linked verse and of free-standing *hokku*, which came to be called *haiku*. And so self-improving townsmen flocked to him for guidance and even peasants in the fields wanted poems from him.

Back to 1666 . . . The servant who wrote haikus as Sobo had acquired the samurai name of Matsuo Munefusa when he came of age. Now his beloved young master Yoshitada suddenly died. Bashō asked the bereaved father for permission to resign from service. When this was refused, he ran away to Kyoto. He studied there, and tried out life. By his own account he was 'fascinated by the ways of homosexual love' (Ueda, 22), but it was probably in Kyoto that he took up with the woman, Juteini, whose reappearance to live with him in his last years contributed to his world-weariness. In 1672 he moved to Edo. He had a growing reputation as a poet such that three years later, when the veteran master Soin (1605–82) arrived in the city on a visit from his base with the merchant class who dominated Osaka, he was amongst those invited to compose linked verse with him.

This clearly mattered a lot to Bashō, since he now changed his pen name to Tosei. Soin and his school had broken radically from traditional subject matter, introducing any and every incident of everyday life. For a time Bashō was playful in his own poems. But in 1680, his life changed, bringing him the name by which we know him and a more profound conception of his art.

Through his network of many students and admirers, a small house was built for him in a relatively isolated spot in a suburb. After he moved in, one of his disciples presented him with a stock of Bashō tree – this was a species of banana. He loved the tree, he said, precisely because its flowers were drab and its wood was useless. First the house, then he himself, was named after it. Here, disillusioned with everyday life, he brooded.

One of his neighbours was a Zen priest, Butcho, and Bashō began to practise meditation under his guidance. He needed new psychological resources. In 1682 fire destroyed the Bashō house. The following year, his mother died. Though students and disciples presented him with a new house, his mind turned to travel, and his mature masterpieces are travelogues, where in exquisite succinct prose – *haikai* prose, known as *haibun* – he reports on landscapes and their historical associations, giving rise to haikus which are included. He wished to travel not as a famous poet but as a man practising discipline which would enable him to dissolve his ego into nature. He must cast worldly attachments and worldly self away and recover his true identity – 'our everlasting self which is poetry', he called it (Yuasa 30). In the spring of 1689, he sold his house and embarked on the arduous 'Narrow Road to the Deep North', walking, walking, walking far away from fashionable civilisation into wild and dangerous country, at first with one disciple, then alone, a round trip of 1,500 miles which took him more than two-and-a-half years. The result was a uniquely beautiful short book.

He by now attached cardinal importance to a quality in verse which he called *sabi*, 'loneliness'. This could colour a poem irrespective of its subject matter. Bashō wrote: 'If a man goes to war wearing a stout armour or to a party dressed up in gay clothes, and if this man happens to be an old man, there is something lonely about him' (Yuasa, 42).

In the spring of 1694 he set off intending to walk to the southern end of mainland Japan. Lingering in Osaka, he succumbed to dysentery and died, 'talking haiku' almost to the last with a faithful disciple summoned to his bedside.

His most famous haiku, which is of course the most famous ever written, has been often translated and subjected to exhaustive commentary. Here is a bare version:

furuike ya	old pond . . .
kawazu tobikomu	a frog leaps in
mizu no oto	water's sound
	(Higginson, 9)

Freer translation, and commentary, establish that the comic character of the frog – which is present – is subsumed under *sabi*, at a moment of intersection combining nature and history with the basic element of water. This is a product not of chance, lively observation, but of profound thought and discipline. (One might add that it figures concisely the concurrence in Bashō's plebeian culture of instantaneous mundane actuality – the frog – and tradition – the old, or 'ancient' pond.)

Stephen Henry Gill and C. Andrew Gerstle, Rediscovering Bashō . . . *(Folkestone) 1999; William L. Higginson*, The Haiku Handbook: How to Write, Share, and Teach Haiku, *(Tokyo) 1985; Donald Keene, ed.*, Anthology of Japanese Literature: To the Mid-Nineteenth Century, *(Harmondsworth) 1968; Haruo Shirane*, Traces of Dreams: Landscape, Cultural Memory and the Poetry of Bashō, *(Stanford, CA) 1998; Ryusaku Tsunoda et al.*, Sources of Japanese Tradition, *(New York) 1958; Makoto Ueda*, Matsuo Bashō, *(New York) 1970; Nobuyuki Yuasa, trans. and introd.*, Bashō: The Narrow Road to the Deep North and Other Travel Sketches, *(Harmondsworth) 1966*

Tom Bass (USA) 1859–1934

Trainer Tom Bass did more than anyone else to promote the development of the American Saddle Horse as a distinct and distinguished breed. Future and current US Presidents sought him out and bought his horses. 'Buffalo Bill' Cody acquired from him Columbus, noble star of his world-famous Wild West Show. Tom, not liking the prospect of sea travel, turned down an invitation to give a command performance for Queen Victoria in London, on the occasion of her Diamond Jubilee. He made the otherwise undistinguished town of Mexico, Missouri, the saddle-horse capital of the world, and with his finest mounts, ridden by himself, won countless prizes in shows all over America.

Tom Bass was born a slave in Boone County, Kentucky. Though his grandfather, Presley Gray, was a freed man, his mother, Cornelia, was the slave of Tom's father, William Hayden Bass. While Cornelia was pregnant, William Bass married his fiancée Miss Irene.

William's grandfather Peter had been one of the pioneering white settlers in Boone County, and his father Eli was a prominent public man. Eli's coachman was Presley Gray. Presley's daughter was wonderfully handsome. William never disguised his paternity. Cornelia served his wife Irene. The Civil War raged, and at its end Eli Bass had to free all his slaves. His great wealth subverted, Eli soon died, but William managed the estate shrewdly. Cornelia went to work in Columbia. Tom was left alone with his devoted grandparents, and William's livestock, prominent amongst which was Helen MacGregor, a favourite elegant mare. Tom helped tend her. Aged seven, he saw her perform at his first horse show. Small though he was, he put her through her paces round the farm, and she followed him about with doggish devotion. He was deeply grieved when she suddenly died.

He was partly consoled by the responsibility of exercising his grandfather's mule, Mr Potts, an especially sullen and unbiddable beast. He tamed it and taught it the five 'gaits' of the show horse. William Bass, now spending most of his time in Columbia, brought his family down one Sunday with two schoolmates of his eldest white son. The latter accused Tom of insolence. 'Don't you know how to act when white people talk to you? . . . Maybe we ought to teach you a few things about riding.' Tom went home, then returned on Mr Potts, wearing Sunday clothes borrowed from his grandfather. The white boys laughed so uproariously that Tom's father left his porch to join them in the corral. Laughter subsided in awe as Tom put the old mule through its immaculate paces, finally astounding them when he made Mr Potts canter backwards, a trainer's feat which no one had ever achieved with a thoroughbred horse. William remarked to the three white lads, 'Maybe I should have Tom give you three a few lessons.' He began to astound his neighbours by buying up notoriously 'renegade' horses. Tom talked to them kindly, never used a whip, and trained them to the point where his father could sell them at a good profit.

Frequenting livestock sales at his father's suggestion, Tom heard tales of the new 'city', Mexico, which was becoming famous for horse breeding. Then, just before his sixteenth birthday, he met Joseph Potts, who ran the biggest saddle-horse business there. Potts suggested that Tom might get a job as bellhop in Mexico's Ringo Hotel, and in 1878, the young man did exactly that. He did wonders with the proprietor's coach horses, and Potts soon asked him to join his company, Mexico Horse Sales. With a bad-tempered, though beautiful, mare, Blazing Black, whom only he could control, he became the first black man to ride in a Missouri show. He was soon known as the rider to beat.

Potts sold up in 1883. Tom Bass bought four undeveloped acres and built his own horse barn. Already the father of twin sons out of wedlock, in 1887 he married a schoolteacher, Angie Jewell. She was a resourceful partner for a man who had had only three years' schooling and couldn't manage even mental arithmetic, perhaps one explanation of his extraordinary indifference to money. She drilled him in mathematics and spelling. But she understood his overwhelming passion for horses, and shared fully in one extraordinary triumph. Tom rescued a handsome, well-bred gelding which had stampeded through a rail fence in a thunderstorm, had a huge splinter gashing its neck and shoulder, and was about to be put out of its misery. He nursed and trained Denver to the point where he was skilled enough to be shown – but no judge would give a prize to a beast still disfigured with jagged scars. Angie, who weekly used hot combs to straighten her own hair, like all genteel black ladies, applied her skills to re-train Denver's silver mane so that it flowed (against nature) over the scarred side of his neck. Denver then won his very first horse show, in Kansas City, and went on to many more triumphs.

Long before that Columbus, his first independently owned star horse, had made Tom's reputation at the St Louis Show. He opened a stable in Kansas City, and set up the first of his Tom Bass Riding Clubs there. For a time he trained Rex Macdonald, greatest of all Saddle Horse stallions. With his dainty silver mare Miss Rex, he took on and beat Lou Chief, the whirlwind queen of Kentucky. Miss Rex was adjudged World Champion at the World's Fair in Chicago. President Grover Cleveland saw this, and came back to the barn to meet her and Tom. Bass rode in Cleveland's Inauguration Parade. Now famous horsemen, millionaires and great public men flocked to Tom's stable in Kansas City. He found a very beautiful gelding for Theodore Roosevelt.

In 1897, Tom rode Miss Rex to an astonishing victory, for a huge new prize, in the Championship Class of the Kansas City Show. It was the first time Rex MacDonald had ever been beaten. Miss Rex's owner insisted that Tom took the prize money for himself. Tom was invited to a banquet for a future President, William McKinley. The candidate whom McKinley defeated, William Jennings Bryan, became another valued customer.

After he had moved back to Mexico, Miss., in 1902, Tom was nearly mortally injured when his favourite Columbus, on whom he was mounted, fell over backwards on top of him at the Show. It was reported that the devoted animal did his best to raise up his stricken master with his hooves and teeth. It was a long time before Tom could ride again. But he bred and trained yet another supreme though tempestuous horse, Belle Beach, 'the greatest show mare in American history'. Tom taught her to dance to music from a gramophone. As a band played at her first show, she waltzed with Tom, then, to general astonishment, stomped into the country dance 'Turkey in the Straw'.

For all the pleasure his displays gave and the cordial friendship of eminent customers, Tom Bass could not escape Jim Crow. Wealthy admirers were often bewildered to discover that normal bans on blacks in bars and railway carriages applied to this courteous and distinguished man. At one point, the contemptuous refusal of his friend the great white horseman John Hook to sign it stymied a petition by many notable showpeople that negroes should be barred from competition. At another, the Iowa State Fair Board, a long way north of the Mason–Dixon line, refused to let him compete. White friends from Missouri wouldn't let him take his sixteen horses away and showed them in every class in which they were entered, winning more than their fair share of ribbons and prizes. Next year Tom went back to the Des Moines show, was allowed to ride, and swept up most of the prizes.

McKinley was assassinated, Roosevelt died, but Tom had another Presidental admirer in Calvin Coolidge, to whom Belle Beach sycophantically kneeled after a special performance. In 1929, when she was twenty-four and he was seventy, Tom decided that he and Belle must retire. Making a small comeback at the St Louis Spring Show in 1931, Tom suffered a heart attack. News agencies put out the story all over the world. Interviewed by the press, he explained what epitomised his utter devotion to horses. 'I'm glad that automobiles came in when they did. Many nights I have lain awake thinking of tired old horses that had been whipped all day to make them do things that their bodily strength did not permit. To a man who loves a horse, to see one abused is as bad as having the whip laid to his own body. So the automobiles after all were a welcome relief to the average horse.' (Downey, 200).

After his death, black people ran his funeral, but Mexico's white people gathered in force to pay their respects to their most famous fellow-townsman. In 1949, the Missouri State House of Representatives voted that he should be honoured with a memorial. A stone erected over his grave shows Tom, upright as ever, riding Belle Beach.

Bill Downey, Tom Bass: Black Horseman, *(St Louis, MO) 1975; Dorothy Bass Spann,* Black Pioneers: A History of a Pioneer Family in Colorado Springs, *(Colorado Springs) 1978; thanks to Polly Rewt*

Belgrade (Britain?) *fl.*1740s

'This singular female, whose masculine features and appearance every way suited the occupation she chose for her livelihood, attached herself to the British soldiery, and followed the camp as a sutler. She was known only by the name of Belgrade, and was so called from being in the noted battle which took place in Hungary, at a city of that name. She came to the brigade of English Horse-guards at Waesbaden on the Rhine in Germany, and continued faithfully serving them with provisions, &c. and was remarkable for exposing her person even in the very heat of action, by assisting the wounded and distressed. All the female followers of a camp do not bear quite so humane and charitable a character; Smollett, in his admirable *Adventures of Ferdinand Count Fathom*, gives an animated picture of his hero's mother, who followed the army, under the same employ as Belgrade; but, unlike the latter, instead of alleviating and assisting the wounded and distressed, the field of battle inspired her with no other feeling but plunder! In the pursuit of which, she kindly eased the wretched victims (not quite dead) of their lives as well as property, for the better security of enjoying the spoils.

'Belgrade was attended in her peregrinations by a favourite dog, named Clumsey, who rendered himself truly remarkable at the battle of Dettingen; when the two armies faced each other, a few minutes before the attack began, there came a French dog from the enemies' front, and immediately our English dog met him in the interval, fell upon him, and beat him back into his line, after which he quietly returned to us . . .' (Caulfield, 33–34).

Tobias Smollett's novel *The Adventures of Ferdinand Count Fathom* (1753) is the grim tale of a swindler, not popular when it was first published. Dettingen, fought near Hanau in the War of Austrian Succession, in June 1743, was a notable British victory, in which George II was the last reigning British monarch to appear in battle.

James Caulfield, Portraits, Memoirs, and Characters of Remarkable Persons from the Revolution in 1688 to the End of the Reign of George II, *vol. 3, 1820.*

Annie Besant (England) 1847–1933

Annie Wood was the only daughter of a businessman who worked in the City of London, a scholarly person and a religious sceptic. Annie was three-quarters Irish, and this mattered to her, but her family were not wild – her brother became a distinguished public servant, and died 'Sir Henry'. Her mother paid to send him to public school, though she was widowed when Annie was five – she moved to Harrow, and took in boy boarders. Miss Ellen Marryat became interested in her daughter when Annie was eight, and offered to educate her, along with other protégées, in her country house in Dorset. Annie got a good education, even though Miss Marryat was a hell-fire Evangelical Protestant.

In her teens Annie yearned for self-sacrifice. When she was eighteen, she accepted the proposal of a shy young clergyman, Frank Besant, thinking that she would devote her life to battling against sin and misery. Instead, she was shocked by sex, and turned out to be no good at housekeeping. Life in a Lincolnshire vicarage was hell. A son, Digby, was born in 1869 and a daughter, Mabel, eighteen months later. Nursing Mabel through a desperate illness, she began to lose her faith in God. In 1873, when she was twenty-five, her husband told her that she must attend his Communion services or leave him. A legal separation was arranged. Annie got custody of Mabel. Frank kept his son.

Annie had published a few stories in a magazine during her wifehood, and now, back in London, earned small sums by writing tracts. She was at this stage a rationalist Theist, not an Atheist, but that changed when she joined the National Secular Society and met its remarkable leader, **Charles Bradlaugh** (q.v.).

The apparatus of British Freethought which he dominated with his pen, voice and legal acumen was a close match of that of an Evangelical Christian sect. Freethought Halls were its churches, it had its Secular Hymn Book, it published a journal and tracts – and leading freethinkers indulged in bitter public splits and quarrels. Bradlaugh needed the support of someone like Annie as much as she needed his inspiration. She was bowled over when she first heard him lecture at his headquarters, the Hall of Science, in the summer of 1874 – this tall man with his massive head and mighty brow, cheered ecstatically by a packed audience. Within three weeks she had a job as columnist and reviewer for the *National Reformer*, and began busily writing, as 'Ajax', about practically everything. She launched her own career as a tireless agitator for Bradlaugh's causes – atheism, republicanism and agricultural reform. Young, comely, with a strong, musical voice, ardent in her platform advocacy, Annie bumped around in farm carts, slept in miners' cottages, was reviled and spat upon – a charismatic heroine for the National Secular Society, of which she was elected vice-president in 1875.

Bradlaugh was separated from his hopelessly alcoholic wife, and his daughters Alice and Hypatia (named after the martyred pagan philosopher, q.v.) spent most of their time with him. But the great atheist was impeccably Victorian in his moral standards. He could not divorce his wife, and Annie, by accepting a legal separation, had debarred herself from divorce from Frank. Bradlaugh's daughter Hypatia, not an uncritical fan of Annie, conceded in her biography of her father that their relationship was 'of so close a nature that had both been free it would undoubtedly have ended in marriage' (Bonner, vol. 2, 13). As it was, they functioned as Presidential Consorts of Freethought. Annie soon became co-editor and co-proprietor of the *National Reformer*. In 1876 the pair collaborated in organising a 'monster petition' against grants from public taxation to the Royal family. A strip of paper almost a mile long when unrolled was trundled to the House of Commons as 'The petition of the undersigned Charles Bradlaugh, Annie Besant, and 102,934 others' (Dinnage, 34).

Annie was now able to acquire a house in St John's Wood. Bradlaugh and his daughters moved to within ten minutes' walk. Bradlaugh would turn up at Annie's with his books and papers and write and write while she got on with her own work. Frank set private detectives on to his wife but they could find nothing incriminating. Bradlaugh would pack up and walk home about 10 p.m. every evening. Annie said he was 'the merriest of companions in our rare hours of relaxation', but it is very hard to imagine either of these earnestly dedicated people actually *laughing*, except perhaps in fierce scorn or haughty triumph.

Meanwhile they achieved notoriety together as advocates of birth control. The principle of the condom was anciently known. Now mass production had started, and the price had dropped to a halfpenny, making protected intercourse only twice as costly, in relative terms, for the Victorian working man as it would be for his present-day counterpart. However, advocates of birth control in Britain, from the 1820s onwards rated the condom lowest amongst possible methods (Mason, 58). There was much moral agitation over men unable to support a family until advanced in years, who were impelled to waste their seed in masturbation or to resort to prostitutes.

In 1832 a doctor in Massachusetts, Charles Knowlton, had published an 'Essay on the Population Question' coyly entitled *The Fruits of Philosophy*. In fact, it had discussed birth control. This book had continued to sell both in the USA and in Britain, where it was published by Charles Watts, who also brought out the *National Reformer* and the many tracts of Bradlaugh and Besant. Knowlton's book had always been wrongheaded, and now it was old-fashioned as well.

In 1876, Henry Cook, a bookseller of Bristol, published it with illustrations which were deemed to be obscene. He was sentenced to two years hard labour. Watts got cold feet, and took the book out of circulation. Bradlaugh and Besant didn't think much of it, but decided that it must be defended. They withdrew all Secular Society work from Watts, set up as printers themselves, and republished Knowlton. On publication day they sold 500 copies from their tiny office in twenty minutes.

They were hauled up before the Lord Chief Justice himself at the Queen's Bench. The jury was completely confused. They agreed unanimously that the book was calculated to deprave public morals, but exonerated the manifestly sincere and respectable defendants from any corrupt motives. The judge had to find the pair guilty, but offered to let them go free on their own bail if they promised not to sell the book for the time being. Sure enough, a Court of Appeal overthrew the indictment. Knowlton's book became available again, and so did a pamphlet on birth control by Annie herself (she recommended a sponge or cotton pessary) which sold 100,000 copies and was translated into several foreign languages. However, her notoriety was a pretext for her husband to deprive her of Mabel by legal judgment.

In 1878, London University admitted women to degree courses. With Bradlaugh's daughters, Annie signed on. She did very well as a science student at first, but kept failing her chemistry practicals and never got a degree. However, her life was expanded. She was attracted to Dr Edward Aveling, a lecturer in science, freethinker, swindler and serial love rat. Now he came to live and work with her – except overnight. In 1884 he took up with Eleanor 'Tussie' Marx, Karl's daughter, and lived with her until her suicide fourteen years later.

Bradlaugh had had a run-in with Karl Marx years before, when both had involved themselves in the affairs of the Paris Commune. Marx had put him down as 'that huge self idolater' (Tribe, 126). Bradlaugh deplored the idea of class war, and as a liberal individualist wanted the state to keep out of the economy. Annie defected from his position as the result of another crush. She went to hear a young Irishman called George Bernard Shaw speak on behalf of the Fabian Society. She had expected to attack him, but stood up to agree with him, and afterwards asked him to nominate her for membership of the society. A lopsided relationship ensued. Shaw, nine years younger, flirted with her. She wrote him poems and drew up a contract for a 'free union' between them like that of Aveling with Tussie Marx. Shaw, whose view was that 'she had absolutely no sex appeal', laughed her off. She demanded her letters back. Her hair turned grey (Nethercot, *First Five Lives*, 235–42).

Annie remained co-owner of the *National Reformer*, but in 1885 she ceased to be Bradlaugh's co-editor. She was now not only a Fabian but a member of the more confrontational, Marxist, Social Democratic Party. In November 1887, after a phase of agitation by and on behalf of the unemployed in a period of sharp depression, police at short notice banned a planned march on Trafalgar Square. Some groups of demonstrators got through and were charged by mounted police, while police on foot struck out with truncheons. Two demonstrators were killed, 130 had to go to hospital, and about a hundred demonstrators were jailed. This would be remembered as 'Bloody Sunday'.

Annie, who was present in the Square, organised defence and bail for the prisoners and soon joined with W. T. Stead, a famous campaigning journalist, to found a new cheap weekly, *The Link*, to speak out for the poor. In the summer of 1888 it carried an article by Annie, 'White Slavery in London', which exposed working conditions in Bryant and May's match factory, where the firm, which was paying shareholders a dividend of thirty-eight per cent, gave women an average of seven shillings for a sixty-hour week in unhealthy conditions. They had gone on strike in 1885 but had got no support from male trade unionists. Annie held a protest meeting where 1,400 match girls agreed to come out on strike. Their cause received widespread backing and after showing impressive solidarity, the strikers were taken back at only slightly improved wages, but with a promise of better working conditions.

So far, we seem to be looking at the story of a typical Labour pioneer, who would surely go on to assist Keir Hardie and his comrades in the foundation of the Independent Labour party, living to see the first Labour Government in 1923. Not Annie . . .

In her day, Liberal Britain had long ceased to burn witches. Practical tolerance of anti-Christian views had on the whole come to stay. In Britain and North America, at least, distinguished minds were permitted to display openly their interest in occult phenomena, and new religions emerged, under the personal spells cast by a wide range of charismatic heresiarchs.

Annie moved on into strange territory, where ancient Neoplatonist ideas jostled with those associated with the mythical origins of various forms of Freemasonry, and the Great Beast Aleister Crowley would before long stand forth as wizard and diabolist. Yet mystical notions supposedly derived from eastern religions existed side by side with the scientific fantasies of H. G. Wells. The prestige of science was enormous, and the word was hijacked for occultist purposes.

In 1889, Stead asked Annie to review for their magazine *The Secret Doctrine*, two volumes by Madame Blavatsky (1831–91). This Russian lady, maiden name Helena von Hahn, had grown up believing in her own magical powers. In 1875 she and Colonel Olcott set up the Theosophical Society in New York. Blavatsky's credo, *Isis Unveiled*, published in 1877, provided an excellent shopfront. She was erudite, persuasive, even witty, in her plea for a return to Plato and 'the recognition of the Hermetic philosophy, the anciently universal Wisdom Religion, and the only possible key to the Absolute in science and theology' – which was Theosophy (Blavatsky, *Isis*, xiii). In 1879, Olcott and Blavatsky moved to India. Land bought at Adyar near Madras in 1882 provided a world headquarters for Theosophy.

The aims of the Theosophical Society seemed to Annie to include and surpass those of Socialism. It intended to form 'a nucleus of the universal brotherhood of humanity, without distinction of race, creed, sex, caste or colour', and to encourage 'the study of comparative religion, philosophy and science'. But these irreproachable humanitarian and academic aims were not what gave the Society appeal. It proposed to 'investigate the unexplained laws of nature and the powers latent in man' and in women such as the irrepressible Blavatsky (Eliade, 464–65).

Blavatsky in 1889 was living in London. Smitten by her book – 'I knew that the weary search was over and the very Truth was found' – Annie sought an audience, and went with Herbert Burrows, her coadjutor in the Bryant and May strike. The pupil of Tibetan Masters made them very welcome. 'She talked of travels, of various countries, easy brilliant talk, her eyes veiled, her exquisitely moulded fingers rolling cigarettes incessantly.' As her visitors rose to go, 'two brilliant piercing eyes' met Annie's and 'with a yearning throb in the voice: "Oh my dear Mrs Besant, if you would only come among us." Annie 'felt a well-nigh uncontrollable desire to bend down and kiss her . . .' (Besant, 340–42).

In the summer of 1889, she joined Blavatsky's Society. Bradlaugh was greatly saddened. Shaw, still her Fabian colleague, was furious. The erstwhile science student Annie insisted that Theosophy was empirical, not 'supernaturalist'. But the occult was to the forefront of her new agenda. The National Secular Society forced Annie out, she left the Fabians and she even repudiated her advocacy of birth control. But to her great delight her two children reappeared in her life and joined her Society.

1891 was a watershed year. In January, Bradlaugh passed away. Blavatsky died soon after. She had made it clear that she saw Annie – despite her regrettable lack of any sense of humour – as her successor, and Annie now became head of Theosophy in Europe and India, and in effect the movement's leader. She would succeed Olcott as world President in 1907.

She went to India in 1893 and lived there for the remaining four decades of her life. Her new views, not popular back in England, raised no eyebrows among Hindus, to whom she stressed that Theosophy was fully compatible with their own ancient learning. When Olcott took her to Adyar and she addressed the Theosophists' annual convention, the local Indian press were ecstatic about the woman who became 'Bari Memsahib', the Great White Lady.

The new man in her life, platonically as usual, was one C. W. Leadbeater, whose fame worldwide would match her own. She saw him as 'a man on the threshold of divinity' (Tillett, 3). If his stories were true, she was right. From his bed in Madras, he dispatched sea spirits to dig atoms for him out of certain mines in Ceylon. But this exploit was nothing compared to his exploration of most of the Sun's planets whilst his body remained on earth. On Mercury, for instance, he found cacti, butterflies, and small, rabbit-like animals. With Leadbeater, Annie discovered her own occult powers. Together, they reconstructed the past lives of the Theosophists, and discovered that Leadbeater himself had once lived as Ulysses in the capital of Atlantis, when it was ruled by one of the Masters whose son happened to be Helena Blavatsky (gender was not a fixed fact in reincarnation) (Nethercot, *Last Four Lives*, 48–49). Annie's fifty-three previous incarnations included a noble-minded monkey resident with Leadbeater on Mars, and the philosopher **Hypatia** (q.v.).

As for his present incarnation, Leadbeater's view of his own biography differed from that found in the documentary record. But with his patriarchal beard and mask-like face, he was a most impressive lecturer on his worldwide tours, and a great force in the Society, despite an awkward phase when he was accused of sexual abuse by the parents of one of the pubescent boys he always carried with him on his travels, for their 'education', which included, as he publicly stated, teaching them how to masturbate.

Leadbeater popularised his conception of the 'aura', a bio-energetic field surrounding the human body. In 1909, he perceived the aura of a boy playing with his brother by the Adyar river and decided that he was the new Messiah, a successor to Krishna and Jesus as incarnation of the Lord Maitreya, the World Teacher. Jiddu Krishnamurti, then fourteen, was the son of an impoverished Brahmin, who did not object at first when Leadbeater took him and his brother Nitya under his wing for schooling, and who then signed legal guardianship over to Annie. She took them to her home in Benares.

In 1899, the Maharajah of Benares had given to her foundation the Central Hindu College, a fine site and building, which became the nucleus of the Hindu University founded in 1916. Here practical Annie was furthering the education of women. But she soon had a battle on her hands, when her boys' father changed his mind and demanded his sons back. She won custody of the boys in 1914. They were sent off to England for expensive education. Nitya had some fun as a dispatch rider on the Western Front, but Krishna was kept out of the army and was miserable, repeatedly failing his university entrance examinations, and wishing that he was not a Messiah.

Leadbeater, whose reputation was bringing Annie's judgement into serious question amongst Indians otherwise well disposed towards her – Gandhi, for instance, took the view that she was a sincere woman 'duped' by her dodgy friend (Tillett, 7) – now took himself off to Australia. He had himself ordained Bishop of the small break-way Old Roman Catholic Church of London, renamed it the Liberal Catholic Church, and wrote his own liturgy for his Sydney congregation, instructing them that Krishnamurti was the new Messiah. He continued to give harbourage to boys amid renewed accusations of abuse.

Annie had always enjoined on her followers support for the Indian National Congress, first convened in Bombay by a Scot, Allan Octavian Hume, in 1885. Hume, general secretary of Congress till 1908, was himself a Theosophist (Fry, 326–27). In general, Annie was a loyal

Briton who wanted for India self-government within the Empire. She was at odds with Gandhi despite her admiration for him (they had first met at Madame Blavatsky's) when he came back from South Africa in 1916 and set forth his programme of passive resistance. In the same year, she launched her own Home Rule League. The police began to hound her, and in 1917 the Governor of Madras had her interned. She was now nearly seventy, and her health broke down. Gandhi suggested a thousand-mile protest march across India in her support, and influential Theosophist friends in Britain secured her release after ninety-four days. She had become now an Indian national heroine, and as such was elected President of Congress in 1918. But her triumph was short-lived. Gandhi's more forceful approach was winning out among nationalists and even her own Home Rule League deposed her as President in his favour.

Her Theosophists were always quarrelsome and fissiparous. Furthermore, Krishnamurti himself was by no means disposed to toe the Theosophical line. In 1929, he stood up before 3,000 members of the Order of the Star in the East which had been founded for him and disowned both the Order and Theosophy. From now on he would pursue a dignified path of his own, teaching a quietist message founded on honesty (Dinnage, 118–21).

When Annie died at Adyar on 20 September 1933, the egregious Leadbeater (who followed her out of this life in February 1934) was on hand to pronounce the First Ray Benediction, which she had written herself, over her body, and to pay tribute at her funeral. Indians thought she had been a great woman. The Bombay Stock Exchange, amongst other institutions, closed all day to honour her. Gandhi and his rival in Congress, S. C. Bose, both sent messages of grief. For three days, the Indian press poured forth its tributes. Streets were named after her in Bombay, Madras and Benares. Krishnamurti informed the *New York Times* that he held her in very high regard (Tillett, 249–50; Nethercot, *Last Four Lives*, 455).

Annie Besant, Autobiography, *1893; H. P. Blavatsky*, Collected Writings, *(Los Angeles) 1954; H. P. Blavatsky*, Isis Unveiled: A Master Key to the Mysteries of Ancient and Modern Science and Theology, *1910 edn; H. P. Blavatsky*, The Key to Theosophy, *1889; Hypatia Bradlaugh Bonner*, Charles Bradlaugh, *1908 edn; Charles Bradlaugh and Annie Besant, eds.* The National Secular Society's Almanack for 1880 . . . 1884 . . . 1890; *S. Chandrasekhar*, 'A Dirty Filthy Book':

The Writings of Charles Knowlton and Annie Besant on Reproductive Physiology and Birth Control and an Account of the Bradlaugh–Besant Trial, *(Berkeley) 1981;* DNB; *Rosemary Dinnage*, Annie Besant, *(Harmondsworth) 1986; Mircea Eliade, ed.*, Encyclopaedia of Religion,. *vol. 14, (New York) 1987; Michael Fry*, Scottish Empire, *(Edinburgh) 2001;* Lucifer: A Theosophical Magazine, *ed, H. P. Blavatsky and Annie Besant, vol. V, 1889–90; Michael Mason*, The Making of Victorian Sexuality, *(Oxford) 1994; Arthur H. Nethercot*, The First Five Lives of Annie Besant, *1961; Arthur H. Nethercot*, The Last Four Lives of Annie Besant, *1963; Gregory Tillett*, The Elder Brother: A Biography of Charles Webster Leadbeater, *1982; David Tribe*, President Charles Bradlaugh MP, *1971*

Billy the Kid (USA) 1859–81

In the summer of 1939, **Aaron Copland** (q.v.) compiled an orchestral suite using about two-thirds of the score of his ballet *Billy the Kid* which had just been premiered by Lincoln Kirsten's Ballet Caravan company. The result was an enduring and very popular addition to the concert repertory.

It begins with an evocation of the 'Open Prairie'. The rattle of the snake and the snarl of the puma are not heard. Instead, we get 'lonesome'-sounding pastoral woodwind and horn, before mounting percussion, with cymbals, produces an ominous atmosphere. We move to a very jolly 'Street in a Frontier Town'. With lively and unexpected harmonies and rhythms, Copland quotes well-known cowboy songs, including –

> Oh, you'll be soup for Uncle Sam's Injuns;
> 'It's beef, heap beef,' I hear them cry.
> Git along, git along, git along, little dogies,
> You're going to be beef steers bye and bye . . .

A 'dogie' was a calf who'd lost his mother, while his daddy had run away with another cow (Lomax 194, 204–05). Born to misfortune, destined to early death, such a beast might remind us of Billy the Kid himself. But it was the American public, not the 'Indians', who gobbled up Billy.

In 'After Billy's Capture', the town's saloon hosts an innocent folk-dance, with out-of-tune piano, before we return, in a final section,

'Billy's Death – Open Prairie Again', to primal America, now characterised by soft strings in elegiac congress with sweet woodwind and noble horns, before the drums and at last cymbals return.

One of several redeeming characteristics attributed to the actual Kid was his great fondness for music. But Copland's tone-poem corresponds hardly at all with the facts – which are numerous, though much disputed – of 'Billy's' brief and violent existence.

He was definitely born, in 1859, as Henry McCarty, in New York City, in a slum where Irish immigrants had gathered, and he had a brother called Joe. If his mother Catherine lived with her spouse Patrick at 210 Greene Street, then he gave his first wail on 17 September, and Joe came later. If Catherine lived at 70 Allen Street with an unnamed male, or no male at all, then Henry was born on 20 November, and Joe was five years his senior . . .

In March 1873 Catherine marries William Henry Antrim in Wichita, Kansas, where she has operated for a couple of years as a hand-laundress. They shortly turn up in Silver City, New Mexico, site of a mining strike not long before. This place already boasts a school. A teacher there will recall 'Henry Antrim' as having 'an artistic nature, always willing to help with the chores around the schoolhouse . . .' (Utley, 6).

Henry's mother dies. Now fifteen, the grief-stricken lad falls in with a wrong 'un called Sombrero Jack. They raid a Chinese laundry together, Henry hides the loot in the boarding house where he and his brother stay with stepfather Antrim. The proprietress finds it and hands Henry over to the sheriff. In September 1875, he make his first jail-break. Over the Arizona border he teams up with a Scotsman, John Mackie, who is hanging around the cavalry post at Camp Grant. Here, Billy learns the cowboy trade, but is soon discharged as not up to it – too wee. With Mackie, he turns to petty theft and horse stealing. In August 1877, a coroner's jury finds him guilty of killing Francis P. Cahill, but 'Henry Antrim alias Kid cannot be found'.

When he resurfaces in New Mexico, Henry has acquired fluency in Spanish. Here is an endearing accomplishment – source of 'the instant rapport and popularity' he enjoys with people of Hispanic extraction (Utley, 15). At 5'7" tall, he is slim, muscular, wiry, upstanding, and weighs 135 pounds. He has expressive blue eyes and slightly protruding front teeth, which account for his degenerate and moronic appearance in a famous photo (which might have been taken expressly to convey the peril which WASP civilisation faces from slum Irishpersons), but apparently don't detract from his charm. Apart from the Mexican sombrero which he affects, he dresses neatly and simply, not the dude. He dances well and is thought of as a ladies' man. He is quick-witted, can read and write and his cheerful, sunny nature is marked by candour and generosity – but he has one hell of a temper.

He has arrived at a nasty intersection in Western history. There are buffalo, still, on their way to near extinction. There are 'Indians', herded in these parts into reservations where Uncle Sam feeds them. There are cavalry to control the natives. And there are cattle, driven on long, long trails by bored and frustrated cowboys who – having endured ghastly winters on the range, and rounded up, branded and castrated animals in spring before they drive herds of about 2,500 beasts north at some twelve miles a day, crouching on the ground to eat their wretched food – will whoop it up with strong drink and whatever wild, wild women are to hand whenever they hit town.

Farmers who tried to homestead in the shortgrass country of the West found it a pitiless terrain for agriculture. But it suited gaunt longhorn cattle, descendants of low-quality beasts which had escaped from Spanish missions in the eighteenth century. When the Civil War ended in 1865, and embittered Confederate soldiers drifted back to Texas, towards five million head of untended feral cattle were ranging the frontier counties. One Charles Goodnight began to drive cattle west to New Mexico and Colorado, where he sold them to contractors who supplied Army camps and 'Indian' reservations. A Texas trail boss who conveyed plenty of cattle to Goodnight was John Chisum. After the Navajo left Bosque Redondo in New Mexico, Chisum acquired squatter and homestead rights along the Pecos River, and soon had 100,000 beasts running on a range stretching 200 miles.

Chisum suspected that Major L. G. Murphy, who kept a saloon and large store in the town of Lincoln, was employing rustlers to raid his herd. Vendetta now commenced, to feed at last the infamous Lincoln County War. Meanwhile, capital from England and Scotland was massively attracted by the opportunities provided by beef ranches, now enhanced by demand from construction crews as the railway drove West.

Murphy and his partner, a German, Colonel Emil Fritz, were backed by a political clique known as the 'Santa Fe Ring'. With rustled cattle, Murphy could undercut honest stockmen. The Sheriff of Lincoln, one William Brady, was an old army comrade, on his side. In the middle of 1874, Fritz died. A young Scottish lawyer, Alexander McSween, was appointed to collect his insurance policy. Having extracted his own fee for doing so, he withheld the remainder, assuming that Murphy would find means to steal it. At the end of 1876 McSween found an ally with the arrival of John Tunstall, a well-mannered English gent in his early twenties, who employed him as legal adviser as he set up not only a ranch, but a bank, and a big store in Lincoln in the most direct rivalry possible to Murphy's, which was now managed by James Dolan.

'The combination of whiskey and guns so prevalent throughout the West seemed particularly volatile in Lincoln County.' A Scottish–English team now confronted the entrenched Irish, but all English speakers had problems with Hispanics, 'intensified by the racism that pitted Texans against "Mexicans," whites against the "nigger soldiers" at Fort Stanton, and everyone against the Indians of the Apache Reservation' (Utley, 18). If the Kid did indeed brag, untruthfully, that he had killed twenty-one men, one for each year of his life, it may be that he did add, as further alleged, 'not counting Indians'.

By October 1877, the Kid was part of the most notorious gang of outlaws in southern New Mexico, varying between ten and thirty in number, led by a twenty-five-year-old called Jesse Evans. 'The Boys', as they called themselves, stole horses and cattle, in alliance with a crooked rancher. Each 'Boy' would sport more than one alias, and the Kid now decided to become 'William H. Bonney', providing himself, it seems simply at whim, with the surname with which he would enter myth and history.

The Murphy–Dolan 'Firm' enlisted 'the Boys' to intimidate their adversaries. When Evans, surprisingly, was jailed, the Kid helped the others get him out. He then drifted off, perhaps thoughtfully, to the Rindoso valley, where he met Charlie Bowdre, a pleasant, older man with a Hispanic wife. By December 1877, the Kid had switched sides and was a cowhand on Tunstall's ranch. The Kid's favourite resort of this time was the hamlet of San Patricio, where Hispanics lived in some fifteen adobe dwellings. They liked Billy, and a woman called Carlotta Baca whom he knew then would recall in 1937 that when 'the Keed' died 'many Spanish girls mourned for him' (Utley, 37). Nevertheless, it is not entirely impossible that he developed a homosexual relationship with his twenty-four-year-old employer Tunstall. He certainly seems to have been impressed by a courtesy and consideration shown by the Englishman such as he had not encountered in his brief life hitherto. He made plans to settle down as a farmer and these were well-advanced when the Lincoln County War erupted.

The Murphy–Dolan 'Firm' eggs on the family of the late Fritz to take action to recover his insurance from the lawyer McSween. An attachment of McSween's property results, and this is extended to that of Tunstall, presumed to be his partner (though that is not in fact their relationship.) A posse, including Jesse Evans, is sent by Sheriff Brady to seize Tunstall's cattle. The Englishman, forewarned, has set off for Lincoln to seek help from the courts. Brady's posse, when this is discovered, rides in pursuit. Tunstall is gunned down. War between two armed camps follows – McSween's 'Regulators' against Dolan's 'Boys'. Unattached robbers, rapists and assassins make hay as law and order break down completely.

The Kid was a relatively minor member of the Regulators. While he participated in all their battles and killings, his bullets were part of a sizeable hail. Though he was tried and condemned for the murder of the Sheriff, five others were with him when Brady was ambushed in Lincoln's main street, and the corpse had sixteen bullets in it. Billy was not the stellar lone shootist of legend. All told, his 'score' by the time he died would be four solo slayings and six deaths in which he had a hand.

The climax of the War came in 15–19 July 1878. Supported by Hispanics from local villages, McSween's Regulators took over the town. The Sheriff, Peppin, appealed to Colonel Dudley, commanding at Fort Stanton. On the morning of the 19th, Dudley marched troops with a howitzer and a Gatling gun into the town. The Kid led a party which got away with one casualty. McSween and various others were gunned down. A mob looted Tunstall's store.

Murphy soon died. Dolan was bankrupted. McSween's widow was

on her own warpath with the help of a cantankerous one-armed lawyer, Chapman. On 18 February 1879, this pair lead three Regulators, including the Kid, to parley with Jimmy Dolan, Jesse Evans and Bill Campbell. An agreement is made – no more fighting, and no one on either side to testify in court against one on the other. The lads get drunk in celebration. Campbell, who is what is known in Scotland as a 'heidbanger', jokingly shoves a pistol up against Chapman's chest and (accidentally, it seems) shoots him. The Kid skedaddles.

Enter Lew Wallace, Governor of New Mexico, a former Union General who would be better remembered as the author of a novel, *Ben Hur*, published in 1880. He was actually more interested in writing that book than in Governing, but thought he should sort out Lincoln County. He had Dolan, Campbell and Evans arrested. Unsurprisingly, they escaped. Most key witnesses of the War are now either dead or fled. The Kid is a man Wallace needs to see – not far off when Tunstall was killed, an aghast witness of Chapman's death, now rustling cattle in the Chisum country around Fort Summer. At a secret meeting with Wallace, the Kid breaks his agreement with Evans and the Boys and agrees to turn prosecution witness in return for amnesty. While the Kid is in jail in Lincoln, Wallace is bemused to find him 'an object of tender regard. I heard singing and music the other night. Going to the door I found the minstrels of the village actually serenading the fellow in his prison' (Utley, 119). The Kid duly testifies about Chapman's killing before a grand jury, but the 'Santa Fe Ring' begins to exert political pressure. A pro-McSween jury indicts fifty men – only two eventually stand trial and both are acquitted. Meanwhile the Kid scuttles back to the relative safety of thieving. Wallace has failed to secure him amnesty.

Enter Pat Garrett, new Sheriff of Lincoln. Son of an Alabama farmer, Garrett (1850–1908) was a man of superior intelligence, well-read, a lifelong religious agnostic. He knew how to impress influential acquaintances (one of his later drinking and gambling cronies would go on to be Vice-President of the US under Franklin D. Roosevelt).

On 19 December 1880, he and his posse surprised the Kid and his gang of former Regulators at Stinking Springs. They killed Tom O'Folliard, pursued the rest into the hills, cornered them in a one-room rock-house, and received their surrender after disposing of

Charlie Bowdre. The Kid was tried for Sheriff Brady's murder and sentenced to hang. He escaped from Lincoln Court House, shooting and killing two guards. He was harboured by Hispanic sheepmen in the Fort Sumner area. Garrett tracked him down there on 14 July 1881. While Garrett was interrogating the Kid's host, one Maxwell, in his dark bedroom, the Kid came in asking '*Quien es*?' – 'Who's there?' He drew, but Garrett fired first and shot him dead through the heart. He was buried alongside Bowdre and O'Folliard in the old Fort Sumner military cemetery. The granite headstone, touchingly, is inscribed 'Pals'.

The local Hispanics were not happy at all. One of them, piquantly, was Garrett's sister-in-law. Legend would have it that she was the Kid's mistress. She cursed Garrett and pounded him on his chest. Nor was the Sheriff's action universally popular elsewhere. Men said that Billy was unarmed when Garrett shot him, a cold-blooded sneak. By some process which defies explanation, the Kid, of all participants in the famous Lincoln County War, was the one singled out for deification by dime novel. Within less than a year, five 'biographies' appeared in dime-novel format. Garrett, anxious to put his own case before the public, turned to an old friend, Ash Upton, frontier postmaster and inveterate journalist. The *Authentic Life of Billy the Kid*, attributed to Garrett, was published in Santa Fe. The last eight chapters of the book are soberly written from Garrett's direct experience. The preceding fifteen display Upton's inventive talents. The introduction did not undersell the subject: 'This verified history of *The Kid*'s exploits, devoid of exaggeration, exhibits the peer of any fabled brigand on record, unequalled in desperate courage, presence of mind in danger, devotion to his allies, gallantry and all the elements which appeal to the holier emotions . . .' (Garrett, 23).

Upton and Garrett devised the operatic idea that the first man Billy killed, at the age of twelve, was a 'filthy loafer' who had insulted his mother, she being, of course, 'courteous, kindly and benevolent . . . a lady by instinct and education' (Garrett, 26–28). The general aim was to make the man Garrett had shot seem more dangerous, but also more romantic, than the Kid had ever been.

In 1926, with Hollywood launched on its course towards world domination, a Chicago newsman, Walter Noble Burns, published *The*

Saga of Billy the Kid, crystallising the legend of an American folk hero – a frontier Robin Hood, friend of poor Hispanic herdsmen, who fought corruption and greed and died a martyr to the essential advance of law and order. It was this notion of Billy as a figure representing the transition from the wild and free frontier to a settled society which informed the idea for a ballet which Kirsten put to Copland. More than a score of movies would develop this and other motifs derived from Billy's sad life.

Like a good Greek myth, the story of Billy came to contain potent elements which could be permutated so many ways. Grief for his mother. Grief for Tunstall, whose death he may vow to avenge by seeking out all the murderous posse to slay them. Bowdre and O'Folliard are his 'pals'. Governor Wallace lets him down. Garrett may be his father-figure. A devoted Hispanic lover grieves for him. The devilish Santa Fe Ring ultimately settles matters its own way . . . As the newsman says in John Ford's great Western, *The Man Who Shot Liberty Valance*, 'If the facts conflict with the legend, print the legend.'

American National Biography *(Billy and Garrett), (New York) 1999; Aaron Copland and Vivian Perlis*, Copland: 1900 through 1942, *1984; Pat F. Garrett*, The Authentic Life of Billy the Kid, *introd. Frederick H. Christian, 1973 edn; David Lavender*, The American West, *(Harmondsworth) 1969; John A. Lomax and Alan Lomax*, Folksong USA, *(New York) 1947; Howard Pollack*, Aaron Copland: The Life and Work of an Uncommon Man, *1999; Robert M. Utley*, Billy the Kid: A Short and Violent Life, *1990*

Charles Bradlaugh (England) 1833–91

Bradlaugh should be universally acknowledged as one of the heroes of English civil liberty. As it is, few people now remember him. He was an outspoken atheist and Republican. Elected MP for Northampton in 1880, he was refused permission to take the oath required for seating in the House of Commons. ('I, [name], do swear that I will be faithful and bear true Allegiance to Her Majesty Queen Victoria, Her Heirs and Successors, according to Law. So help me God.') The same constituency returned him in three successive by-elections before, at the fifth time of asking, after a general election, he was allowed to take the oath in 1886. His own Oaths Bill of 1888 was passed by a substantial majority, consolidating the right of non-Christians, and others with objections to oath-taking, to 'affirm' rather than 'swear' in various legal contexts.

Bradlaugh suffered posthumous neglect, I fancy, because he was a man of boringly irreproachable integrity, in many respects an archetypal 'Victorian'. His vehement individualism, and detestation of Socialism, ensured that he would not join Morris and Shaw in the roster of pioneers of the 'Labour Movement', members of which, with their proneness to Methodism, would largely have found his atheism abhorrent. Republican sentiment, quite strong in Bradlaugh's heyday, was thereafter very little voiced in Britain down to the 1950s.

It was a jibe of his enemies against Bradlaugh that he wanted to do away with the Queen so that he could be elected President. That such an aspiration could be regarded as inherently vain and ridiculous demonstrates the gulf between attitudes in Britain and the USA, where a self-made man with a strong intellect, great power as an orator, and organisational skills, would long have been regarded as a viable candidate for Presidency.

His early life was hard. Son of a solicitor's clerk, he went to work as an office boy, aged twelve, in his father's firm, at fourteen becoming clerk himself, to a coal merchant. Having failed to make his way as a coal agent, he enlisted in the Army at the end of 1850. After his family bought him out of his degrading situation in 1853, he turned back to the law, and before long was promoted from message boy in his solicitor's office to manager of the common law department. Though never qualified, he developed a prodigious knowledge of English law which saw him, often with success, through a lifetime of almost incessant litigation. He became a mighty soap-box orator and in 1858 he began his national campaign for the cause of atheism, stumping the provinces, hiring halls for lectures, and covering his expenses if possible by taking whatever profits accrued – but for many years there usually were none. He recounted in later life how once, having proceeded from Edinburgh to Bolton in bitter winter weather with enough money only for a ticket as far as Preston, he had had to leave his bag with the guard of the train as security for his unpaid fare. Unfed and weary, he had arrived in an unheated, foggy Unitarian chapel, where in discussion after his lecture an opponent upbraided him for the life of luxury he was leading as a paid propagandist against the Lord (Tribe, 60).

His lively young wife Susannah tried to share as much as possible in his campaigning while looking after their two young daughters. But before long, her attraction to alcohol was worrying Bradlaugh, a strict teetotaller, and when **Annie Besant** (q.v.) came into his life he was, sadly, both married and separated – alone.

The *National Reformer* was founded as an organ of freethought in 1860. Two years later, Bradlaugh bought it. Under the pseudonym 'Iconoclast' he was a strong writer, to the fore in the growing Republican movement. Amongst his scores of pamphlets, he published, in 1871, an *Impeachment of the House of Brunswick*, based on lectures he had given up and down the land, which attacked Victoria's Royal Family *ad hominem*. 'I loathe these small German breast-bestarred wanderers, whose only merit is their loving hatred of one another. In their own land they vegetate and wither unnoticed; here we pay them highly to marry and perpetuate a pauper prince-race' (Tribe, 131).

His attempts to represent Northampton in the House of Commons involved multiple legal actions – as when he sued the Deputy Sergeant-at-Arms for assault. He shifted his ground from his right to affirm to the right of a declared atheist to swear upon the Bible. The General Election of 1885 produced a new Speaker of the House, who refused any objection to Bradlaugh's at last taking the oath. Legally seated in the Parliament which he revered, he proved an exemplary member, noted for particularly hot support for Indian Home Rule. As he lay, worn out by his labours, on his death-bed, the Commons unanimously voted to expunge from its journals its resolutions expelling him.

Hypatia Bradlaugh Bonner, Charles Bradlaugh, *1908 edn; David Tribe*, President Charles Bradlaugh MP, *1971*

Lady Butler (England) 1846–1933

The Roll Call was without doubt the hit of the 1874 Royal Academy Exhibition in London.

On Varnishing Day, 28 April, the painter arrived at the Academy to find a knot of artists in front of the picture, including the very famous John Everett Millais. 'I could hardly do the little helmet alterations necessary, so crowded was I by congratulating and questioning artists and starers.' Next came the customary private view for Royalty. The Prince of Wales wanted to buy *The Roll Call* and was told that it already belonged to a Manchester businessman, Charles Galloway, who had commissioned it. By 4 May, when the exhibition at last opened to the general public, Royal attention to the picture had been publicised, and the painter found 'a dense crowd before my grenadiers'. Two days later it disappeared temporarily from view. Reclusive Queen Victoria herself had demanded to see it at Buckingham Palace. Eventually, Galloway drove a bargain with Her Majesty. She got the picture. He retained copyright on engravings, which he sold to J. Dickinson and Co. for £1,200. They asked relatively high prices – four guineas for the cheapest print, fifteen for the luxury version. But the first edition of 1,150, published on 13 July, sold out. *The Roll Call* went on to adorn homes all over Britain, and ultimately the world (Butler, 83–89; Usherwood and Spencer-Smith, 28–29, 41).

How much did this furore have to do with the fact that the painter was a woman, aged twenty-seven?

Naturally, that created curiosity. Elizabeth Thompson's picture was far from girlish romantic fantasy. *The Roll Call* depicts Grenadier Guards mustering after a battle in the Crimean war of 1854–56. Several guardsmen can hardly stand. One has fallen face down in the snow. Each of the thirty-odd figures had been individually sketched from life. Elizabeth's family doctor, Pollard, had helped her track down authentic Crimean War accoutrements in Mr Abrahams' 'dingy little pawnshop in a hideous Chelsea slum' (Butler, 80–82; Usherwood and Spencer-Smith, 57–59, 177–79). And the public responded to the sober authenticity and compassion of a composition which simply arranged soldiers in full or part face right across the canvas, with a mounted officer in profile and an arc of birds punctuating the blank sky.

Her interest in soldiers went back to a tomboy childhood in Genoa, in the days of Garibaldi's Risorgimento. Her father, Thomas James Thompson (1812–81), had inherited private means. He travelled in Europe and pursued his cultural interests. He was a widower when his friend Charles Dickens introduced him after a public piano recital to the young performer, Christiana. They married in October 1845 and Elizabeth Southerden Thompson arrived in their lives in Lausanne, Switzerland, just over a year later. In 1847 along came sister Alice, who would achieve great literary fame as a poet and essayist under her married name, Meynell. Father's independent means did not make him wealthy and Europe was cheaper to live in than England. The Thompsons moved between the home country and Italy, never abiding in any house for long.

In Genoa Elizabeth, 'Mimi', saw Garibaldi himself en route to his epic landing in Sicily and the eventual Liberation of Italy. She sketched 'charges of Garibaldian cavalry on discomfitted Neapolitan troops'. Back in England, she witnessed the upsurge of the Volunteer Movement to defend the island against invasion by Napoleon Ill of France. 'I stuffed my sketchbook with British volunteers in every conceivable uniform' (Butler, 5, 7).

She joined the elementary class in the Female School of Art in South Kensington at the age of fifteen, but soon left, after objecting to being trained merely in design, copying scrolls and patterns. However, it was almost the only place in Britain where women could study to be painters. She returned, aged nineteen, to demand the hardest instruction the School could offer, including the Life Class. Her first oil after completing her training was on a religious subject, *The Magnificat*. If the Royal Academy had accepted this painting for exhibition, Elizabeth might just have specialised in sacred subjects. But it was turned down. Then, in 1872, her father took her to see autumn manoeuvres by the Army near Southampton. One of the generals in attendance was interested in her work and hoped she would 'give the British soldiers a turn' (Butler, 78). She became aware of the achievements of French painters – Meissonier, de Neuville, Detaille – who were bringing the ethos of 'realism' to bear on battle paintings. Now Mimi, in the era of dawning mass democracy, would make a hero out of the common soldier.

Elizabeth, by the 1880s, would face competition from male British painters, such as Robert Gibb whose *The Thin Red Line* of 1881, depicting Highlanders at Balaclava in the Crimea, would give a familiar expression to the language. The pre-eminent and ultimately triumphant rival to all 'battle painting' – photography – impinged distastefully on her life at her moment of triumph in 1874. Critics exalted her. Royalty praised her. As a celebrity, she must be photographed. She resisted. 'The idea of my portraits being published in the shop windows was repugnant to me.' But she had to give in. Then, one of her aunts, 'passing along a street in Chelsea, was astonished to see her rueful niece on a costermonger's barrow among some bananas' (Butler, 91–92).

Meanwhile, she was working in her obsessively methodical way on her next big canvas, *The 28th Regiment at Quatre Bras*. This evoked an actual event in the war against Napoleon, on 16 June 1815. The regiment formed square to receive the last charge of Marshal Ney's cuirassiers and Polish lancers.

Again, she used a plethora of models. In the 1870s, most men wore moustaches, as had not been the case in 1815, so she found policemen, whose upper lips were still shaved, particularly useful. She also hired a musketry instructor to get her drill details just so. She was rewarded at the opening of the 1875 Royal Academy Exhibition by the sight of 'a dense, surging multitude in front of my picture'. Galloway had tried to get it at the same price as *The Roll Call*, but he was beaten up to £1,126 – and then sold copyright to Dickinson for £2,000. (Butler, 100–17; Usherwood and Spencer-Smith, 61–62).

In 1876 she triumphed again, with *Balaclava*. Her subject was the Crimean battle of 24 October 1854 in which the Light Brigade of cavalry, charging, famously lost nearly three-quarters of their number in twenty minutes. She showed shattered men from the shattered brigade returning from the battle. The central figure was modelled by an actor named Pennington who had actually been there as a Light Brigade trooper. Nevertheless, he was criticised as unreal. Further criticism concerned her decision to exhibit not at the Academy but at a private gallery, the Fine Art Society's premises in Bond Street. 'Fine Art Society' was the new name of Messrs Dickinson, whose gross profits on *Quatre Bras* and *Balaclava* would total, by 31 December 1876, £34,232. They had paid her £3,000 for the copyright of her new picture. Fifty thousand people viewed it at the Fine Art Gallery, and then it toured the country, so that when it arrived in Liverpool in January 1877, 100,000 had flocked to see it.

The 'brightest spring' of Elizabeth's life came in 1877. She got engaged to Major William Butler. Both were Catholics and Cardinal Manning himself married them in June, when the guests were mostly Butler's comrades from the recent Ashanti War. With 'the droll inventiveness of her conversation' (*DNB*) and his traveller's tales and forthright opinions, they must have seemed an enchanting couple to guests with strong brains and a sense of humour. William Butler, though authoritarian in his own household, was libertarian in his view of the world. Born in Co. Tipperary in 1838, he had seen the worst of the great Irish famine in childhood. His vehement Irish patriotism and feeling for the Irish poor were acquired early and lasted till he died.

William became a friend, and devout admirer, of Charles Stewart Parnell, who led the Irish Home Rulers in Parliament. His anti-Imperialist views began to influence his new wife's paintings. When she returned to the Academy to exhibit in 1879, *The Remnants of an Army: Jellalabad, January 13th 1842* evoked one of the worst disasters in British military history. In the First Afghan War the British expeditionary force occupying Kabul had been forced to retreat through arduous terrain under constant harassment. When Dr Bryden, a surgeon, arrived alone at the gates of Jellalabad, he was thought to be the sole survivor of some 16,000 men, though a few others eventually struggled in. Elizabeth, who depicted the wounded Brydon barely clinging on to a near-crippled horse with broken knees and bloodshot eyes, had been inspired by indignation, shared with her husband, against a second ineffectual invasion of Afghanistan launched by the Disraeli Government in 1878.

Two famous canvases followed before critics turned decisively away from her and the long decline of her 'serious' reputation began. *The Defence of Rorke's Drift, January 22nd 1879* was commissioned by Queen Victoria, who wanted Elizabeth to paint something from the recent Zulu War. Elizabeth was in a quandary. Her *Times* obituary would quote her as saying, 'Thank God, I never painted for the glory of war, but to portray its pathos and heroism. If I had seen even a corner of a real battlefield, I could never have painted another war picture.' But the Queen wanted Rorke's Drift, the one episode in the Zulu War which smacked of triumphant British valour. Eleven Victoria Crosses had been awarded to members of the eighty-four-strong garrison which had defended a mission station against up to 4,000 of Cetewayo's Zulus. So Elizabeth interrupted work on what is now her most celebrated composition, *Scotland Forever* (1881), in which the Scots Greys charge at Waterloo. They broke the French infantry before them, but then rashly continued galloping into a hail of fire from the French guns. They made some impact, but as they were returning, a counter-attack by French cavalry cut them to pieces. Elizabeth knew that the men whose faces we see above the heads of the horses charging towards us – ardent, grimly determined, or apprehensive faces – are mostly doomed. The picture is more scary than inspiring. Reproductions are on sale in British shops to this day.

Elizabeth bore William six children, of whom three boys and two girls survived infancy. He was knighted in 1885, so Elizabeth became Lady Butler. She went on painting battle pictures and exhibiting at the Academy, but her vogue was past. The Boer War could hardly inspire her. In October 1898, Sir William had been appointed commander-in-chief in South Africa. When he arrived, he became also Acting Governor of Cape Colony and High Commissioner in South Africa, in the absence of Sir Alfred Milner, who held the latter post. The 'Outlander' adventures in the Boer state of Transvaal, backed by the kind of people whom Sir William habitually denounced as 'usurers', were trying to stir up war with their spurious grievances. Lieutenant-General Butler refused to forward their petition to the British Government. Relieved of his civil duties when Sir Alfred got back, Sir William continued to do his best to prevent war. The War Office in London did not like this, and in July 1899 he was forced to resign. Back home 'the Radical General' was given harmless employment as commander of Western District. Retired in 1905, he returned at last to his homeland, where he served on the King's Irish Privy Council and interested himself in education, continuing to fire off his heterodox views from his home, Bansha Castle, Co. Tipperary, where he died in June 1910.

Elizabeth had imbibed his Parnellite sentiments. But she did not oppose Irish involvement in the Great War, in which one son served as a British officer, another (a Benedictine monk) as a front-line chaplain. Her work during the war was anodyne, making no attempt to rise to the scale of horror which she did apprehend. But the last painting she exhibited at the RA, in 1920, was a return to her old subject matter – the aftermath of grim battle, *In the Retreat from Mons: The Royal Horse Guards*. It had, for her, to be cavalry again. Compared with other Scottish regiments, the Greys sustained relatively very few casualties in the Great War. That was because there was little use for horsemen.

The tank arrived in 1916. Cavalry was obsolescent, like Elizabeth's pictorial techniques.

She was very annoyed when, as civil war preceded the creation of the Irish Free State, Republicans took over Bansha Castle in 1922. She went to live with her younger daughter, who had married Lord Gormanston, at Gormanston Castle in Co. Meath, and ended her days there, very deaf, a long way from the sunny Italy of her high-spirited girlhood.

Her paintings were by then thought of by 'serious' art-lovers as relics of discredited British imperialism. This was grossly unfair. But she had lost out to the challenge of photography. Official War Artists in 1914–18 – Nash, Nevinson – had actually managed by modernist techniques to register the new horrors of mechanised war – she couldn't. Movies accentuated her supersession. Her horses convey a suggestion of motion – Hollywood could display horses actually moving. No fair judge, though, surely, can deny her an accolade, as the pre-eminent British battle painter of the Victorian era, and a woman of great unsentimental humanity.

Elizabeth Butler, Autobiography, *1993 edn, orig. pub. 1922;* Dictionary of National Biography; *Pamela Gerrish Nunn, 'Lady Butler', in Delia Gaze, ed.,* Dictionary of Women Artists, *vol. 1, 1997; Simon Pepper, 'Battle Pictures and Military Scenes', in Jane Turner, ed.,* The Dictionary of Art, *vol. 3, 1996; Paul Usherwood and Jenny Spencer-Smith,* Lady Butler: Battle Artist, *(Gloucester) 1987*

Muriel Calder (Scotland) 1494/5?–1570s

When I was about four years old, my mother bought me a kilt. (This was my first and last kilt – my family couldn't afford a bigger one.) Even then I was puzzled to learn that the greeny tartan of it belonged, according to books, to the 'Campbells of Cawdor'. My father later told me the story he had had from his father of how the Campbells robbed the Calders of their independent clanship. I was delighted one day in the National Library of Scotland, where I was looking for something else, to discover, in a volume of *Highland Papers*, published in 1914 by the Scottish History Society, 'A Succinct Account of the Family of Calder', written by the Reverend Lachlan Shaw, who was Minister of the parish of Calder from 1719 to 1734. Shaw had got from his flock, orally, much the same story as my father had transmitted to me.

Sometime around then, in the 1970s, back briefly to East Africa, where I'd taught for three years, I told this story to Okot p'Bitek, the leading Ugandan poet and folklorist. Okot had picked up the traditional tales of his own Acoli people, very noted warriors. But he was genuinely, visibly, appalled by mine. He had no idea that people could behave so badly. I think I know why Okot was shocked, and will explain later . . .

It was late in the day that Calder was transformed to Cawdor. This must have been due to the influence of William Shakespeare, who thus miscalled it. Macbeth, formerly 'Thane of Cawdor' in Shakespeare's great play, in fact suppressed the Thaneship of Calder, but his successor King Malcolm restored it, and the Calder chiefs, also Sheriffs and Constables of Nairn, retained the title of Thane till the 1490s.

Then William, Thane of Calder, died in 1503. His son John had predeceased him, leaving just one child, a red-headed little girl called Muriel, born around the turn of 1494–95. Her mother's father Hugh Rose of Kilravock intended to marry her to his grandson, and took her into his own household. But the Campbells of Argyll had begun their long and greatly detested march to dominance over huge tracts of the Scottish highlands. The Earl of Argyll was great pals with King James IV, who looked to him to pacify less obsequious clans. When Kilravock's son and the Laird of MacIntosh plunged into a scrap with Alexander Urquhart of Cromarty, who launched a criminal prosecution against them for spoiling his lands, Argyll, being Justice General of Scotland, got young Kilravock off with a fine, on condition that he himself acquired wardship over Muriel and the right to dispose of her hand in marriage to one of his own kinsmen.

'Tradition', says Shaw, 'bears that she was brought to Argyll as follows.'

In the autumn of 1505, Argyll sent Campbell of Inverliver up the Great Glen to secure possesion of Muriel and bring her to Inverary, under the pretext that she should be educated in the south. The report that Inverliver took sixty men with him suggests that some fighting was foreseen. Muriel's grandmother, Lady Kilravock, knew a bit about the Campbells. Fearing that the lassie might be impersonated in marriage by a counterfeit, she plunged a great key into the fire and branded her hip. Inverliver grabbed the child, but returning through Strath Nairn, he saw a big band of Calders led by Alexander and Hugh, Muriel's uncles, coming up in hot pursuit.

Aha! Inverliver stripped Muriel and sent her, presumably shivering, off down the Great Glen with an escort of five. He dressed a sheaf of corn in Muriel's clothes and set it on a wagon as decoy for the Calders.

Fight raged around it and the Calders killed, amongst others, four of Inverliver's own sons. When the Campbell thought that the real Muriel was beyond catching, he ordered a retreat and abandoned the fake Muriel. It is said that as they rode down the Great Glen one of his men chided Inverliver, with words, in Gaelic, to this effect. 'I fear you've been very, very foolish. Look – you've lost four fine sons battling those Calders, and all for a wee mite who may catch the smallpox this winter and die.' To which Inverliver, who maybe hadn't noticed the brand mark, memorably riposted, 'She'll never die, that one, so long as there's a red-haired lassie by the banks of Loch Awe.'

Muriel, we are informed, did not die. In 1510 she was married to Sir John Campbell, son of the Earl of Argyll. She lived to a ripe old age, while the Campbells of Calder established themselves as a powerful satellite Campbell dynasty in their own right. As such, they were responsible for ousting the Macdonalds from the island of Islay, by 1619.

Now, just why was Okot p'Bitek so shocked by the tale of Muriel and Inverliver? His Acoli folk, like most African peoples, are unremittingly patriarchal. I think Okot could not comprehend how a man would sacrifice his *sons*, as Inverliver so coolly did, for such an insecure advantage. But that's the old Gaelic clan spirit for you, as when hundreds of Macleans pushed forward to be slaughtered by Cromwell's troops at Inverkeithing in 1651, each man crying out, as tradition has it, 'Another for Hector', Hector being their chieftain. The Campbells, for all the suave political manners of their Earls and Dukes, remained a Gaelic clan, and were foremost amongst the majority of Gaels who opposed Prince Charles Edward in 1745, loyal to their own clan chiefs, not to some Stuart foreigner.

W. D. Lamont, The Early History of Islay, *(Dundee), 1966; J.R.N. Macphail, ed.,* Highland Papers: Volume 1, *(Edinburgh) 1914, pp. 118–39; Spalding Club,* The Book of the Thanes of Cawdor . . . 1236–1742, *(Edinburgh) 1859*

J. L. Carr (England) 1912–94

James Carr was one of those English writers, including the great historian E. P. Thompson, who have striven, with scant success, to remind their fellow countrymen that they are the heirs of an egalitarian, revolutionary tradition. Unlike most very funny novelists, he was never seriously cruel – indeed, he was anti-cruel. Crabwise, with amazing originality, he managed also to be truly profound.

A Yorkshire Methodist by birth, he eventually pitched his defiant literary camp in those English Midlands which are not only 'sodden and unkind' but to Scots like myself so flat as to seem almost featureless. From Kettering, Northamptonshire, a place not much frequented by the muses, he published an eccentric list of books and booklets. His 'Little Poets' were designed to sell by bookshop tills like sweeties in supermarkets. When I wrote to him in 1989 to invite him to take part in a literary event in Glasgow, he replied with some enthusiasm and enclosed his tiny *Poor Man's Guide to the Revolt of 1381*. (It might have been his equally minuscule dictionary of *Kings' Wives, Celebrated Paramours, Handfast Spouses and Royal Changelings*.) I cherish the gift and greatly regret that because the London Arts Council wouldn't sponsor English writers to visit Scotland, we never met him in Glasgow.

Carr had begun working life as a primary school teacher. He became a published novelist in middle age. His reputation was established in 1980, the year when he didn't win the Booker Prize. No one now can remember who did. But *A Month in the Country*, shortlisted for the Prize, gave Carr more than his previous cult following, and was quite well filmed. Since it is not a long book, I suppose it is now a 'minor classic'. Not much happens. Two survivors of the Great War trenches meet in 1920 in a Yorkshire village where one of them is uncovering and restoring a medieval painting on a wall of the church. The other, a homosexual, is tracing a grave in the next field. In a coup typical of Carr, it turns out that the occupant, crusader ancestor of the local squirearchy, was denied burial on sanctified ground because he had converted to Islam. Carr's superbly atmospheric writing evokes an 'Englishness' which is in no way a cushion for conservative values but is anciently, anarchically, unstable.

Lovely though *A Month in the Country* is, it does not eclipse Carr's other fiction. *A Season in Sinji* (1967) derives from Carr's Second World War experiences and centres on a cricket match in West Africa. *The Harpole Report* (1972) is a subversively accurate, excruciatingly witty, account of primary school life. As Carr himself had done, the protagonist of *The Battle of Pollock's Crossing* (Booker shortlist, 1985) goes for a year to teach in South Dakota, where mayhem occurs. My own dearest favourite is *How Steeple Sinderby Wanderers Won the FA Cup* (1975). Kick by kick we learn how a Leicestershire pub team reach the Final in the first year when the Cup is opened to Scottish sides, and defeat the mighty Glasgow Rangers . . . The book is exciting, wildly funny, and ultimately sad – because the epic team, of course, splits up. (One hero goes to teach on a tiny Hebridean island by which passing boats from Oban linger so that Rangers supporters can have 'long brooding looks through binoculars at his school and cottage').

The Club Chairman, Mr Fangfoss, a cross between Alf Garnett and Oliver Cromwell, converts the disused Primitive Methodist chapel into a Cup Final Museum. The Press have had a field day with this 'very remarkable man', the voice of Deep English prejudice against more or less everything, and *The Thoughts of Chairman Fangfoss* have sold in tens of thousands . . .

Carr's love of English land and history survived without any taint of piety or illusion. Rueful, bolshie, kind-hearted yet sharp as a knife, he'd surely have felt at home with the Ranters and Diggers of the 1640s, the Nore Mutineers of 1797 – and, of course, the Revolting Peasants of 1381. To quote his day-by-day account of John Ball's rebellion:

> JUNE 13, Thursday
> John Horn, London aldermanic negotiator, lost his nerve and advised the Kent rebels to cross to the seat of power on the river's north bank. So, destroying business premises, substandard tenements housing brothels in the Southwark stews owned by Walworth the Mayor, the tremendous host appeared before London Bridge. Alderman Sybile, in whose ward the bridge lay, betrayed it and released a human flood, only a little less dangerous than Scots football supporters, down the city's narrow streets. London anarchists, pyromaniacs, jailbirds, small-time gangsters, medieval skinheads and amateur eliminators now took a hand.
>
> The Fleet Prison was burst open, New Temple and Chancery records burnt, lawyers murdered wholesale, the Bishop of Lichfield's gargantuan cellars drunk dry, the Clerkenwell HQ of the Knights of St John gutted and John of Gaunt's magnificent

Palace of the Savoy, one of Europe's architectural glories, was blown up. By the waterside, a race riot with economic overtones swelled into the cowardly slaughter of a colony of hardworking Flemings . . .

JUNE 15, Saturday
Flying pickets from Essex failed to provoke a rising in Guildford, where cricket had just been invented. Bedfordshire men, slow on the uptake, got round to a half-hearted attack on Dunstable Priory. The Mayor of Cambridge led student militants against Barnwell Priory. Buckinghamshire bands ranged the Ashridge district. And a Huntingdon spigurnel* led a flying column of minor officials and their relations to the relief of Ramsey Abbey.

*[Carr's note] *Readers should not write to ask what a spigurnel was. I don't know either . . .*

JUNE 21
Leading a posse of cavalry, the bloodthirsty Bishop of Norwich, Henry Despenser, left his Rutland holiday home, terrified Peterborough back into its normal (and continuing) drab awfulness and disappeared into the east.

Perhaps Carr's memory is not too fragrant in Peterborough . . . Gey queer people, those English East Midlanders. Last time I was in Peterborough, I watched Manchester United's extraordinary European Cup Final against Bayern Munich in Barcelona in the residents' lounge of the Station Hotel . . . An elderly gent who reminded me of Fangfoss had a lively lady from Alaska with him. He was explaining to her simultaneously how the rules of soccer work and why Man United were certain to lose. Then Man United confounded him by scoring two goals in the dying minutes. It was pure Carr.

Cheng Ho (China) 1371–?1433

In certain political systems, in ancient times, eunuchs had been assigned important political roles. This happened under Persian rulers from the sixth to the fourth centuries BCE, and in Rome under emperors from

Claudius to Titus. Above all, in China, eunuchs at court were a factor from the Chou period (*c.*122 to 221 BCE) down the end of the Ching Dynasty in the twentieth century.

Under the Ming Dynasty which ruled from 1368 to 1644, indigeneous Chinese took over the vast empire formerly and afterwards controlled by foreign invaders. Ming generals mopping up on the frontiers as the new regime settled in were ordered to recruit eunuchs for central service. Thus, Fu Yu-te, pacifying, in 1381, the mountainous southwestern province of Yunnan, arranged the castration, amongst others, of Cheng Ho, who became the most notable eunuch in history. He was assigned to the retinue of Chu Ti (1360–1424), the fourth son of the first Ming Emperor, Chu Yuan-chang. He attracted favourable attention as a soldier campaigning against Mongols on the Great Wall in the 1390s. He grew into a mighty figure of a man. We need not credit the family tradition that he was seven feet tall and that his waist had a circumference of five feet, but may believe that he had glaring eyes and 'a voice as loud as a huge bell' (Chang Kuei-sheng, 194–200).

When the founding Ming died in 1398, rule in his capital Nanking passed to his grandson Chu Yun-wen. Chu Ti did not like this, and launched fierce civil war, with Cheng Ho as one of his most trusted and successful henchmen. When Nanking was captured and burnt in 1402 Chu Ti's nephew either did or did not perish in the flames. If the deposed emperor had survived and fled abroad, Chu Ti wanted to find him, and this was one motive for the great series of maritime expeditions which he quite soon mounted, under the command of Cheng Ho. 'Yung-lo' – 'Lasting Joy' – was the era name assigned to Chu Ti's reign. One might have found joy in the political success which extended Ming influence into Burma and Siberia and annexed Annam (in Indo-China) briefly to the empire, in the transfer of the capital to Peking in 1421, and in Cheng Ho's astonishing treasure ships. But as we shall see, exuberant Ming expansionism did not last and it was probing voyages down the African coast initiated by Prince Henry 'the Navigator' in the tiny European kingdom of Portugal which launched a world trading economy linking all the great oceans directly.

China at this time was far ahead of Europe in technology. The vast state-directed operations which created Cheng Ho's navy were inconceivable anywhere else. By 1405, Cheng Ho was equipped with hundreds of ships. The sixty-two largest, so-called treasure ships, were as much as 440 feet long and more than 180 feet wide. Each of these had a crew of 400 or 500 men. With nine masts, these junks would have shamed anything to be seen in European waters. The rest of the fleet ranged down to relatively poky battleships, 180 feet long, but armed with cannon.

Cheng Ho first sallied forth in the summer of 1405 with 27,800 men under his command. That peaceful diplomacy and trade were prime objects of his expedition was shown by the silk embroideries and other luxuries which his ships carried. But that his fleet could act with politically decisive effect anywhere it went was shown when he smashed the power of the pirate Ch'en Tsu-i who had dominated the straits of Malacca. It is disputed whether five or six more such voyages followed. But Cheng Ho definitely ranged from the Philippines by the Pacific to the Swahili ports of East Africa. The third expedition, of 1413–15, returned with envoys from nineteen different countries to pay tribute in the Ming court. Cheng Ho set up forward bases from which side-missions visited yet more countries (thus, parts of his fleet may have sailed down the Mozambique Channel nearly to the southern tip of Africa, and reached furthest south in Kerguelen Island, towards Antarctica. Chinese sailors at this time may well have landed in Australia).

On board. Cheng Ho carried Muslims able to communicate as co-religionists with rulers who had adopted that fast-expanding faith. He himself was interested in Buddhism and took the Buddhist name Fu-Shan. Unlike the Portuguese, Cheng Ho's men had no crusading or proselytising religious agenda. Without much difficulty, they overawed peoples from Borneo to Zanzibar. Demand for fine Ming products overseas stimulated handicraft industries in China, especially in silks and porcelain. And geographical and scientific knowledge were greatly extended. Beside useful herbs, there were those giraffes . . .

The expedition of 1417–19 brought back an amazing menagerie for Chu Ti – lions, leopards, dromedaries, ostriches, zebras, rhinos, antelopes – but the Emperor of Lasting Joy was chiefly interested in giraffes. A previous expedition had retrieved one. This was most gratifying. The giraffe was identified with a mythical animal, the *chhi-lin*, 'which according to age-old legend was one of the greatest auspicious signs appearing in nature to signalise an imperial ruler of perfect virtue' (Needham, 530). So it was good that in 1419 the ruler of Malindi, on the Swahili coast, just visited for the first time, was one of the tribute-paying rulers who supplied Chu Ti with giraffes.

The emperor's death in 1424 unleashed those who had been critical of the voyages. There was an immemorial conflict between court eunuchs and the Confucian bureaucrats, trained in ancient philosophy, whose labours kept the mighty Empire going. Confucianism despised unnecessary foreign luxuries. The treasure expended on ostentatious voyages could have been better used on agricultural improvements in China itself. Under Chu Ti's successor, Cheng Ho and his fellow eunuchs (who had provided most of the commanders of his fleet) were out of favour. The new emperor Chu Kao-chih soon died himself, and his successor Chu Chan-chi authorised what proved to be a final voyage. From 1431 to 1433, this re-established relations with countries which had paid tribute and returned with still more giraffes, as well as elephants. Cheng Ho himself may have died in Calicut in 1433, or back in China two or three years later. He had 'sailed the longest distance and covered the widest expanse of water during his lifetime of anyone in the world up till then' (Chang Kuei-sheng, 198).

For several reasons, Ming rulers thereafter lost interest in maritime expansion. Before the end of the fifteenth century, the records of Cheng Ho's voyages were burnt, as unsuitable for human inspection. Beside the anti-eunuch resentment of the bureaucrats which this vandalism represented, there were serious economic and military factors inspiring what we might call 'Chinese isolationism'. Problems with barbarians pressing on the north-west frontier got worse. Severe currency depreciation meant that overseas trade would have required expenditure of precious metals. Perhaps most crucially, improvements under Chu Ti in the Yuan Grand Canal meant that it was possible to transport grain in China without going to sea. The shipyards were diverted from seagoing vessels to shallow-draft sailing barges, and that nursery of deep-water sailors, the maritime grain service, was disbanded in 1415. The craft of the shipwright declined. By the 1470s, only 140 ships of the great fleet of 400 vessels were left, and early in the next century it was actually made a capital offence to build a seagoing junk with more than two masts. As the Portuguese rounded the Cape of Good Hope and reached India, as Columbus made landfall in a New World, as Magellan's men exceeded Cheng Ho's records and actually circumnavigated the globe, the greatest power on earth turned its back on the oceans and left them to insignificant Western barbarians.

Chang Kuei-sheng, 'Cheng Ho' in L. Carrington Goodrich, ed., Dictionary of Ming Biography 1368–1644, *vol. 1, (New York) 1976; Joseph Needham with Wang Ling and Lu Gwei-Djen*, Science and Civilisation in China, *vol. IV, part 3, (Cambridge) 1971*

Henri Cochet (France) 1901–87

Lawn tennis was developed from the ancient indoor sport of 'real' (royal) tennis in England in the 1870s. It was an immediate hit among the English upper-middle class, and caught on so rapidly wherever the manners of that class were aped that Tolstoy instantaneously introduced a tennis match between Russian aristocrats into his ongoing masterpiece *Anna Karenina*, published in instalments from 1874 to 1878. The first Wimbledon championship was held in 1877. The first US championship, played under English rules, followed in 1881. The Davis Cup was first contested between Britain and the USA in 1900. Other national teams emerged to vie for it. By 1927, when major tennis matches attracted huge crowds, there were twenty-six in competition. That was the year when France won the Cup for the first time. It was also the year of Henri Cochet's almost supernatural victory over the great American player 'Big Bill' (or 'Beel', as French opponents called him) Tilden, in the semi-finals of the men's singles at Wimbledon.

Tilden (1893–1953) dominated tennis in the 1920s as Michael Schumacher did Grand Prix racing in 2002. He was almost unbeatable. If the 1920s were the Golden Age of tennis, their great drama was the assault of France's 'Four Musketeers' on Tilden's supremacy. The oldest of the four, 'Toto' Brugnon, though good enough in singles to be seeded, was chiefly a great doubles expert, who could keep the game going single-handed while his partner Borotra retrieved himself from the lap of whichever enchanting lady in the crowd one of his spectacular leaps had introduced him to. Jean Borotra (1898–1994), 'the Bounding Basque' who always played in his ethnic beret, featured in Wimbledon singles and doubles from 1922 through to 1963 – and still returned after that to grace the veterans' competition. Lacking supreme finesse, he dominated opponents with athletic volleying and incomparable gamesmanship. Rene Lacoste (*b.* 1904), scion of a rich family, with no need to earn a living, became the greatest tennis swot, practising insatiably, and nightly poring over notes on his opponents' styles of play. In complete contrast, Cochet was a 'natural'. He hated practice, and one plausible explanation of his propensity to win five set games after falling two sets behind was that he needed time to warm up on court before he really got going.

So it was three against one. The great male French singles players won their own Paris Championships nine years running – 1924 to 1932. Between 1924 and 1929, each of them won Wimbledon twice, and on five of these six occasions the runner-up was also a Frenchman. In 1926 and 1927, Lacoste beat Borotra for the US Singles title, and in 1928 Cochet won it. The Musketeers competed rather fiercely with each other, but combined wholeheartedly *pour la gloire* to end US dominance in the Davis Cup, which France won from 1927 to 1932. Cochet himself wrote, in 1936, that of nine million tennis players around the world, three-and-a-half million lived in the USA – and only 200,000 in France (Cochet, 9). Triumph over the emergent superpower was special joy for a nation ravaged by the Great War.

Norah Cleather, secretary of the Wimbledon club during those years, wrote: 'On the courts Henri Cochet was the fastest player alive. The beautiful Mme Vlasto, who often partnered him at Wimbledon, said to me, "*Pour Henri c'est toujours l'impossible qui est plus facile.*" At Wimbledon Cochet's mixed partner would always be the prettiest girl in the tournament (it was probably for this reason that the mixed was the one event he never won there). Whenever Cochet played a mixed double, the crowds were always around the court in thousands' (quoted in Smythe, 43).

Cochet, with his cheeky charm, has been picturesquely described as a 'street gamin from Lyons with little culture' (Baltzell, 189). In fact, his father was secretary of the local tennis club, where the boy Henri chased balls and practised in off-hours. Tilden thought him the 'greatest' of the Musketeers. His backhand was relatively weak, but his exceptional reflexes made him an inimitable master of mid-court play, of the 'half-volley and rising bounce shot'. He also introduced the use of sharply angled soft drives from the baseline across the forecourt. 'There has never been any player with the ease of execution and speed of instinctive reaction that was Cochet's at his prime.' In spite of this, Tilden found their 1927 Wimbledon semi-final 'the most mysterious match in tennis history . . . in which for nearly three sets I played the greatest tennis of my life, when suddenly my entire game collapsed' (Tilden, *Aces, Places and Faults*, 56–58).

Tilden had an awe-inducing all-round game. '. . . If inspired or mad enough at the crowd or his rival, he would serve out the match by somehow holding five balls in one huge hand and then tossing four of them up, one after another and pounding out four cannonball aces – bam, bam, bam, bam; 15–30–40-game – then throwing the fifth ball away with disdain' (Defford, 20). His cannonball serve was incomparable, but he used it sparingly. He also deployed the 'American Twist' serve, arched in, kicking high and away to his opponent's backhand, and a slice serve which pulled the ball into a slide from right to left. He didn't care to volley much himself, but was great against people like Borotra who did. His dropshots were especially delicate. On that day in 1927 he overwhelmed Cochet 6–2 in the first set, took the second 6–4, then became almost unplayable in the third, when at one stage Cochet won only two points in three games. Cochet served to save the match at 5–1 down. He took the first point. Tilden took the second. The match, after forty minutes, seemed to be over. A women's match was scheduled to follow and the contestants had appeared at the entrance to the court.

The next time Tilden won a point was when he was 30-love down at five games all. Cochet won seventeen consecutive points.

Cochet took the third set 7–5, then the fourth and fifth at 6–4 and 6–3. After the match had lasted just seventy-five minutes, Tilden sprawled exhausted on the grass as he tried to reach Cochet's winning shot. 'He sat up and played the "harp" on his racket, which allowed the crowd to relieve their tensed-up feelings in gales of laughter' (Smythe, 65).

How on earth had this turnaround happened? Tilden dismissed the theory that a group of Hindus had hypnotised him. 'I think if an explanation must be found', he wrote, 'it was the heat. It was the first hot day of the tournament and I may have had too much sun. I know that what Cochet did had nothing to do with it. He played the same tennis all the way through the match . . . in no way did he produce anything sensational to save the match.'

Hmmm . . . Games players at all levels are familiar with moments when you 'lose your bottle'. A pass is missed, a tackle is muffed, a catch is dropped, and suddenly the opposition is inexplicably unstoppable. It is like a waking nightmare. Cochet, at the crunch, had more 'bottle' than Tilden. He proved this in the 1927 final. Borotra, his opponent, always aimed to rush at his opponents with tremendous energy, win two sets, relax in the third, then come back when his technically superior rival had been lulled into a false sense of security. Against Cochet that year, he won two, lost two, and counter-attacked to 5–2 up in the final set. Then Cochet saved no fewer than six match points and won the trophy.

Cochet eventually joined Tilden on the US professional circuit, where Big Bill usually beat him. He later lived out his days as the owner of a sports-goods store. But had he perhaps been the greatest tennis player ever?

E. Digby Baltzell, Sporting Gentlemen: Men's Tennis from the Age of Honor to the Cult of the Superstar, *(New York) 1995; Henri Cochet*, The Art of Tennis, *1936; Frank Defford*, Big Bill Tilden, *1977; Edward C. Potter*, Kings of the Court, *(New York) 1963; Sir John Smythe, VC*, Jean Borotra: The Bounding Basque, *1974; W. T. Tilden*, Aces, Places and Faults, *1938; W. T. Tilden*, Me – The Handicap, *1929*

Aaron Copland (USA) 1900–90

Copland, Jewish and homosexual, was *a priori* an unlikely person to become, between Gershwin and Bernstein, the key figure in the development of a native American idiom in classical music, especially as the bright boy from Brooklyn (where his father Harris was president of the oldest synagogue) saved up enough to go to Paris when he was twenty. In Europe he fell under the influence of Stravinsky, experienced the Diaghilev ballet, made contact with Prokofiev and Milhaud, and travelled to Austria where he encountered the music of Bartok and the Second Viennese School, whose dodecaphonic music impressed him.

But European avant-gardists were fascinated by US jazz, and so was

Copland. He applied 'blue' intervals to his own compositions. Back in the USA from 1924, he would return to Europe frequently, but a trip to Mexico in 1932 took him further into the creation of 'New World' idiom. He was back in Paris in 1938 when Lincoln Kirsten asked him for the score of a ballet about **Billy the Kid** (q.v.) for his Ballet caravan company. Several factors persuaded the composer to settle down with three books of cowboy songs which Kirsten had given him and work to the scenario provided by a choreographer. His strong left-wing opinions went along with the belief that 'simplicity was the way out of isolation for the contemporary composer'. He found the words of cowboy songs and the manner of their delivery very attractive, but the tunes themselves 'often less than exciting' (Copland, 278–79). However, he had already expressed his love of Latin popular music successfully in his exhilarating *El Salon Mexico*. And as he retorted to people who queried how someone with his background could present the spirit of the West, his mother, born in Russia, had grown up in Illinois and Texas before the Koplan family of retailers into which she married set up its thriving base in Brooklyn.

The choreographer, Eugene Loring, had never been west of the Mississippi. But with Copland he elaborated a most effective scenario, which used silence to mark the shot whenever Billy killed a man, but had the Kid perform a double pirouette each time before firing 'as though an explosion of fury is going through his body' (Copland, 280). The ballet, in which Loring himself danced Billy, was a triumphant success. At its first performance in Chicago, Copland met a young dancer named Jerome Robbins who was taking a minor part. At its New York premiere in May 1939 it was preceded by a ballet, *Pocahontas*, by the subsequently important composer Elliott Carter. Its reviews were all good. It was much performed and well received in Latin America, popular at home in the States. In San Francisco an old-timer appeared back stage and told the performers that he'd known Billy and they'd got him right – except that the Kid shot left-handed.

The concert success of Copland's suite confirmed the importance of his music in the development of American culture. He had written the definitive music of Frontier America. When Copland devised a four-hand arrangement for piano, a bright young musician named Leonard Bernstein was the first to play it with him. He became a kind of father-substitute for this immensely gifted bisexual. As the first 'all-American' ballet, *Billy the Kid* paved the way for Bernstein's *West Side Story*, choreographed by Jerome Robbins, as well as much other musical theatre. A second Wild West ballet by Copland, *Rodeo*, launched Agnes de Mille, who commissioned it for Ballet Russe, on a mighty career. His reputation with other composers peaked and he began to write influential scores for Hollywood films – eventually eight in all – to set beside his symphonies and a Clarinet Concerto (1948) composed for the great Swing bandleader Benny Goodman. He became a congenial Grand Old Man, with the Norton Professorship of Poetics at Harvard and frequent appearances on TV.

He was a man of the left, and his *Fanfare for the Common Man* expressed the democratic faith with which idealistic Americans went to war against Nazism. Possibly his best-known work is *Appalachian Spring*, commissioned as a ballet score by Martha Graham and first performed in 1944. It includes the catchy Shaker melody otherwise known in the hymn 'Lord of the Dance'. Always 'contemporary' in idiom, Copland's music was usually very accessible, at a time when other modernists often seemed to write only for their fellow composers.

Aaron Copland and Vivian Perlis, Copland: 1900 through 1942, *1984; Howard Pollack*, Aaron Copland: The Life and Work of an Uncommon Man, *1999*

Jhenne Darc (France) 1412–31

The story of Joan of Arc is now so familiar that we are in danger of forgetting how very amazing it really is. At the height of a war in which the survival of his dynasty is at stake, a major European monarch turns for aid to a teenage girl, who, dressed in armour, leads his forces successfully in battle. Attempting to do a deal with one of his adversaries, the king then turns his back on her and lets his main enemies execute her by burning at the stake, as a heretic. Add the fact that the virgin heroine is, much later, canonised by Rome . . .

Joan's tale is quite lavishly documented and most of the familiar outline must in some sense or up to a point be true. Jhenne Darc, pronounced 'Jane Day' (the c is silent and she never calls herself Jeanne d'Arc, with the particle *de* implying noble birth), is the youngest of five children of Pierre, a peasant of Domremy, a small village in the Vosges mountains, on the edge of Lorraine. The family is prosperous, and she will resent the suggestion that she has been a 'shepherd girl'. Jhenne turns to silence in her teens, repelling young males who take an interest in her. She has never learnt to read or write, but her mother has taught her to recite the Pater Noster, Ave Maria and Credo, the local vicar has made a pretty good job of expounding the essentials of the faith on Sundays, and she is equipped to recognise the voices of St Michael, St Catherine and St Margaret when they come to her, aged thirteen, in visions, urging her to save France.

The so-called 'Hundred Years War' – in fact a series of wars between 1337 and 1453 in which English kings try to make good their claim to the whole of France – is going badly for the French in the 1420s. The English, allied to Philip, Duke of Burgundy, have controlled the whole country north of the Loire since Henry V of England won at Agincourt. Now his son, also Henry, has been proclaimed King of France at his father's grave at St Denis. France lacks even a titular king, since the Dauphin Charles has not been crowned yet according to tradition at Rheims. It is said by the English that he is not the true son of his father, Charles VI, who died raving mad. Propelled by her visions, Jhenne heads off, aged sixteen or so, to Vaucouleurs, the nearest stronghold still loyal to the French monarchy, hoping that Robert de Baudricour, in charge there, will facilitate her introduction to the Dauphin. Naturally enough, he rebuffs the strange young woman.

But after the English have invested Orleans, the key to the South of France, Jhenne goes back to Baudricour with her plan to relieve that town and go on to crown the Dauphin. This time, the governor gives her an escort, she gets through to the Dauphin's court at Chinon and asks to see him. Popular opinion is on her side, and the Dauphin's advisers, after a couple of days, decide that he should meet her. (One imagines fifteenth-century political 'spin' at work – 'Troops' morale is low – folk have lots of faith in these prophets who are buzzing around all over the place these days – might be worth trying.') The young Dauphin is a walking disaster area. He is impoverished, apathetic, unwarlike, and depressed himself by the idea that he isn't truly his father's son. It will be related that Jhenne wins Charles to faith in her mission by picking him out where he stands disguised amid a crowd of courtiers, by reassuring him about his own legitimacy, and by her knowledge of a particular prayer inspired by his doubts about it which is secret between God and himself. If this is true, she has attributes of a witch. Anyway, she bucks him up.

These are awkward times for the Church. The dreaded Bohemian heretic Jan Hus was burnt in 1415. His followers still hold out. The

Great Schism which saw rival Popes in Rome and Avignon was healed only in 1417. Great care has to be taken. Learned doctors examine Jhenne for three weeks, find that she is a sound enough Catholic and advise the Dauphin to use her. A council of matrons confirms her chastity. During April 1429, she is given her own armour and a squire, Jean d'Aulon, and her brothers Jean and Pierre arrive from Domremy to join her. As from 'the Maid of God' she sends her famous letter of defiance to the Lancastrians telling them to clear off, or else . . . 'I am a leader in battle, and in whatever place I shall come upon your people in France, I will make them to go out . . .' (Calmette, 247). At the head of several hundred men, with a standard painted for her by a Scot named James Power, displaying Christ Pantocrator in Judgment, Jhenne rides forth as a splendidly arrayed chivalric knight to relieve Orleans.

The cause of the Valois dynasty is now a Holy Crusade. News of Jhenne's divine mission has preceded her. Her presence inspires the beleaguered French, led by Dunois, the 'Bastard of Orleans', to sally forth and bash the English, who lift their siege and retreat on 7 May. Because it is Sunday, Jhenne won't let the French pursue them. She also prohibits swearing in the army. Jhenne is now the 'Maid of Orleans', 'La Pucelle', the Virgin Militant.

The English in further fights are driven back over the Loire, routed at Patay on 18 June. Now the Dauphin is persuaded that he must be crowned in Rheims Cathedral, though this is in Anglo-Burgundian territory, behind enemy lines. Towns on the way yield to the Dauphin, Jhenne and their army and he is is duly confirmed as Charles VII on 17 July. Jhenne is to the fore, holding her standard, beneath the altar where her king is crowned. Tears in her eyes, she clasps him round the legs and says, 'Gentle King, now the will of God is accomplished' (Warner, 86). In not much more than two-and-a-half months, Jhenne, it seems, has revived his cause.

But now Charles wants, very sensibly, to negotiate with Burgundy. A truce is made. Jhenne and her friend the Duc d'Alencon nevertheless attack Paris in September. The assault fails, Jhenne – bravely to the fore in battle as usual – is seriously wounded and her mystique is sullied. Now, though her family are ennobled as Du Lys in December 1429 – a move of which Jhenne herself does not approve – Charles's court finds her an awkward nuisance. Operating as a freelance warlord, after further trivial encounters, she is captured by the Burgundian general John of Luxemburg when she is defending Compiegne, in May 1430. The Archbishop of Rheims, formerly a fan of hers, comments that she has 'failed in her mission because she did as she pleased out of a proud heart, without humility', and takes up another lower-class prophet instead, Guillaume the Shepherd, who bears the stigmata – wounds of Christ – on his hands and feet. But this new Valois military mascot will himself soon be captured by the English . . . (Warner, 88–89). Easy come, easy go . . .

What follows, it seems, must largely be understood in relation to the ambitions of the University of Paris, where the presiding clerics, like most academics, have a yen to be 'involved in the actual exercise of power' (NCMH 7, 235), and support the Anglo-Burgundian regime, and of Pierre Cauchon, Bishop of Beauvais, a pro-Burgundian who has lost control of his see due to the forays of Jhenne . . . She is in effect sold on to the English, for 10,000 crowns, in November 1430, on the understanding that she will be tried by a church court, an Inquisition, fronted by Cauchon and dominated by local academics. Her accusers and judges are French. She is not to be treated as a captured military leader, worth a bob or two in ransom money, but as a suspected heretic and witch. Seventy charges against her are investigated in a series of interrogations from January 1431. Basically, the charges attack Jhenne's attitude. She claimed for her actions the authority of divine revelation. She professed to be sure of her own salvation. She followed what she took to be direct commands of God through her 'voices' rather than the advice of the Church. The fact that as a soldier she wore men's clothes is also held against her. This is odd, because – see **Wilgefortis** – the medieval church does not usually oppose cross-dressing by women. Indeed, the archbishop of Embrun publicly defends Jhenne's transvestism. Underlying the hostile reactions of other clerics is the current fear of sorcery. In the early fifteenth century 'Sorcerers were the new heretics, taking over from Cathars and Waldensians; to fight them was a matter of urgency' (NCMH 7, 218). The aim is to get Jhenne to admit her heresy and repudiate her 'voices'. Otherwise, she must die . . .

* * *

Jhenne keeps up her end very sturdily, sincerely convinced that she is a perfectly good Catholic Christian. The seventy charges are reduced to twelve, but, ill in prison, she is still badgered. Eventually, on 24 May, her sentence is read out publicly in Rouen. She has been browbeaten to the point where she signs an abjuration of her heresy. She is sent back to prison, apparently for the rest of her life. But soon, a visitation discovers her wearing male clothes again. She prefers them. She now avers that St Catherine and St Michael have ticked her off for her treason, in abjuring her 'voices'. She is held to have relapsed. On 30 May, she is burnt at the stake in a Rouen street. Her head is shaven and she wears a tall mitre like a dunce's hat on which she is proclaimed to be heretical, relapsed, apostate and idolatrous. The three saints of her visions are shown as devils, Belial, Satan and Behemoth. But her last cry, as the flames destroy her, is 'Jesus! Jesus!'

This, of course, is not the end of the story. In England she will be remembered as a typically nasty Frog adversary. As Shakespeare and his collaborators display her in the first, in historical chronology, of three plays later named, as a sequence, after Henry VI – this one is performed with tremendous success in 1592 – 'Joan' is a burly, cunning Amazon, and crude witch. In a travesty of historical events (she is seen taking part in a battle of 1451) she sweet-talks the Duke of Burgundy over to the French side. When an attack on Paris fails, she summons fiends to her aid, but they hang their heads in silence and will not help her, and she is captured. Having claimed noble birth, she is exposed as the daughter of a mere shepherd, who urges her captors to burn her – 'Hanging is too good' – when she snobbishly refuses to acknowledge him as her father. While faggots are being piled up, she shrieks 'I am with child, ye bloody homicides. Murder not then the fruit within my womb . . .' She says Alencon is the father, then, when mention of this deadly enemy merely increases zest for her incineration, avers that Rene, King of Naples, impregnated her. Oho! So the Maid has been sleeping around – 'Strumpet! Thy words condemn thy brat and thee.' Jolly patriotic stuff . . .

While the defection of Burgundy to the Valois side in 1435, rather than the relief of Orleans, was the true turning point of the Hundred Years War, even before it was over Charles VII was moving to rehabilitate Jhenne, and in 1456 the Pope revoked the sentence passed upon her for heresy. Beatified in 1906, she would be canonised, as Jeanne, by Benedict XV in 1920, after a Great War in which she had served as a symbol of French valour and righteousness and her native Lorraine had been reclaimed from Germany. An annual public holiday in her honour was instituted by the French Parliament.

The fact seems to have been that Jhenne was an entirely practical visionary, with straightforward military aims – to clear the Lancastrians out of France, then proceed to crusade against the Hussites and the Mohammedans – but succeeded as far as she did because she was regarded as a miracle-working prophet of a type given credence in her times by masses and monarchs alike. When she met failure outside Paris she was judged not as a soldier who'd lost one battle, but as a prophet from whom God's favour had been withdrawn. Meanwhile, the learned Parisian academics were tormented by fantasies about witchcraft and were desperate to prove that the self-proclaimed virgin was in fact an unholy harlot. 'The coexistence of heresy and chastity in one person created intolerable tension' (Warner, 116). Hence the slur that she was actually randy and promiscuous which Shakespeare and *et al.* eventually echoed was first circulated in France around the time of her burning. But her judges, it seems, could not convince even themselves that she was either a harlot or a witch. It appears that she was permitted to receive communion before her execution – implying that she was in a state of grace, as pagans and heretics could not be.

Though Jhenne repudiated the name Du Lys conferred on her family by Charles VII, the name d'Arc, when people got round to pronouncing the final 'c', around 1600, not only had a ring of nobility but irresistibly suggested the bow, favourite armament of the Goddess Diana and of the Amazons of revered classical antiquity. By the twentieth century, the erstwhile Jane Day's mystique combined the appeals of national resistance, simple peasant piety, and chivalric Amazonian valour, with kinky sexual allure thrown in.

C. Allmand, ed., New Cambridge Modern History, *vol. VIII, (Cambridge) 1999; Joseph Calmette, 'France: The Reign of Charles VII and the End of the Hundred Years War' in* Cambridge Medieval History, *vol. VIII, (Cambridge) 1936; William Shakespeare [et al.], 'Henry VI Part I', in Stanley Wells and Gary Taylor, ed.,* The

Complete Works, *(Oxford) 1988; Barbara G. Walker,* The Woman's Encyclopaedia of Myths and Secrets, *(San Francisco) 1983; Marina Warner,* Joan of Arc: The Image of Female Heroism, *1983 edn*

Esca Brooke Daykin (Sarawak/Canada) 1872–1953

Ten Years in Sarawak, published in 1866, still makes very agreeable reading. Its author, Charles Brooke, 'Tuan Muda' of Sarawak, has an evident love of this northerly portion of the Indonesian island of Borneo.

'It cannot be denied', he writes, 'that rain in abundance does fall here . . . but let the most depressed soul behold a few evenings of fine weather, with the bright moon, and it repays him for a year's gloominess.' The great painter Turner 'could only attempt to emulate' such beauty (Brooke, vol. I, 9). Brooke was also enthusiastic about the region's people. Beside Mohammedan Malays on the coast, the interior was occupied by Dyaks, famous for their practice of headhunting, otherwise dependent on rice-growing. He admired Dyak women. They married early and separated frequently before they found a partner who pleased them. 'In many cases they are more adept politicians than their husbands, and their advice is often followed in serious business' (Brooke, vol. I, 65–72, 75).

When back in England, Brooke confessed, his weaknesses were opera – a love which even the jungle had not destroyed in him – and riding. Going about, he was disgusted by the 'poverty-stricken appearance and discomfort of a great portion of the English peasantry . . . In point of creature comforts, the Dyaks certainly have the best of it.' But white settlers in the tropics die out. They must interbreed with the natives, Brooke thinks. '*An infusion of native blood is essential to the continuance of the race.*' White people 'may lose their fantastical notions and prejudices of the nursery respecting dark-coloured people ere long . . . All the idle follies of one race being better than another will vanish' (Brooke, vol. II, 213–14, 330–37). The future of the tropics should depend, according to Brooke, on half-castes. He put his ideas into practice, but only up to a point . . .

Charles Johnson (1829–1917), who took the surname Brooke, was nephew and political heir to his uncle Sir James Brooke, a hero of boys' fiction transported to real life. James (1803–68), born in Benares, served as an ensign in the Bengal Army. In the 1830s, he tried out Eastern trade and developed the view that the 'Eden of the Eastern Wave', as he called the Indonesian archipelago, was being ruined by Dutch oppression from Java. He announced that he was going to Borneo to make friends with the Dyaks and assess the chances of an English settlement. With a small schooner, he arrived in Kuching, at the mouth of the Sarawak river, at just the right moment.

The Sultan of Brunei, who claimed the northern coastline of Borneo, was a half-wit. Arabs descended from adventurers from Yemen dominated each river system. There was conflict with and among the Muslim Malay aristocracy and between them and the aboriginal Dyaks. When Brooke got to Kuching he befriended the Governor, the Sultan's nephew, Rajah Muda Hassim, and helped him to put down a rebellion of local Malay chieftains supported by Biduyah Dyaks. As a reward, Hassim gave him the title of Rajah of Sarawak, then a tiny province towards the western edge of the Sultan's domain. He proved to be a cuckoo in the Sultan's nest. 'On the pretexts of extending peace and civilisation, of punishing pirates and eliminating head-hunting', with the support of the local Malay elite and the Dyak chiefs, James and Charles Brooke extended their tiny river state into a country of 50,000 square miles, while Brunei, squeezed also by the operations of the British North Borneo Company in what is now Sabah to its east, was reduced to little over 2,000, but saved from oblivion in 1914 by the discovery of oil (Woodcock, 78–79).

James had always said that he wished to preserve whatever was good in native life, and the paternalist rule of the Brookes in Sarawak – James from 1841 to 1868, Charles till 1917, Vyner till he abdicated in 1946 – was not oppressive. The court of justice was a room in the Rajah's house. In 1877, Charles needed only nineteen European officials and a handful of Eurasian clerks to run his domain. The Brookes did not tax severely. The status of James Brooke's regime was debateable, since he was nominally the subject of the Sultan. The British Government at first got round this by making him Governor of the tiny colony of Labuan, acquired from Brunei in 1846. In 1865 Sarawak was recognised as an independent state, then it became a British protectorate in 1888, and finally a colony when Vyner abdicated. It is now part of the Federation of Malaysia.

Charles Brooke, whose clergyman father had married James's sister, had first seen Sarawak in the heady early days of his uncle's reign, when as a plucky fifteen-year-old midshipman on HMS *Dido* he had taken part in a four-day battle in which the Rajah's Dyak allies in their *prahu* longboats had bested other Dyaks deemed pirates on the Batang Lupar river, taking many heads. Two years later Charles was back again, on HMS *Wolverine*. With six other navy vessels, it joined in a successful assault on Sharif Osman and his native allies at Marudu Bay.

For years Brooke wooed Charles Johnson to join him. After he succumbed, in 1852, James gave his favourite nephew the title of 'Tuan Muda', 'young lord'. Up-country, Charles 'Brooke' dressed in Malay or Dyak fashion, learning to interpret the calls of birds as omens referring to the all-important cycle of rice cultivation, the *padi*. He was a welcome visitor in longhouses lined with human heads, where at festival time men would drink rice wine for days on end. As a single man, he was entitled to sleep with any unmarried woman, and he availed himself with gusto of this sensible arrangement. 'Every young man was expected to journey far beyond the longhouse and bring back a head as proof of his manhood, so that he could have his hand tattooed and take a wife' (Pybus, 5). So when a spear was sent round the longhouses announcing war, Dyak braves eagerly took up their sharp *parangs* and jumped into their sixty-man *prahu* war canoes. The Brookes' tactic was to divert this enthusiasm towards whatever enemy or rival the Brookes had in their sights – not *any* head: *those* heads. Thus, when immigrant Chinese goldminers rose up in 1857 and took control of Kuching, killing four whites, Charles was happy to make a present of their heads, at least a thousand in number, to his Dyak allies, saving Rajah Brooke's skin and the whole Sarawak venture.

Charles Brooke consolidated his own power base amongst the Dyaks. Then he married Dayang Mastiah, the adopted daughter of an important Malay aristocrat, up-country at Simanggang, where as Tuan Muda he had set up his seat of government. When he had to go to Kuching, he took her with him. Their son Esca Brooke was born on 27 August 1867.

James Brooke, whose sexual predilections had not been such as to encourage him to marry, had died two-and-a-half months before.

Charles, proclaimed Rajah on 3 August, had inherited enormous debts. He simply had to marry a rich English wife.

The prospect did not enthuse him. On leave in cold, old England after years up-country in Sarawak, he had found its pale girls inspid compared to his lusty Dyak concubines. But needs must. The dying James had drawn his attention to long-forgotten cousins, the de Windts. On his return to England, Charles sought them out and married Margharita de Windt, 'Ghita', who, renamed, became his Ranee Margaret. Naturally, he divorced Dayang Mastiah. Margaret was not quite as rich as he had hoped, but her money definitely helped to keep his beloved Sarawak going.

Providing an heir legitimate in British eyes was a problem – a daughter and twin sons died of cholera en route to England in 1873 – but three more sons mercifully followed. Meanwhile, Margaret had become aware of her husband's previous and continuing dalliance with native women, and she had been made really angry by her discovery of little Esca's existence, when he was about four. She was appalled to see local Malay deferring to him as the Rajah's son. Sarawak was well-stocked with Charles's children by native women. They didn't count dynastically. But a son legitimately conceived by a high-born mother, a 'Dayang', daughter of an 'Abang', was an important figure in local eyes. Margaret therefore decided to get him out of the country.

In 1874 Charles agreed to pay the curate of Sheepstor in Devon, James Brooke's English home, to look after little Esca, who would grow up believing William Daykin to be his father. Daykin's wife Mary was childless. Esca became very fond of his ailing 'mother'.

There was something – it is just not clear what – dodgy about William Daykin, an impressive, tall man with a sonorous voice. Maybe his accepting in 1866, from James Brooke, the offer to serve as no more than a curate in the tiny village of Sheepstor, after he had been expelled from a prosperous rural deanery for reasons not on record, had to do with the High Church, ritualistic views which he shared with his new patron. But a careful historian has 'a niggling suspicion that there is something else about Daykin and his relationship with James Brooke' (Pybus, 147).

It is equally odd that Daykin should go out in 1875 to Natal as Archdeacon, in Durban, of the breakaway Church of the Province of

South Africa. The Church of England had upheld the position of Bishop Colenso of Natal, controversial because of certain heretical views, and still more because he stood up for the Zulus. James Brooke had been a friend and supporter of Colenso. But Archdeacon Daykin, again for reasons unclear, soon fell into disfavour with the schismatic Bishop Macrorie – there was something in his 'character' which the 'Colenso party' might 'get hold of' – and by mid 1877 Daykin was on his travels again. How he passed the next seven years is not known. He was certainly in Canada by October 1884, when he became the incumbent of **Madoc**, Ontario – named after the legendary Welsh discoverer of America, q.v. – a malarial frontier settlement transformed by a recent gold rush, now over.

Here he was a missionary priest expected to service six parishes without lay readers to help him, and with a core constituency of anti-ritualistic Irish Protestant Orangemen who put as little as possible into his collection plate. But he found a scholarship which enabled Esca to attend the prestigious Trinity College School at Port Hope, as the son of Archdeacon Daykin, born in Devon in 1868. Norely, the cricket professional there, spotted his potential and added this new boy to the side for the grudge match against traditional rivals, Upper Canada College, in Toronto. 'As the tail-end batsman for the trailing team, Esca held his crease for an hour and a half to build a stunning winning partnership with the captain' (Pybus, 108). Instantly a hero, he went on to be an outstanding cricketer, footballer and athlete, mixing with the school's sporting dandies, himself a sharp dresser, Head Boy in his final year. He was probably never so happy again.

After a year at the Presbyterian Queen's University, Kingston, he joined his father as an assistant, lay reader, in wild impoverished rural parishes. Esca, however, developed excellent woodcraft and enjoyed hunting and fishing – which helped to feed his penurious, elderly parents. Locals suspected that he was a Native American half-caste.

In the brash but thriving town of Mattawa, where his family washed up, Esca went into business, setting up a store which soon collapsed. The capital had probably come from an inheritance received by his ailing 'mother'. When she died in 1896, husband and 'son' decided they must leave town. William at last – though only briefly – got a comfortable parish, on the outskirts of Ottawa. Esca, with his dark good looks and dress sense, was a round peg finding a round hole as a floorwalker in one of Ottawa's leading stores. In 1897, the Archdeacon married him to Edith Webster, who had worked beside him as a window trimmer, daughter of a well-regarded Ottawa family. In the church registry, Esca recorded that he had been born in Borneo, son of Rajah Charles Brooke.

It is not clear when he had learnt that this was the case. Before they left Mattawa, Harry de Windt, the Ranee's brother, in transit through Canada, had visited them, probably to make double sure that Esca would be steered well clear of Sarawak, at a delicate time when the Rajah's heir-apparent, Vyner, a perpetual absentee in England, was so out of favour that Charles was threatening to cut all his three sons by his estranged wife Margaret out of Sarawak entirely. (She was having a fine time back in Europe, where she befriended Oscar Wilde, Henry James and the painter Edward Burne-Jones, who was ardently smitten with her. Such fun cost Charles a lot of money.) But in August 1897 Vyner at last agreed to his father's demand that he should work in Sarawak. From March 1898 Esca began to receive regular cheques from the Sarawak Treasury.

Charles became a magnificent eccentric. To stay in during the Sarawak wet season, he bought a house in Cirencester, Gloucestershire, where he established a huge aviary of Eastern birds and a Sarawak museum with a thirty-foot preserved python as its centrepiece. Aged eighty-two, hunting, he lost an eye when his horse threw him. From the nearest taxidermist, to replace it, he bought a selection of glass animals' eyes – tiger, leopard, albatross – which had a chilling effect in company. Yet this stern old man whose heart seemed made of stone retained the reputation of a great seducer to whom wives of his white subordinates in Borneo and those of neighbours in England had come as easy as his many Dyak mistresses. He continued to assert in print his conviction that the British Empire, doomed, as he rightly foresaw, to collapse, due to the contempt of its rulers for indigeneous peoples, could only have a lasting legacy through miscegenation. He must have regretted the loss of Esca. But Esca was not to know that, or that his mother, remarried, remained a formidable force in the Malay community. Charles never replied to his many letters.

Back in Sarawak, Rajah Charles lived alone except for Malay servants, who heard him humming snatches of opera as he paced the wide verandah of his 'palace' in Kuching. He died in May 1917. William Daykin had died two years before, and Esca for the first time had received the documents which provided a few clues to his early life in Sarawak.

After many years as a floorwalker, he had moved to Toronto in 1912 and tried his hand at business, again unsuccessfully. By good fortune, David Dunlap, an old Mattawa acquaintance who had acquired a rich strike of silver, and proceeded to become a magnate with mining operations all over Canada, made Esca his private secretary from 1916. Esca joined the Toronto elite, with a big house which Dunlap bought for him, children at expensive private schools, membership of elite clubs. He also served as a warden of the prestigious St Clement's Church of England. In his new position he was not going to boast about his quasi-royal birth. His children, in race-conscious Canada, would not thank him. But after Dunlap died in 1924, leaving Esca a lot of money while he remained personal secretary to his widow, with all his children well married, Mrs Edith Daykin was emboldened to start chasing her husband's Sarawak relations.

She went to England in 1926, visited Sheepstor, and paid a call on the Dowager Ranee Margaret at her home in Ascot – who refused to see her. Next year, newspapers reported that the new Ranee, Vyner's wife Sylvia, would visit Toronto. A cousin of Edith's, Alex Webster, who performed as Esca's agent, dropped a bombshell, with a letter to the *Star* which informed readers that the rightful heir to Sarawak was a respectable citizen of Toronto. The story ran wild from Canada to almost every newspaper in England, where vivacious Ranees were noted figures in society, and Vyner was about to receive a knighthood. In deference to this honour, however, newspapers dropped the story. Poor Esca was now blackmailed by his cousin-in-law, who threatened to publish Vyner Brooke's assertion that Esca was merely Charles's bastard son. One way and another, the business had cost him a lot of money. Though he continued to live comfortably, he was embittered against his half-brother Vyner, who would not respond when he wrote, and he became, after a teetotal lifetime, a heavy closet drinker in old age. He was infuriated that Vyner received millions of pounds in compensation from the British Government when Sarawak became a regular colony in 1946. He wrote to the British Government asking for a similar deal for himself. This claim was ignored. Instead, the Colonial Office, while paying pensions of £500 p.a. to key Sarawak employees of the Rajah, added one for Edith Brooke Daykin. Such a slimy expedient made a fitting end to a story conferring discredit on almost everyone closely involved except Mary Daykin, and the beautiful boy whom she had brought up with love.

Charles Brooke, Ten Years in Sarawak, *1866; Cassandra Pybus*, White Rajah: A Dynastic Intrigue, *(St Lucia, Old) 1996; The Ranee of Sarawak [Margaret Brooke]*, My Life in Sarawak, *1913; George Woodcock*, The British in the Far East, *1969; thanks to Cassandra Pybus*

Vera Delf (England) 1904–99

My father was vice-chairman of the committee of public men and women who set up the Campaign for Nuclear Disarmament in January 1958.

CND certainly had much historical effect. It canalised the energies of Youthful Protest in the era of Rock and Roll. Its marching politics helped revive the comatose Liberal Party and set the Scottish National Party on course to transformation from a little clique of hairy men in kilts into a serious, election-winning force. But CND was in many ways heir to the Victorian Liberal conscience. Its quixotic, guiding conception that the renunciation of nuclear weapons by 'Great' Britain, on whose Empire the sun had never set, would overawe the consciences of rulers everywhere harked back to the delusion that abolition of the UK slave trade by the Westminster Parliament in 1807 had somehow caused the abolition of slavery. There were some decidedly Victorian personalities in CND.

John Pilgrim, whom I got to know many years later, came into the 'peace movement' from another angle than mine. A lifelong capital-A Anarchist, he was a working-class Outer Londoner, somewhat notable in early CND days as the washboard-player in a Skiffle group called The Vipers which apparently influenced the Beatles, the Stones and everyone else. Later in life, John found a niche writing newspaper obituaries of old jazzers and anarchists. Living in rural Suffolk, he witnessed the last days of Vera Delf, a belated Victorian heroine of the peace movement, and with his permission I select here from his obituary for her in the *Independent*.

> Born Vera Hart to a fourth-generation colonial family in Cawnpore, India, in 1904, she grew up in surroundings which did not make for radicalism. Her earliest letters show this clearly. 'I don't know why the Indians want us out of the country', she once wrote, 'I've never seen anybody being beastly to the Indians.' This changed quickly and the children of old India hands still speak fearfully of the remonstrations she visited on colonial wives caught being unpleasant to her beloved Indian friends.
>
> In 1924 she attended Glasgow Art School for a year but typically had little patience with the academic methods of the time. She became a non-academic painter of fresh, direct portraits. Her ability to capture likeness had been evident at an early age and her confidence and economy of line put her work, especially portraits of children, much in demand.
>
> Her approach to painting was at one with her approach to life and politics. Patient research or mastery of detail never interested her. It was the broad brush and the immediate impact that characterised both her life and her painting. Her friend Jill Tweedie was once heard to remark that Delf 'could not be bothered with anything more complicated than what she already knew . . .'
>
> Despite a stern parental injunction against shipboard romances and 'joining the bridge-playing clique', she typically ignored their warnings enough on a journey from England to India to fall in love with an army officer. Charles Delf then neglected to ask his superior for permission to marry. Taken to task, he told his commanding officer that it was none of his business. Vera had found a soulmate . . .
>
> Her unshakeable conviction of her own rightness caused some problems. At one point during a dysentery epidemic in India she embarked on a campaign to clean up the British military kitchens. Her daughter Deborah Ardizzone remembers that the ominous sound of her approaching pony and trap signalled a bout of feverish fly-swatting audible a quarter of a mile away. 'Properly fed soldiers

are less vulnerable to infection,' she announced as she replaced much of the normal stodge with chilled consommé, salads and fresh fruit. Nothing more substantial was offered and soldiers who had survived with relative equanimity the worst theatres of the Second World War revolted. It took all Brigadier Delf's diplomacy to avert a serious mutiny and both army and India Office breathed a sigh of relief when Vera Delf departed for England in 1946.

But army conventions were never safe in her vicinity. Finding that troopship conditions had resulted in more than 50 women to a bathroom she grandly commandeered one near her that was, she declared, 'always empty'. She handed it over to the heterogeneous collection of army wives of all ranks. It turned out to belong to the Officer Commanding Troops. He stationed a sentry to keep the women out but Delf simply swept past with her friends. Faced with increasing numbers of unbathed angry women and children the O/C succumbed and gave up for the duration of the voyage. It was her first taste of direct action success and she relished it hugely.

Like her husband she began political life as a Liberal voter. This in itself was enough to alienate the more Neanderthal elements of Suffolk's deep blue county set – where the Delfs went to live after returning from India. They had expected to find natural allies in Brigadier and Mrs Delf. She spent a brief spell as a prospective Liberal candidate but resigned with a typically coruscating letter attacking the local party organisation and the 'swamp Tory tendencies of its members', as she put it.

However, her letters of the time show an acute awareness that the day of the amateur MP had already ended and that her own impatience with detail made her unfit for the work of the post-war House. Her attention turned to single-issue groups where her role of general gadfly could be more effective. Inevitably these included CND and Vietnam, but as with many far younger her mind was focused by Suez, Hungary and Sharpeville. Her home in Yoxford, Suffolk, became a hubbub of committees meeting round her gigantic kitchen table, arguing conflicting ideas and planning stunts to upset what she regarded as the American occupation force in East Anglia . . .

Surprised American tourists invited back for the special coffee

Delf had sent up from London found themselves unwilling recipients of lectures on their country's foreign policy. She convinced everyone that she mattered.

Her opposition to nuclear power stations brought the manager of nearby Sizewell A to her home in a fruitless attempt to convince her that nuclear power was safe. The American ambassador wrote her an apology for the hate mail she received following publication of one of her letters in the *New York Times*.

She poured out a constant stream of letters to the world's English-language press. In much of this she had her husband's support. As the horror of Vietnam gradually became more apparent he took a grim pleasure in attacking the Vietnam War in *The Times* and signing his letters 'Brigadier Retd'. While opposed to the proliferation of nuclear weapons, he drew the line at the Aldermaston March his wife and daughter insisted on attending. 'But', she explained to him happily on her return from the second one, 'you meet such a nice class of person on the Aldermaston March.'

As well as writing Delf travelled for pleasure and peace, invariably mixing both activities to the bewilderment of Iron Curtain apparatchiks and indeed officialdom everywhere. As a grandmother, she felt fervently that her grandchildren should have a world to inherit. The women she met tended to be apolitically conservative and she set out to change this in Britain and worldwide. Through Russia, Poland, East Germany, Sweden, China, America, Italy, Portugal, France and Greece she travelled, lectured and made lifelong friends, solving the language problem with drawings and occasional lapses into Urdu.

A veteran of Greenham Common women's peace camp and protests in Grosvenor Square, she gradually withdrew from demonstrations and lecture tours as age took its toll. She concentrated instead on letter-writing and on the art gallery she had set up, with the help of Julian Trevelyan and Mary Fedden, in the grounds of her Suffolk home in the early Sixties. A number of successful artists exhibited there and many more donated pictures for the causes like Medical Aid for Vietnam that she supported.

Oddly for an army officer's wife she never really understood rank and hated any authority apart from her own. 'Authoritarian anarchist' was a phrase used by both friend and foe about her attitudes. In particular she virulently opposed racism and applauded its opponents. She was delighted by the release of Nelson Mandela and in her last months, crippled and chairbound, she insisted on being wheeled past a hall portrait of Nelson Mandela so she could formally bid goodnight to the man she had written to so often on Robben Island.

Independent, 30 March 1999

Devil (Middle East and Europe)

Nasty spirits exist in abundance in Oriental, African and Native American systems of religion. Amongst 'tribal' communities these are often thought of as deceased ancestors requiring propitiation. Ancestor worship and exorcism of demons exist also in more complex cultures. Chinese Taoism has picturesque dragons and demons, and the *asuras* of Hindu scripture are a manifold and dangerous band of spirits. In Buddhist tradition, Gautama is tempted by a spirit called Mara. But the personification of all Evil in a single powerful figure is really a middle-eastern development.

In the ancient Iranian religion founded by Zoroaster, the world, in this temporal epoch, is a scene of conflict in which the creator-God, Ormazd, is opposed by Ahriman, from whose corrupted children, called *daevas*, come all the evils around us. According to their deeds, humans are consigned to heaven and hell. Eventually, in a decisive struggle, Ormazd will break the power of evil for ever, and all believers will live happily in perpetual sunshine, each possessed of an inexhaustible cow . . . Zoroastrian understanding of life is not far from Christian beliefs, as these evolved from the ancient Semitic lore which is the foundation of both Judaism and Islam.

In the 'Old Testament' of the Jews, as Christians came to call it, Satan is a latecomer, not prominent overall. In Genesis, notably, it is a serpent, not Satan, which tempts Eve – it was St Paul who first saw the snake as the Devil. Satan's name derives from a root meaning 'to oppose'. In the great Book of Job, composed some time between 600 and 200 BCE, he is a member of God's council who becomes God's 'opponent' in a bet. Can Job be brought to curse God or not? Afflictions are rained on this notoriously good man, testing his faith, but while Job rails against his plight, he acknowledges God's omnipotence and calls on the Creator to explain himself. God, speaking out of a whirlwind, eventually silences Job's complaints. How can Job question and complain when he does not understand God's creation and its rules? Did Job make the stars or those amazing monsters, Behemoth, who can drink up Jordan, and Leviathan of the deep? 'Canst thou draw out Leviathan with an hook? or his tongue with a cord which thou lettest down? . . . Who can open the doors of his face? his teeth are terrible round about' (Job, 41).

What we call 'Evil', according to Jewish scriptures, exists philosophically 'within the concept of God and within his purpose'. Christianity carried this tradition forward. The first successful Protestant heretic, Martin Luther, declared that 'The Devil is God's Devil' (Sharma, 82).

In the Mohammedan Qur'an, al-Shaytan, under the name of Iblis, is deposed from God's company for refusing to bow in homage to Man, but is given licence to tempt mortals. In Islamic tradition he can assume any form – snake, goat, dragon or lovely angel. Lesser *shaytans* assist Iblis, the Great Shaytan, in leading from God's law those already inclined to go away. The Christian New Testament had already assembled a comparable system. Taking all references together, Satan is a former angel expelled from heaven for his pride and revolt against God. He gets other names – Lucifer ('bearer of light'), Beelzebul ('lord of flies'), Beelzebub ('lord of dung'). He personifies evil, he physically assails and possesses humans. Above all, like the Buddha's Mara, he is associated with temptation and death. He tempts people to sin and either destroys them or enlists them in his ongoing struggle against God and Christ. Leading a host of evil spirits – fallen angels or demons – he accuses and punishes sinners. Though this is devilish work, it serves God's purpose. In contrast with Judaism and Zoroastrianism, where God will triumph only at the end of Time as we know it, Christ is actually winning his contest with Satan as time goes on. On and after the Day of Judgment, Satan will still have his function, taking custody of all those condemned to Hell.

In the descent through Hell in Dante's great *Inferno*, begun perhaps in 1307, the poet's confrontation with Satan himself in the bottom-most pit is not an anti-climax, exactly, but gives an impression that the ultimate source of sin and evil has been reduced to the condition of an enormous, miserable punishment-machine, chewing away in accordance with God's Judgment. 'The Emperor of the woeful kingdom stood forth at mid-breast from the ice, and I compare better with a giant than with his arms . . . I saw three faces on his head; one in front, and that was red, the two others joined to it just over the middle of each shoulder and all joined at the crown. The right seemed between red and yellow; the left had such an aspect as the people from where the Nile descends . . . With six eyes he was weeping and over three chins dripped tears and bloody foam. In each mouth he crushed a sinner with his teeth as with a heckle and thus he kept three of them in pain; to him in front the biting was nothing to the clawing, for sometimes the back was left all stripped of skin.' Dante's Master, Virgil, tells him that the one in front, head in Satan's mouth, is Judas Iscariot, obviously the greatest of sinners since he betrayed Jesus Christ. He is flanked by Brutus and Cassius, hanging head downwards, who betrayed Julius Caesar – and like stalwart ancient Romans they bear their lesser torment stoically (Dante, 421–23). According to Dante, the Christian God punishes pagans who knew nothing about him and his commandments, and Satan, a.k.a. 'Lucifer', his instrument in this, represents in his three sad faces the 'races' of humankind, white, yellow and black.

Indeed, we may, if we wish, see the Devil, as I will call him hereinafter, at work everywhere in the world. James McAuley (see **Ern Malley**) merely expressed a frequent Christian response when he thought he had encountered him in the native rites of New Guinea. To Christians, **Ogun** and **Kali** (q.v.) have seemed Devilish in aspect. And of course all the gods and spirits worshipped in Europe before Christianity might be assimilated with the Devil, and their continuing adherents might justly be executed as witches and warlocks.

The word Devil derives most obviously from the Greek *diabolos*, meaning 'accuser' or 'traducer', but is surely related to the Iranian *daeva*, which simply reverses the connotations of the Hindic word *deva*, applied to wholly beneficent spirits. Devils in the plural 'may have been originally benign, or may be capable of acting in either a benign or malign way (Sharma, 'Devils', 319). This is clearer if we call them 'demons'. The Greek sense of *daimon*, adopted by the writers of the

New Testament to refer to nasty creatures, actually denotes a guardian spirit, or source of inspiration. The Authorised Version in English of the Bible blurs all this etymology by turning demons into devils, and so assimilates them with Satan, who becomes The Devil. Cultures under Christian influence may be divided in attitude, with some people abhorring The Devil, all his works, and all the other devils, and many getting on very well with particular beings regarded as devils by orthodox Christians, who represent good old gods and goddesses, like the ex-African *loas* of Haitian *vodun*. The Muses themselves are ancient pagan spirits. Extraordinary achievements in the arts may seem to be energised by personal 'demons'. An envied, inspired musician driven by a 'demon' might be suspected of making a pact with The Devil – but who is to gainsay the results?

Robert Burns, from a Calvinist culture where the ruling theology had damned most mortals to Hell fire, wrote an 'Address to the Deil' (1786) which on one level, from a rationalist, 'Enlightened' position, but in jocular demotic language, simply dismisses by ridicule the whole Godly conception of this infernal potentate:

O Thou! whatever title suit thee –
Auld Hornie, Satan, Nick or Clootie
Wha in yon cavern grim and sootie
Clos'd under hatches
Spairges about the brunstane cootie
To scaud poor wretches.

Hear me, *auld Hangie*, for a wee,
An' let poor *damned bodies* be;
I'm sure sma' pleasure it can gie,
Ev'n to a *deil*,
To skelp an' scaud poor dogs like me
An' hear us squeel!

(Canongate Burns, 37–41)

It is pleasantly relevant here that the word 'Clootie' which derives here from the Devil's cloven hooves is also applied to the beloved 'clootie dumplings' of Lowland Scottish cuisine, which are boiled in 'cloots' – cloths. The Devil, 'sloshing around a dish of brimstone to scald poor wretches', is to be pitied for the menial kitchen-like drudgery assigned to him. Other poets of the Romantic era were struck by the virtuosity of Devils rather than the triviality of their malice. Goethe's Mephistopheles who successfully tempts Faust (1808) represents a 'demonic' principle of energy, needful whatever its negative consequences. He is charming. Satan in Milton's epic *Paradise Lost* (1667) is more than that – perversely tragic. Amongst British Romantics, William Blake famously remarked that Milton was of the Devil's party without knowing it. His younger contemporary Byron was happy to stand forth as a member of that party, which, in his satirical *Vision of Judgement* (1822), he clearly identifies with his own, that of the aristocratical, libertarian, British Whigs. The Devil arrives in Heaven to claim the soul of George III as a handsome, witty grandee ready to upbraid God's bureaucratic angels with the senseless slaughter of the Napoleonic Wars.

The Devil turns up again too with serious satirical purpose in the next century, in Mikhail Bulgakov's novel *The Master and Margarita* (1938). Arriving in Moscow, he slashingly exposes the hollowness of Soviet society. He is now a magician named Woland, attended by the shabby Koroviev whose pince-nez have one lens missing, little Azazello with his red hair and one protruding fang, and a huge black cat first seen by one victim 'sprawled in a nonchalant attitude on the pouffe, a glass of vodka in one paw and a fork, on which he had just speared a pickled mushroom, on the other' (Bulgakov, 92). The accomplished beast is named Behemoth, after the Hebraic monster invoked in the Book of Job. This troupe are at once hilarious and terrifying. There is still diabolic life in the old Devil, as numerous other writers have latterly demonstrated, though none have been more lively than Bulgakov.

The trouble is that *we* get into bad trouble if we give in to the Devil and find his temptations more glamorous than Good. In that very beautiful book *Pilgrim's Progress* (1678), John Bunyan, tinker's son and itinerant illegal Baptist preacher, shows us a decent, ordinary man, Christian, reaching the Heavenly City and achieving Salvation after transit across an allegorical version of Restoration England – that hideous society dominated by people who were preoccupied with screwing in two senses: shagging anything female which moved and ripping off the conveniently numerous poor. The political philosopher Hobbes had not long before extolled the 'Leviathan' state as the proper master of all. Bunyan's very notable Devil, Apollyon, is like Leviathan with an English voice. Bestriding Christian's path he asks him, 'Whence come you, and whither are you bound?' The Pilgrim replies, 'I am come from the City of Destruction, which is the place of all evil, and am going to the city of Sion.' 'By this,' retorts Apollyon, 'I perceive thou art one of my subjects, for all the country is mine; and I am the prince and god of it.'

At this point, we can locate the Devil in his actual place in the modern nation state, which is quite different from his familiar presence in old-fashioned country districts like Burns's Ayrshire. There will always be learned toadies – lawyers and academics – ready to praise Leviathan and his System: the Napoleonic post-Revolutionary secular state, Stalin's Russia, or the globalising activities of the mighty multinational corporations. The System deals out Justice, based on carefully pondered rational principles or it flourishes pseudo-rational Business Plans. Because it perceives that its own security depends on being respected and, if at all possible, loved, it is generous to those who play along with it and serve it unreservedly. It usually offers some variant of the Welfare State, in which no one is to be allowed to starve or die of hypothermia if this can be managed without undue inconvenience to the rich. All the price that it charges for its handouts and fringe benefits is docile conformity.

Apollyon remarks to Christian, 'there is no prince that will . . . lightly lose his subjects.' Christian retorts that he likes God's 'service, his wages, his servants, his government, his company, and country better than thine.' Apollyon mocks this. God's people commonly come to bad ends, 'shameful deaths . . . but as for me, how many times, as all the world very well knows, have I delivered, either by power or fraud, those who have faithfully served me, from him and his, though taken by them; and so I will deliver thee'. In short, 'play the game my way, and I'll see you're all right'. Christian remaining defiant, Apollyon attacks him, with flaming darts, then closes in and they wrestle for half a day before Christian (with a bit of timely help from the Archangel

Michael) gives his adversary 'a mortal wound', upon which Apollyon spreads his dragon wings and speeds away (Bunyan, 90–95).

Few if any of us can now aspire to wrestle with the Devil himself. He is richer than the hundred poorest 'developing countries' put together and lives on an island patrolled by many security guards, controlling his universal empire with the aid of astute computers. A present-day Christian would have to be a brilliant computer hack armed with a really ingenious anti-Devil virus. However, the Devil's subordinates move quite casually amongst us. I will introduce them so that you will recognise them and be on your guard to thwart them as best you can.

Clootie, or 'Cloots', Burns's acquaintance, drinks in our locals, offers useful tips on the horses, points out the likely lasses, and mingles with our football crowds jovially inciting them to devilment. Watch out for him at weekend demonstrations and big international conferences about world trade, developing countries and ecological problems. He mixes with peaceful protesters and suggests acts of provocation which will be used to justify heavy intimidating violence by Leviathan's hired thugs – police, whatever. Then he slips outside the cordon to join his snivelling little sidekick, Toerag, in some safely distant café.

Toerag is a wretch to be shunned at all costs. He lures us into windowless bars reeking of semen spent in vain to watch bored strippers wave their legs in a mockery of Terpsichore. He provokes youths bursting with lager into senseless fights. He is always prompt with remarks to make insecure men jealous of good loyal women (and vice versa). Broken bottles, half-finished pizzas and hefty spew mark, on Sunday-morning pavements, Toerag's itinerary from pub to nightclub. Nightly darg done, he disguises himself as a beggar, shouting abuse at citizens who pass him by without dropping coins in his filthy bonnet.

Meanwhile, in pubs which serve three-course lunches of 'home-made' food fresh from packet to microwave, Beelzebub mingles with the Lesser Executive Class. The repertoire of the Seven Deadly Sins is at his fingertips. He gets Pride going. Inane boasts about Pride's new motor provoke Envy to sneers and counter-fantasies. Lust 'harasses', as we now say, the lass who is serving the food (though coming from Australia, she takes that for granted). Wrath has a row at the bar which nearly ends in blows over the cost of the last round.

Gluttony and Sloth belch their way back to the office together to slumber through yet another afternoon when their secretaries inform callers that they are 'in meetings'. Avarice, much more sober, is chuckling over a good dodge for cheating the taxman which Beelzebub has just unveiled for him.

Bigger prey is assigned to Mephistopheles. He operates at what could be called the 'human heart' of Leviathan's System, if we could believe that it has such a thing. He lobbies in Parliament, lunches with choice targets in the Club, arranges further meetings over Golf. He is not interested in the mere Sins of the politicians, top civil servants, bankers, lawyers and company directors with whom his business lies. It is Clootie's business to lure them to perilous nightclubs and casinos, Toerag's to introduce them to rough trade and cunning bimbos, Beelzebub's to manage their routine adulteries and offshore transactions. Mephistopheles is the suave and cordial proponent of Evil. As he confided recently on *Parkinson*, 'I live for my clients. I see them as my best friends.' In Britain, his favourite recent clients were Jonathan Aitken and Jeffrey Archer, but his routine work involves devising brazen lies as answers to Parliamentary questions, cover-ups of embezzlement, malpractice and sheer incompetence, rationales for bungled military operations in which thousands of innocent people get killed, excuses for making business deals with murderous dictators, and lofty legal judgments in favour of major crooks.

But Leviathan's most visible instruments are people like you and me. Our cousins and drinking companions are such folk as handle documents relating to the Army's cover-ups of alleged suicides by soldiers or the latest persecutions of non-white asylum-seekers. The mass compliance of employees in Leviathan's doings, as his System compels them to sustain it, on pain of the sack, is engineered by my last Devil.

His name is Poshlost. The meaning of this Russian word conflates with 'mediocrity'. Poshlost is the Toerag of the offices. Like Mephisto, he deals in much more significant matters than mere Sins (some of which, by the way, can be highly enjoyable). Poshlost is the master of mundane Evil. Once he controlled the clerks who kept the books in Auschwitz and wrote the Soviet record down as Stalin wanted. Now we find

Poshlost, after his daily stint in the offices of bent accountants, at ease in douce suburban gardens, discussing over tea with Jim Normal and his wife, *née* Murdstone, why naughty children have to be treated like criminals. Well-briefed, Poshlost's modestly suited client agrees with his superior, who in turn defers to his, and so on up the chain to the Cabinet, that every possible public service should be privatised, since it is intolerable that anything should happen out of which no one, not even Rupert Murdoch, is making unearned cash. The lights which Poshlost displays to his people, chatting in luncheries, muttering in buses, are those of Realism and Common Sense. The great Russian fiction writers of the nineteenth century spotted Poshlost at work everywhere in Leviathan's Tsarist system. Gogol was his most hilarious biographer, Tolstoy his most systematic analyst. Poshlost persuades ordinary people, as pen-pushers, pc-tappers and call-centre operatives, to connive in deeds which are variously – or simultaneously – corrupt, crazy, murderous, and just plain incompetent, all performed in accordance with Realism and Common Sense.

But just occasionally, Poshlost's people, addicted, as they think, to Moderation, are confronted by an immoderate eruption of Real Reality which devastates the jerry-built mindsets they have lived in. Amongst the ruins, Christian can square up again to Apollyon. The scale of incompetence in Russia exposed by the Crimean War precipitated the demise of Leviathan's cherished System of serfdom. Watch this space . . . The System in Britain is committed by windbag politicians to the concept of the Family as essential to the preservation of all we hold most dear, such as David Beckham free kicks, game shows, hamburgers, Wimbledon, Cliff Richard and Real Ale. Surely it will suddenly become clear to almost everyone, quite soon, that the Family is now atypical, that it was in its heyday a horrible, sexist, oppressive institution, that where it still exists it is the likeliest arena of child abuse, that single parenthood has worked perfectly well for millennia, and that new structures – new 'building blocks of our society', to pinch a humbug term – need to be developed, outside Poshlost's sphere, to bind individuals together in community. Such a crisis of perception as I have in mind might as well be called 'revolutionary'. It would be akin, on a different scale, to the conviction which came to be shared by more and more poor people, from about 40 CE onwards, that remarkable events had occurred around the execution and entombment of the agitator of obscure origins whom Bulgakov identifies as Yeshua Ha-Notsri.

Mikhail Bulgakov, The Master and Margarita, *trans. M. Glenny, 1969 edn; John Bunyan,* The Pilgrim's Progress, *ed. Roger Sharrock, 1965;* The Canongate Burns, *ed. Andrew Noble and P. S. Hogg, (Edinburgh) 2001; Dante Alighieri,* The Divine Comedy – I: Inferno, *trans. John D. Sinclair, 1971; Arvind Sharma, 'Devils', in Mircea Eliade, ed.,* Encyclopaedia of Religion, *vol. 4, (New York, 1987); Arvind Sharma, 'Satan', in ibid., vol. 13*

Eliza Emily Donnithorne (Australia) 1826?–86

No sensitive reader can ever forget Pip's encounter, in Dickens's novel *Great Expectations* (1860–61), with the rich recluse Miss Havisham. Living almost alone in her big inherited house, when the boy arrives she is just completing her dressing – in rich ancient bridal attire. 'I saw that the dress had been put upon the rounded figure of a young woman, and that the figure upon which it now hung loose, had shrunk to skin and bone.' Clock and watch have been stopped, a long time ago. On his next visit, Miss Havisham sends Pip into a large, dark room '. . . Every discernible thing in it was covered with dust and mould, and dropping to pieces. The most prominent object was a long table with a tablecloth spread on it, as if a feast had been in preparation when the house and the clocks all stopped together. An epergne or centrepiece of some kind was in the middle of this cloth; it was so heavily overhung with cobwebs that its form was quite indistinguishable, and, as I looked along the yellow expanse out of which I remember it seeming to grow, like a black fungus, I saw speckle-legged spiders with blotchy bodies running home to it, and running out from it . . .' (Dickens, 87, 12–13).

It has long been known that Dickens had particular women in mind as models for Miss Havisham, who stops the clocks when her fiancé jilts her on her wedding day, and leaves the wedding feast untouched for decades after. James Payn, a minor novelist, claimed to have told Dickens about one of these women, with whom he was acquainted, and said that the master's portrayal was 'not one whit exaggerated' (Dickens, 512).

Furthermore, it is likely, though not proven, that Dickens knew of a close counterpart to Miss Havisham living in Sydney, Australia, as he wrote the novel – in which Magwitch actually goes to Australia as a convict, so his creator had to take some interest in that country. What Dickens could not have known, since she died sixteen years after he did, was that Eliza Donnithorne, like Miss Havisham, would stick it out to the end.

Born at the Cape of Good Hope, she was the daughter of an Englishman who served the East India Company – a boy writer in 1792, finally a judge and senior merchant in Mysore. Eliza's early memories would have been of the subcontinent, where such customs as suttee consigned women to what seemed to Westerners exotic destinies. Her jolly father settled around 1836 in Sydney, where he became famous for public spirit and 'unbounded hospitality'. He died in 1852, predeceased by his wife, survived by two sons who had entered the British Army and by Eliza, who inherited most of his estate and the family mansion, Cambridge Hall, in the suburb of Newtown.

Here, on a fateful day in 1856, she and her bridesmaid were dressed for her wedding. The wedding breakfast was laid in the long drawing room. The guests had assembled. The groom – a naval man – did not turn up.

Eliza never again left the house till her coffin was carried from it thirty years later. The front door of the Hall was fastened with a chain which permitted it to open only a couple of inches. When it was absolutely necessary for her to talk to a visitor, Miss Donnithorne would converse through the nearly closed door. She admitted to see her only her clergyman, physician and solicitor. Her wedding breakfast, untouched, gradually mouldered to dust. It was supposed that she continued always to wear bridal dress – but long before her passing, locals would have associated her with that notable character in that famous novel. James R. Tyrrell, later a bookseller well-known in Sydney's literary circles, came to live in Newtown in the 1880s. 'In my day, the Donnithorne residence . . . came under the rude designation of "haunted", and I was still young enough to keep to the other side of the road in passing it, especially at night. Still, I would glance fearfully over to its front door, which, by night or day, was always partly open, though fastened with a chain' (Tyrrell, 22).

When Miss Donnithorne died in 1886, her estate, which included land and houses in Sydney, Melbourne and Britain, was valued at £12,000. The chief beneficiary was her housekeeper, Sarah Ann Bailey.

She is said to have found solace in reading. Perhaps she also found solace in the company of Sarah. Her brother's children got jewellery and books. The diocese of Sydney and the British and Foreign Bible Society got £200 each; £50 was left to the Society for the Prevention of Cruelty to Animals, and 'an annuity of £5 for each of my six animals and £5 for all my birds'. She was buried beside her father in Camperdown Cemetery.

In 1969, the English composer Peter Maxwell Davies was at a party celebrating the first performance of his *Eight Songs for a Mad King* – George III. His librettist was the Australian poet and novelist Randolph Stow, who suggested that they should now try something more cheerful. But *Miss Donnithorne's Maggot* is a dark piece. Eccentric frustrated sexuality is the maggot at the centre of the work. Stow takes the self-confessed liberty of assuming that Miss Donnithorne sometimes went berserk and got drunk:

> Gracious Apollo! Why am I sitting on the floor?
> I declare, it must have been the sunflower wine . . .

Naughty boys in the street outside plague her with indecent taunts. She hears them recite a ballad attributed to the major drunk poet Henry Lawson, about the application of a rural thug to join a tough Sydney gang, or 'push':

> 'But you wouldn't fuck your mother,' said the captain of the Push.
> 'I've fucked my bloody brother,' said the Bastard from the Bush.

It is a lively work. I should like to hear it again.

Australian Dictionary of Biography, *vol. 4, 1850–1891, 1972; Peter Maxwell Davies,* Miss Donnithorne's Maggot, *1996; Charles Dickens,* Great Expectations, *ed. A. Calder, (Harmondsworth) 1965; James Tyrrell,* Old Books, Old Friends, Old Sydney, *(North Ryde, New South Wales) 1987, orig. pub. 1952*

Bettie Du Toit (South Africa) 1915–2002

In May 1935, in Industria, a suburb of Johannesburg, the women who worked in the big Consolidated Textile Mills enterprise were out on strike. With police escorts, scabs were getting in to do their work. Johanna Cornelius, the twenty-three-year-old President of the Transvaaal Garment Workers Union, asked another young Afrikaner woman, Bettie Du Toit, to organise pickets outside the works, from 3 a.m., in case scabs tried to slip in early. Bettie at this stage was 'unaccustomed to leadership, or even to the basic principles of trade unionism' (Du Toit, 22). But she went to it.

Two blonde sisters with policeman boyfriends were organising scabs. Cornelius, with twenty-year-old Lucy Combrink, decided, secretly, to sort them out. Mrs van der Westhuizen went with them, because she knew where the sisters lived. A notable rammy ensued, as Bettie and her co-workers heard back at the picket. Much mirth resulted from the idea of the bulky Mrs v.d. Westhuizen, pinned on the ground by two scabs and two policemen, not defending herself but calling for help from Cornelius. As the fight had started before dawn, neighbours had poured out of their homes to see what was happening. One little lady had stopped Lucy Combrink and aggressively said that she had never thought she would witness nice Afrikaans girls brawling in the street like common women. Lucy had taken her firmly by the shoulder and said, 'Stand aside, lady, I'll deal with you later.' The lady had fled back to her home. The strikers noted with pleasure later that one of the blonde sisters had a black eye.

This was the bitterest action in 'an arena of intense struggle during the 1930s', where a tough clothing workers' strike in 1932 had led the way. Women were to the fore here. Between 11 and 13 May 1935, 300 employees at Consolidated stopped work. Anti-scab action was effective. By 2 June, thirty people who had returned to work had rejoined the strike. Only fifty women were actually working. Clashes between strikers and police were frequent. On 28 June, five women were convicted for assaulting scabs when on a picket line – Cornelius, Combrink, Du Toit and Johanna Raats (twenty-four), four Afrikaners, with one Anglo, Mary Masson (seventeen). Offered a choice between fine and jail, they went to jail. As Bettie Du Toit recalled, decades later, two of the arrested women protested that they could not go to prison – 'Our husbands will kill us.' Cornelius replied, 'And if you don't come, I'll kill you. You bring toothbrushes, and you come.' Five days together in Johannesburg fort followed. When settlement of the dispute was shortly reached, all the strikers were rehired as workers, and there was some improvement in wages and conditions.

Undoubtedly, the fact that most of the Consolidated workers were Afrikaner women enhanced solidarity. It also led to a displeasing conflict of principles. One cause of the strike was that the millowner had announced a holiday on Jubilee Day, 6 May, the twenty-fifth anniversary of King George V's accession to the Crown Imperial. Women whose fathers had fought the British weren't too keen on that, and were still less pleased by the fact that they lost pay for the day. On 7s 6d a week, they could barely pay their rent anyway. But another factor was a management decision to save on wages by replacing eighty European spinners with black African workers. Then blacks were brought in as scab labour during the strike. White workers in the Rand goldmines supported the women enthusiastically when they came in collecting for strike pay. They had vivid memories of the 'Rand Revolt' of 1922 when British and Afrikaner miners had struck against Africans being promoted to semi-skilled jobs, and had taken control of Johannesburg. Troops had been called out, martial law had been declared and four British leaders had been executed. Now, in 1935, the South African Labour Party conference passed a resolution urging all other workers to 'support these women workers who are defending the great principle of a white South Africa' (Berger, 109–13).

The sad truth was that skilled white immigrant workers in South Africa, often enough from militant Labour backgrounds in Britain, were set on maintaining their privileged position in the Rand where hundreds of thousands of migrant Africans from all over the south of the continent worked in appalling conditions for despicable wages in the gold mines which were the Union of South Africa's *raison d'être* and provided three-quarters of its exports. Pious Afrikaner farmers who had opposed British greed in the war of 1899–1901 were now prey to the propaganda of the Nazi-style Greyshirt movement founded by Louis Weichardt in 1933 and a Blackshirt rival financed by the German foreign office. The Afrikaner nationalism which would triumph electorally in 1948 and proceed to consolidate apartheid was aggressively on the march. Meanwhile, two million whites had established total supremacy over a million Asians and Coloured people and six-and-a-half million blacks. Prosperous and educated blacks in Cape

Province were deprived of the vote in 1936. Pass laws governed the movements of black people. Segregation of African from white residents in towns was mandatory from 1937.

The basic industries of farming and mining had been supplemented after World War I by expanding light industries supported by tariffs against foreign competition. These recruited women workers. They came cheap and were thought to have an innate talent for working in cloth and preparing food. There was a drift to the towns in years of worldwide agricultural depression. Especially among Afrikaners, white women came to outnumber white men in the cities (where prostitution was a fallback option). '. . . The cash contributions of daughters working in the cities were more essential to family survival than their labour potential on the farms' (Berger, 50). Country-bred Bettie Du Toit represented that movement out from the heart of Afrikanerdom. Adjustment to any vision beyond that of the Dutch Reformed Church was, for such women, extremely hard. Johanna Cornelius remarked later that 'It took me years to get used to the notion that even the English – let alone the natives – were human beings' (Berger, 123).

The only political organisation in South Africa firmly and constantly committed to the idea of one person, one vote, irrespective of race, was the Communist Party. Many of its leaders were Jews from eastern and central Europe with their own reasons for detesting racism. For seven decades, until the Communist lawyer Joe Slovo took his place as of right, revered, in Nelson Mandela's post-apartheid cabinet, the CPSA, while trotting out Leninist slogans and ostensibly toeing the Moscow line, was the rendezvous of women and men of conscience, of all classes and every colour, determined to overthrow racist barriers. So Bettie Du Toit naturally joined it. Not long after the Industria strike in 1935, the name of the Textile Workers Industrial Union was amended to add '(SA)' and the constitution to commit it to organising 'all South African textile workers irrespective of race, colour or creed' (Du Toit, 28). This was the cutting edge of anti-racist unionism, deliberately trying to indoctrinate white women in class loyalty. The TWIU organised rallies against racism and Nazism, set up libraries and sports clubs, published poems by members and produced plays by them, and when Afrikaners celebrated their cultural identity, in 1938, the centenary of their Great Trek away from British rule, garment workers 'donned bonnets and long skirts' and took part in the grand re-enactment 'explictly as union members' (Berger, 123).

Solidarity paid off – in the late 1930s, Transvaal garment workers were the highest-paid women in industry.

Cape Province beckoned. In 1938, Bettie went to Cape Town as the only waged organiser in the TWIU, paid £10 a month from a levy on the membership. She had trouble with the white–Coloured split in the textile workforce. After she had organised a non-racial branch with equal white and coloured representation on the organising commitee, the two groups decided to have separate fundraising dances. In 1979, Bettie would recall how she danced with the coloured union chairperson, who went back to the mill and boasted to whites, 'Oh yes, Bettie Du Toit's not like any of you, she danced with me, a coloured man.' The resignations 'came in fast and furious. Oh, my heart was broken.' With great tact, she rebuilt the branch, though never to quite its former strength (Berger, 113).

The Consolidated works at Huguenot was more intractable. This was a sleepy village in the delectable Paarl region of fruit farms and vineyards amid the Drakensberg mountains. Bettie moved in realising that she could do nothing at this stage with black workers – 'to ask Afrikaner girls on the *platteland* to unite with black African labour would be very provocative'. But the boss, Morris Mauerberger, as a Jew, was worried by the rise of Afrikaner Nazism. On condition that she told no one that he had done this, he gave Bettie a job. Staying with other countrywomen in the Dutch Reformed Church hostel, she helped make the 'beautiful coloured pure wool blankets, which the Africans of Basutoland bought to wear as cloaks to keep out the bitter winter when they walked or rode on horseback through the snowy mountains of the Drakensberg'. Before long, she had persuaded almost every white co-worker to join the union. Then . . .

Away in Cape Town for the weekend to report, she returned to find placards in the streets of Huguenot declaring that a Communist viper had raised its head there. Every Dutch Reformed *predikant* had preached against her. Her belongings at the hostel were ransacked and a letter from a black friend was shown around as proof of her utter immorality. The Greyshirts were out to smash the union. Pressure on her colleagues was too much. All Monday workers came up to her loom, tore up their union cards and threw them in her face. The manager warned her to expect a thrashing after work. She was very frightened, but concealed her fear, and reckoned that was why no one lifted a finger against her. However, even those still loyal to her couldn't associate openly with her. She was thrown out of the hostel and could find no other lodging. If she boarded a bus, everyone else got out. If she walked along the street, people crossed to the other side. She could do nothing but go back to Cape Town.

There she learnt that the Dutch Reformed Church and the Afrikaner nationalists had hired Paarl town hall for a meeting against the Communist threat. A senior trade unionist told her she just had to be there. The occasion was saved for her when a farmer sitting near her asked in a loud voice, 'Man, waar is hierdie vreeslike kommuniste?' ('Who is this terrible Communist?') Girlish Bettie stood up and announced in a small voice, 'Dis ek, Meneer' – 'It's me, sir.' She had, as Nadine Gordimer would write, 'the pert, delicate square face and black hair of her French Huguenot ancestry'. 'Marr jy's blerry mooi!' ('My, but you're bloody pretty!') exclaimed the farmer. The whole hall laughed, and when she spoke she got a sympathetic hearing. The Greyshirts and Blackshirts present didn't touch her (Du Toit, 3, 40–46).

But the union was bust in Huguenot, and a second attempt in the 1940s failed in the face of the same nationalist opposition. Bettie meanwhile roved outside the textile industry. Her paths crossed those of another remarkable woman. Ray Alexander had arrived in South Africa from Latvia in 1929, a Jewish Communist, who organized unions in many industries. The multiracial Food and Canning Workers Union which she founded in Cape Town in 1941 was especially significant. Wartime conditions, with food in great demand, favoured it, and it won pay increases in successful strikes. Betty Du Toit began its Johannesburg organisation and became branch secretary. But that wasn't her stopping place. She featured as national secretary of the Laundry, Cleaning and Dyeing Workers Union. She got work in a match factory in Pretoria and organised the Match Workers Union. She helped Johanna Cornelius organise Transvaal Tobacco Workers.

South African industry expanded fast. Just twelve textile factories in 1934 became 104 by the 1960s, when the great majority of workers were African and white women were a small minority. There weren't enough white workers to go round. But apartheid legislation in the 1950s ended multiracial trade unionism. In 1953 all strikes by African workers were declared illegal. The umbrella Trades and Labour Council of unions dissolved in 1954 to be replaced by the Trade Union Council of South Africa which excluded blacks. Fourteen mixed-race unions hived off to form the South African Congress of Trade Unions, with an African general secretary and an Afrikaner president, but this was soon forced to operate in exile. The Suppression of Communism Act was the means of banning militants from union activity – fifty-six in just five years. Bettie Du Toit was the first woman banned, in 1952.

Her first marriage had been to an Englishman, her second to Yusuf Cachalia, whose family were famous in anti-racist politics since days of association with Mahatma Gandhi. That had ended when Nadine Gordimer, whose fiction would eventually win her the Nobel Prize for Literature, met Bettie in 1953. 'Bettie became a close friend of my husband, Reinhold Cassirer, and the closest woman friend I have ever had. She was important in my political commitment, bringing me into touch with and action with the grassroots of the anti-apartheid movement. She became virtually a member of our family; our three children were her children. When Reinhold and I went abroad, she lived in our house and was a mother to them' (Gordimer).

She shifted to organise co-operatives. Though forbidden to enter the black township of Orlando outside Johannesburg, she ran a successful co-operative store there, 'her bulldog "Pod" a sleepy symbol of defiance in the back of her car' (Du Toit, 4). She handed the store over to Africans as a flourishing concern and worked for Kupungani, a voluntary organisation concerned with nutrition, after free school meals for African children were withdrawn. At last Special Branch spotted her in an out-of-bounds area. She was detained for months in Pretoria Central Prison – Nadine Gordimer posed as her sister to get access to her. After a further spell of illegal activity, she was tipped off that Special Branch were about to arrest her again. Disguised as a Hindu woman amidst an Indian family, she fled South Africa without a passport in 1963. With Gordimer's help, she reached Ghana.

Here she worked for the federation of trade unions, then as a researcher for Ghana Radio. Every weekend she swam in the Atlantic breakers off Accra. Seawater in her ear set up an infection, Steven

Johnson's Syndrome, through which she lost the sight of both eyes. She went to London for treatment and stayed there, cared for by friends. Reinhold Cassirer eventually bought her a flat, where she looked after herself, even cooking, though totally blind. In 1976, Nadine Gordimer contrived her return to South Africa, discovering in the process that Du Toit was not her real name. Funds from sale of the London flat supported her, and eventually a long-lost brother emerged, whose daughter took charge of her till she died, sadly senile, in an old-age home – the remnant of what Gordimer called 'a remarkable, brave and warm personality'.

Iris Berger, Threads of Solidarity: Women in South African Industry 1900–1980, *(Bloomington, IN) 1992; Bettie Du Toit,* Ukubamba Amadolo: Workers Struggle in the South African Textile Industry, *1978; Nadine Gordimer, letter to A. C., 27 November 2002; thanks to Liz Calder, Mike Hathorn and Pat Haward*

Egil (Iceland) *c.*810–*c.*890

Egil was grandson of a nightwolf. His grandfather Ulf got so bad-tempered in the evenings that no one could speak to him, then went early to bed. So people suspected that he changed at night into a wolf, and he was accordingly known as Kveld-Ulf. As a young man he used to leave Norway on raiding trips, *for i viking*, looking for plunder. His mate on these forays was a tough character called Berle-Kari, who was a berserk, meaning that he went into fearless blind rage in battle. They got back to Norway rich and Kveldulf married Kari's daughter Salbjorg. She was full of spirit and very good-looking, whereas her husband was notably ugly. Of their two sons, Thorolf must have taken after her. He was a cheerful charmer. Grim, though a great blacksmith, carpenter and fisherman, looked just like Kveldulf, horrible, with a foul temper. He went bald very young, so he was called Skallagrim.

Harald the Shaggy, who had land in Oslofjord, made himself the great power, 'King', in Norway. Thorolf Kveldulfsson joined him and gave him good service. But Harald believed slanders against him and killed him. Having decided to up sticks for Iceland, Skallagrim and his father watched out for Hallvard, who had slandered Thorolf, ambushed a ship he commanded, and slaughtered him and some fifty of his men, taking possession of his good vessel. Kveldulf died at sea. But Skallagrim settled at Borg in the west of Iceland.

Some time in the middle of the ninth century CE, Scandinavian seamen driven off course had discovered a huge island inhabited only by a few stray Irish monks. It was most actively volcanic, and its hot springs were an asset but the centre was occupied by glaciers: it became Iceland. There were no dangerous beasts, rivers and sea teemed with fish, and there was excellent grazing land. At least 10,000, perhaps 20,000, people settled in Iceland between about 870 and 930. By the mid tenth century, a general assembly, the Althing, had emerged to give law and common direction to the island. Around the necessary pursuit of genealogy, important in claims to land, a wonderful body of stories was fleshed out in prose sagas, written down in the thirteenth, fourteenth and fifteenth centuries.

With its huge sweep of time and space, the significance of the political events which it presents – the family of Kveldulf are at feud, not with local rivals, but with Kings of Norway – and a hero both mythic and humanly complex to compare with Odysseus, *Egil's Saga* is by any standards a major work of literature.

Like Skallagrim himself, Egil grows up under the shadow of a tall, strong, handsome brother called Thorolf. He himself inherits his father's extreme ugliness and, it will soon transpire, something from his shape-changing and berserker genealogy. By the time he is three, he is as strong as a boy of six or seven. When his father-in-law, Yngvar, invites Skallagrim over to party, he refuses to take his little prodigy, telling him, 'You're difficult enough to cope with when you're sober.' Egil is angry, jumps on a farmhorse, somehow finds his way through marsh and over ridge, and gets a warm welcome from grandad Yngvar, whom he promptly praises in skaldic verse. This wins him general praise, but his next recorded exploit is not so charming. Aged six, losing at a ball game to a boy four or five years older, he strikes his opponent angrily with his bat and gets beaten up in return, to the jeers of other boys. So he borrows an axe, comes back, and drives his weapon into his enemy's brains, prompting a battle in which seven people are killed. His mother is pleased with Egil, though. She thinks he'll make a good Viking and bring home rich plunder.

As he goes on, Egil kills often, but always in self-defence, or in pursuit of what he considers to be justice, or in honourable quest for plunder or reward. He controls whatever irrational berserker tendencies he has inherited. With women, he is shy, modest, even tender. He is a heroic fighter, usually against steep odds – if ten men oppose him, he will kill them all. But he also has the virtues of a very good farmer, a loving father, and a master poet, exploring his own feelings bravely.

On a visit to Norway, young Egil gets extremely drunk and makes up scurrilous verses in the home of a man called Bard who is entertaining new King Eirik and his Queen Gunnhild. Exasperated, Bard appeals to the Queen and they try unsuccessfully to poison Egil, who kills Bard and flees. Gunnhild's enmity is especially dangerous. She is the daughter of a Russian chieftain named Ozur Toti, and is a great sorceress with all kinds of alien lore. But Egil escapes, and goes off with Thorolf to plunder Latvia and Denmark.

The brothers arrive in England in time to fight for the Saxon king Athelstan (*c*.895–939) in the battle of Brunanburh, where Olaf, King of Dublin, and his Scottish allies, are routed. According to the saga, Egil changes the history of Britain by his valour and sagacity in command of Athelstan's foremost troops, but Thorolf dies through the cunning of a treacherous Welsh earl, whom Egil of course destroys face to face. 'No ravens went hungry' concludes one of the poems which Egil made on the battlefield.

Egil's ugliness is now completed by premature baldness. He is far above normal height and has shoulders much heavier than those of other men. His eyebrows join in the middle, accentuating a trick he has of quizzically sinking one right down to his cheek while pulling the other way up his big forehead.

Eirik is thrown out of Norway, deposed by his brother Hakon, and sets himself up as King Eirik Bloodaxe of Northumbria, with his capital at York. Perhaps because of a spell cast by Gunnhild, Egil is shipwrecked in Eirik's territory on his way to see his old friend Athelstan about possible employment. Luckily, his blood-brother Arinbjorn left Norway with Eirik and is a favourite at court. But it looks as if Gunnhild, when Egil turns up in York, will have her way and see him killed. Arinbjorn advises him to sit up all night and write a poem in praise of Eirik. Egil composes and learns by heart a wondrously sycophantic effusion and uses an unusual and difficult verse form for it, not just alliterative but end-rhymed as well. It is not clear that Eirik Thicko fully appreciates this masterpiece of studied insincerity, but he tells Egil that for Arinbjorn's sake he will spare him on condition that he never sees him again.

Egil fights many more battles. Near Sweden, he sets a world puking record after a treacherous man called Armod has kept serving his party especially strong ale. Forewarned, Egil simply drinks what is given to his companions, so that they won't fall over, and finally goes up to Armod, lets it out, and covers the man in vomit from head to foot . . Next morning, he spares Armod's life but gouges one of his eyes out.

Egil's people at Borg prosper, but the ageing hero is nearly killed by grief. One son dies, then a second is drowned in the fjord. Egil refuses food and says he wants to die, but his daughter Thorgerd persuades him to express his grief in a poem. 'Lament for My Sons' is his masterpiece.

A few years after his death the Icelanders adopt Christianity by law and his heir builds a church. This is demolished when a new one is built nearby and under the altar huge bones are found. These must be Egil's. The priest picks up the very big skull, which is ridged all over like a scallop shell, suggesting enormous pressure from within. He sets it on a fence, and to find out how thick it is, bashes it with the reverse side of a heavy axe. It doesn't break or even dent. It simply turns white. Some skull. Egil's bones are then reinterred on the edge of the new churchyard. Not in the middle.

Jesse L. Byock, Viking Age Iceland, *2001;* Egil's Saga, *trans. Hermann Palsson and Paul Edwards, (Harmondsworth) 1976;* The Sagas of Icelanders, *introd. Robert Kellogg, 2000; thanks to George Gunn*

Johnny Faa (Romany) 16th–17th c.

A document shows that in February 1540 King James V of Scotland recognised the right and title of Johnnie Faw as 'Lord and Erle of Little Egypt' and called on all Sheriffs and other people in authority to assist him in 'exicutione of justice vpon his company and folkis' (Gardner, 616). Romany people were thought to have originated in Egypt. Hence, in Britain, they were called 'gypsies'. James V was accepting their presence and delegating to their leader power to discipline his own 'folkis'. This didn't work. In June 1541, an Act of the Lords of Council ordered their expulsion from Scotland because of the 'gret thiftis and scaithis [thefts and harms] done be the saidis Egyptians vpon our soverance lordis liegis . . .' In accordance with this decree the Edinburgh magistrates forbade all gypsies residence within the city limits. It seems pretty clear that they moved just over them to squat in an area which became known as 'Little Egypt'. Since the Israelites under Moses had left Egypt to return to Palestine, the local stream eventually attracted the name 'Jordan Burn' and 'Canaan Lane' retains its presence in the notoriously genteel suburb of Morningside. In any case, Johnny Faw's people did not leave Scotland (Smith, 100–02).

It is now agreed that the Romanies originated in northern India. Their own language is closely allied to tongues from that region. Bands reached Western Europe in the fifteenth century. Though authorities everywhere proclaimed their banishment, they hung on, to inspire music by Brahms and poems by Lorca, and to secure, in Scotland as elsewhere, traditional songs, music and customs in danger of extinction as the peasantry were uprooted by agrarian and industrial revolution.

They squatted where they could and otherwise travelled the roads, plying trades which secured them a place on the edge of settled society. The men dealt in livestock, provided veterinary services, and worked as tinkers, mending broken metal things. As circuses developed, their skills in training animals would literally find new arenas. The women, adept at begging, also told fortunes and sold potions. Both men and women were welcomed as entertainers, stringed music propelling song and dance. James IV (1505) and then James V of Scotland (1529) received them at court in that capacity.

They did not 'integrate' with the *gadje*, as they called all non-gypsies. A gypsy 'Lord and Earl' would be chief-for-life, *voivode*, of a band of upwards of ten households. He would rule through a council of elders in consultation with *phuri dai*, the senior women. Under the code of customary law, *kris*, the ultimate sanction was excommunication from the band. (One can see how this might limit Johnny Faw's usefulness as a policeman – a gypsy kicked out would be more likely to steal than ever.)

The name 'Johnny Faa' (as it came to be spelt) became generic for gypsy chiefs. In 1611, two years after an act of the Scottish Parliament had again ordered the expulsion of gypsies, Johnne, alias Willie Faa and three others 'of the name' – members presumably of the same kinship group – were sentenced to be hanged. Another Johnny Faa was executed in 1616. Then in 1624, 'Captain' Johnny Faa and seven of his tribe were tried and hanged as 'vagaboundis, sorneris, common theieves, callit . . . Egiptianes' (Child, 63–4; Gardner, 616). 'Sorner' roughly means 'sponger', and carries the associations of idleness (preying on others for subsistence) and 'blackmail', in its then-current sense – extorting goods or money by threats. So it was a serious charge sheet, but it did not include 'abducting an aristocratic lady by magical enticement'.

Nevertheless, song collectors have been prone to associate the great ballad of 'Johny Faa, The Gypsy Laddy', with the Captain who perished. In it, a gypsy band lures from her home a fine lady, and tradition in Ayrshire eventually insisted that this had been the wife of the Earl of Cassilis. Foundation or accidental credibility was given to this legend by the fact that a tune to which the ballad is sung is found as 'Lady Cassilis Lilt' in the important manuscript collection of music compiled by John Skene in the 1620s (Grieg, Song cx). Hard evidence insists that the actual Lady Cassilis of 'Captain' Johnny's day died in 1642 mourned by her husband, whereas an extreme form of the folk-tale had her immured for life in a tower in Maybole, Ayrshire, after her irate lord had retrieved her from Faa clutches and hanged her gypsy raptors . . .

All but one, it must be, since in most of many variants of the song one voice is that of a gypsy survivor.

The best-known variant is that originally published by the great collector (and major poet) Allan Ramsay in the mid eighteenth century.

The gypsies came to our good lord's gate,
And wow but they sang sweetly!
They sang sae sweet and sae very compleat
That down came the fair lady.

Johnny Faa's band at first appear in the role of gypsy entertainers, parading their artistry and hoping for patronage. But they develop grander intentions . . .

And she came tripping down the stair,
And a' her maids before her;
As soon as they saw her well-fared* face *good-looking*
They coost the glamer oer her.

The word 'glamour', which entered the English language from Scotland in the nineteenth century, is now abjectly debased, to refer to mere film starlets and bimbo models. Originally it was a very serious word indeed. The gypsies here cast a magical spell over the lady.

Perhaps because Ramsay didn't realise their possible significance, his version omits the exchanges of gifts mentioned in other variants (Child, 65–74). She gives the gypsies good wheat bread. They give her ginger, nutmeg, both, or sweetmeats. She strips a ring off one finger – or several off several – to present to the 'gypsy laddy'. As in so many Scottish ballads first collected and printed in the 'modern' period, something very old is hinted at here, customs and beliefs predating the actual arrival of gypsies in Scotland. There is 'glamour' in these exchanges of elemental breadstuff, exotic spices, betrothing rings.

The great American collector Child printed in the 1890s eleven versions of 'The Gypsy Laddy', from printed sources, from manuscripts and from contemporaneous singing. Some are from Scotland, but the song had spread (as great songs do), so that Child had versions from Shropshire, from Ireland, from New England and from New York. All agree on the main point, which is that the lady runs off with the gypsy and his band, renouncing lord, creature comforts, children, everything. To revert to Ramsay:

Yestreen I lay in a well-made bed,
And my good lord beside me.
This night I'll ly in a tenant's barn,
Whatever shall betide me.

At this point, variants begin sharply to reflect differences in values and world-view between different singers at different times in different places.

A broadside, possibly published in the north of England, gives us the lovely:

Oh what care I for houses and land?
Or what care I for money?
So I have brewd, so will I return;
So fare you well, my honey!

In some versions the lady is happy with her new circumstances, in others she regrets them. Some singers lay so much stress on her getting drunk with Johnny Faa that one might suspect that her chief motive for absconding was alcoholic rather than sexual. Anyway, fun or no fun, her time with Johnny is short.

Ramsay again:

And when our lord came hame at een,
And speir'd* for his fair lady **asked*
The tane she cry'd, and the other replied,
'She's away with the gypsy laddie.'

'Gae saddle to me the black, black steed,
Gae saddle and make him ready,
Before that I either eat or sleep,
I'll gae seek my fair lady.'

The end, depending on your own values, or those of the singer, is either sad or happy. The lord swiftly catches up with the gypsies and executes summary justice. Says Ramsay's gypsy survivor (or ghost):

And we were fifteen well-made men,
Altho we were nae bonny;
And we were a' put down for ane,
A fair young wanton lady.

Like many other great songs, this ballad, however sung, dodges between possible truth and ancient narrative patterning. The Lady Cassilis of history, blameless (at least in gypsy matters), is ineluctably linked forever with the Romany captain, earl or king, the Other representing sex and booze and freedom. A Cornishman, Sir Arthur Quiller Couch, picked for the *Oxford Book of Ballads* (1910) the most radically pro-Johnny version of the ballad known to me, in this case called 'The Gypsy Countess'. Here Earl Cassilis picks his *brown* mare – 'For the black was ne'er so speedy.' He implores his Lady to come home, but apparently to no avail. Her rousing last words are:

'The Earl of Cassilis is lying sick;
Not one hair I'm sorry;
I'd rather have a kiss from Johnny Faa's lips
Than all his gold and money.'

Francis James Child, The English and Scottish Popular Ballads, *vol. 4, (Cambridge, MA) 1892; Alexander Gardner*, The Ballad Minstrelsy of Scotland, *(Paisley) 1893; Gavin Grieg*, Folksong of the North East, *(Hatboro, PA) 1963; Emily Lyle*, Scottish Ballads, *(Edinburgh) 1994; Sir Arthur Quiller Couch, ed.*, The Oxford Book of Ballads, (*Oxford) 1910; Charles L. Smith*, Morningside, (*Edinburgh) 1992*

Bet Flint (England) *fl.* 1750s

On 8 May 1781 James Boswell dined with Dr Johnson at Mr Dilly's. Another guest was the formidable erstwhile rabble-rouser John Wilkes. He had once been Johnson's *bête noire*, but the two men were now fully reconciled. After both great men had enjoyed teasing Boswell with jokes against his Scottish compatriots, Johnson 'gave us an entertaining account of Bet Flint, a woman of the town, who, with some eccentric talents and much effrontery, forced herself upon his acquaintance. Bet (said he) wrote her own Life in verse which she brought to me, wishing that I would furnish her with a Preface to it (laughing). I used to say of her that she was generally slut and drunkard – occasionally, whore and thief. She had, however, genteel lodgings, a spinet on which she played and a boy that walked before her chair. Poor Bet was taken up on a charge of stealing a counterpane, and tried at the Old Bailey. Chief Justice ——, who loved a wench, summed up favourably, and she was acquitted. After which, Bet said, with a gay and satisfied air, "Now that the counterpane is my own, I shall make a petticoat of it"' (Boswell, vol. IV, 103).

Boswell's modern editors contribute more of interest on Bet. She was tried in 1758, when the Lord Chief Justice was Willes. Of Willes, the gossip and annalist Horace Walpole remarked that 'he was not wont to disguise any of his passions. That for gaming was notorious; that for women, unbounded. There was a remarkable story current of a grave person's coming to reprove the scandal he gave, and to tell him that the world talked of one of his maidservants being with child. Willes said, "What is that to me?" The monitor answered, "Oh, but they say that it is by your Lordship." "And what is that to you?"' Such a character makes Bet's story seem well-founded, but it appears, from the published report of the trial, that the technical reason for her acquittal was that she had taken the counterpane, and five other articles, from another woman who could not prove that they really belonged to her and not to a certain captain, whose servant she said she had been, and who was now abroad. (Note in Boswell, loc. cit.)

Boswell noted down Johnson's conversations as soon as he could after they occurred. On this occasion, he left a blank in his notes after 'Bet composed a poem', not having registered exactly what Bet was supposed to have written. He sought advice from a mutual friend, probably the novelist Fanny Burney, and was thus able to include Bet's opening lines, which Johnson had quoted, in a footnote in his great Life of his friend and hero:

When first I drew my vital breath
A little minikin I came upon earth,
And then I came from a dark abode
Upon this gay and gaudy world . . .

But Bozzie's 'minikin' replaced his interlocutor's word 'diminutive'. Perhaps he thought it sounded more Bet-like (Reed and Pottle, 349–50).

The point of plunging here not only into the reeking lowlife of Hanoverian London, but into the delicious minutiae of pedantry, is to recover, beside Bet, Samuel Johnson's wonderful generosity towards erring and unfortunate fellow creatures. His own household included, as his amanuensis, Frank Barber (*c.*1735–1801), a freed black slave whom he educated for five years in Bishop's Stortford Grammar School at his own expense, and whose 'eminently pretty' white wife, and children, he eventually boarded also as part of his own family. Johnson left him money and made him his residuary legatee. Frank settled in his late master's home town, Lichfield, and named a further child, Samuel, after him. This boy grew up to become a Primitive Methodist preacher in Staffordshire. Descendants of him through his own six children presumably passed for white in the aptly named Black Country. Himself of lowly provincial origins, coarse in toilet and table manners and notably ugly, Johnson gave to such people as Bet an affection and even respect which he did not accord to pompous and pretentious fools and bores of his own middle class, or inane aristocrats whom he encountered in the society circles to which his immense erudition and talents gave him a passport.

James Boswell, Life of Johnson, *ed. G.B. Hill, rev. L. F. Powell (Oxford) 1971 reprint; Peter Fryer,* Staying Power: The History of Black People in Britain, *1992 edn; Joseph W. Reed and F. A. Pottle,* Boswell: Laird of Auchinleck 1778–1782, *(New Haven, CT) 1977*

Margaret Fountaine (England) 1862–1940

Notable lone female travellers of Anglo-Saxon provenance are not few. But for gallant craziness, surely no one beats Margaret Fountaine, ace lepidopterist and unquenchable romantic?

She was the second of eight children of the rector of a tiny parish in Norfolk. When he died in 1878, his widow moved the family to Norwich. The two boys were sent away to school, the six girls were educated at home. Their lives were genteelly circumscribed. With twenty-two aunts and uncles and a huge cousinage, Margaret did not lack company, but the limits of acceptable social intercourse were strict. Only one of the Fountaine girls would marry.

A habit of wistful crushes overcame Margaret. After several such, she fell for a chorister employed at Norwich Cathedral, one Septimus Hewson. Both were twenty-one. She was a fairly talented artist. Long desperate days sketching in the Cathedral elided into discreetly immodest pursuit of the object of her adoration. Horror! He was sacked for drunkenness and returned to his native Ireland. Joy! Rich Uncle Edward Fountaine died and left £30,000 to be divided between the six sisters and a random cousin. From now on, Margaret had a tidy independent income, several hundred pounds a year, increased later by sad deaths of sisters from consumption. She hunted Septimus down in Limerick, and experienced her first kiss at the age of twenty-eight. Back home, she announced her engagement. Her mother wrote to enquire about Septimus's financial circumstances. He never replied. She had been betrayed!

Next year she travelled to Switzerland and Italy and took up butterfly hunting. A *Vanessa* whirling through Florence – a Camberwell beauty far from south London – roused her to rapture. In Italy she took singing lessons, but at the age of thirty-one decided that the life of an opera singer was not for her – she detected a casting-couch system and was deterred. However, she was clear that foreign parts inhabited by *risqué* males were much more fun than Norwich. In what became obsessive lepidopterous roamings through Europe – Sicily, Germany, Austria, Hungary, Greece, snaring *M. Pherusa* here, *P. Clemene* or *Suvarovius* there – she repelled many propositions and proposals, revenging Septimus's perfidy upon the male gender. But in 1901, she met nemesis in Damascus.

She hired a dragoman named Khalil Neimy. At first she took little account of this low-class member of a lesser breed without the law, distracted from him by the beauty of the fiery red *M. Didyma*. When one evening it became clear that he was smitten with her, and he kissed her on the arm through the sleeve of her silk blouse, she thought 'that never had I come into contact with quite such a weak, contemptible character before' (Fountaine, *Love Among the Butterflies*, 133).

The enigmatic Khalil was indeed more timid than his goddess, but otherwise a Deep Character. He was twenty-four years old, Greek Orthodox Christian, apparently a subject of the loathsome Turkish Empire, but had fair hair and grey eyes. A spell in the USA had left him with a strong American accent but little capacity to spell English. Margaret responded to his urgent devotion. In the shadows of the great rocks of Baalbek she agreed to be his wife. Shocked but not diverted by subsequent information that he had a wife already, she travelled on with him as long as he lived.

The course of passionate tenderness did not run smooth. In Spain in 1905, Margaret absurdly accepted the proposal, by post, of the mediocre British Vice-Consul of an obscure place in Turkey she had visited – but soon mustered strength to jilt him. She had ample bottle for trips to Southern Africa, the Caribbean, Ceylon and the borders of Tibet (*Acraea acrita, Papilio agamemnon, Mylostris agathina*). She could quell a roomful of putative Circassian robbers with the untruthful announcement that she was related to the British Consul, or assert her indignation conclusively elsewhere with a string of uncomprehended English swear-words. She despised drunken English expatriates, often encountered in the tropics, but came to enjoy cigarettes (she once smuggled sixty cigars from Manila into England) and was highly proficient at cards and billiards. While in the tropics, she found that a creosote bath once a week served to keep off leeches.

She reflected late in her life on how she always got on better with foreigners than with Englishpersons – 'no doubt the latter have their points, but with my own countrymen rarely if ever have I felt that magnetism and moral affinity which draws me to men of any alien race' (Fountaine, *Butterflies and Late Loves*, 114). However, the pound sterling was almighty and Britannia still ruled the waves. Apparently indifferent to Empire as such, Margaret nevertheless deployed its authority. And she could not possibly have become a Turkish subject by marriage.

In Australia during the Great War, she tried settling down with Khalil, renamed 'Charles' – by residing in Australia he would acquire British citizenship and become fit lord and master for an Englishwoman. They attempted to farm 160 acres in north Queensland, but 'Charles' cracked under the strain, took to drink, and accused her – in her fifties – of infidelities. He got his naturalisation, but marriage to such a demented person seemed impossible. Margaret left him with a shop in Sydney, while he completed the year's residence required to secure him a passport, and sailed for the USA. She loved Hollywood in its pre-Tinsel awakening, but higher taxes due to war had eroded her British income, and she had to turn pro. She successfully completed a contract to supply spiders to a 'Natural Science Establishment' in the Eastern US, then took regular work at twenty-five cents an hour for a butterfly collector in Pasadena. Now Charles was able to supply her with money from his shop, but then some unnamed illness detained him in Australia, and he further sent news that his wife, presumed dead, was still alive. Yet they met again, in Wellington, New Zealand, in 1920.

Margaret returned to dreary old England after nine years' absence in 1921. It could not detain her. Next year she was off again to South East Asia and the Philippines, picking up Charles in Port Said. After all this time, she was still squeamish about being caught out by fellow Englishpersons when sharing a bedroom with her lover. And travelling in West Africa without Charles in 1926, her faithfulness was tried (but triumphed) when she developed a crush on Herr Rein, manager of a big cocoa concern in Cameroon.

Charles met her in Marseilles. A cousin who was an Orthodox bishop had at last dissolved his marriage. The problem still, in this passport-mad new era (see **Traven**), was that Charles was Australian rather than properly British until he had spent an unbroken year in Britain. Now portly, with an array of gold teeth, Charles could not settle in London and fled back to Damascus. In 1928 he died, after a fever, in Syria. For twenty-seven years, Margaret wrote, he had 'been everything to me' (Fountaine, *Butterflies and Late Loves*, 120).

But she was soon off again, up the Amazon, enraptured by her first flight in an aeroplane, aged sixty-seven, in Venezuela. She sorted out the affairs of her scapegrace ex-dipsomaniac brother Arthur and his wife and young sons in Virginia, and flew joyously thence to New York through blue heavens where 'no early Victorian lady in her sedan chair', she reflected, 'could have travelled in greater comfort or safety' (Fountaine, *Butterflies and Late Loves*, 137). In East Africa she picked up hookworm to add to her recurrent malaria. Aged seventy-four, she was still getting menopausal hot flushes which had afflicted her for seventeen years. But undeterred by all infirmities she steered for Indo-China, where under the shadow of coming war she hunted out of Hanoi for *Zetides* and *Pathysa* with an especially charming and enthusiastic boy helper. When war arrived she headed for Trinidad, a natural choice, since there were almost twice as many species of butterfly there as there were in the whole of Europe. Years before, she had befriended the monks of Mount St Benedict. In April 1940, with battle raging far away in Norway, one of them found her collapsed with a stroke by the roadside.

Her will bequeathed her entire collection of 'diurnal lepidoptera and other natural history specimens' to the Castle Museum in Norwich, to 'be known for all time as "The Fountaine-Neimy Collection".'

Margaret Fountaine, Butterflies and Late Loves, *ed. W. F. Cater, 1986 edn; Margaret Fountaine,* Love Among the Butterflies, *ed. W. F. Cater, 1980; thanks to Tom Lowenstein*

Ganesha (India)

In 1992, staying in the famous and by no means overrated Victoria Falls Hotel in Zimbabwe, I went out on a wee nature-safari one morning. It was very early, but in the adjacent village, people were setting out to work. Our guide, driving the Land Rover, told us almost casually that an elephant had killed a villager here the previous week. Right on cue, on the outskirts we came across an extremely nasty-looking elephant taking his *petit déjeuner* by chewing up a tree.

This confirmed my impression, collected on earlier sojourns in Africa, that, after buffaloes, the elephant was probably the most dangerous beast for a human being to get close to. These things can run at up to 25 mph . . . Granted the elephant's tree-chewing proclivities, we might think of ivory poachers as unwitting eco-warriors, working to preserve vegetation in Earth's increasingly denuded tropics.

Ah but, you say, that is the *African* elephant. The *Indian* elephant, surely, is a benign creature, best friend to man, his faithful servant in peace and war, a lovable, sage beast remarkable for long memory . . .

There were trunked animals fifty million years ago but the true elephant's family tree extends only about seven million. Two 'recent' genera, *Mammuthus* and *Elephas*, go back about four million years. Elephants spread all over, except to Australia. A fossilised specimen from Kent stands fourteen feet high. The modern Asian species, *elephas maximus*, is a relatively recent arrival, found in India, Sri Lanka, Malaysia and Sumatra. Its average height is about ten feet. Its differences from *Loxodonta*, its African counterpart, are relatively minor. Indian females don't have tusks, Africans do. *Loxodonta* has longer legs and much bigger ears and averages about eleven feet.

Elephants were tamed in India in early times, as draught animals and awesome vehicles in war, and were much involved in the history of humans, not least, through the elephant god, Ganesha.

Elephants were originally identified with their supposedly prodigious sexual energy. Despite a gestation period for baby elephants of twenty to twenty-two months, Krishna's sexually insatiable consort Radha was named after the She-Elephant. Ganesha was in one emanation the Lord of Hosts, and in this capacity, in the fifth century BCE, fathered the Buddha upon the Virgin Maya. The Hebrew god Yahweh in those misty times opportunistically assumed the title Lord of Hosts and elephantine characteristics, since the elephant cult was big in Egypt and the Middle East. Judaeo-Christian scholars later refused to believe that he had done anything so base as to couple, as an elephant, with a human lady . . . An Egyptian version of the Elephant-God seems to have entered the Jewish scriptures as Behemoth, who later became an elephant-headed **Devil** (q.v.) in medieval Europe.

But the lovable Ganesha of our own day arrived in the scriptural Hindu pantheon only in the early CE. Other names for him are Vinayaka (leader), Gajanana (elephant-faced), Ekadanta (one-tusked), Lambodara (pot-bellied) and Siddhadata (giver of success), but Vighnaraja – 'lord of obstacles' – best sums up his role. He creates obstacles to your undertakings, but also makes you grateful by removing them.

The god Siva was still firmly hitched to his posh consort Parvati before Dirty **Kali** (q.v.) got her hands on him. Parvati was not unclarty herself. She rubbed a substance, sometimes called *mala* – dirt – off the surface of her body and formed it into a handsome young man. While Siva was away meditating on some mountain or cremation ground, Parvati told her nifty creation to guard her private quarters against all – emphasis, *all* – intruders. So when Siva came back, the novice attendant barred him. They fought, and Siva beheaded the youth. Parvati was wrathful. Siva sent out his attendants – *ganas* – to find the first available head. This happened to be an elephant's. Siva revived the corpse, gave it the elephant's head, and put the result in charge of his *ganas* as Ganesha, 'Lord of the Group'. Instructions went out from Siva that Ganesha must be worshipped first before all enterprises, ritual or otherwise, or else they would founder.

In Maharashtra a sect of Ganapatyas arose amongst high-caste Hindus who regarded this god as a form of ultimate reality, and centred their devotion on eight shrines clustered around Poona. This sect rose to prominence in the seventeenth to nineteenth centuries CE when the Marathis dominated north-west India. Ganesha had previously been important in South India, whence his most famous devotee, Moraya Gosavi (*d.*1651) had emigrated to settle 70 km south-east of Poona, in Moragaon, now a centre of annual pilgrimages.

The Indian elephant remained a tough creature, typically sculpted to hold up massive temples, or presented in effigy as a bouncer guarding doors. In his *Jungle Book*, Kipling gives us Kala Nag – 'Black Snake' – a big old bruiser nearing seventy. (Elephants normally last for fifty years in the wild, but one captive in India lived to 130.) Kala Nag served the British Indian Army in the Afghan war of 1842, then carried a mortar on his back in the Abyssinian War. Afterwards set to haul teak in the Burmese timber-yards, he has now been recruited to assist the Raj in its regular drives to capture wild elephants for training. Once forty or fifty monsters from the hills are rounded up in the Keddah stockade, Kala Nag's role is to pick out the biggest and wildest of them all and batter him to submission while the rest are roped and tied . . . The great animals seen in the ceremonial processions of the Raj, as in those of previous Indian emperors and of contemporary Princes, represented, didn't they?, the capacity of men in authority to tame for public use the true King of the Beasts, who could shrug off a lion and reduce a tiger, as Kipling put it, to 'a fluffy striped thing on the ground for Kala Nag to pull by the tail'. Good old Ganesha, likewise, represents horrendous martial and sexual energies brought companionably within the human orbit.

Encyclopaedia Britannica; *Mircea Eliade, ed.*, Encyclopaedia of Religion, *vol. 5*, (New York) *1987; Rudyard Kipling*, The Jungle Book, *1894; Barbara G. Walker*, The Woman's Encyclopaedia of Myths and Secrets, *(San Francisco) 1983*

Gerutha (Denmark)

In the *Danish History (Gesta Danorum)* written by Saxo Grammaticus at the end of the twelfth century CE, Gerutha is the daughter of Rorik, an entirely legendary King of Denmark, who marries Horwendyl, governor of Jutland, and becomes the mother of Amleth. Horwendyl is murdered by his brother Feng, joint governor, who usurps his marriage bed, telling Gerutha that he slew her husband because he was a nasty man who was out to harm her. 'So gentle that she would do no man the slightest hurt', Gerutha swallows this lie (Bullough, 62). To protect himself, Amleth feigns insanity, and eventually exacts revenge by slaying Feng.

Though Saxo's book was printed, in Latin, in 1516, William Shakespeare almost certainly didn't read it. What he presumably did come across was the version of Saxo in the fifth volume of *Histoires Tragiques* by Francois de Belleforest, published in 1570, though this wasn't translated into English till 1608. The Frenchman 'modernised and moralised' Saxo (Bullough, 10). Feng becomes 'Fengon'. Gerutha is made to commit adultery with him before her husband's murder, in which she is fully complicit, lying to Amleth about it all. This makes her later actions harder to understand. Amleth, addressing her in her chamber, is spied on by an unnamed lord who has volunteered to find out if he's really mad, as Feng suspects he isn't. Finding this chap lurking in the straw, Amleth kills him, chops him into pieces, and slings these into an open sewer, where pigs find and eat them. Then he returns to upbraid his mother for 'wantoning like a harlot' and redeems her 'to walk in the way of virtue' (Bullough, 65–66). When Feng sends Amleth to see a tributary king in England, carrying sealed orders that the king should execute his nephew, Amleth asks his mother to hang the hall with tapestries and, if he's not back after a year, give him funeral obsequies there. Saxo's Amleth is an intriguing mixture of Holy Fool, trickster and wizard. Having found and changed the sealed orders so that Feng's tools, his companions, are executed themselves, he successfully demands blood money for them, and also convinces the English king that he must give him his daughter in marriage. Returning to Jutland secretly, he daubs himself in filth to resume his imbecilic character and turns up – to uproarious laughter – at his own funeral. Once Feng's court are thoroughly drunk and snoring he cuts down the hangings which Gerutha has faithfully woven, so as to cover them, hammers them down with stakes long prepared, sets them on fire, and disposes of Feng, who has retired, in the latter's bedroom. Amleth justifies his deeds to the people and is acclaimed King of Jutland.

Then he goes back to England. The king there, a blood brother of Feng, is honour bound by deepest oath to dispose of Amleth, so cunningly sends him as his ambassador to Scotland, to court on his behalf the notorious Queen Hermutrude, who had slain all her previous suitors. However, she is utterly smitten with Amleth and persuades him to marry her. His English wife, so far from reacting against this, tips Amleth off that her father is out to kill him. So Amleth gets his retaliation in first and returns with his two consorts to Jutland.

But his luck runs out. Wiglek has succeeded his father as King of Denmark and has been harassing poor Gerutha. He now challenges Amleth, who is slain. Hermutrude thereupon marries Wiglek . . .

By the 1580s, Londoners liked 'revenge tragedies'. Revenge had a topical political resonance. In 1587, Elizabeth I executed Mary Queen of Scots, long her prisoner, after Catholic plotting in her favour. Would the Queen's putative heir, James VI of Scotland, seek to avenge his mother? (As it happened, James wasn't interested. In any case, he had good reason to suppose that Mary had connived in the murder of his own father, Darnley, so the issue of 'revenge' was rather complicated . . .) Meanwhile James courted a Queen for himself, Anne, in Denmark . . . By 1589, when James married Anne, a play about 'Hamlet', presumably drawing on Belleforest, had been performed in London. We do not know if Shakespeare wrote it, and scholars incline to attribute it to Thomas Kyd. This, or another, Ur-*Hamlet*, seems to have been performed in 1594, when Anne gave birth to an heir.

Avoiding hideously complex questions surrounding the five earliest printed versons of the play which is known to be (mostly) by Shakespeare. I will merely observe that the enigma of Hamlet's character is compounded by the senseless desire of editors to conflate 'Fl', the Folio text of Shakespeare's works published by colleagues in 1623 seven years after his death, with 'Q2', the Second Quarto, of 1604–05. These represent two different versions of a popular, much repeated work. To quote Stanley Wells and Gary Taylor, 'major additions and omissions co-exist with massive verbal variations . . .' They detect in Fl 'the hand of a revising author co-operating with his professional colleagues' (Wells and Taylor, 400–01).

One entirely sound point put across in that delightful skit, the movie *Shakespeare in Love*, was that many ideas, and even some deathless lines, in Shakespeare's works must have come from his fellow-actors, evolving through rehearsal and repeated performance. And conflated texts of the play not only make it, rather tediously, longer, but introduce (for instance) two different reasons for Hamlet's attitude towards Laertes in the final scenes.

Saxo's wondrous tale clearly drew on the Roman story of Lucius Brutus, who feigned insanity to escape execution by Tarquin the Proud, whom he eventually overthrew. The author of the Ur-*Hamlet* in turn added the Ghost of Hamlet's Father, from popular (Catholic) tradition, and his murder by poison inserted in the ear is derived by Shakespeare from a relatively recent episode in Italy. Latinising Feng to Claudius, Shakespeare harks back to Saxo for 'Gertrude'. His strange play creates an image of the endangered intellectual in a corrupt state which proved especially potent in Russia and eastern Europe from the nineteenth century onwards and provided one of the great archetypes of Western 'civilisation'.

But a fine actress can make Gertrude also, even in Shakespeare's relatively scant presentation of her, into a compelling tragic figure. An ancient Greek dramatist might well have fashioned an eponymous drama round Gerutha – this woman cozened by the evil Feng who eventually conspires with her son in the slaughter of her husband and his courtiers, and whose tale distantly echoes those of Homer's Penelope and Aeschylus's Electra.

Geoffrey Bullough, ed., Narrative and Dramatic Sources of Shakespeare, *vol. 7, 1973; Alastair H. Thomas and Stewart F. Oakley,* Historical Dictionary of Denmark, *(Lanham, MD) 1998; Stanley Wells and Gary Taylor,* William Shakespeare: A Textual Companion, *(Oxford) 1987*

Helen Gloag (Scotland/Morocco) 1750–?

In the beautiful centre of Scotland where Lowlands and Highlands mingle was the village of Muthill. Nearby, where a stone bridge carried the road from Stirling to Crieff over a river, was a hamlet called Mill of Steps . . . And there, in the early nineteenth century, stood a cottage which was the residence of an old woman who was known as the mother of the Empress of Morocco . . . This empress had a brother who was a sea-captain. He died in the cottage at Mill of Steps. A local antiquarian, nosing around, was shown 'several articles, particularly of china, which he brought home from that country, and were in the possession of the family of John Bayne, farmer, Lurg, who remembered her very well. She was a good-looking woman: he occasionally played at cards and other games with her . . .' (Shearer, 54–55).

'Other games', in a book published around 1860 at the climax of Victorian prudery, makes a rather lively impression. Otherwise, Shearer's account provides more puzzles and confusions than hints.

A late twentieth-century antiquarian depones that a blacksmith at Muthill, Andrew Gloag, and his wife Ann Key, were blessed with a daughter in January 1750, baptised Helen. The family moved to the cottage at Mill of Steps. Helen's mother died, her father remarried. Archie McKerracher has found out somehow that Helen grew up a striking beauty, with green eyes, golden red hair and high cheekbones in a pale oval face. She couldn't get on with her stepmother. Bayne, the neighbouring farmer, was eleven years older, but she used to go over to 'play cards' with him . . . At nineteen, she and several girl friends decided they had had enough of Perthshire and headed off in a party to Greenock, intending to emigrate to South Carolina (McKerracher, 182–83). In that prosperous colony, attractive young women would easily find places as servants and in time would surely acquire substantial husbands – and more than a few African slaves.

So (this is 1769) the vessel carrying them is accosted and captured on the high seas by the dreaded Sale corsairs. Moriscoes – Muslims expelled from Spain in 1610 – had established a base on the Moroccan coast whence they roamed widely in their xebecs. These were swift three-masters, heavily armed, which could slip over the sand bar in Sale harbour mouth leaving larger pursuers helpless in their wake.

They had raided as far as Orkney for slaves, and in one famous incident in 1631 had taken 250 people from a village on the west coast of Ireland. They were genetically a mixed bag by now. Whether for Byronic or merely pragmatic considerations, numerous Europeans had abjured Christianity and joined them.

The corsairs put the men they captured in chains and sent them into servitude. Those women whom they deemed less attractive were handed over to the 'Moorish' soldiery. The Moroccan royal army was known as the '*abid*, meaning 'slaves'. The despot Mulay Ismail, who had ruled from 1672 to 1727, had built up an army composed solely of uprooted black Africans from southern lands, whose children automatically became soldiers. Helen, with other women the corsairs thought especially desirable, was sold at auction. The merchant who bought her, we are told, presented her to the ruler of Morocco.

Sidi Muhammad, who ruled from 1757 to 1790, was a man of scruple. Mulay Ismail's death had been followed by a quarter-century of turmoil, with the '*abid* as power-brokers. The black army had four times levered Mulay 'Abd Allah inconclusively into position as sultan. When he died in 1752, they offered the job to his grandson Sidi Muhammad. But he magnanimously refused the title – he did the work while his father, formerly governor of Marrakesh, assumed the prestige. Sidi Muhammad was attracted to the austere doctrines of the Wahhabi reform movement within Islam, which was emerging amid the sands of Arabia. His predecessors had gone shares with the Sale corsairs. Now he wanted a modern fleet. If Helen Gloag had brains as well as beauty, these could well have been useful to him. But perhaps she wasn't even fully literate. Whether through her brother or not she must have been in touch with Bayne and other folk at home, otherwise her tale would not have emerged and survived. But letters from her – which surely would have been preserved? – have evaded antiquarians past and present. Anyway, it does seem possible that she became one of Sidi Muhammad's four official wives – does that make her a quarter-sultana? – and had children by him.

Christian captives had long had a peculiar position in the continuous, hot-and-cold history of dealings between first English, then British governments and the Sultanate. Morocco had much to offer by way of trade. It was also of vital strategic importance after the English had captured Gibraltar in 1704. Its provisions fed the garrison there. Siding with France or Spain, Morocco could cause problems. From time to time the British redeemed from the Sultan, for money or armaments, besides persons captured by the corsairs, others castaway by shipwreck on Moroccan shores.

In 1735, Britain bought off Morocco with £60,000 in protection money, and corsair captures dwindled. Sidi Muhammad wanted an Arabic-speaking British consul based permanently in his country, and lots of naval stores. What he got, in 1756, was an extremely rude young naval captain as *ad hoc* ambassador. Outraged, he unleashed his corsairs, and by 1758 had nearly four hundred captives to trade. Captain Milbanke, RN, now arrived with the new Consul-General, Joseph Popham, and redeemed most of these for 200,000 Spanish dollars. A new Treaty of Peace and Commerce was signed.

Assuming that Helen Gloag arrived in 1769, good relations still prevailed. This could explain why the British Government seems not to have concerned itself about her fate, and that of other survivors, from whatever ship it was she had sailed in. It was otherwise in 1771 when a Liverpool ship, the *Lark*, was wrecked off Cape Bon and its crew were sold, by the tribesmen who found them, for thirty Spanish dollars a head to the Governor of Agadir, who sent them on to the Sultan. Sidi Muhammad was so unaccommodating that the British Consul-General in Tetuan fled for his life to Gibraltar . . But that place badly needed Moroccan food. Next year a new Consul-General brought presents to the Sultan and redeemed all his English captives at the cost of £697 per head. Sidi Muhammad sent envoys to London. In 1784, a 'personal' message from George III announced that he had ordered thirty large cannons with complete carriage to be sent to 'Your Imperial Majesty' and expressed 'how very sensible we are of the humanity you have shown to some of our seamen and subjects shipwrecked on your coast, who were afterwards made slaves by the wild Arabs'.

Good relations then prevailed for a couple of years, until Sidi Muhammad became agitated about the delay in return of a clock and watch which he had sent to Britain for repair, and raised by one-third the export duties charged for provisions to the Gibraltar garrison. During the War of the American Revolution the Sultan at first sided with the British, but then, in 1781, expelled their Consul-General and twenty others from Tangiers and handed that port and another to Spain for a year (in return, of course, for a cash payment). In September 1782, a British fleet relieved the siege of Gibraltar. Britain had lost thirteen colonies, but otherwise had won the war. Sidi Muhammad could not have been more gracious when the commander of naval forces in Gibraltar, Sir Roger Curtis, came to see him. The Sultan actually went down to the coast to meet Sir Roger. In May 1783, additional articles to the Treaty of Peace and Commerce were signed. But grievances soon returned. The Sultan sent three ships to Gibraltar for repair. The Governor refused to repair two of them and asked 5,000 guineas to refit the third. Sidi Muhammad got his two gold watches at last in 1787, but remained stroppy . . .

Not to say, daft. Helen Gloag, as was the custom with wives over thirty, would have been sent away from court years before, but may have been aware that the father of her children was going off his rocker. He gave the British consul a demand for a huge carriage clock which would record the days of the month according to the Christian calendar, as well as striking as loudly as possible four times a day. When an English merchant named Layton hit an old Moroccan woman so that she fell to the ground and lost teeth, the Sultan ordered a blacksmith to extract some of Layton's own teeth to send to her as compensation. But then he decided to make Layton his foreign secretary. He lauded him to the skies in public audience and ordered that as a mark of the highest royal favour he should be known henceforth as 'Milbanke' (after, that is, the kind envoy of yore). Within months of this absurdity, in April 1790, Sidi Muhammad died (Rogers, 96–123).

According to Perthshire preference, what followed was this. Helen's two sons were too young to rule. Mad Mulay Yazeed, son of Sidi Muhammad by a 'German concubine', seized power, and during his reign of terror Helen – who had been quartered in Fez – appealed to the British Government for help! A fleet prepared to sail to her aid!! Lt-Col. Jardine was sent to assess the situation but before he arrived the two princes seem to have been murdered!!! At which point the British fleet was diverted to help Mad Yazeed throw the Spanish out of Ceuta . . . (McKerracher, 188).

As the last incongruity suggests, that story doesn't hold up. In 1789 an English doctor, William Lempriere, had been permitted to penetrate the harem of Sidi Muhammad, who wished him to examine 'Lalla Zara', one of his four official wives. Guarded by eunuchs, he found there between sixty and one hundred concubines, several of them European, who mobbed him with pleas to examine their complaints. He saw 'Lalla Zara', a ravaged beauty whom the sultan had to keep on because she had borne him two children, and 'Lalla Batoom', the senior wife, aged about forty. Both these women were 'Moorish', but the favourite wife, 'Lalla Douyaw', was a woman originally from Genoa, shipwrecked on the Barbary Coast aged eight and reared in the harem until she was beddable. She read and wrote Arabic well and was said to have 'much influence', despite which she suffered from scurvy and was losing her teeth. 'At the time' the fourth wife was in Fez. She was said to be the daughter of an 'English renegado' (Lempriere, 362–404). She was the mother of Mulay al-Yazid, who was in fact the favourite son of Sidi Muhammad. She was perhaps an Irish rather than English woman. Mulay al-Yazid's temper had always been erratic, and he did indeed behave badly during his brief rule, following bloodthirsty whims and attacking Jews and Christians. But the brothers whom he saw as rivals, and who did oppose his succession, were not Helen's sons. He was friendly towards Britain and reduced the export duty on cattle destined for Gibraltar. He did indeed want to drive the Spaniards out of Ceuta, but Britain was now in harmony with Spain and wouldn't join him. Major Jardine had been designated ambassador to congratulate him on his accession, but this was cancelled for fear of endangering relations with Spain. Yazid died in 1792 of wounds incurred in battle against his brother Mulay Hishan. But it was Mulay Sliman, Sidi Muhammad's second favourite among his sons, who by 1796 gained control of Morocco and ruled for more than quarter of a century. Really, nothing definite seems to be known of the fate of Helen after she left Perthshire (Julien, 267; Rogers, 124).

Had one an adequate command of Arabic, French and Spanish, it would be a compelling and instructive labour to search archives and secondary sources for the references which must exist to Helen's life in Morocco. But they would often be as casual, I think, as the statement that tells us of Yazid's 'Irish' mother. In the Islamic world in which these women moved, persons of their gender were not supposed to be historical. The girl, perhaps 'not as good as she should be', who ran away from Perthshire vanished – on a vessel with no name – into the blue yonder and returned as a figment of imagination.

Linda Colley, Captives: Britain, Empire and the World 1600–1850, *2002; C. A. Julien*, History of North Africa, *1970; William Lempriere*, A Tour from Gibraltar to Morocco, *1793 edn; Archie McKerracher*, Perthshire in History and Legend, *(Edinburgh), 2000 edn; P. G. Rogers*, A History of Anglo-Moroccan Relations to 1900, *1992; John Shearer*, Antiquities in Perthshire, *(Perth) c.1860*

Juan Gomez de Medina (Spain) *fl.*1588

For the story of this Armada admiral's wreck on Fair Isle in his ship *El Gran Grifon*, and subsequent finding of succour for himself and his men at Anstruther in Fife, see under **Archie Angel**. Gomez was a tough and experienced seaman – as it happened, he had already seen action against a flotilla of English privateers in the Spanish Main before he joined Philip II's Armada in the important role of commander of the supply ships – 'hulks'. He was a big man of dignified appearance, grey-haired and very polite. As the most senior Spanish officer from the dispersed and wind-tossed fleet to land in Scotland, he became a magnet for intrigue by the pro-Spanish party in the country, mostly consisting of Catholics, but with an opportunist Protestant, the Earl of Bothwell, to the fore. An English agent, Thomas Fowler, reported from Edinburgh in January 1589 to Elizabeth's spymaster, Walsingham, that 'Don John de Medina and divers captains of the Spaniards are going hence with great credit from divers of the nobility, as Huntley, Bothwell, Seaton and others. On Sunday night I dined at Bothwell's, where I found four Spanish captains whom he entertains . . .' Gomez seemed to go along with talk of Spanish support for a rising in Scotland – 4,000 well-trained soldiers and plenty of cash was what Bothwell asked for – and was given a forty-ton barque in which he secretly slipped away. He took with him only a small number of men – priests and Irish exiles who were especially vulnerable to English rage – and left the bulk of his people languishing in the port of Leith. News of his disappearance did not go down well with them, and two captains wrote to Philip II accusing him of treachery and petitioning for vessels to take them home. But Gomez had always intended to see to that.

It is estimated that 660 Spaniards from various wrecks were corralled in Scotland at the end of 1588. To take them to Dunkirk, Scottish skippers were demanding a fare of ten shillings and a letter of safe conduct from Elizabeth I in case weather forced the ship into an English port. The Queen herself didn't like the idea of troublemaking Spaniards north of her border and tried a spot of gunboat diplomacy. In June 1589, two English warships dropped anchor in Leith while a third mounted guard at the entry to the Firth of Forth. James VI was happy enough to see them, and invited the crews ashore. There was a nasty incident when a Spanish soldier killed an English trumpeter in a brawl, but by August the Queen had confirmed the safe conduct of 600 Spaniards on four Scottish vessels bound for Dunkirk. But almost in sight of that port, as Elizabeth knew would happen, they were ambushed by Dutch 'Sea Beggars', rebels against Spain allied with England, under the command of Justin of Nassau. One ship was captured and all Scots and Spaniards aboard were tossed into the sea. The other three ships, trying to escape, were wrecked and broke up in the surf under heavy fire. About 300 Spaniards died.

The Spaniards who had decided to stay on in Scotland as servants might just have made the best decision. Gomez himself, returning to Cadiz, was lucky to escape from a further wreck, off Cape St Vincent.

Colin Parker and Geoffrey Martin, The Spanish Armada, *1999 edn*

Grimsby Chums (England) *d.*1917

In May 2001 French archaeologists were excavating a battlefield site in farmland east of Arras, in Normandy, anticipating the building of a new factory there. They came upon the skeletons of twenty British infantrymen in one shallow grave, lying on their backs in a single line with their elbows overlapping, as if arm in arm. In March 2002, they were reinterred at the Commonwealth War Graves Commission Cemetery at Pont au Jour.

It may be that all these men were from the 10th Battalion of the Lincolnshire Regiment. Four of them had 10th Lincoln shoulder flashes and it was exactly at this point that the battalion attacked the

German lines on 9 April 1917. Twenty-four were killed, and the bodies of twenty were never recovered.

The head of the Arras archaeological service, Alain Jacques, commented: 'The fact that the bodies had been arranged so theatrically suggests to us very strongly that they were from one unit. By arranging them arm in arm, their comrades were saying, 'These people were friends.' The bodies must have been collected in the heat of the battle, before the limbs had stiffened. That again suggests that they all came from the same battalion.'

So newspaper headlines evoked the Grimsby Chums. This had been the nickname of one of the many 'Pals Battalions' created in the fervent early days of the 1914–18 war when fathers, sons, brothers, cousins, men who were comrades at work or at play, signed up to fight alongside each other. Thirty thousand men from the Welsh coalfields joined up in 1914 and 1915. Amongst over a million men who had volunteered by the end of 1914 in 'one of the most impressive mass movements ever witnessed in British history' (Stevenson, 47–48), there were contingents of 'pals' from factories, offices, trade unions, churches, sports clubs, old boys societies and many more of the myriad types of organisation with which British males identified themselves. Lord Derby, 'The King of Lancashire', launched the Pals movement at a crowded meeting in St George's Hall, Liverpool, on 28 August 1914, guaranteeing that if the city's clerks joined up together they would serve together. Battalion subtitles such as 'North-East Railway', '1st Football', 'Arts and Crafts' and 'Church Lads' testified to the appeal of palship. About a quarter of a million men enlisted in over 300 battalions raised on this basis. The Grimsby Chums were gathered on the initiative of a local headmaster, from the fishing port itself and from neighbouring parts of Lincolnshire.

At the Battle of the Somme, which began in July 1916, the volunteer regiments were mangled. The first day of botched assault on the German lines was so lethal that the London Scottish (for instance), 856 strong at dawn, were reduced by death or wounds to 266 by nightfall. John Keegan, in his classic account, muses over the fate of a 'vanished party of the 12th York and Lancasters, whose bodies were discovered five months after the attack in the heart of the German position. That a party could disappear so completely, not in the Antarctic wastes but at a point almost within visual range of their own lines, seems incomprehensible today, so attuned are we to thinking of wireless providing instant communication across the battlefield' (Keegan, 260).

The military authorities perceived, through the Somme débâcle, that 'pals' recruitment had its downside. A whole street in a small industrial town might simultaneously be plunged into mourning. It was decided that the Pals Battalions should be diluted. So only a third of the Lincoln's casualties on the first day of the Battle of Arras came from the county – the rest were drawn from many parts of England, South as well as North.

Arras was another disaster to compare with the Somme. The idea was to suck in German reserves and help a French attack further south, at Reims. This failed badly, and widespread mutinies in the French army followed. British and Canadian troops at Arras advanced four miles with 142,000 casualties. The Germans had 85,000 casualties. The twenty men in the trench were probably victims of 'friendly fire'. One British gun in the rolling barrage under which they advanced was firing short and disposed of many men in the 10th Lincolns.

But if the twenty men whose bodies were found forming a spectral frieze were mostly not from Lincolnshire, and were the disillusioned victims of gross incompetence to their rear, it does not follow that their 'arm in arm' postures were a bogus and sentimental imposition. Asking the big question, Why do men go on fighting, even in conditions like those in the First World War trench country? historians conclude unanimously that 'bonding' is the crucial factor.

Out there among the shells, you do not fight for Empire, for King and Country, for Liberal Democracy, or whatever other slogans politicians and propagandists are deploying. You fight for the guys who are fighting around you. Even a new chum who has spent only a few days in the line with you may seem like your dearest brother. Even your family at home may seem so remote from the world in which you suffer that you almost despise them. The soldiers in your unit, whatever part of Britain they come from, are all the nation and all the family you care about. The men who, as the battle raged on, buried twenty comrades at Arras in the way just revealed were expressing the highest values which the Poor Bloody Infantry could sustain, what the Australians called 'mateship'.

John Keegan, The Face of Battle, *(New York) 1977 edn; John Lichfield, 'Arm in arm they lie, Grimsby Chums . . .'* Independent, *20 June 2001; John Stevenson,* British Society 1914–45, *1984;* The Times, *21 March 2002; thanks to Bill Swainson*

Che Guevara (Argentina) 1928–67

After Ernesto ('Che') Guevara was captured and executed by the Bolivian Army during his fruitless attempts to generate a revolution amongst the peasants of that very poor country, those who had killed him felt compelled to wash his corpse, comb his hair, trim his beard, and display his smiling visage to a photographer who would prove to the world that they really had disposed of the legendary Che. His bearded image matched that of Jesus Christ in iconic power on posters, T-shirts, on merchandise all over the world – seized and exploited by just such capitalist marketeers as he had denounced. But the legend endures of the asthmatic young doctor moved by poverty and oppression, and hatred of the US capitalism which had enslaved Latin America, to sail from Mexico with Fidel Castro's little band of eighty-two in August 1956 and raise peasant revolt on the Sierra Maestre in Cuba which in little more than two years swept the America-backed dictator Batista out of Havana. Che became the leading organiser and theorist of Castro's revolution, then sought to extend the struggle against imperialism, first abortively in the Congo, before Bolivia. A Marxist with independent ideas, he was never a puppet of Moscow. Failure to get on with the Bolivian Communist Party was one cause of his ultimate failure. Young idealists everywhere could identify with Che as his, and their, own man.

He had begun life as scion of a decayed aristocratic family in Argentina, where his father, Ernest Guevara-Lynch, blundered through a succession of business failures, but still found resources to sustain a middle-class lifestyle. The Guevaras were on the liberal wing of the bourgeoisie – supporters of the Spanish Republic against Franco and the Western Allies against Nazism – but Che when a student was not markedly political. His asthma did not prevent him taking an avid interest in outdoor activities (above all, motor-cycling) and sport. Soccer had become the favourite game of the Argentinian proletariat and would bring the country long-term World Cup success. But rugby football was the preferred code of the wealthy elite, which created huge clubs and eventually, after Che's death, a world-class team.

Che was passionate about the game, and launched a rugby magazine called *Tackle* which lasted for eleven issues. He wrote severely analytical articles for it under the pseudonym 'Chang-Cho' (Anderson, 56). Castañeda, his biographer in Spanish, gives a strange account of Che's active involvement in the sport, which he played at the Atalyia Rugby Club of San Isidro. Castañeda describes him as performing as 'half-scrum' and presents the specious but actually nonsensical idea that this position suited both his asthma and his personality, being 'static' and 'strategic'. He could 'develop his skills as a leader' without running from one end of the pitch to the other. (Even so we are told that he sometimes suffered asthma attacks while playing, and had to rush off the pitch and inject himself with adrenalin through his clothing [Castañeda, 17].) The 'scrum-half' does indeed have a key 'leadership' role, involved with the forwards when they move into scrums and line-outs, then getting the ball they heel or pass to him out to the backs. But this means that he has to stick close, running a lot, to both forwards and backs. Matilde Sanchez is more plausible. Che found that running left him breathless while playing, but actually helped him improve his breathing at other times. His family had nicknamed him 'Ernestito' or 'Tete', but 'on the rugby field he rebaptised himself with his battle cry of "Out of the way! Here comes Furibundo!" This name (shortened to "Fuser") meant "wild" or "furious". Ernesto/Fuser played at such a hard pace that because of his asthma he did not always survive till the end of the game' (Sanchez, 19).

Jon Lee Anderson, Che Guevara: A Revolutionary Life, *1997; Jorge G. Castañeda*, Compañero: The Life and Death of Che Guevara, *1997; Ferdinando Diego Garcia, Oscar Sola and Matilde Sanchez*, Che: Images of a Revolutionary, *1997*

Ruth Handler (USA) 1917–2002

'Barbie', most celebrated of all dolls, was born in 1959. She was named after Barbara, the daughter of her creator, Ruth Handler.

Mrs Handler was the youngest of ten children of a Polish blacksmith surnamed Mosko who had emigrated to the USA to avoid conscription into the Russian Army, and had settled in Denver. Aged nineteen, Ruth headed (naturally) for Hollywood. Films being full up, she studied industrial design and married a boy on the same course. In a converted garage, they started Mattel, initially producing plastic houseware, then moving into toys. Their prosperity was modest until Ruth, on holiday in Switzerland, met a German-made doll named Blonde Lili, 11 inches tall. Her measurements were improbable, her clothing exiguous, her sordid intent was clearly to turn on young men.

Back in the US, Mrs Handler took the sex out of Lili. Barbie had no nipples, nor even a belly button. Her statistics were still ballistic – about 39–18–33 had she been human – but her target was little girls: 351,000 Barbie dolls were sold in the year after her debut, at $3 each. She became an icon, seized as such by Andy Warhol. A Danish group called Aqua produced a big hit record, 'Barbie Girl' ('life in plastic/

Is fantastic . . .'). She was placed in the official US time capsule when it was buried in 1976, the bicentenary of the American Revolution. Into the next century, more than a billion Barbies have been sold in 150 countries. At the time of Mrs Handler's death, Barbie's manufacturers were quoted as alleging that an American girl up to age eleven is likely to own ten Barbies. French children stick at five. But millions of grown women cherish Barbies, and there are Barbie collectors of both sexes, who might pay $5,000 for an original 1959 Barbie in good nick. An 'illustrated identifier' to over 140 Barbie and related dolls, published in 1998, makes it clear that constant diversification has been the key to Barbie's success. Five different versions were issued in the first two years. By the next century, Mattel was devising 150 new dolls a year, with 120 new outfits.

If Barbie were alive she would be severely handicapped. Her fingers are joined together so that she cannot grip or hold anything. She cannot stand unassisted. But at least her virtue is impregnable. She is supremely 'nice'. Her chief function is to have accessories, and apart from miniaturised fashion clothes, she is heavily into technology, from kitchen gadgets to sports cars. In 1997 she got her own pc. She takes a lot of care. The 'illustrated identifier' advises that really dirty Barbies can be reglamorised with Castrol SuperClean, a degreaser used on motor cars, which 'works wonders without taking off face or nail paint'. Yellowed wedding gowns and other white dresses can be revived with denture cleaning tablets (Fennick, 11, 13–14).

Feminists hated Barbie. Mrs Handler retorted that, so far from offering girls a bimbo role model, Barbie represented choice. And it is true that Barbies have been offered attired as policewomen, astronauts, doctors. She even ran for President (party unspecified). There are Chinese Barbies and black Barbies. Though Barbie has a younger sister, Skipper, friends Midge and Christie and a boyfriend, Ken (named after Ruth Handler's son), she has never married to reproduce the babies which were what dolls mostly were before she came along. Whatever role she plays is independent.

She still inspires fascinated anger. Anti-globalisers are incensed by the fact that since 1987, when Mattel closed the last US Barbie factory, she has been manufactured solely in countries where wages are low and conditions for employees are appalling. Talking Barbies appeared in the 1990s. One shamefully cheeped, 'Math class is tough.' A New York-based 'Barbie Liberation Organisation' swapped voice boxes with those of GI Joe, an all-action male doll made by Hasbro, and slipped them back on toyshop shelves, where 're-educated Barbies bellowed muscular lines such as "Vengeance is mine!", while the boy dolls chirped "Let's go shopping"' (*Economist*, 'Life in Plastic'). Meanwhile academics of all kinds have buzzed around Barbie. In a study of *Barbie Culture* by a professor of sociology, the ten-page small-print bibliography includes – beside such predictable titles as 'Barbie as a Site for Cultural Interrogation', and much on sexuality and gender – Brownell, Kelly D. and Melissa A. Napolitano, 'Distorting Reality for Children: Body Size Proportions of Barbie and Ken Dolls', *International Journal of Eating Disorders* 18 (3) (Rogers).

Alas, Mrs Handler's own success story was flawed by most un-Barbie-like behaviour. Mattel began to diversify in the 1970s and the Handlers were forced out of the company they had started. In 1978 Ruth was indicted for mail fraud and false reporting to the Securities and Exchange Commission. She pleaded no contest, was fined $57,000 and sentenced to 2,500 hours of community service.

Economist, *Obituary, 4–10 May 2002;* Economist, *'Life in Plastic', 21 December 2002–3 January 2003; Janine Fennick,* Barbie Dolls, *1998;* Herald, *Obituary, 29 April 2002; Mary F. Rogers,* Barbie Culture, *1999*

Hildegard of Bingen (Germany) 1098–1179

An authoritative multi-volume *Dictionary of the Middle Ages* produced in the USA from 1978 has a substantial entry on St Hildegard of Bingen – 'probably the most important woman of her time'. It notes the visions – *Scivias* – which she committed to writing from 1141 with the help of the monk Volmar, her fame as a physician and healer, consolidated by a medical handbook which was still in great demand among physicians in the fifteenth century, and her correspondence – 391 surviving letters – with the great men, lay and clerical, of her day (including Frederick Barbarossa, the Holy Roman Emperor) who sought the advice of this brilliant abbess. As for the morality play attributed to her – the earliest known medieval drama by more than a century – and scores of liturgical songs, this dictionary reckons they aren't authentic . . . (Strayer, 278–79).

Quarter of a century on, Hildegard has become the most famous of all medieval creative writers in Latin and all female composers – poet and musician first, scientist and saint second. She was the tenth child of well-born Rhineland people, Hildebert and Mechtild, who accordingly promised her as their 'tithe' to the service of the church. She became a novitiate under the recluse Jutta, sister of Count Meginhard, who with her followers occupied a cell in the Benedictine monastery of Didisbodenberg. Aged fifteen, she took the veil. Jutta was not noted for learning, but at least taught Hildegard to read, though joined-up writing, as we now call it, was never her forte – hence the importance for her of the monk Volmar until his death in 1173, as her secretary and copy-editor. When Jutta died in 1136, Hildegard succeeded her as superior of her cell. By 1150 she overrode ecclesiopolitical problems to found her own convent on the Rupertsberg, in the Rhine Valley near Bingen, and settled there with eighteen sisters. Letters of protection drawn up by the Emperor Frederick in 1163 referred to her as 'Abbess' – her point was made. She then expanded her operations, founding in 1165 a daughter convent at Eibingen on the opposite bank of the Rhine. Preaching tours through Germany extended her formidable reputation as the 'Sybil of the Rhine'. She remained controversially active down to her venerable death. Her Church found it hard to cope with such a woman, orthodox in theology but not in the ways in which she acted and expressed herself.

She had visions from the age of three. She claimed that none of them were the result of ecstasy. Their context was illness. 'Without losing consciousness or ordinary perception, the girl was able to see hidden things, such as the colour of a calf in its mother's womb, and to foretell the future.' Late in life, she characterised her *visio* as 'a non-spatial radiance . . . "the reflection of the living Light"', and in it she saw 'the complex symbolic forms that fill her visionary writings'. A voice from heaven, addressing her in Latin, helped her to interpret these forms, sometimes speaking as God in the first person, sometimes talking about him in the third. This voice dictated her books and letters. Beside illness – perhaps migraine – and the stress which preceded all the important decisions of her life, she was also acutely sensitive to weather, especially storms and wind. She compared her own voice, in music, to that of a trumpet resounding by the breath of God (Newman, 2–3, 30–31). This was a variant of her favourite saying that she was a feather borne up by the breath of God.

When she was forty-three, she was terrified by a divine command to set down her visions. She took to her bed in pain. Her dearest friend, the nobly born nun Richardis von Stade, and Volmar, the provost of her convent, saw her through the *Scivias*, which took her ten years to complete. Based on twenty-six visions, three books set forth the divine scheme of creation, redemption and sanctification, alternating visual descriptions with much longer allegorical passages expounding God's doctrines. Halfway through this, Pope Eugenius III heard of her efforts. He dispatched legates to the monastery of St Disibod to get a copy of Hildegard's writings, and later sent her a letter of apostolic blessing and protection.

Now she was a holy celebrity there was no stopping her. The fame of her avant-garde songs had spread as far as Paris and in the early 1150s she collected them as her *Symphonia armonie celestium revelationum*. Despite a bad patch, when disgruntled sisters left her new convent because it was so damn poor, Richardis and her Pope died and her admirer Heinrich, Bishop of Mainz, was deposed for embezzling church funds, she now held such cards as her protégée, the nun Elizabeth of Schonau, who in 1156–57 had visions that usefully explained the recently noted presence of male bones among those uncovered in a cemetery in Cologne fifty years earlier, which had been supposed to be those of the 11,000 massacred female virgin martyrs who had followed **St Ursula** (q.v.). The male intruders were now seen to be devout bishops, so countless profitable relics were still guaranteed to be holy. Hildegard's medical encyclopaedia, the *Physica*, listed the wholesome or toxic properties of trees and herbs, gems and metals, animals, fishes and birds and defined their medicinal uses. A companion volume on *Causes and Cures* dealt with physical and mental diseases. For these scentific works, she claimed no divine inspiration.

Other Latin poets of the day used rhyme. Hildegard wrote what we would now call 'free verse', with proto-Surrealist imagery. Without formal training in music, she produced settings in which emphases took no account of the significance of particular words. She would race up and down the octave several times in the space of one word. She was addicted to melisma. Her words are strange and passionate, the music is lovely, like floating with mildly erotic thoughts in safe though agitated sea. Hildegard's artistic vision is wonderfully straightforward. When Adam before his Fall sang, with the angels, his voice, she declared, was 'resonant', like 'the sound of a monochord' (Newman, 31). This ancient one-stringed instrument had been used for many centuries for teaching elementary laws of harmonics and singing. By Hildegard's day it had acquired extra strings and greater sonority, and she may well have used one to pick out her new melodies. Music was basic holiness. The **Devil** (q.v.) could not sing. But Hildegard could depict his fall by flying between extreme upper and lower ranges of the human voice in her 'Antiphon for the Angels':

It could be said that Hildegard's currently huge reputation is the result of a lucky coincidence – in the 1970s the Women's Movement, looking for neglected female stars, bumped into the Early Music Movement which sought to revive medieval scores. But her ascent depended on the scholarship of two nuns at her abbey at Eibingen who proved the authenticity of her works beyond all doubt in 1956. Hildegard was quite as extraordinary as her admirers ask us to believe.

Joseph L. Baird and Radd K. Ehrman, trans. and ed., The Letters of Hildegard of Bingen, *(New York) 1994–98; Ian D. Bent, 'Hildegard of Bingen', in* The New Grove Dictionary of Music, *vol. 8, ed. Stanley Sadie, 1980; Jane Bobko, ed.,* Vision: The Life and Music of Hildegard of Bingen, *(New York) 1995; Sabina Flanagan,* Hildegard of Bingen: A Visionary Life, *2nd edn, 1998; Hildegard of Bingen,* Selected Works, *ed. Mark Atherton, 2001; Fiona Maddocks,* Hildegard of Bingen: The Woman of her Age, *2001; Barbara Newman, ed. and trans.,* Hildegard of Bingen: Symphonia, *2nd edn, (Ithaca, NY) 1998; Heinrich Schipperges,* The World of Hildegard of Bingen, *(Tunbridge Wells) 1997; Joseph R. Strayer, ed.,* Dictionary of the Middle Ages, *vol. 6, (New York) 1985*

'Joe Hill' (Sweden, USA) 1879–1915

In 1941, Pete Seeger, Lee Hays and Millard Lampell set up, in New York, what is claimed to be 'the first urban folk-singing group ever assembled'. They called it, rather oddly, 'The Almanac Singers'. They lived and worked communally, sharing all proceeds equally. To amass their rent, they used their loft for Sunday afternoon concerts. Up to a hundred people would crowd in, non-musicians paying 35c. Participants included the legendary black ex-convict Leadbelly, Burl Ives, Blind Sonny Terry and Josh White. Another singer, an erstwhile Okie hobo, Woody Guthrie, joined the Alamanac founders. Drifting around in the West, he had encountered, in the so-called 'jungles', the camps where men in search of work gathered, many old radicals, 'all of whom seemed to be named Mac', who would pull out red cards after a time to prove that they had once been members of the International Workers of the World, the legendary Wobblies (Klein, 82, 186, 190).

And at the Almanac HQ, in the autumn of 1941, arrived Elizabeth Gurley Flynn, now a leader in the Communist Party, formerly a heroine of the IWW, bringing with her many private papers of the man who called himself 'Joe Hill', hoping that new singers would find inspiration in them (Klein, 206). Joe Hill was by common consent the greatest of the Wobbly balladeers featured in the movement's *Little Red Song Book*. He had corresponded with Flynn while in jail awaiting execution, she had spent just one hour with him there, and he had written with her in mind his last song – 'The Rebel Girl'.

'Hill' was born Joel Hagglund in Gavle, Sweden, in October 1879. He was one of six surviving children of a railroad conductor, Olof. The Hagglunds were musical. Olof built a four-octave organ which the whole family learnt to play, and Joel also learned piano, accordion, guitar and violin. But Olof died from an industrial injury when Joel was eight, and he had to work as a child to help support the family, first in a rope factory, then as a fireman on a steam-powered crane. In 1902, his mother died, the family broke up, and Joel and his elder brother Paul set off, like so many Swedes in that era, in search of wealth in the rising USA.

At first, Joel found odd jobs in New York City. Then he headed West. By 1905, he had been in Chicago and Cleveland and had changed his name, first to 'Joseph Hillstrom', then to 'Joe Hill'. Never smoking, never drinking, never gambling, working hard at this and that, Joe Hill travelled widely. It seems he was in Philadelphia, then in San Francisco during the 1906 earthquake, the Dakotas, Portland in Oregon, Hawaii. The closest he came to settling was in the Californian port San Pedro, where in 1910 he joined the IWW local. 'I am just one of the rank and file – just a Pacific Coast wharfrat – that's all' (ANB, 788). It was probably in Malgren's Hall, the Wobbly centre in San Pedro, and the local Sailors' Rest Mission, that Joe tried out the songs which began to make him famous from 1911, when the third edition of *The Little Red Song Book* carried his first and greatest hit, 'The Preacher and the Slave'.

You will eat, bye and bye,
In that glorious land above the sky;
Work and pray, live on hay,
You'll get pie in the sky when you die.

(Smith, 20)

The last line of that refrain acquired classic power in the Great Depression and the hungry years of the Thirties.

Songs weren't just optional afterwork entertainment for the Wobblies. They were integral to the Union's organisation.

Major capitalist trusts had increasingly grossed monopoly power in the USA. Centralised big business dominated pauperised labour, with 'Progressive' liberal politicians nervously attempting to provide fair play. When the Wobblies talked about employed workers as 'slaves', what they had in mind was typified by Lawrence, Massachusetts, a sizeable town where over half the working population were employed in textile mills. Wages were so low and living conditions so bad that a local physician estimated that more than a third of employees died before they were twenty-five (Renshaw, 48–50; Smith, 26).

The chief organisation mobilising workers to achieve improved pay and conditions was the American Federation of Labor. Three points about the AFL help to explain the irruption of the IWW. Firstly, while union membership rose sharply around the turn of the century, and the unions affiliated to the AFL accounted for half of it, around two million unionised workers were less than ten per cent of the total workforce. Secondly, the AFL grouped together craft unions, each organising only one skilled sector of the workers within a given industry – at a time when advancing technology was increasingly eliminating the need for skilled men. Finally, though many delegates to AFL conferences were Socialists, its leader Samuel Gompers didn't want to operate 'politically', still less to challenge capitalism.

In half a century from 1860 to 1910, the population of the USA tripled, to ninety-two million. Mass immigration accounted for this. Increasingly, incomers from Britain, Germany and Scandinavia, whose paleface culture was compatible with previous North American norms, were outnumbered by swarthier persons – Catholic, Orthodox and Jewish – from southern and eastern Europe. Between 1891 and 1910, eight million out of twelve-and-a-half million immigrants came from Italy, Poland, Hungary, Bohemia, Slovakia, Croatia and Greece (Renshaw, 30, 47). Bosses in the eastern USA saw the advantages of 'divide and rule', employing an ethnic mixture in the labour force where differences of language and culture would impede collective action on wages and conditions.

Meanwhile, the West, famously, had been stolen from its red aboriginals and opened up to capitalist exploitation. There were hordes of migratory workers such as Gompers' craft unions could never hope to organise, working seasonally, like Joe Hill, in logging camps and lumber mills, in mines and on construction projects, building and maintaining railroads, in orchards and planting and harvesting fields. The impetus which created the IWW came from the West. In 1897, the strong new Western Federation of Miners withdrew from the AFL. Its leaders met, in a secret conclave in Chicago in January 1905, with people from other unions and organisations (including a maverick Catholic priest) to draft an invitation to comrades in the USA and Europe to found a new big union on 'industrial' lines. Two hundred delegates attended a founding convention in Chicago in June.

The aims of the IWW were clear, and sweeping. Workers, whose interests were everywhere and always opposed to those of capital, must combine against it in industrial unions. When strong enough, these would seize control, by direct action, of the economy and society and would initate a new commonwealth where the rights of human life and happiness would be emphasised over the rights of property.

The General Strike of all workers would be the instrument of revolution. By 1908, 'Big Bill' Haywood, who had come from the Western Federation of Miners, a huge man, blind in one eye, whose face, according to the great Red journalist John Reed, was like a 'scarred battlefield', was the iconic leader of a movement with no leaders. Rarely more than about 100,000-strong in its era of effective existence, from 1905 to 1924, the IWW had such a huge turnover of membership – 133 per cent per year from 1905 to 1915 – that maybe a million workers at one time or another held IWW cards. Explanations of the nickname 'Wobblies' tend to hover round a legendary Chinese restaurateur on the west coast who is said to have tried to ask, 'Are you IWW?' but could only manage 'All loo eye wobble wobble?' (Renshaw, 21–22, 71–72).

The impact of the Wobblies in their brief heyday was enormous. Accused by righteous capitalists and politicians of fomenting anarchist violence, they were as committed as Gandhi himself to non-violence, except when the bosses themselves used violence. Wobblies set out to organise any and every kind of worker – blacks along with whites, women as well as men, folk of whatever ethnic origin. In the West 'Any IWW member could become a "jawsmith" or organiser while pursuing the regular routine of a transitory worker. He supplied himself with membership cards, dues books and a notebook, and samples of IWW literature, and carried the gospel with him on his job.' 'Job delegates', as the organisers were called, made the red IWW card a necessary ticket for those travelling on freight cars to find work. In the 'jungles' they set up committees to arrange hygiene and sanitation, and organised supplies of food for communal cooking. And such men would carry with them the little cards on which were printed the words of Wobbly songs (Foner, 115, 118–19).

Songs were the Wobblies' trademark and lifeblood. Hymn tunes and those of commercial hits of the day were hijacked. Humorous words and noble expressions of Wobbly values were carried away even by those who left the movement, to fuse with the body of existing folksong. In the West, singing provided community, identity and self-respect for lone drifters; in the East, their easy English could be shared with Italians and Polish Jews making their first stumbling steps into the language of their new country.

Thus, Joe Hill hit, and hit hard, in the action of Southern Pacific Railroad employees in 1911. A sentimental ballad had recently come into popular currency in honour of a Deep South railwayman called

Casey Jones. John Luther Jones, born in the town of Cayce, Kentucky, stood 6' 4¼" tall and had a heart to correspond. He was an engineer on the Illinois Central Railway, pushing the crack Cannonball Express from Memphis, Tennessee, to Canton, Mississippi. One night in April 1906 he pulled up in Memphis, ready to go home, when the engineer on the outgoing southern run turned up sick. Casey volunteered to take his place, and crashed into boxcars at Vaughan, Mississippi. He was found in the wreck with one hand on the brake and the other on his whistlecord. His whistle – somehow identified by those who heard it as manifesting its operator's Irish genes – was famous along the line. One admirer of Casey and his whistle was Wallis Saunders, an African-American engine cleaner in the roundhouse at Canton, who wiped Casey's blood off the cabin and wrote a song in his memory. This came to the attention of a vaudeville singer, Taliferro Lawrence Sibert, and by 1909, printed, it had become a popular hit as a 'ragtime ballad' (Lomax, 248–50).

From September 1911, 35,000 shopmen on the Illinois Central and other lines owned by Harriman, including the Southern Pacific, were in dispute over sixteen demands presented by nine craft unions acting together and demanding recognition as a federation. When, on 30 September, the entire crew of 300 SP shopmen walked out in San Pedro, and 1,400 struck in Los Angeles, the bosses brought in non-union labour, and kept the trains running, thanks to the refusal of Casey Jones's equivalents – the engineers, firemen and brakemen organised on a craft basis – to come out with the shopmen. 'NO SCAB SO DESPICABLE AS A UNION SCAB' roared the IWW poster. Hill's song, 'Casey Jones – The Union Scab', imagines the eponymous engineer driving a 'junk pile' of a train deprived of maintenance until his 'wheezy engine' runs 'right off the worn-out track', his back is broken, and he takes 'a trip to heaven on the SP line'. In heaven, St Peter welcomes him – 'just the man' – since the musicians are on strike and he needs scab labour. But the Angels Union Local No. 23 chuck the scab down the Golden Stair where the Devil sets him to slave work shovelling sulphur . . . Hill's ditty eventually became more popular than the original which it parodied, and passed current in labour unions everywhere (Smith, 21–23).

Joe was an impressive, tall, slim figure, with his vividly blond hair, deep blue eyes and long, thin face. He made eloquent prose contributions to the Wobbly press, and was rumoured to be a ladies' man. He was free, surprisingly, of a police record . . . In 1913 he showed up in Utah, where the founding Mormons had lost out in the 1908 senate race to an extreme right-wing pro-business party, but had fought back. The state now had a Mormon governor pledged to crack down on business and Wobblies alike.

While working unpaid for Wobbly Local 69 in Salt Lake City, Joe was arrested for the murder of a grocer, John Morrison, a former policeman, and one of his sons in their store during an armed raid on the night of 10 January 1914. One of the masked raiders had been shot himself, and Joe had been treated that night for a gunshot wound by a doctor who noticed on him a revolver in a shoulder holster. Arrested three days later Joe claimed he had been wounded in a fight over a married woman, whom, for reasons of gallantry, he could not name. No weeping woman came forward to save him. Meanwhile, Joe's room-mate, Otto Applequist, had vanished in the wee small hours on the night of the raid, and was never seen again. Applequist had suffered a gunshot wound on a night in the previous September when the Morrison store had been attacked. Scenarios multiply. Did Joe kill Applequist, who himself might have been working out a grudge against the former policeman? Joe stayed mum, did not stand in the witness box. The weakest part of his literary output was the sickly, sentimental lovesongs which he seems to have written while in Utah. Maybe *chercher la femme* was always the best path for researchers into his legend to follow . . .

Though a second son of Morrison had witnessed the killing and survived, Joe was never positively identified as the murderer. But on 28 June a jury found Hill guilty. The IWW claimed that his trial was part of a conspiracy to do down the Wobblies by the all-powerful Utah bosses.

Until he died by firing squad on 19 November 1915, Joe Hill handled himself calmly in jail like a man conscious of his own immortal destiny, even noting in a letter that he had reached the age when Christ was crucified. Protests rolled through the USA and echoed round far continents, not muted by the outbreak of World War I. Even the AFL weighed in with a protest unanimously agreed at its 1915 convention, to the effect that Joe had not had a fair trial. President Woodrow Wilson twice asked Governor Spry to reconsider the case – appeals rejected as unwarrantable interference in the affairs of Utah. Joe ensured his undying fame as a martyr by a wonderful message to Big Bill Haywood – 'Goodbye Bill: I die like a true rebel. Don't waste any time mourning – organize!' (Smith, 166–74).

After a first funeral in Salt Lake City on 21 November (music provided by the Swedish Temperance Society), Joe's body was conveyed by rail to Chicago, where 5,000 people crammed into an auditorium and the streets outside were clogged for blocks in all directions by hordes of mourners. After cremation, Hill's ashes were placed in envelopes and distributed to IWW locals in every state bar Utah, to South America, Europe, Asia, South Africa (where Wobblies brought black and white workers out on strike together), New Zealand and Australia.

Amongst many songs and poems inspired by Hill's death, one written in 1925 by Alfred Hayes, set later by Earl Robinson to music, became, as rendered by Paul Robeson, a worldwide perennial:

> I dreamed I saw Joe Hill last night,
> Alive as you and me.
> Says I, 'But Joe, you're ten years dead,'
> 'I never died,' says he,
> 'I never died,' says he . . .
>
> 'From San Diego up to Maine,
> In every mine and mill,
> Where workers strike and organize,'
> Says he, 'You'll find Joe Hill,'
> Says he, 'You'll find Joe Hill.'

(Seeger and Reiser, 110)

American National Biography, *vol. 10, 1999; Philip L. Foner,* History of the Labor Movement in the United States, *vol. 4,* The Industrial Workers of the World, 1905–1917, *(New York) 1965; Woody Guthrie,* Bound for Glory, *(New York) 1943; Joe Klein,* Woody Guthrie: A Life, *1981; John A. Lomax and Alan*

Lomax, eds., Folksong USA, *(New York) 1947; Patrick Renshaw*, The Wobblies: The Story of Syndicalism in the United States, *1967; Pete Seeger and Bob Reiser, eds.*, Carry It On! A History in Song and Picture of the Working Man and Woman in America, *(Poole, Dorset) 1986; Gibbs M. Smith*, Joe Hill, *(Salt Lake City) 1969; thanks to James A. O'Neill and Polly Rewt*

Dorothy Crowfoot Hodgkin (England) 1910–94

Back in the early sixties, some of us Cambridge students travelled to Oxford for a CND or Committee of 100 demonstration outside a rocket base. Elizabeth Hodgkin took us to her family home. I think I was already much aware of Thomas Hodgkin, her father, as a distinguished left-wing scholar and educationalist who had become a pioneer in African studies in the era of emergent nationalism. (I still have a paperback copy of his *African Political Parties*, published in 1961). That her mother Dorothy, FRS since 1947, was not only Fellow of Somerville College but also Wolfson Professor of X-Ray Crystallography was not perhaps then clear to me. I recall a cheerful, housewifely person bustling about to provide for her young visitors while mighty Thomas brooded in his study. Memory insists that she was wearing an apron.

In 1964, she won the Nobel Prize for Chemistry. Other international honours followed, along with an Aida-scale procession of honorary fellowships, memberships of learned societies, and honorary degrees. For eighteen years from 1970 she was Chancellor of Bristol University, suggesting a modest willingness to be of service close to home.

In *Who's Who* she referred to her publications as 'various, on the X-ray crystallographic analysis of structure of molecules, inc. penicillin, vitamin B12 and insulin'. Elizabeth had two brothers. Dorothy listed her 'recreations' as 'archaeology, children'.

I don't want to suggest that Thomas Hodgkin was a vain man or an unsupportive husband – just to demonstrate that first impressions, especially those of young people, may be wildly misleading, and to pay tribute to the basic friendly humanity which that towering scientist communicated.

Billie Holiday (USA) 1915–59

Grotesquely emaciated, her once luscious body sadly ravaged by booze and illicit substances, Billie Holiday died in the Metropolitan Hospital, New York, on 17 July 1959 in the midst of legal wrangling over her latest possession of drugs – a nurse had just found her supply of cocaine. A subsequent friend of mine, who played washboard on the British skiffle and blues scene, had sat with her in a pub during her last UK visit. All he can remember the goddess saying was 'Big Sid Catlett [a notable jazz drummer] – he had the biggest cock of the lot.' She was habitually 'coarse' in her speech. Though she wasn't illiterate – indeed, she taught her mother to write – she read nothing more substantial than comic books and slushy romances. She was very pleased to seduce other women, claiming the white star Tallulah Bankhead amongst her trophies. But she was also heavily into sex with men, and her choice of those she stuck with for any length of time was consistently bad. Opinion about her performances in the fifties varies between deep embarrassment over the wreckage of her talent and the view that – rather like Titian, say, in his late great painting 'The Flaying of Marsyas', or Yeats in his raging as an old man – Billie, full of booze and shit, was a great artist awesomely baring her suffering.

In any case, she had smaller resources as an artist than almost anyone of equivalent stature. The critic Henry Pleasants points out that 'Billie had a meagre voice – small, hoarse at the bottom and thinly shrill at the top, with top and bottom never very far apart. She had hardly more than an octave and a third' (White, 123). Brothels figured as prominently in the orphaned early life of Ella Fitzgerald, her only rival for the title of greatest jazz singer of the day, as they did in Billie's. But Ella had a voice to disarm the most bigoted 'classical' canary fancier. Billie's voice was redolent, while it transcended them, of the disastrous social conditions which formed her and killed her – bad housing, bad sex, bad booze and Jim Crow.

'Mom and Pop were just a couple of kids when they got married. He was eighteen, she was sixteen, and I was three' (Holiday, 1). The opening sentence of Billie's 'autobiography', *Lady Sings the Blues* (1956), matches in epigrammatic memorability those of *Pride and Prejudice* and *Anna Karenina*. Like Jane Austen's and Tolstoy's, it commences a work of fiction. The book is copyrighted by Eleanora Fagan and William Dufty. Mr Dufty was a devoted, long-time friend of the singer. His child became her petted and adored godson. A lot of fiction arises because publishers simply refused to print the bawdy truth as he wrote it out for her. But that is not why the tale of her parentage is intricately fictional. Why in this case Billie – whose given name was certainly Eleanora – chose to be 'Fagan' is not clear. Her illegitimate birth in Philadelphia on 7 April 1915 was registered as that of Eleanora Harris. Her mother Sadie said she was eighteen. The father's name was recorded as 'Frank De Viese'. But Sadie always told Billie that her father was Clarence Holiday, a teenager from Baltimore who served in the US Army from 1917 to 1919. He was a jazz musician, good enough to play for the famous Fletcher Henderson band in the thirties, when Billie caught up with him at last.

According to *Lady Sings the Blues* she knew a grandmother who had been a slave and told her about old plantation days. Her Grandpop was half-Irish, named after his own father, Charles *Fagan*. But on Christmas Eve 1926, one Wilbert Rich was accused of the rape of Eleanora *Gough*. Sadie had briefly been married (1921–23) to a man called Philip Gough. Rich was jailed for three months. Billie was sent back, briefly, to the House of the Good Shepherd for Coloured Girls, a Catholic institution where she had suffered nine months of torment. Running errands for a local brothel, she waived payment on condition that she could listen to records of Bessie Smith and Louis Armstrong on the house's victrola gramophone. That was her self-education in jazz music. Having commenced her singing career in Baltimore bordellos, Billie followed Sadie to New York early in 1929. Their landlady ran a whorehouse. Sadie made a living as a prostitute, and Billie also plied the craft of sex-worker – '20 dollar call-girl' – till she was arrested in a general raid on the establishment and spent four months in hospital and workhouse. Thereafter, she began to sing in clubs for pennies thrown on the floor. She changed her name to 'Billie' after her favourite film star, Billie Dove, and settled on her father's surname. Lady had taste, in fact. She hung around, and jammed with, the band led by the great Benny Carter, one of the aristocrats of jazz. An English musician, Spike Hughes, spotted the very young Billie singing in a Harlem club – 'a tall, self-assured girl with rich golden-brown skin . . . black swept-up hair and a pair of paste earrings . . . I found her quite irresistible' (Ingham, 5). The trademark white gardenia in her hair came later.

Enter John Hammond, rich Yale dropout. He turned up in Coven's club in Harlem one night early in 1933 expecting to hear Monette Moore, a favourite singer. Billie had replaced her. Lady's fame began when Hammond at once wrote about her in his regular column for the UK journal *Melody Maker*. He brought a young white clarinettist, Benny Goodman, to hear Billie. Goodman's sudden advent as the most charismatic bandleader of the swing era was still a year ahead, but it was nevertheless notable that he dated her, and joined her in her first recording session for Hammond in November 1933.

Better recordings for Hammond soon followed, thus: the repeal of Prohibition at the end of 1933 created a booming market for records to be played on jukeboxes in now-legal bars for poor black people. Like the fiction of Charles Dickens, the great Teddy Wilson small-group tracks originated at the bottom of the market to fill a perceived niche in popular culture. Wilson was a young pianist (born 1912) from a background diametrically different from Billie's. His father had been head teacher of English Literature and Language at the famous Tuskegee College for black students in the Deep South. He was trained not just in practice but in the theory of music. A charmer who, as one record sleeve puts it, was attractive to both sexes, Wilson became a John Hammond protégé. Hammond, as producer for the Brunswick label, employed him to organise a recording session for the jukebox market every month. From July 1935 till early 1939, Billie took part in these sessions.

As and when the notable bands they worked for were back in New York, Wilson hired, to play, in various combinations, the finest soloists of the day, including the incomparable **Lester Young** (q.v.). 'I succeeded', Wilson would say, 'in getting them on the recordings at rates which, to put it mildly, were only a pittance compared with what they were earning outside . . . Nobody really cared about the money they were getting, they were only interested in the excitement of playing with seven men who were all as good as they were' (Wilson 23–24).

On 1 June 1937, for instance, Wilson brought together the great

Basie rhythm section – guitarist Freddy Green, Walter Page on bass, Jo Jones on drums – with Buck Clayton on trumpet, Young's tenor sax and Buster Bailey, virtuoso clarinettist with John Kirby's polished little band. They recorded 'Foolin' Myself', 'Easy Living' and 'I'll Never Be the Same'. At Wilson's sessions, the musicians turned up not knowing the items to be played. Wilson had prepared mininimal 'orchestrations', establishing a running order for them but leaving space, within the bare three minutes available for each song, for passages of improvisation. Billie could not read music, and Wilson would normally rehearse her several times between sessions – 'just the two of us at the piano' (Wilson, 25). Billie does not dominate proceedings as Ella Fitzgerald would do in her hit recordings. Hers is one jazz voice among several, her smoky, wry tones contrasting with the elegance of Clayton and Bailey, and the lyricism of Young.

Alarmed by rats in his hotel bedroom, Lester came to board for a while with Billie and her mother. Young dubbed Sadie 'The Duchess' and augmented Billie's nickname to 'Lady Day'. Billie's riposte derived from her sincere, and sound, conviction that Young was the most astonishing saxophonist of that moment. 'The greatest man around then was Franklin D. Roosevelt, and he was the President. So I started calling him the President.' Young accepted this to the point where he started addressing all his male acquaintances as 'Pres', and Billie's nickname defined him for the rest of his life, and for posterity. They became as close as brother and sister.

What was probably the happiest part of Billie's life, paradoxically, followed the sudden and traumatic death of her father Clarence, struck down with pneumonia while touring in the South, and denied, by the Colour Bar, timely admittance to hospital. John Hammond had stepped in to reorganise her life. He had his eye very much on the promising Count Basie Band and reckoned it needed a female vocalist to complement the great blues singer Jimmie Rushing. So Billie toured for eleven months with Basie. Despite all the discomforts of travelling, Billie had fun, hanging out with Pres and Buck Clayton – 'the Unholy Three' – and bedding down with the guitarist, Freddy Green. Basie tried to mitigate the sufferings of his team by finding self-catering accommodation, where Billie took charge as an excellent cook. The amiable and superb trumpeter Harry Edison, whom Pres nicknamed 'Sweets', said the tour was 'most beautiful . . . because everybody loved Lester and everybody loved Billie' (Ingham, 11).

Then Goodman's main white rival, Artie Shaw, was brave enough to hire her. As black singer with a white band, Billie encountered the worst of Jim Crow. In the South, there were towns where no toilet was open to her and she couldn't stay on stage when she wasn't singing. The crunch came at a hotel in New York, named, ironically, after Lincoln. Playing there was important for Shaw and his band, because their music would be relayed over radio coast to coast. So Shaw couldn't protest when Billie was forced to use the back entrance and the freight elevator and was forbidden to use any of the hotel's public spaces. She quit.

Hammond introduced Billie to Café Society. This was a brave venture in New York run by an idealist named Barney Josephson in deliberate contrast to the rest of the city's night life, as 'the Right Place for the Wrong People'. The doormen had all fought for the Abraham Lincoln Brigade against Franco in Spain. Black people were warmly welcomed. Located in a former basement speakeasy in Greenwich Village, the original Café Society generated another in midtown Manhattan. To these places flocked labour leaders, leftists, intellectuals, Nelson Rockefeller, Charlie Chaplin, Errol Flynn, and the black cultural leaders Langston Hughes and Paul Robeson.

When Billie was singing in the Village venue, a white schoolteacher called Abel Meeropol turned up to show Josephson a song which he had written under the pen-name 'Lewis Allan'. It had already been performed here and there in left-wing circles. Now he wanted Billie to sing it. At first she was suspicious. The lyric was a poem – technically, a good one – remote from jazz and popular song. It was about a lynching in the Deep South. At first, Billie didn't understand it. But she tried it out at a party in Harlem. Everyone fell silent. The pianist just got up and walked away – there could be no more music after that.

'Strange Fruit' became for Billie both an imposition to be endured and a weapon to be wielded. She claimed that the song had been written specially for her. She resented other singers taking it up. Josephson turned her nightly performance into an agitprop event. 'Before she began, all service stopped. Waiters, cashiers, busboys were all immobilised. The room went completely dark, save for a pin spot of Holiday's face. When she was finished and the lights went out, she was to walk off the stage, and no matter how thunderous the ovation, she was never to return for a bow' (Margolick, 52).

There are many impressive testimonies to the shock which listeners experienced from 'Strange Fruit'. Though lynchings of black people by the 1930s were far less common than they had been in the decades immediately after the Civil War, there were recent, well-publicised instances. In 1934 Claude Neal, lynched in a Florida swamp, had been made to eat his penis and testicles. His body had been dragged to a certain home where thousands of people from all over the South watched further mutilation, till what remained of him had been hung from a tree in the town's courthouse square. In the following year, an anti-lynching bill had been passed by the House of Representatives, but blocked in the Senate. 'Strange Fruit' connected with profound fears and profound feelings of guilt. Columbia Records, to whom Billie was contracted, wouldn't touch it. She took it to a small left-wing company, Commodore, run by Milt Gabler. The record was a success. *Time* magazine reported on it, and published a photo of Billie which, Josephson claimed, was the first ever of a black person in its pages (Margolick, 76–77). Jazz purists, including John Hammond, objected that 'Strange Fruit' was not jazz. Similar objections could be made to later additions to Billie's repertoire – the 'Hungarian suicide tune' called 'Gloomy Sunday', and the complexly mournful 'God Bless the Child', which Billie claimed to have written herself after a quarrel with her mother about money. 'Strange Fruit' was, till her death, very much a trademark song for Billie, still too controversial to be commonly broadcast, still capable of freezing audiences to silence.

The plump good-time girl had become something more; a prophetess, a precursor of the Civil Rights and Black Power movements which would force Jim Crow into the shadows. Billie often referred to herself as a 'race woman'. Interviewed by *Tan* magazine in 1953, she spoke freely of her sordid upbringing and claimed that 'the corner hoodlum, the street walker, the laborer, the numbers runner, the rooming house ladies and landlords, the people who existed off the twenty-five- and thirty-dollars-a-week salaries they were paying in those days . . . were the ones who wanted to see me "go", to get somewhere. It was their applause and help that kept me inspired' (Davis, 162–63). Many of those who knew her well didn't see her at all as a victim. She was a remarkably tough woman who could use her own fists to remarkable effect when, for instance, she was subjected to racist insult.

But by the mid fifties, with a TV programme *Comeback* in which she talked about her addictions and her spell in prison (1953) and the publication of her autobiography (1956), Billie herself was capitalising on her image as victim and 'survivor'. The triumphs of her later career – the 'comeback' concert at Carnegie Hall after her release from jail in 1947, which broke box-office records and had to be repeated, the reunion with Lester Young (who had fallen out with her over her heroin habit) at the first Newport Jazz Festival in 1954, singing with the Jack Parnell band to 6,000 people in London's Royal Albert Hall in the same year – related to a hold on her admirers based on her capacity to struggle through misery, her manifestation of human vulnerability, in contrast with the ageless, always assured, transcendently on-top, Ella Fitzgerald.

Billie and Pres last performed together in a telecast, *Sound of Jazz*, in December 1957. Lester was now desperately ill. Early in 1959 he was holed up in the Alvin Hotel in New York, just opposite Birdland, the jazz venue named after another self-destructive maestro, a disciple of his, the already-dead Charlie Parker. He didn't eat at all. He drank a lot. He had a heart attack. He died on 15 March. Billie followed four months later.

John Chilton, Billie's Blues, *1975; Donald Clarke*, Wishing on the Moon: The Life and Times of Billie Holiday, *1994; Angela Y. Davis*, Blues Legends and Black Feminism, *(New York) 1998; Billie Holiday, with William Dufty*, Lady Sings the Blues, *1958 edn; Chris Ingham*, Billie Holiday, *2000; David Margolick*, Strange Fruit, *2001; Stuart Nicholson*, Billie Holiday, *1995; Lewis Porter*, Lester Young, *1985; Rex Stewart*, Jazz Masters of the Thirties, *(New York) 1972; Teddy Wilson, with Arie Ligthart and Humphrey van Loo*, Teddy Wilson Talks Jazz, *1996; thanks to John Pilgrim*

Anne Hutchinson (England/New England) 1591–1643

Anne was the daughter of Francis Marbury of Alford, Lincolnshire. He was an Anglican parson who had been silenced and imprisoned for long periods by his bishop for his criticisms of the church. In 1612, she married William Hutchinson, a successful merchant. They had no fewer than fifteen children. Only two died in childhood – a remarkable record for the time.

Arminius is not much mentioned these days, but this good-natured Dutchman (1560–1609) earned the kind of demonisation suffered by Tom Paine and Leon Trotsky. The most convincing theologian of the Protestant Reformation had been Jean Calvin. His all-knowing, all-powerful God, must logically have decided in an instant of eternity (so to speak) which human creatures would be saved to enjoy Heaven, and which would suffer for ever and ever in Hell. So there was damn all that anyone could do in this life to change her or his immortal destination. Arminius argued against this. God was unceasingly loving, and by human free will his proffer of salvation might or might not be accepted. The movement of Remonstrant Arminianism which developed in Holland after his death eventually won tolerance in Calvinist Holland. In England, Calvinist Puritans, without real foundation, perceived the influence of Arminius behind changes in the church instituted by Charles I's Archbishop of Canterbury, William Laud. These included enhancing the power of Bishops and introducing liturgical changes which smacked, to Calvinists, of Catholicism.

Also to the point was Charles's struggle with parliament over the reluctance of the English gentry to be taxed. In the 1630s he seemed to be winning. So the great Puritan emigration to 'New England' was spurred by a combination of doctrinal recalcitrance and political and economic unease. A pastor admired by the Hutchinsons, Rev. John Cotton, fled to Massachusetts in 1633 to avoid arrest. They followed him. In the village-port named after Boston in her own English county, with the wild seas before it and dense forests behind, Anne's powerful personality was at first most welcome. Congregations who turned up in the colony hoping to stick together under their minister from England had trouble fitting into the existing Massachusetts church structure. Cotton encouraged Anne to hold weekly prayer meetings in her home. When Rev. John Wheelwright, a parson from Lincolnshire married to her husband's sister, turned up in mid-1636, he was not allowed to form his own church. A pattern seems to have emerged where Wheelwright preached in the Hutchinsons' house, and

Anne conducted meetings for women excluded from public lectures and weekday sermons. Up to eighty people might gather at once in her house, including prominent merchants and the newly elected Governor, young Sir Henry Vane, who sympathised with their difficulties in a godly colony where a trader could receive a very heavy fine for taking what were considered to be undue profits.

Women also flocked to hear Anne. While Puritan women worked alongside their husbands in farm and counting house, and enjoyed under Massachusetts law degrees of security and independence not accorded them in England, male colonists cherished as biblical the father's right to teach and chasten servants, women and children alike. Anne's assertion that 'I live but not I but Jesus Christ lives in me' was a counter-expression of complete spiritual equality.

The hot theological controversy in Boston was over the issue which had engaged Arminius. Could humans co-operate with divine Grace to their own spiritual benefit? Did good works demonstrate that they were saved? Or were they totally reliant on God's Grace? Cotton took the latter view, and Anne followed him. Now, various awkward, or perhaps agreeable, thoughts might arise from attributing total responsibility to God. If He had already decided that one would be Saved, no naughty action of one's own whatsoever could affect one's immutable election. A Saved merchant, for instance, might trade in slaves or charge exorbitant interest on loans without altering his condition of eternal sainthood. This kind of thinking was called Antinomian. Cotton, Wheelwright and Anne Hutchinson were not conscious Antinomians. However, the notion that good works – which might be performed by hypocrites – did not prove grace and salvation, only the conviction of the person saved by grace, was certainly conducive to the heresy. 'At the moment of conversion, the saint, like an empty vessel, is cleansed and filled with Christ's love, and by the motion of the divine, the chosen are freed of accountability under the law and assured of election' (Lang, 6–7). Smearing Anne with Antinomianism was not implausible. Furthermore, as a woman, she was not expected to pronounce on such matters at all . . .

The Puritans of Massachusetts, eschewing bishops, were grouped in independent Congregationalist churches. But the ministers of these meeting together had complete authority, if magistrates agreed with them. Both sorts were scunnered by the spectacle of a woman, Anne, giving men ideas. One of the orthodox wrote sarcastically, 'The weaker Sex prevailed so farre, that they set up a Priest of their own Profession and Sex, who was much thronged after . . . Come along with me, sayes one of them, i'le bring you to a Woman that Preaches better Gospell than any of your black-coates that have been at the Ninneversity . . . I had rather hear such a one that speakes from the meere motion of the spirit, without any study at all, then any of your learned Scollers' (Johnson, 127). But as trouble blew up, Wheelwright was initially the more contentious figure. A majority of the Boston First Church wanted him as their pastor. The incumbent Rev. John Wilson resisted this 'Antinomian' interloper. In January 1637 he was allowed to preach in the church, but what he said provoked charges of sedition, as did a petition from church members in his support. The battle lines were drawn. Wilson was in cahoots with John Winthrop, who had lost the Governorship to Vane and wanted it back. Their allies were ministers in villages outside Boston.

Vane was manoeuvred out, Winthrop was back in. The colony's ruling General Court refused four times to censure Wheelwright, so Winthrop dissolved it and engineered a more tractable one. The first-ever Synod of the Congregational Church was called in 1637 to deal with the 'Antinomians'. The Synod decided that dissenters must be got rid of. Wheelwright was banished by the General Court. At Anne's formal civic trial before it in January 1638 the chief charges against her were her 'keeping two public lectures every week in her house' and her reproaching all ministers save Cotton for 'not preaching a covenant of free grace, and that they had not the seal of the spirit, nor were able ministers of the New Testament'. For such subversive anti-patriarchalism, Winthrop's judgment was that she should 'be banished out of our liberties and imprisoned until she be sent away' (Winthrop, 132–33). She was put under house arrest in Roxbury.

Boston was seriously split. Winthrop thought the opposition to his regime so dangerous that he ordered the guns of its members to be confiscated. Anne was ill. She was suffering a 'phantom pregnancy', thought now to be a neoplastic growth. Despite her weak state, she was hauled before the Boston First Church for two further grillings. Frail and confused, she still admitted to no heresy. But she was excommunicated anyway. Her staunch friend Mary Dyer (*d.*1660) walked out of church beside her. Mary, wife of a successful milliner from London, struck Winthrop as a 'very proper and fair woman', but he added that she was 'of a very proud spirit and much addicted to revelations' (Winthrop, 140). We shall see how he tried to cut her down to size.

While Anne was still detained in Roxbury her followers, knowing that expulsion was inevitable, headed towards Narragansett Bay in 'Indian' country.

Amongst them, William Coddington (1608–78), also from Lincolnshire, richest merchant in Boston, Mass., had sacrificed his imposing brick house there, but could at least trade on successfully without Puritan magistrates questioning his profits. He had bought Aquidneck, which was eventually renamed Rhode Island, and Anne now settled in his town 'Portsmouth'. Massachusetts meanwhile claimed sovereignty over the Narragansett Bay area, and its rulers continued to harass Anne. When her young son Francis went to Boston formally to request permission to leave the church there and join his own, he and his brother-in-law, the Rev. Collins, were arrested without charge, jailed for months, fined enormously and released under penalty of death if they came back. After her husband died in 1642, Anne up-sticksed with her remaining family to settle on territory claimed by the Dutch on Long Island, in what is now the Bronx district of New York City. The following year, local Indians massacred the Hutchinsons, all save one young daughter, taken as hostage, who, when she reappeared among whites after three years, had lost the use of the English language.

A rather detailed account of the massacre was written up by a staunchly orthodox Massachusetts man, Captain Edward Johnson, in 1650 or 1651 (Johnson, 186–87). Since Winthrop's earlier account in his journal mentions no surviving witnesses some scholars now believe that Johnson could only have got his details from a white man actually present, with the Indians. The Massachusetts authorities, anxious to discourage other English settlers from following the Hutchinsons' example, are thought to have set up, or at least connived in, their destruction. Occam's Razor disposes of this, I think, with two cuts. First, Anne's death was one of many in a general, fierce uprising of local Native Americans deprived of their land, against white settlers, provoked by the actions of one Kieft, and causing the terrified Dutch leaders to retreat into their fort on Manhattan Island. Second, while it is easy enough to imagine English settlers intriguing with Indians against their Dutch rivals in trade, Winthrop was very clearly no unprincipled, worldly Macchiavel. On the contrary, he combined his Calvinism with old-fashioned godly superstition, as he showed in the matter of the Monstrous Births.

He kept his now-famous journal primarily to record the operations of God's Providence in Massachusetts, noticing in particular 'judgements' on evil doers who died after trespassing against the general welfare. In it he recorded that Anne Hutchinson's friend Mary Dyer had been delivered of a stillborn child in October 1637. A woman present spread the rumour that the child was a monster. Winthrop recorded her claims in disgusting detail. The child had no head, ears on its shoulders, hard and sharp horns over its eyes, two mouths, scales on its back, claws like a chicken instead of toes. Next April he had Mary's alleged monster dug up, 'and though it were much corrupted yet most of these things were to be seen, as the horns and claws, the scales, etc.' Winthrop believed a story that the bed had shaken beneath Mary when the creature inside her died and that there was a smell so noisome that those present were 'taken with extreme vomiting and purging'. These were signs that the Devil was in her. Delighted by this evidence that God had turned against the Antinomians, Winthrop sent details to Governor Bradford in New Plymouth (q.v. **Tisquantum**), Roger Williams in Providence, and friends in England (with a drawing of the monster, now lost) (Winthrop, 140–42).

Equally 'providential' was a second monstrous birth next year, to Anne Hutchinson herself. Her phantom pregnancy resolved itself in a sorry mess, which her doctor – a follower of hers who presumably saw nothing discreditable in her sickness – did not scruple to describe to Winthrop on request. He had, in a scientific spirit, made dissections amid a mass of nearly thirty lumps tangled in 'strings'. Inside most of the lumps there were 'globes', and inside these 'partly wind and partly water' (Winthrop, 146–47).

Mary Dyer, who had a son with the wonderful Old Testament name of Mahershalalhashbaz, found in Book 8 of Isaiah, settled in Rhode Island (Winthrop, 139–40). In 1652 she went with her husband on an embassy to Cromwell's Parliament in London. He returned within months, she stayed on, and was converted to Quakerism. This was then a way-out, ultra-radical creed, inimical to State and Church alike, taking Anne's belief in 'inner light' to an extreme. Thomas Hutchinson, Anne's great-great-grandson, who would suffer for his own beliefs – his loyalty to the British Crown as assistant governor of Massachusetts in the days of the American Revolution – believed that Anne, who he thought had been a danger to morality and 'immoderately vain', would have joined the Quakers had she lived ten years longer, and acted as a restraint on their excesses (Bailyn, 22). But in its early days Quakerism was intrinsically excessive, because its adherents were extremely brave.

When Mary returned to New England in 1657, she was immediately jailed in Boston, till her husband paid a heavy bond to get her out. Massachusetts made Quakerism a capital crime. Nevertheless, she felt compelled to return to Boston to visit persecuted Quakers in prison. She was jailed herself, under foul conditions, then banished for ever on pain of death. Again, she returned to see fellow-Friends, and was spared execution only on the intercession of John Winthrop Jr, Governor of Connecticut, a much more tolerant man than his father. There was public revulsion when two of her co-thinkers were hanged, but no one could save Mary when she reappeared a third time to 'bear witness' against the capital law. She was summarily convicted and hanged within hours. But a fourth Quaker executed in 1661 was the last so to suffer. In England, Quakerism was moving quite rapidly towards respectability, assisted by the success of Friends in trade. William Coddington converted to Quakerism in the 1660s, and this did not prevent him serving as Governor of Rhode Island in 1675.

American National Biography, *vols 5, 7, 11, 23 – 'Coddington', 'Dyer', 'Hutchinson' and 'Williams', (New York) 1999; Bernard Bailyn,* The Ordeal of Thomas Hutchinson, *1974; Angus Calder,* Revolutionary Empire: The Rise of the English-Speaking Empires from the Fifteenth Century to the 1780s, *1981; David D. Hall,* Worlds of Wonder, Days of Judgement: Popular Religious Belief in Early New England, *(Cambridge, MA) 1990; [Edward Johnson],* Johnson's Wonder-Working Providence, 1628–1651, *ed. J. Franklin Jamieson, (New York) 1959 edn; Amy S. Lang,* Prophetic Women: Anne Hutchinson and the Problem of Dissent in the Literature of New England, *(Berkeley) 1989 edn; M. J. Lewis, 'Anne Hutchinson', in G. J. Barker-Benfield and Catherine Clinton, ed.* Portraits of American Women: From Settlement to the Present, *(New York) 1991; John Winthrop,* The Journal of John Winthrop 1630–1649, *ed. Richard S. Dunn and Laetitia Yeandle, (Cambridge, MA) 1996*

Hypatia (Alexandria) *d*.415

Edward Gibbon, scourge of the hypocrisy, superstition and bigotry of early Christians in his incomparable *Decline and Fall of the Roman Empire* (1776–88), evinced especial dislike of Cyril, the patriarch of Alexandria in the early fifth century CE, under the Byzantine Emperor. Originally living as a learned hermit, he succumbed to worldly ambition and assumed leadership of the Christians of the great city of Alexandria. As archbishop-patriarch, Cyril, who controlled a dangerous mob, effectually ruled the city:

> His voice inflamed or appeased the passions of the multitude; his commands were blindly obeyed by his numerous and fanatic *parabolani* [members of a privileged and corrupted charitable corporation] and the praefects of Egypt were awed or provoked by the temporal power of these Christian pontiffs.
>
> (Gibbon, 15–17)

Cyril opened his reign by oppressing the harmless Novatian set and without any civil authority, says Gibbon, led an attack on Alexandria's Jewish quarter, plundering their wealth and expelling the survivors. Gibbon was not sure whether Cyril prompted, or merely accepted, the murder of Hypatia. This woman, a virgin, was the daughter of a noted mathematician named Theon, and had followed in his footsteps, writing mathematical and astronomical commentaries. She was also a philosopher, of the Neoplatonist school derived from the third-century Greek thinker Plotinus, whose idealism has echoed on through European thought and affected many Christian thinkers. The Alexandrian Neoplatonists were more scholarly and less dogmatic than their Athenian contemporaries, and Hypatia, who had a chair of philosophy at Alexandria's academy, lectured on Aristotle as well as on Plato. Her most brilliant pupil was Synesius of Cyrene, who became a bishop. This brilliant pagan was certainly not unfriendly to Christians. But Cyril might well have resented the influence, which spread throughout Egypt, of a woman whose gender Pauline Christianity deemed inferior.

Let Gibbon continue . . . 'In the bloom of beauty, and in the maturity of wisdom, the modest maid refused her lovers and instructed her disciples; the persons most illustrious for their rank or merit were impatient to visit the female philosopher; and Cyril beheld with a jealous eye the gorgeous train of horses and slaves who crowded the door of her academy.' Politics provided pretext. 'A rumour was spread among Christians that the daughter of Theon was the only obstacle to reconciliation of the praefect and the archbishop, and that obstacle was speedily removed. On a fatal day, in the holy season of Lent, Hypatia was torn from her chariot, stripped naked, dragged to the church, and inhumanly butchered by the hands of Peter the reader and a troop of savage and merciless fanatics: her flesh was scraped from her bones with sharp oyster-shells, and her quivering limbs were delivered to the flames. The just progress of inquiry and punishment was stopped by seasonable gifts' – that is, Cyril and his creatures bribed the civil authorities – 'but the murder of Hypatia has imprinted an indelible stain on the character and religion of Cyril of Alexandria' (Gibbon, 17–18).

This stain did not inhibit Pope Leo XIII from canonising Cyril as a saint in 1882.

Edward Gibbon, The Decline and Fall of the Roman Empire, *vol. V, 1994 edn; Barbara G. Walker*, The Woman's Encyclopaedia of Myths and Secrets, *(San Francisco) 1983*.

Herbert Ironmonger (Australia) (1882–1971)

Nowadays, top-class cricketers have to be athletes. The one-day international game exacts the highest fielding standards from players. Even in five-day Test Matches, there is now a premium on grudging runs.

It was not ever thus. Leaving aside James Southerton, who played successfully in the very first Test Match between England and Australia in 1877 at the age of forty-nine, Miran Bux was the oldest international debutant, for Pakistan versus India at Lahore in 1955 aged forty-seven years and 284 days. He played two Tests, his offspin claimed two wickets.

Bert Ironmonger was a more remarkable case. When he was picked to play for Australia against England at Brisbane in 1928–9, he numbered forty-six years and 237 days. When he played his last Test for Australia, against England again, at Sydney in 1932–33, he was fifty plus 327 days, and junior at international level only to the incredible Wilfred Rhodes of England, who was nearly a year older when he played against the West Indies in Jamaica in 1929–30. In between debut and exit Ironmonger had returned astonishing figures with his lively-paced left-arm spin bowling – seventy-four wickets in fourteen

Tests at an average of just under eighteen, making him one of the most destructive international bowlers of all time. He took eleven wickets for twenty-four runs (in twenty-three overs) against South Africa at Melbourne, his home ground, in 1931–32, and twenty-two wickets for under fifteen runs apiece against the 1930–31 West Indians.

It is hard to reconstruct the mindsets of those involved in selecting teams in the hot summer of 1928–29, when the England side led by Percy Chapman vanquished Australia on Oz soil. Jack Hobbs (*b.*1882, same year as Bert) was one of England's star batsmen. Phil Mead (*b.*1887) and Ernest Tyldesley (*b.*1889) also appeared, as did high-scoring Patsy Hendren (*b.*1889), and a farmer from Somerset, Jack White (*b.*1891) was bowling slow left arm for England on his first overseas tour. Superfine fielders though Hobbs and Hendren had certainly been when younger, it is hard to imagine their feet at this later time flying across the turf as the long afternoons neared their close. As for Australia, which would these days dismiss from consideration any player not excellent in the field, having set a new benchmark of senility by picking Ironmonger, they surpassed it when they selected Don Blackie to play his first Test a fortnight later. Blackie, the offspinner who partnered Bert for Victoria and the St Kilda club in Melbourne, was actually sixteen days his senior, and remains the oldest Australian debutant to this day.

Bert was simply too good a bowler to be considered a freak, but he was certainly unique. In youth he lost the top joint of his left index finger operating a chaff-cutter on his family's farm in Queensland. He thus became one of the notable spin bowlers (Muralitharan of Sri Lanka springs to mind) who have made a physical defect or peculiarity into a source of mystifying virtuosity. Even so, his debut for his State, Queensland, came relatively late, in 1909–10. He was persuaded to move to Victoria in 1913–14 to become a ground bowler in the nets for Melbourne Cricket Club. He played at once with great success for his new state, but then, of course, the Great War stopped first-class cricket. After touring New Zealand with an Australian side in 1920–21, he tried to run a pub in Sydney, but his hopes of modest prosperity in that line were baulked by postwar economic recession. He retreated to Melbourne, where he worked as a gardener for the local council, and took trams to Melbourne Cricket Ground when summoned there by state or country.

Bert was not a fixture in the Victoria side until 1927–28. But his overall first-class record would be outstanding. In ninety-six matches, he took 464 wickets for 21.50 apiece. Though his trajectory was flat enough to deter batsmen from jumping out of the crease to attack him, by spinning the ball off the stump of his index finger he achieved vicious turn even on the flattest and smoothest of wickets. When hot Antipodean sun hit a wicket which had been affected by rain, he was, as they say, 'unplayable'. Don Bradman – whose record as a batsman is simply half as good again, statistically, as that of any cricketer ever – admired Ironmonger's bowling vastly.

Bert, with broad Ocker irony, was nicknamed 'Dainty'. He was a big man, not highly mobile. English cricket historians have variously described him as 'a batsman so negligible that he might as well have taken a table leg to the crease and sat on it' (Illingworth and Gregory, 56) and 'the worst batsman in the history of Test (or any) cricket' (Batchelor, 176). A well-loved story has a friend, or perhaps his wife, phoning him at Melbourne Cricket Ground. Told that Bert has just gone out to bat, this person replies, 'Oh that's all right, I'll just hold on.' In thirty-five of his 127 first-class innings, he scored no runs. His Test batting average was 2.50, highest score twelve. The Australian crowds found his ineptitude endearing, and were furious when Chapman put on his fastest bowler, Larwood, to hurl thunderbolts at Ironmonger at Sydney and Melbourne in 1928–29.

Yet from the notorious 'Bodyline Series' of 1932–33 come stories suggesting that Bert quietly got his own back. The mean Scotsman Douglas Jardine, who captained England, had instructed Larwood and his other pace bowlers to pitch the ball short on or outside the leg stump, and mounted a phalanx of close fielders on the leg side. This meant that batsmen had to take evasive action and were sometimes hit. Similar tactics had been used before, and would often be used again, but in this particular case they jeopardised friendly relations between the United Kingdom and the Commonwealth of Australia. The aim – to stifle Bradman's astonishing accumulation of runs – was only partially fulfilled. In the second Test, at Melbourne, Bill Bowes got him out for 0 in the first innings, but in the second Bradman scored 103 not out in an overall total of only 191. When Ironmonger, last man in, appeared in the middle, 'the Don' was still in his nineties. But Ironmonger, memorably, said, 'Don't worry, son, I won't let you down,' stayed there long enough for Don to get his century, then ran himself out for a duck trying to present him with the strike (Bradman, *Farewell to Cricket*, 62). 'Though the England fast bowlers twice bowled Australia out for small scores . . . Ironmonger and O'Reilly bowled England out for smaller ones, Australia winning on the fourth day by 111 runs . . .' (Le Quesne, 21–22).

Bradman, loyal to the helpful Bert, discounted the view that he was the worst batsman ever. '. . . I remember that in one Test match Ironmonger cut Larwood for two successive fours' (Bradman, *My Cricketing Life*, 113). That must have been the eight, his highest score of the series, in the Brisbane Test which England won easily. One imagines the 'strokes' in question – Ironmonger, shifting prudently backwards out of line, waves his bat at two ferociously fast balls and somehow connects. In the fifth Test at Sydney, Larwood played a notable innings, hitting his way rapidly to ninety-eight. Aiming for his century, he skied the ball towards 'Dainty', fielding at mid-on (one position which in days of yore was regarded as suitable for cricketers not lissome). Ironmonger moved smartly to his right and bent to take the catch below his knees. It is recorded that he achieved thirty catches in his ninety-six first-class matches – not a bad rate at all.

Ironmonger's last first-class cricket was played in 1935–36, with a team touring India, where sadly he contracted typhoid and had to drop out. Looking back, he must have cherished in particular one late memory from his egregious career. In a joint Testimonial game for himself and Blackie in his final Australian season, 1933–34, he had taken his last chance to dismiss Bradman.

Denzil Batchelor, The Game of a Lifetime, *1953; Don Bradman*, My Cricketing Life, *1938, and* Farewell to Cricket, *1950; Richard Cashman et al., eds*, The Oxford Companion to Australian Cricket, *(Melbourne) 1996; E. W. Docker*, Bradman and the Bodyline Series, *(Brighton) 1978; Ray Illingworth and Kenneth Gregory*, The Ashes, *1982; Laurence Le Quesne*, The Bodyline Controversy, *1983*

Mirza Sheikh I'tesamuddin (Bengal) *c.*1730–*c.*1800

In 1827 a strange book was published in Leadenhall Street, London: *Shigurf Namah i Vilaet . . . Being the Travels of Mirza Itesa Modeen in Great Britain and France – translated from The Original Persian Manuscript into Hindoostanee, with an English Version and Notes by James Edward Alexander, Esq., Lieut., Late H.M. 13th Light Dragoons and Adjutant of the Body-Guard of the Honourable the Governor of Fort St George.*

In an introduction datelined 'Bangalore, Mysore, 1825', Lieutenant Alexander explained that a copy of the Mirza's manuscript account of his far travels had been purchased by his own 'Moonshee' (*munshi* = secretary) from the head servant of the son of Captain Swinton, the Scot whom the Mirza had accompanied to Europe. His chief object in translating it into the 'common dialect' of Hindi 'used in the Madras Presidency' of the East India Company was to tempt young men, 'tyros', employed by the British Raj, into studying 'that most useful language, the acquirement of which is so indispensably necessary for those who mean to sojourn in our Eastern possessions' (Alexander, vi, x). The vast intrinsic interest of the Mirza's text is presented as a secondary consideration. Alexander presumably thought that it would reinforce, amusingly, the prevailing British view that Indians were backward and superstitious people.

Yet at the time of the Battle of Plassey, fought just sixty years before Alexander's translation was published, British 'possessions' in India had amounted to little more than three trading 'factories' in Bombay, Madras and Calcutta. The East India Company was licensed by the British state to monopolise trade with the subcontinent and points east. When its mercenary army, commanded by Robert Clive, defeated the Nawab of Bengal, Siraj-ud-Dowla, at Plassey in 1757 and installed his uncle Mir Jafar as his successor, the EIC was able to commence the 'rape of Bengal', plundering the territory and its taxpayers freely. The power of the Moghul Emperor in Delhi was in freefall, challenged by native opponents. In 1765 he decided to implore protection of British troops from King George III. Clive, an EIC employee, could not place British troops at the disposal of a foreign ruler, so it was decided that a letter should go to London with Shah Alam II's request, accompanied by a present of 100,000 rupees. Captain Swinton would take it, and Mirza Sheikh I'tesamuddin would go with him to explain the finer points of the Persian language in which it was written.

When the Mirza was born, Bengal, a province of the Moghul Empire, was second in prosperity to nowhere in the world – an immensely fertile country, with fish teeming in its huge rivers, and craftsmen superbly skilled in textile production and all manner of other work. It was governed, like the other Moghul provinces, by descendants of Islamic incomers from the north-east. Along with these had entered the family of the Mirza, anciently established in Persia, which claimed descent from the prophet Mohammed himself, and was greatly distinguished for its scholarship. He was trained as a *munshi*. Such a scribe, skilled in the official language, Persian, was indispensably useful in the fields of administration, diplomacy and law. The Mirza entered the service of the EIC. This was not treachery to his native land, just a pragmatic recognition of job opportunity, as if a British lad nowadays were to get work with a Swiss bank in London. For a short time, anyway, he left the EIC to serve his Emperor, who conferred on him the title of 'Mirza', corresponding to a knighthood.

So he was an obvious, heavyweight choice to go to England with Swinton and the Emperor's letter. Numerous people from the subcontinent must have reached Britain before – as sailors ('lascars'), as servants, as entertainers and as pedlars. But no learned, polished and self-assured Indian gentleman had left a record of his experiences before the Mirza.

After three weeks at sea, the Mirza learnt from Swinton that the infinitely rapacious Clive had held back the letter, saying that the present which went with it hadn't yet arrived, and promising to follow them to England with both letter and money. But when they arrived in England they would find that Clive had suppressed the letter and presented the money on his own behalf – with EIC interests, and his own, in mind, he didn't want direct contact between the Emperor and the British Crown.

But the Mirza spent nearly three years away from home on his aborted mission. Sophisticated though he was, the sea was a complete novelty to him, and each place his ship called at was a fresh surprise. He was fascinated by markets, comparing goods and prices with those he knew at home, and shrewd about local economic conditions and architectural styles. However, he was credulous of tales of 'satanical' cannibals in areas not seen by him, and a section of his memoirs describing sea-creatures includes, alongside flying fish and whale, the mermaid.

Perhaps because of long contact with Britons of the EIC, the Mirza, distinguishing between different kinds of 'hat-wearing Feringhees' – Europeans – had a contemptous view of the French. When, after six months at sea, his ship docked at Nantes, the Mirza was astonished to find the French poor shuffling about in clogs – 'There are poor people in England, too, but they do not suffer for want of leather boots and socks' (Haq, 50–51).

The Mirza, devout though he was, was immensely susceptible to women. In this respect, England proved quite heavenly, since he also had the common subcontinental preference for pale-skinned beauty. At a dance, where his turban, robes and shawl earned 'wide-eyed amazement', the ladies 'continued to stare at my clothes and countenance, while I gazed at their astonishing loveliness . . . I could not distinguish between the brightness of the lamps and the splendour of their appearance.' Common people in the streets flocked to see the Mirza. Children ran into their houses 'crying, "Look! Look! A black man is walking down the street!" – at which their elders would rush to the door and stare at me in amazement' (Haq, 53–54). But it can't have been his colour which surprised people – there were at this time 10,000 or even 20,000 African and Afro-Caribbean people in London (Fryer, 68). It must have been the Mirza's gorgeous clothes. But he was a serious man, not a pantaloon, always ready to debate theology with intelligent Christians, and deeply interested in British political practices and social customs.

He was vastly impressed with London, which was indeed the most advanced city in the world, with its wide paved roads, oil lighting in its streets, and a weekly supply of drinking water piped to every house. He marvelled at the British Museum, where he saw Hindu and Persian scriptures and treatises in Arabic, musical instruments and fruits peculiar to India, stuffed animals and birds, as well as Egyptian mummies. He revelled in stage plays, which might be attended by royalty and noble 'emirs' paying an *ashrafi* (gold sovereign) for the best seats, but which were open to ordinary citizens for just eight annas a head. 'Truly, the Firinghees can accomplish great things at little expense. In India, on the other hand, luxurious young men squander a couple of hundred rupees on an evening's nautch party; and lakhs of rupees of patrimony . . . take wing in a short time' (Haq, 67). But above all he was smitten by a giantess exhibited in Haymarket. 'When I stood before her, I only reached up to her armpit . . . Her face was so beautiful and her figure so desirable, that neither my pen nor my tongue is adequate to sing the praises of her fairness' (Haq, 70).

In Oxford he met the great oriental scholar William Jones who later, as a judge in Calcutta, was the centre of eager research in Indian literature. In an observatory, he strove to match his understanding of the universe in terms of 'seven heavens' to post-Newtonian Western astronomy, but gave up – only scientists could sort out that controversy. Travelling towards Scotland he saw snow for the first time. Ice in severely cold weather, he noted, could bear the weight of an elephant. Skaters entranced him. 'As they glided along in their white robes the Europeans appeared like angels who had descended on earth', whizzing along faster than 'the wind or an arrow or a swift bird' (Haq, 76–77). He met Swinton's family in Edinburgh and learnt that the Captain had trained as a surgeon, but had fled for fear of his life after it was discovered that he had submitted a living man to vivisection in order to study the functioning of veins and arteries, skulking in Malacca and Pegu before he joined the EIC service as a soldier

While Clive had sordidly cheated him, Swinton does seem to have been a somewhat shifty character himself. His idea was to exploit the European market for tuition in oriental languages, using the Mirza's skills as teacher. The Mirza said he'd be happy to travel about, but only if he could take his own cook with him. 'Ablutions must be performed and prayers to Allah offered, which cannot be done by one who isn't a Muslim. Beside, you cook without salt, spices and ghee, so that the offensive odour of raw meat is not dispelled from the meat. How can I swallow such food?' Swinton said that carrying a cook around would be too expensive. So they parted after eighteen months together in Britain and at last, in 1769, the homesick Mirza got back to Bengal, where he became a local celebrity, known as 'Vilayet Munshi', because Vilayet was the Indian word for Britain and Europe.

In his second spell in the employ of the EIC, he was involved in long diplomatic dealings which finally ended the Company's war with the Mahrattas. He wrote his memoirs, he tells us, at the request of friends, but also to distract him from the sad chaos into which the subcontinent had fallen. His erstwhile master the Emperor was now a puppet of the Company, which, with a mixture of willy and nilly, was taking over more and more Indian territory. In his memoirs the Mirza contrasted the hard-working, frugal British with the hedonistic, spendthrift native rulers of India. But staunch in his faith in Islam and his contempt for mere wealth, the Mirza was in no way a Quisling. He observed with all-too-much insight the takeover of his land by the hat-wearing Feringhees who knew so much about deep-sea sailing and piped fresh water.

J. E. Alexander, Shigurf Namah I Vilayet . . ., *1827; Peter Fryer*, Staying Power: The History of Black People in Britain, *1984; Kaiser Haq, ed. and trans.*, The Wonders of Vilayet: Being the Memoir, originally in Persian, of a Visit to France and Britain in 1765, *(Leeds) 2000; thanks to Kaiser Haq*

Mother Jones (USA) 1837–1930

Fred Mooney, who became secretary-treasurer of District 17 of the United Mine Workers of America from 1917 to 1924, closely observed the natural phenomenon called Mother Jones.

The Cabin and Paint Creek area of the West Virginia bituminous coalfield had been non-union since 1904, when gunmen hired by the 'coal barons' had crushed the UMWA. A call for a strike in 1912 prompted the owners to bring in gunmen again, mainly from the notorious Baldwin-Felts agency. The miners saw themselves as heirs of the pioneers who had rampaged their way into West Virginia generations before, slaying Indians, distilling whiskey and creating farms since bought up by coal barons. They acquired ex-army rifles for less than $2 each. Several of the owners' guards were shot. Martial law was declared by Governor Glasscock.

Martial law meant that while people could barely move in the designated area without permission, even to buy groceries, drumhead courts were sending miners to jail for up to twenty years. Outside that area, miners held protest meetings and committees were elected to go see the Governor in the state capital Charleston and ask him to withdraw his proclamation. Mooney and thirty-four others were joined on such a committee by Mother Jones. She travelled light, could walk without flagging for hours. She was '. . . The white haired angel of the miners . . . Her hair was snow white, but she was yet full of fight . . . The miners loved, worshipped, and adored her . . . She called them "her boys," she chastised them for their cowardice, she criticised them for their ignorance. She said to them "Get you some books and go to the shade while you are striking. Sit down and read. Educate yourselves for the coming conflicts"' (Mooney, 15–21).

A report reached the police that not thirty-five but 3,500 miners, led by Mother Jones, were coming to kill Glasscock and dynamite Charleston. As the committee walked from the railway station, Mother Jones was picked off, thrown into a car, and hurried away to be imprisoned in a bull pen at Pratt. After days incommunicado, she got a message out to a Senator she had had useful dealing with, John W. Kern of Illinois. Kern's resolution in the Senate calling for an investigation into conditions on the West Virginia coalfields led to the setting up of a sub-committee of the Committee on Education and Labour. Its report condemned the coal barons for bad wages and dreadful living conditions. Meanwhile, all strikers sentenced under martial law had been released.

Mooney thought that Mother Jones was in her eighties at this time. So she would have been, had her claim to have originated in Cork in 1830 been true. Certainly, she celebrated her 'hundredth birthday' in 1930. But documents suggest that Mary, the daughter of Richard Harris, labourer, was born in that Irish town on 1 August 1837. Her father, in the late 1840s, emigrated to North America. He got a job on railway construction in Toronto, where his family joined him in 1852. By 1860, trained as a teacher, Mary Harris was working as such in a convent school in Monroe, Michigan. She also learnt the trade of seamstress, and was briefly a dressmaker in Chicago. Just before the Civil War, she moved to Memphis, Tennessee, where she married George Jones, a member of the iron moulders' craft union.

In 1867 her husband and four children all perished of yellow fever. She moved back to Chicago, where she opened a small seamstress' shop with a partner, but she lost this in the Chicago fire of 1871. Now in her mid-thirties, she began to eventuate as the stormy petrel of the nascent Labor movement. She joined the secretive, quasi-masonic Knights of Labor in the 1870s. She claimed to have worked in California for the Workingmen's Movement, to have been in Pittsburgh for the great railway strike of 1877 and in Chicago for the Haymarket Riot of 1886, when martyrs perished under police attack. In 1894, working with textile operatives in Alabama, she developed her passionate detestation of child labour. Meanwhile, the Union of Mine Workers of America had been founded in 1890. This would provide the main, though far from sole, stage for Mother Jones's agitations.

The 'craft unions' banded in the American Federation of Labor (AFL), led by the remarkable Samuel Gompers, deployed the leverage of skilled and specialised men. The UMWA, in contrast, was an 'industrial union', on the lines of the so-called 'New Unionism' which had emerged in Britain. It recruited men, skilled and unskilled, of all trades employed on the coalfields. Its constitution banned racial, ethnic and religious discrimination, and gave the rank and file power to elect its leaders. At this time, West Virginia's coal production was small, compared to the output of the 'Central Competitive Field' stretching through Western Pennsylvania, Ohio, Indiana and Illinois. But as competition from West Virginia intensified, the coal owners of the CCF, who recognised the UMWA in 1897, pressurised the union to organise the West Virginia field, where their rivals openly declared their intention to defy the union. The state had weak traditions of law enforcement. Hence the ambience of violence in which Mother Jones at various times displayed her remarkable courage as a UMWA organiser.

Colorado was still wilder country, 'Wild West'. Here Mother Jones was on hand when, in September 1913, District 15 of the UMWA led a strike against the Rockefeller-controlled Colorado Fuel and Iron Company and two other big firms. Conditions here were bad beyond belief. The companies owned all houses, land and water; 7.3 miners out of 1,000 died in accidents in Colorado in 1912, double the average for the USA, which country had the worst mine safety record in the world. Miners, paid by the ton, were cheated by weighing machines which grossly underestimated their production, then charged outrageous prices in company stores. The owners' mineguards were deputised by county sheriffs, mounted surveillance in every town, saloon and camp, sexually harassed miner's women with impunity and screened, and ejected at will, any outsider trying to enter the coalfield. Of 14,000 Colorado coalminers, only some thirty per cent had English as their first language. By deliberate 'divide and rule' policy, the Colorado Fuel and Iron Company used Italian, Greek, Eastern European and Mexican labour.

Mother Jones had been tried before a military court for conspiracy to murder and sentenced to twenty years imprisonment for her part in the West Virginia strike. She was freed after nationwide outcry, and of course headed for Colorado. She was not the first UMWA organiser to penetrate this Inferno-above-and-below-ground, but her arrival on 2 September 1913 meant that the days of clandestine organisation were over. A District Convention was called in the town of Trinidad for 15–16 September. Hundreds flocked into the streets. The 'opera house' was packed and many were turned away. Mother Jones held all spellbound for two hours. She pleaded for arbitration by the Governor of the state, but at her peroration cried, 'If it is strike or submit, why for God's sake, strike – strike until you win!' Wild cheers responded – the *Rocky Mountain News* reported 'veritable pandemonium' (Priscilla Long in Laslett, 350–51).

When the strike began on 23 September it was more than ninety per cent solid. The Union gave strikers food, coal, water and relief pay. It policed the tent villages set up on land which it rented just outside the bounds of company property. Here mining families began to dissolve their ethnic differences in close-knit multicultural communities. But gun battles soon began between miners and guards. On 28 October, Governor Ammons, under pressure from business interests, sent in the Colorado National Guard. Company guards appeared in CNG uniforms, stole and vandalised miners' property as they conducted searches, even committed armed robbery with impunity. Miners retaliated. In January 1914, Mother Jones was deported from the strike region. Governor Ammons declared that he thought three-quarters of the strikers' violence was attributable to her 'incendiary' utterances – though in fact here, as elsewhere, she always counselled non-violent action.

Of course, Mother Jones came right back in. Without charge, the

CNG detained her in a hospital. Then it attacked a big demonstration by women demanding her release. Five congressmen turned up to investigate what was happening. Violence abated, only to resume when they departed. The CNG was now wholly dominated by company guards in state uniform. In an appalling climax on 20 April, its troops fired all day on Ludlow Tent Colony, home for more than 1,000 people – devout US patriots, by the way, who opened all union meetings with singing of the National Anthem. At dusk, the tents were burnt to the ground. Amongst the dead were two women and eleven small children. Mary Petrucci regained consciousness next day in a cellar and found thirteen corpses beside her including those of her own three children. Ten days of armed rebellion by the miners followed until President Woodrow Wilson ordered in the US Army. This brought about the defeat of the strikers, but Mother's testimony before Congress had ensured that 'Ludlow became a byword for the oppression of miners, the greed of operators, and the courage of Mother Jones' (ANB, 230–31).

In such grim coalfield wars, Mother Jones gained many battle honours. But her scope was far wider. She carried the logic of 'industrial union' to its quixotic height when she attended the inaugural meeting in Chicago in 1905 which set up the Industrial Workers of the World (see **Joe Hill**). But her involvement with the IWW was fleeting. Her relationship with her usual employers, the UMWA, was not an easy one. Officials of its locals feared her scalding tongue, and found it hard to live with her highly personal methods, some based on her real or imagined hotlines to men prominent in public life, whom she likewise sometimes overawed. (Visiting Governor Hunt of Arizona when he went West armed with an out-of-date letter of introduction from Mother, Fred Mooney was show by him a large autographed photo of her which hung, behind discreet lace, in the gubernatorial office. 'You know, boy,' said Hunt, 'I think she is unquestionably the greatest woman this nation has ever produced' [Mooney, 132].) She despised professional union organisers who chomped steaks paid for by the dues of 'her boys' who were starving. She execrated the remarkable John Mitchell (1870–1919), President of the UMWA, who built up its membership from 30,000 to 300,000 in ten years, but secured gains for his people at the price of compromise with the coal owners.

US textile manufacturers employed child labour at starveling wages. Mother Jones, in 1903, led a children's crusade of a hundred from Pennsylvania to New York, then a smaller contingent of women with just three children on to interview President Teddy Roosevelt at his summer home at Oyster Bay. On this occasion, she did not get her audience, but she had achieved a lot of publicity. Not long after, the state of Pennsylvania prohibited factory work by children under fourteen. In 1905, she supported striking machinists on the Southern Pacific railroad. In 1907, she helped Mexican revolutionaries with results observed by Fred Mooney, who went there with her in 1921. Their train was waylaid short of Mexico City by cabs carrying about forty strikers from a certain jewellery factory. They blocked it, boarded it and showered 'Madre Yones' with crimson carnations and blue violets 'until only her head and shoulders could be seen'. With much tooting of motor horns, they bore her and Mooney into the city. They were allowed to pay for nothing. President Obregon was grateful to Mother Jones for preventing his extradition when he and others had fled across the US border during the Revolution (Mooney, 79–85). In 1909 she helped organise New York shirtwaist workers. She helped the militant Western Federation of Miners shut down the Arizona copper mines in 1910. She assisted New York City streetcar and garment workers just before World War I and steel workers after it ended. But the coalminers remained 'her boys' and she was buried alongside victims of the Virden (Ill.) Massacre in the Union Miners Cemetery in Mount Olive, Illinois.

American National Biography, *vol. 12, (New York) 1999; Mother Jones,* The Autobiography of Mother Jones, *introd. Fred Thompson, (Chicago) 1977 edn; Fred Mooney,* Struggle in the Coalfields: The Autobiography of Fred Mooney, *ed. J. W. Hess (Morgantown) 1967; John H. M. Laslett, ed.,* The United Mine Workers of America: A Model of Industrial Solidarity?*; (University Park, PA) 1996; Patrick Renshaw,* The Wobblies: The Story of Syndicalism in the United States, *1967; thanks to Beth Junor*

Kali (India)

In a wondrously bad RKO movie of 1939, *Gunga Din*, 'three lusty sergeants' (I quote the video blurb) played by Cary Grant, Douglas Fairbanks Jr and Victor MacLagen, are found serving in the British Army in India. Thanks to the eponymous native water carrier, extrapolated from a great poem by Rudyard Kipling, they thwart a plot by crazed fanatics, gathered in a huge but surprisingly secret temple, to overthrow the Raj in the name of Kali. This impressive subcontinental deity had been a byword for oriental evilness since the word 'thug' entered the English language in the early nineteenth century.

Deriving from the Marathi for 'cheat, swindler' – *thag* – it was applied to a brotherhood of professional robbers and murderers, worshippers of Kali, who typically ingratiated themselves with travellers, then strangled them.

Kali is actually just about as complicated as even a goddess could be. One might say that there are two Kalis, merging yet separable. One is the benign source of all gods and all goodness, mother of everything. The other is a gutsy streetfighting black kid from some despised ethnic minority in the boondocks who claws her way socially upwards to be Big God's chief wife, even the dominant partner, or as the scholar Kinsley puts it (84–85), 'eventually transcends her origins'.

To take Dirty Kali first . . .

In the great Indus Valley civilisation which flourished from around 2500–1500 BCE, goddesses played a prominent part. There are several goddesses, though not Kali, in the *Rig Veda*, the most ancient Vedic texts, but thereafter high-caste male writers made sure that male deities dominated. So the goddesses who got into the Hindu literary tradition in the so-called 'Epic' period (400 BCE to 400 CE) shoved forward despite patriarchal prejudice. Sarasvati began as a river goddess, but she moved on to embody wisdom, learning and cultural refinement, so is now looked up to by school swots. Lakshmi, a more worldly creature, embodied the wonderful vitality of vegetation. She came to represent royal authority, kingly bounty and, more prosaically, good luck and prosperity. You thank her when you win the Lottery. Hitched as consort to Visnu, the heavenly king, she represents the order and fertility arising from his just rule. Siva's consort is (but watch this space) Parvati, originally a mountain goddess. Like a certain schoolgirl in Muriel Spark's monumental *Prime of Miss Jean Brodie*, Parvati is 'famous for sex'. Siva is aloof and ascetic, his godly energy untapped until Parvati seduces him and channels it for the world's benefit. Hence the central feature of most Siva temples is the image of *linga* (phallus) and *yoni* (vulva) conjoined.

This cosy pantheon was threatened, in the early medieval period, by a demon who could only be defeated by a female. So the male deities combined their energies to create Durga. She has many arms, each wielding a weapon. She is very beautiful and rides on a lion. She appears in the world when it is threatened by demons, or in response to the pleas of her devotees.

But while Durga is a male creation, Kali is an entirely female intruder.

Non-Aryan 'tribal' peoples first knew about her. As she sneaks into literary tradition, she is the kind of tribal goddess who is worshipped by hunters, tinkers and thieves. The golden-haired, cruel demoness Nirrti makes way for her as she comes. In the vast epic *Mahabharata*, which dates from five or six centuries BCE, she turns up after the treacherous slaughter of the sleeping Pandava army by the only three Kaurava warriors to survive the great battle of Kuruksetra. She is holding a noose to lead the dead away.

She is black. Her hair is dishevelled. Her teeth are like fangs. Want more? Here is her description from an ancient Sanskrit text:

> She is dark as a great cloud, clad in dark clothes. Her tongue is poised as if to lick. She has fearful teeth, sunken eyes, and is smiling. She wears a necklace of snakes, the half-moon rests on her forehead, she has matted hair, and is engaged in licking a corpse. Her sacred thread is a snake, and she lies on a bed of snakes. She holds a garland of fifty heads. She has a large belly and on her head is Ananta with a thousand heads. On all sides she is surrounded by snakes . . . She has . . . corpses for ear ornaments. (Kinsley, 81)

So that's Kali. She lives in cremation grounds. She is black, tends to be naked, is adorned with bits of human bodies. She gets drunk on the blood of her victims, and lusts for blood sacrifices from humans. Her rampages threaten all stability. When she dances the world shakes as if to shatter.

She is integrated into the Hindu Great Tradition in a scripture of early CE, *Devimahatmya*. The demon brothers Sumbha and Nisumbha have subdued the gods, who call on the Great Goddess for help. As Parvati, she calms the gods, then sallies forth as Durga to battle the demon hosts. The demon heroes Canda and Munda are sent against her. This makes Durga lose her temper. Her face becomes dark as ink. Then, out of her forehead, Kali leaps. She has a garland of human heads, wears a tiger's skin, and waves a staff with a skull handle. She is hellishly gaunt, her sunken eyes are red, her mouth gapes, her tongue lolls, she emits a terrifying roar. She flings demons into her mouth and crunches them between her jaws, then wades on, crushing and decapitating. Laughing and howling wildly, she bears down on Cana and Munda, grasps both by the hair, and takes their heads off with her mighty sword, then carries these away as a gift to Durga.

But the Divine Duo still have problems. When the demon army is nearly done for, Raktabija remains unvanquished. If he is wounded and bleeds, other replica demons are instantly born from his blood.

Durga summons Kali again. Kali merely swoops on the field of battle and opens her colossal mouth. She swallows up the demon clones and drinks up all the blood from Raktabija's wounds, before finally sucking all the blood out of his body. Upon which, he falls down dead. Game, set and match.

(Kali's Thuggee followers told this tale differently. They said that with a horde of creatures whom she had spawned for the purpose, Kali *strangled* all the blood-born demons, so killing them bloodlessly. As you see, this would halt the process of demon-reproduction from blood. Then she told all her minions to go forth and make their livelihood by strangling. Queer, that – Kali is usually supposed to be a glutton for blood.)

In the scriptural account, Kali is wholly subservient to Durga, who summons her up as a kind of pinch-hitter, and Durga herself is only an aspect of the greater Great Goddess. But once she got in, Kali kept going. At quite an early date she was acclaimed in widely separate parts of India, appearing, for instance, in ancient Tamil epics. A growing mythology linked her with Siva. They had tastes in common. Siva also abode in cremation grounds, and also frequented wild places and mountains. Kali turned up dancing with Siva in all sorts of contexts. She revealed her potent sexuality. In tales, she usurped Parvati's place and became Siva's consort. Normally, he remained dominant. But sometimes he couldn't control her. By the sixteenth century CE, Kali was big in the Tantric cults which foregrounded the feminine.

In many Tantric texts, she was the supreme deity, equal to the all-founding God Brahma. With her spouse Siva she made and destroyed the world. The Tantric practitioner, *sadhaka*, sought salvation through bodily and mental rituals intended to bring to unity the polarised world of male and female, sacred and profane. Once the essential worth of the forbidden was acknowledged, it would lose its power to pollute, degrade and bind people. Nothing was more forbidden, so to speak, than Kali, who represented Death itself. So the *sadhaka* would meditate in a cremation ground on every loathsome aspect of Kali, thus achieving salvation. Tantric texts might describe Kali as smiling and bounteous, a symbol not only of death, but of triumph over death.

Kali achieved great glory in Bengal, then the most fertile and wealthy part of India, before Clive and his fellow-Brits despoiled it. Her shrine at Kalighat, a little village in mangrove swampland beside the Ganges, was a centre of pilgrimage when Job Charnock of the East India Company founded a settlement nearby in 1690 which anglicised the name to 'Calcutta'. Whatever else can be said for or against Kali, it is undeniable that one of the hugest and most interesting of all human cities is very specifically her place.

By the eighteenth century, Bengali poets were taking Kali to their hearts. Ramprasad Sen (1718–75) was a writer whose songs appealed to masses and intellectuals alike. In hymns he invoked Kali as she who shows us what life is really like, the 'mistress of a mad world'. For him she was stony-hearted, bestowing wealth capriciously on some not others, yet he also saw her as 'mother', a caring presence. 'Though she beat it, the child clings to its mother, crying "mother".' Ramprasad got across the idea that if you petitioned her openly like a persistent child, Kali might give you comfort and peace.

> Oh Mother! is it a virtue of Thy family that Thou placest thy feet on Thy Husband?
> Thou art nude; Thy Husband is nude; you both roam cremation grounds.
> Oh Mother! we are all ashamed of you . . .
>
> (Kinsley, 115–20)

Kali's most important modern champion, Ramakrishna (1836–86), was born in a peasant family and never learnt any language but Bengali. As priest at a new temple for Kali just north of the city, he insisted on Kali's weird nature. As a scholar summarises Ramakrishna's view: 'The world is created by Kali in play and for her amusement . . . Man, as her plaything, her toy, her puppet, finds fulfilment in joining Kali's play, in clapping his hands in delight, in giving himself up in self-surrender to her mad escapades.' By loving her through thick and thin, as a child loves a mother, man can tether Kali, make her dance. A disciple recorded Ramakrishna's own behaviour in his temple – reeling like a drunkard up to Kali's throne, touching her chin affectionately, singing and joking, laughing and dancing like a child (Kinsley, 120–24).

Kali was to the fore in emergent nationalism. Around 1905, for instance, a Bengali journal called: 'Rise up, rise up, O sons of India, arm yourselves with bombs, despatch the white Asuras [demons] to Yama's abode. [Yama is the lord of death.] Invoke the Mother Kali; nerve your arm with valour . . . The Mother is thirsting after the blood of the Feringhees . . . Satisfy her thirst' (Kinsley, 127). But nationalistic Bengali intellectuals, of whom there were plenty, were not all enamoured of Kali – the great Rabindranath Tagore did not like her at all.

Kali, though second to Durga, is still immense in Bengal. Her images stand in thousands of temples, and thousands more are set up on Kali Puja Day, which in Bengal supplants Diwali, the Hindu Festival of Lights. Then immense images of Kali appear in one of south Calcutta's biggest cremation grounds. Shortly after midnight, huge crowds there shout 'Victory to Kali! Victory to the Mother!' Several black goats are beheaded and offered to Kali, as they are every day in the nearby Kalighat temple.

'But', Kinsley reports, 'alongside many of her images on this day, Ramakrishna and his wife are shown sitting placidly. Kali stands behind them, looking terrible as ever, but her hands are placed gently on their heads. There she stands, lolling tongue, blooded sword and all – but comforting her trusted children. She is tamed' (Kinsley, 124).

In Kerala, South India, males have implicitly tamed Kali in a quite different way. Kerala's Tamil culture has been modified by sea-contacts with China, Greece, Rome and the Mediterranean. Muslims settled from the seventh century CE. Their community was matrilineal. Woman had high status among them, and unlike the Keralan Hindu women who went bare-breasted until the mid-twentieth century, Muslim women wore red cotton blouses.

In Kerala the great Goddess Bhagavati is the supreme Hindu deity, associated not only with the Sanskritic Goddesses of Hindu tradition, but also with village goddesses identified with various diseases. Nevertheless, until Indian Independence in 1947 was followed by the election of a Communist state government in Kerala which redistributed vast properties to bonded labourers, all temples were owned privately by patriarchal upper-caste families, descended from Aryan immigrants after the fourth century CE. In the preceding non-Aryan Sangam culture, the Goddess Kottavai had ridden about on a tiger, drinking the blood of her enemies. In apparent allusion to the very dark colour of the peoples of the mountainous regions between Kerala and Tamil Nadu, her skin was black, or blue. Her devotees accompanied male warriors to battle. Female court bards glorified the bravery of the king.

All versions of legendary history emphasise that an indigenous culture was conquered and that Kali derived from and represented that culture. But in the devotional folk-drama form *mutiyettu*, Kali now wears a red jacket evoking the garb of Muslim women, with brilliant naked red breasts shown outside the blouse.

These have to be artificial breasts since Kali is always enacted by a male. 'As upper-caste art forms . . . developed, low castes, and women of all castes, were denied the right to portray the deity in possession performances' (Caldwell, 25).

Kali's story in folk drama, transmitted orally, involves her killing of Darika. This local Kerala demon is like Raktabija in scripture. Every drop of his blood gives birth to a thousand *asuras*, and he can only be slain by a woman. The Earth Goddess appeals against Darika's cruelty, and Siva accordingly incarnates Kali, who frightens even the God himself. Devotees assume that Kali herself is an *asura* (demon), not a *deva* (divine being). She is made even uglier when Siva's consort Parvati plots with the wife of Darika the demon to kill her with smallpox. Siva creates a brother to cure Kali's smallpox by licking (OK, this does have to refer somehow, boringly, to cunnilingus) but in modesty he stops short of the face, so in *mutiyettu* Kali's facial makeup includes blood-bursting pox-pustules.

Enough of Dirty Kali. Now for Divine Kali.

Suppose that Bhaghavati is simply a manifestation of Kali or rather of Kali Ma, the Dark Mother, whose name is cognate with the Hindu *Kharma* – fate. Consider the view of the Nirvana Tantra that 'Compared to the vast sea of Kali, the existence of Brahma and the other gods is nothing but such little water as is contained in the hollow made by a cow's hoof.' Suppose that Kali is 'the basic archetypal image of the birth-and-death Mother, simultaneously womb and tomb, giver of life and devourer of children, the same image portrayed in a thousand ancient religions'. Consider that one of her names is *Shakti*, meaning 'power', without which humans can do nothing at all. Suppose that her

Om or Sacred Word is the origin of the concept of the *Logos* – 'In the beginning was the word and the word was god' – in the Christian Bible. Imagine that before the Christian Trinity there were the three colours of Kali's Trinity – white for the Virgin, red for the Mother, black for death – but that black was Kali's fundamental colour because it 'meant the formless condition she assumed between creations, when all the elements were dissolved in her primordial substance' (Walker, 488–94).

She is also said to have invented Sanskrit, the root of all Indo-European languages. Observe that Kali's title *Devi* – goddess – is clearly related to the Latin *diva* from which we draw the English word 'divine'. (And note in passing the worship of the great Diva, Maria *Callas*, by countless record-collectors, and that 'Diana', adored as Greek goddess and English princess, is an alternative form of Devi's ancient Minoan title *diwi*.) Grant that Romany Gypsies worshipped Kalika as a disease-causing Goddess whom they called 'Aunt', and that Kalma, the Black Goddess of the Finns, haunter of tombs and eater of the dead, is clearly Kali Ma. Concede that the Celts and Sassenachs who contended for the North-West European Archipelago both worshipped Kali, so that all the folks called Kelly in the world are descended from the kinship-groups which produced her priestesses (*kelles*), and all the Irish and Scottish placenames beginning with 'kil' are likely to refer back to her, while the Saxons knew Mother Earth as *Kale*, who put forth new shoots in their spring month of Sproutkale . . .

Your conceptions of Kali, thus broadened, will form a spectrum extending from Earth's oceans, the source of all life, to blood-loss in birthing and to menstruation gauged by our monthly Calendar (or Kali-endar), and from the mighty wars of Gods and Titans, Pandava and Kurava to diurnal butchery at Kali's Bengali altars, from which her worshippers take away the meat to eat, while she retains the blood. Jungians and New Age god-sippers will have a rare old time with Kali. But can a mere sceptical humanist snatch out of her whelming vastness any useful proposition for purposes of argument except the statement that God is (but of course!) a woman? Theologically, psychologically and devotionally she is a huge holdall containing infinitely more goods than one mind, or (shall we say?) soul could use. A poet, however, can revel with her as

Kali's curvaceous long lecherous tongue woos
Shiva as it hangs loose, while she
tramples Him, stamping her beloved's breast, who
lies passive under her feet, breathing still, as he
watches her wild . . .
crusade-ridden, victorious
bedecked, dripping thick in blood and luxurious . . .

('Kali in Ottava Rima', Sen, 175)

Sarah Caldwell, Oh Terrifying Mother: Sexuality, Violence and Worship of the Goddess Kali, *1998; Mircea Eliade, ed.,* Encyclopaedia of Religion, *vols 2 ('Bengali Religion') and 6, (New York) 1987; David R. Kinsley,* The Sword and the Flute: Kali and Krsna, *(new edn, Berkeley) 2000; Sudeep Sen,* Postmarked India: New & Selected Poems, *(New Delhi) 1997; Barbara G. Walker,* The Woman's Encyclopaedia of Myths and Secrets, *(San Francisco) 1983; thanks to Balraj Khanna*

Howard Kippenberger (New Zealand) 1897–1957

Though Karl Kippenberger, head teacher and Methodist preacher in the town of Ladbrooks, south of Christchurch, was the grandson of a German immigrant of 1862, his wife had the pre-eminently English surname Howard, and this was given as first name to their son, who became New Zealand's favourite war hero.

'Kip' was expelled from Christchurch Boys High School for slack attendance and poor performance. But with the Great War raging, he enlisted in the Army in January 1916, adding eighteen months to his age so that he could serve overseas. He duly joined the New Zealand 'Div' on the Somme in September. During twenty-three days on the front line all his closer friends in the Canterbury Battalion were killed or wounded. Kip himself suffered a severe arm injury through 'friendly fire' and was invalided home and discharged from the Army in April 1917. This did not put him off soldiering.

He now turned law student, qualified as a solicitor, then as a barrister, and ran the branch office of a Christchurch law firm in a small place called Rangiroa. Here he was a pillar of the community, serving as a borough councillor, captaining the cricket team as a wily slow bowler, helping found the golf club, of which he became President.

But his passion was the Territorial Army. He steeped himself in military history. By 1936, he was ranked Lieutenant-Colonel and commanded the first battalion of the Canterbury Regiment. In January 1940, he sailed towards his second war as commander of the 20th Canterbury-Otago Battalion.

The New Zealand Division, the 'Div', was organised on a territorial basis, so that men from the same area served together, enhancing the factor of 'bonding' or 'mateship' so crucial to infantry morale. Maoris were also grouped by tribal areas, in a unit attached to others as need arose. 'The NZ Division was in the best sense a great amateur combination – a gifted civilian body that had learned the craft of war the hard way and excelled in it' (Majdalany, 102).

The Div had its first chance to show its mettle when sent into Greece in the spring of 1941 to resist the incoming Germans. Kippenberger did well, but with Britons and Australians, the Div had to retreat to Crete, where a New Zealand General, Freyberg, commanded the Empire forces during a major military disaster. The Wehrmacht brought off the only unsupported victory by parachutists in military history, on an island where the imperial troops had been left with no aeroplanes to oppose the Luftwaffe, which bombed and strafed them unimpeded. Eventually the Royal Navy evacuated 18,000 men, but 12,000 were left behind as prisoners. Kippenberger received a DSO, however, for his heroic conduct. 'His quick thinking and command abilities prevented a rout of panicking New Zealand troops.' During the appalling Imperial retreat over the White Mountains to the tiny port of Sphakia where the Navy awaited them, 'while suffering from a sprained ankle, Kippenberger kept an iron grip on the 20th Battalion when many other units disintegrated' (Harper, 269–71).

As the Div fought on against Rommel in North Africa, Kippenberger, now a brigadier, was one of twenty men who made a daring escape after capture by the Germans. He earned a bar to his DSO. When the Div proceeded to Italy, he succeeded Freyberg as its commander. He was in charge as it tried, coming close to success, to capture Monte Cassino from the Germans during one of the longest and bloodiest battles of the Second World War. Preparing for the next assault, he stepped on an anti-personnel device. One foot was blown off, the other had to be amputated. This was a terrible blow to the whole Eighth Army, where 'Kip' had become an icon, but especially to the Div . . . 'That night more than one soldier said, "There goes our best man. He is irreplaceable" (Majdalany, 170–71).

After hospitalisation in England, Kippenberger was given artificial feet, the rank of Major-General, and a desk job, overseeing the repatriation of NZ prisoners of war. On his return to his homeland in 1946, an inspired appointment made him editor-in-chief at the War History Branch of the Department of Internal Affairs, leading a team which told the story of New Zealand's war in twenty-three volumes. It was a proud tale. New Zealand with a population of only 1,630,000 people had suffered proportionately the highest casualties of any part of the Empire. The volume on Crete, written by Dan Davin, a gifted novelist and short-story writer, is a big book and could be called a masterpiece. It contains a very detailed account of the action on 25 May 1941 at the village of Galatas which epitomises Kippenberger's special touch as a commander.

He was in charge of an awkward assortment of men, minced in Greece and further disorganised in Crete, including gunners and service corps mobilised as infantry in a Composite Battalion, latterly reinforced by the relatively battleworthy 18th Battalion. On the 25th May, the New Zealanders were flushed out of Galatas by the advancing Germans. On a ridge above the village, Kippenberger rallied men whose morale was teetering, 'shouting', he recalled, '"Stand for New Zealand!" and everything I could think of' (Kippenberger, 65). His line included the Kiwi Concert Party, entertainers sent in to relieve the anticipated boredom of army life. When two British tanks arrived looking for action, they found Kippenberger, a trim, alert man, not tall, pipe in mouth, still exuding courage. He ordered them to reconnoitre and shoot up the village. As reinforcements turned up, Kippenberger ordered a charge in the gathering dusk, led by the two tanks, now returned. His motley crew surged downhill with a yell analysed by one of its leaders, Captain Sandy Thomas, as a composite of all the Maori-style *hakas* – war chants – performed at rugby matches commenced by school and college teams throughout New Zealand. Another officer characterised it as a 'deep-throated wild beast noise'. With both tanks out of action and scores of casualties in fierce close fighting, the Div recaptured Galatas. This little epic provides a crux in military history to compare and contrast with **Pickett**'s charge (q.v.). The recapture of Galatas might seem gratuitous. Next day Kippenberger had to pull his men out and join the general retreat to Sphakia. But his counterattack had ensured that the 4th NZ Brigade could retire during the night without German harassment. And 'after days of frustration, of tiredness, of retreat, of impotence in the face of the fighters and divebombers' it 'demonstrated with terrible exactitude just what New Zealand infantry could do' (Barber and Tonkin-Covell, 96–97). Galatas came to symbolise the fighting spirit and hard-sustained morale of most, if not all, of the Div under strains which cracked up British soldiers. Irrelevant to the general outcome on Crete, Kip's charge had long-term historical significance.

Given a knighthood after the war (as well as membership of the US Legion of Merit), Kip had huge success with a modest but gripping volume of war memoirs, *Infantry Brigadier*, which was translated into seven languages and was still used as a textbook in military tactics in the NZ Army half a century after its publication in 1949. But in the same year, he faced a last battle he couldn't win. A New Zealand 'All Black' rugby team was picked to tour South Africa which, out of deference to their hosts' racist prejudices, omitted star Maori players. Kip denounced this in the press. If Maoris were good enough to fight with the Div, they should damn well represent New Zealand in black jerseys. But the *pakeha* – NZ white – obsession with a sport in which their country had become pre-eminent ensured that the compromised tour went ahead. Remembering the courage of the Maoris on Crete and at Cassino, Kippenberger wrote to a friend, 'I say it with some bitterness, Rugby is king and the dead are only bones' (Harper, 271).

Laurie Barber and John Tonkin-Covell, Freyberg – Churchill's Salamander, *(Auckland) 1989; Angus Calder, 'Mr Wu and the Colonials: The British Empire's Evacuation from Crete', in Paul Addison and Angus Calder, eds.,* Time to Kill: The Soldier's Experience of War in the West 1939–1945, *1997, Dan Davin,* Crete, *(Wellington) 1953; Roy Farran,* Winged Dagger, *1954 edn, orig. pub. 1948; Glyn Harper, in* Dictionary of New Zealand Biography, *vol. 5, (Auckland) 2000; Howard Kippenberger,* Infantry Brigadier, *1949; Fred Majdalany,* Cassino: Portrait of a Battle, *1981 edn, orig. pub. 1957*

Mwana Kupona (Swahili Coast) *c.*1810–60

When I went to Lamu in 1970, though familiar already with the old towns of Italy and Spain, I thought it was the loveliest place I had ever visited. It is an island, part of a chain off what is now the north-east coast of Kenya, hard to get to by land and ferry, but fully accessible by sea for countless centuries, trading with Arabia and with the *banyan* merchants of India. Swahili people had also interbred with the immigrant population from Indonesia established in Madagascar from about 500 CE. Children at play in the streets of Lamu ranged in pigmentation from pale 'white' to jet black, with every shade in between. Though shysters from North America had moved in to buy up some of the marvellous, distinctive carved doors, it continued to radiate its own culture, leisurely paced, yet actively cosmopolitan. In the nineteenth century it had become the chief centre of Islamic scholarship and Swahili poetry on the East African coast and it was here that Mwana Kupona, knowing that she would soon die, wrote, in 1858, over a hundred stanzas in the *utendi* metre giving advice to her daughter Mwana Hashimabinti Sheikh (1841–1933).

Swahili had evolved among coastal Africans, converts to Islam, over a thousand years or more, as the language of trading ports stretching from Kisimayo in what is now Somalia to Quelimane by the Mozambique Channel. Traders from the coast seeking slaves, ivory and other commodities took it deep into the interior, so that it became a lingua franca understood in what are now Uganda, Congo and Malawi. It is the main language of Tanzania and an official language in Kenya. By at least as early as the seventeenth century, Swahili poets were adapting the tradition of religious verse which had arrived from Arabia, extending it to epics and eventually to African communal ritual songs. Arabic script was used, rather awkwardly, since it had no signs for certain sounds common in Swahili. A very humid climate and heavy rains, not to speak of white ants and cockroaches, militated against the conservation of manuscripts and only about half a dozen survive from before 1800. They are all from Pate, an island in the same archipelago as Lamu.

The Portuguese, erupting into the Indian Ocean in the sixteenth century, conquered Mombasa, and built Fort Jesus there as part of their eastern trading system. Arabs from Oman captured the fort in

1698, and before long established themselves in Zanzibar. But it was not until 1828 that Sayid Sa'id, ruler of Oman, based himself on Zanzibar and sought to dominate the Swahili coast. The rulers of Lamu went along with his ambitions in return for support against their rivals in Pate and Mombasa, but Bwana Mataka, the leader of Siu, a town on Pate island conveniently surrounded by thick mangrove swamps, resisted to such effect that the Sultan of Pate town was inspired to expel its Omani garrison in 1839. Sayid Sa'id sent his son with a new expedition to conquer Siu in 1844. Mataka captured all its guns. Next year Sayid came in person from Zanzibar, based himself in Lamu and dispatched his trusted general Hamad bin Ahmad to take Siu. Hamad was killed and his troops drowned as they tried to escape. Siu continued to resist after Sayid died. While his son ruled Oman his brother Mayid made Zanzibar his independent fiefdom, which by the 1860s was itself dominated by the British, now, through their navy, the chief power in the Indian Ocean. Meanwhile, Mataka, who had passed away in 1848, had become a Swahili folk hero.

Mwana Kupona, his widow, achieved fame to match his own through her great poem. Swahili women were freer than their sisters in Arabia. Female circumcision was not practised. Some traditional cultures – that of Gaelic Ireland, for instance – have proscribed the writing of poetry by women, but in what is now Tanzania, female poets were even permitted to perform their own verse in public. (All Swahili poetry is written to be sung, or intoned.) The *utendi* form which Kupona used is as difficult as Dante's *terza rima*. The first three lines of each stanza rhyme together. The syllable ending the last line is rhymed right through all successive stanzas.

Swahili verse always had a didactic function. The first known woman poet in the language, Saada Taji li Arifina, composed a 'Lament of a Wife' towards the end of the eighteenth century when her husband was seeking to divorce her. It is addressed to older friends, who advise her that there is nothing she can do about it. Mwana Kupona's poem is equally conservative. Hashima is instructed in household management. She is told to be kind to the poor, but not to get too friendly with her household slaves. Kupona claims that in ten years of marriage she never quarrelled with her husband. When Hashima marries, she must be always-obedient and ever-smiling. She is told how to anoint and massage her husband, as well as how to conduct her own toilet. On the Day of Resurrection her husband will determine her ultimate fate. According to his decision, she will either enter Paradise or go to Hell fire. Kupona ends her poem with a devout personal confession of faith in God.

A male Kenyan scholar has recently produced a book about Kupona in a series presenting the lives of African heroes which is clearly aimed at school students. It tackles what is now the thorniest issue for young people, that of arranged marriages, and gets across the view that these may be successful. It gives Kupona herself grave, wise dignity and evokes delightfully the spicy, relaxed atmosphere of Lamu. I was reading this with enjoyment on 11 September 2001 when a friend phoned and said I must switch on my TV, which I did just in time to see the second World Trade tower collapse. One of my first reactions was that the book I had in front of me convinced me that the suicide hijacks had nothing at all to do with the true spirit of Islam.

J.W.T. Allen, Tendi, *1971; Lyndon Harries,* Swahili Poetry, *(Oxford) 1962; Kitula King 'ei,* Mwana Kupona: Poetess from Lamu, *(Nairobi) 2000; Jan Knappert,* Four Centuries of Swahili Verse, *1979*

Hedy Lamarr (Austria/USA) 1913–2000

Hedwig Eva Maria Kiesler was a very gifted and intelligent woman who has been widely referred to as the most stunningly beautiful of all Hollywood stars. But she had a very silly life, in which bad luck was compounded by her own perversities.

She was an only child in Sigmund Freud's Vienna. Her father was a bank manager, her mother a thwarted concert pianist. She was lavishly educated, sent to finishing school in Switzerland, then appeared at the acting school of the great Max Reinhardt, who was so smitten with her 'potential' that he took her on as a personal pupil. To little avail – as soon as she visited a film set, men started casting her. In 1933 she achieved a major *succès de scandale*. A Czech director, Gustav Machaty, made her the first screen actress to be seen totally nude, in *Symphonie der Liebe*, renamed *Extase* in France, where it was a great hit, seen in English-speaking lands as *Ecstasy*. According to Hedy, Louis B. Mayer summarised the film thus: 'There are several censorable scenes in it. In one she runs bare-assed through the woods and dives into the water. In another she gets humped by some young stud and the camera catches her expression.' The close-ups of a female reacting to sex were undoubtedly much more provocative than long shots of Hedy going to bathe in a lake. What the US censorship (which banned the film from 1936 to 1940) did not know was that Machaty had cued her erotic reactions with a safety pin in her backside (Lamarr, 25, 40). While *Ecstasy* was making her world-famous she married Fritz Mandl, a filthy-rich munitions manufacturer. Mandl considered that he had purchased a classy item. He tried ineffectually to buy up every copy of the film in which his new consort had disgraced herself, and to prevent its screening at the Venice Film Festival, where Machaty got best director award.

Hedy was queen of Mandl's parties where Hitler kissed her hand and Mussolini held her chair, but was otherwise a prisoner in her husband's palace. In 1937 she drugged her maid, borrowed her clothes, and fled thus disguised to the railway station. In Paris she won a divorce; in London, a Hollywood talent scout, Bob Ritchie, introduced her to the mighty Mayer, who hummed and hawed (her tits were not as enormous as he would wish), made her an offer she rejected as insultingly low, but finally signed her for MGM and suggested the name 'Lamarr'. Her first hit was opposite Charles Boyer, who met her at a party, reacted as most men did, and insisted she must appear in *Algiers*, in which he did not actually say to her 'Kom wiz me to zee Casbah', but she did shape up a turban for herself in the wardrobe room which launched a new fashion. She was typecast, mostly in poor films, as a woman of exotic mystery. One of her performances would prompt the unkind judgement that her 'idea of acting seems to be limited to smiling like the Mona Lisa' (Carey, 259). She turned down starring parts in both *Casablanca* and *Gaslight* – in each case Ingrid Bergmann was the lucky actress who got the role. Her second marriage – to Gene Markey, a scriptwriter (1939) – having failed, she turned to the star John Loder (1943), with whom she committed the solecism of having a daughter, then a son. After her daughter's birth, she did not work for a year, she quit MGM and, though pregnant, quit Loder, and with more guts than commonsense she set up an independent production company. Two poor movies resulted. But her ugsome apotheosis as a screen siren was then arranged by the ineffable Cecil B. De Mille, with Paramount.

De Mille, a devout man, wanted to direct the biblical tale of Samson and Delilah. He was a stickler for authenticity, so, since the Old Testament book of *Judges* did not give an exact report of Delilah's appearance, he sent researchers forth to find reproductions of all Old Masters, Rembrandt etc., in which she was depicted. None was to his liking, so he had a contemporary painter create an image – then, though she didn't match it, cast Hedy, with Victor Mature as Samson, on the grounds that 'they embody in the public mind the essence of maleness and femininity'. (Unwittingly, he had acted according to the principles of eighteenth-century neoclassicism, according to which the most 'natural' human image is the most highly typical.) Production was lavish. It was put out that every feather in Hedy's gorgeous 'peacock robe' had been personally collected by De Mille on his ranch. Critics loathed the movie. The paying public loved it (Essoe and Lee, 195, 202).

Her fourth husband, Ted Stauffer (1951), was a former bandleader, down on his luck when she met him running a hotel in Acapulco; her fifth, W. Howard Lee (1953), was a Texas oilman so rich that she tried further independent productions. In *L'Eterna Femmina*, shot in Italy, she played, amongst other sirens, Helen of Troy. This was more plausible than her shot at **Jhenne Darc** (q.v.) in *The Story of Mankind*. She bowed out, showing that she could act a bit, as an ageing, drunken film star on the skids in *The Female Animal* (1957). She returned to her avocation of marrying, but number six, a divorce lawyer, Lewis Boies (1963), lasted only a couple of years. In 1965 she was accused of shoplifting, but eventually got off. Next year, she exploited herself in a sensationalist autobiography, *Ecstasy and Me* – with typically Hedyesque bad luck, the devaluation of its key word ensured that by the end of her life her title would suggest, banally, that its author had been a teenage raver using a demonised but normally harmless party drug. Anyway, she shortly sued her ghost writers for misrepresenting her. She lived out her obscure later years in New York, where she turned her hand to painting, and made a surprise reappearance as the author of cabaret songs, performed publicly in 1984.

The truly sad thing about Hedy's silly life was that she could have been seriously brilliant. She was strongly anti-Nazi. In 1940, at another of those Hollywood parties, she fell in with another remarkable misfit, the composer **George Antheil** (q.v.), whose past of *scandale* was, temporarily, as disabling as hers, and who shared her avid interest in weapons of war, her first husband's *metier* . . . Between them they devised a radio-controlled torpedo. This was never actually put into production, but their inspired anti-jamming system of 'frequency hopping' has found manifold commercial and military applications in our neo-electronic era. Hedy was a very bright lady.

Mark Burgess, Letter, The Times, *29 January 2000; Gary Carey,* All the Stars in Heaven: Louis B. Mayer's MGM, *1982; Gabe Essoe and Raymond Lee,* De Mille: The Man and His Pictures, *(South Brunswick and New York) 1970;* International Directory of Films and Film-Makers – 3: Actors and Actresses, *3rd ed., (Detroit) 1997; Ephraim Katz, ed.,* The Macmillan International Film Encyclopaedia, *rev. edn, 1998; Hedy Lamarr,* Ecstasy and Me, *1966*

Li He (China) 790–816

An autumn wind blows over the earth,
The grasses die,
Mount Hua becomes a sapphire shadow
In the chill of dusk,
Though I have reached my twentieth year,
I've missed my goal.

('Song: Throwing Off My Sadness . . .', trans. Frodsham, 128)

'Li He was frail and thin, with eyebrows that met together and long fingernails. He wrote at great speed. Every day at dawn he would leave the house riding a colt, followed by a servant lad with an antique tapestry bag on his back. When inspiration struck him, he would write the verses down and drop them in the bag. He never wrote poems on a given topic, forcing his verses to conform to a given theme, as others do. At nightfall he would go home and work these verses into a finished poem. If he was not blind drunk or in mourning, every day was spent like this.'

Thus, an 'official' biography written some 250 years after Li He's death. Legend pushed him further towards the extreme – 'the demon-talented (*guei-cai*) poet, tall and cadaverous, his hair white as snow round his haggard face, who on his deathbed is summoned to heaven by a spirit-messenger riding a red dragon' (Frodsham, xv–xvi). The Chinese tradition of verse-making paid tribute to the Confucian 'golden mean'. Poetry should be 'moderate and mellow'. This had been breached by the 'decadent' Palace Style verse associated with Chen Houzhu (553–604), last emperor of the Chen dynasty. While his enemies were on the verge of capturing his capital, the emperor and his favourite poets, drunken and surrounded by singing girls, composed one erotic poem after another. Li He, and others of the Late Tang dynasty, adopted the diction and subject matter of such verse, but turned them inside out. Palace Style stuff was easy to read. Li He's language was dense, his meanings were hidden in subtle allusion. His subject matter went beyond the loves of courtesans to extremes of weirdness, so that one modern critic subtitles a chapter on him 'The Poetry of Beautiful Women and Ghastly Ghosts' (Fusheng Wu, 2, 77–116).

The result was that Li He, though never quite forgotten, was banished from the tradition of Chinese verse for many centuries, excluded from the great familiar anthologies. His rediscovery in the twentieth century followed after the collapse of the Chinese Empire and the development of 'Modernist' verse in Europe and America, which paid great, if ill-informed, respect to Oriental precedents. Li He was freely compared to favourite European writers. Like Keats, he died young of tuberculosis. As with Donne, his eroticism was involved with knotty and surprising ideas. Like Baudelaire, he was melancholy and naughty. His often bizarre imagery anticipated Symbolism and Surrealism. As a devotee of the most difficult Buddhist text, the *Lankavatara-sutra*, he knew that Mind was the only reality, that language created the world which his senses relished so avidly, yet language itself was subject to birth and destruction, unsteady, 'mutually conditioning' – so he would have been perfectly at home on the further-flung shores of post-structuralist and post-modernist thinking (Graham, 89–92; Frodsham, xxxvi–xxxix).

He despised the Taoist thinking which persuaded the emperor of his day that he might live for ever if he kept ingesting chemicals which in fact were killing him, yet subscribed to the Taoist idea of afterlife in Heaven, with the characteristic rider that he thought even Heaven might pass away in time. Furthermore, he was in tune with pre-

Confucian shamanistic traditions, still active in the China of his day through female practitioners – 'witches', as we would call them – and in tune with those of 'barbarian' people north of the Great Wall. Spirits could be called down by music, dancing, incantation. Zoomorphic demons could be exorcised by magic –

Blue racoons are weeping blood
As shivering foxes die.

Two hundred and forty-two of his poems survive. Versions by A. C. Graham and J. D. Frodsham give a vivid impression of a highly distinctive poetic intelligence – a lucky man, because he was so gifted, unlucky because his gifts did not earn him the start of a distinguished career, which disease anyway would have cut short.

He was born into a family claiming descent from a Prince Zheng of the Tang royal house, but despite this distinguished lineage, his father was no more than an obscure provincial magistrate, who in any case died when He was eighteen, leaving him to support his beloved mother and a younger brother. He attracted, by his precocious skill as a poet, the patronage of Han Yu (768–824), a highly esteemed Confucian scholar. At this time, and ever after, securing official posts in the Chinese Empire was dependent on passing examinations. He would have got through the provincial exams of 809 with no trouble. Then, sponsored by Han Yu, he went on to the crucial Doctoral exam held in the capital Chang-an. The capacity to write poems, of two types, was central to this. So He should have done supremely well. But his sheer promise excited jealousy. From a highly competitive system, only a handful out of, say, 3,000 strong candidates would eventually get posts. Some rival or high-placed enemy sabotaged Li He thus: under a system of taboos attached to names, bizarre to Westerners but important to Chinese people, He was forbidden to take the Doctoral exam, *jin-shi*, on the grounds that his father's name had been Jin-su. He was nevertheless allowed to take the final Selection exam, where candidates were vetted for their personal qualities. But he would not get a worthy job.

He became Supervisor of Ceremonies in the Court of Imperial Sacrifices, then Harmoniser of Pitch-pipes – a promotion from the ninth to the eighth rank. His salary was low, his mother needed money, and he was tantalised by the manifold pleasures of Chang-an, a city of nearly a million inhabitants, drawing in fair-haired, blue-eyed prostitutes amongst other people from very distant places, and very visibly dominated by princelings and courtesans who lived in luxury. In 814, frustrated, and ill, he retired to his run-down family estate in Chang-gu (now Yi-yang), set in a countryside which he loved and about which he wrote very beautifully. But he needed a career, and now sought a military one.

For more than half a century the Tang emperor's central government had been losing power to military governors. Now Xian-zong (ruled 805–20) was seeking to bring these warlords to heel. Li He got a post under a loyal general, Xi Shi-mei, and headed north-east to the military border town of Lu-Zhou. For my money, the most haunting of all Li He's poems evoke the world of frontier soldiers:

> Barbarian horns have summoned the north wind . . .
> The road to Green Sea vanishes into the sky,
> Along the Wall, a thousand moonlit miles.
> While dew falls drizzling on our flags,
> Cold metal clangs the watches of the night,
> Barbarian armour meshes serpent scales,
> Horses whinny where Green Grave gleams white . . .

('Song: Beyond the Frontiers', trans. Frodsham, 181)

His translator glosses the last line quoted thus – 'Green Grave is the name of the place in Central Asia where Wang Zhao-jun, the Chinese princess who married a Han chieftain, is buried. The horses of the nomads who have massed for the attack have eaten all the grass round the spot and stripped it white as the desert sands' (Frodsham, 275–76).

White for Chinese is the colour of mourning and misfortune. He's death was not far away. He left his general fighting rebels and returned to die in Chang-gu. Over twelve centuries, though, he still speaks to us – and sings, since over half his poems were modelled on old ballads and were meant to be sung. In a preface to a song, 'Bearded Shen Playing his Tartar Horn', He recalls the party at which he composed the verses for a 'northern friend' whose servant Shen was. Delighted, the friend called his concubine in to sing them as a duet with He himself, while Shen accompanied them. From where I sit, this looks like a damn good ancient Chinese ceilidh . . .

J. D. Frodsham, trans., Goddesses, Ghosts and Demons: The Collected Poems of Li He . . . , *1983; Fusheng Wu*, The Poetics of Decadence: Chinese Poetry of the Southern Dynasties and Late Tang Periods, *(Albany, NY) 1998; A. C. Graham, ed. and trans.*, Poems of the Late T'ang, *(Harmondsworth) 1965*

Gregor MacGregor (Scotland) 1869–1919

The last decade of the nineteenth century, through into the Edwardian era, has been widely remembered as the Golden Age of English Cricket. Apart from the general tendency to perceive Golden Ages in various departments of life before the leaden era of 1914–18 dispelled so many aureate illusions, the chief reason must be this – it was the last period in which the Public School Amateur dominated the game at the highest level. This fused with hegemonic ideology in the heyday of Imperialism. Cricket was the pre-eminent expression of the values which made Britons uniquely fit to rule differently pigmented persons in far continents. 'Fair Play!' 'Keep a straight bat!' 'Play up, play up – and play the game!' The lower-middle and working classes – which provided the talented professional cricketers who actually sustained the First Class Counties and England's international Test sides, with their doggedness, reliability and guile – were prepared to flock in huge numbers – say, 50,000 for a three-day match at Lords – to watch the young bloods at their princely pleasures. In disillusioning fact, certain top 'amateurs', through expenses, perks, fees and sinecures, earned far more from the game than plebeian 'professionals'. And some of them

– the great Dr W. G. Grace himself to the fore – while they 'knew the rules', were guilty of every sort of gamesmanship and plain cheating.

These were never alleged against Gregor MacGregor. An Edinburgh-born Scot, he represented Scotland at rugby, but was educated at Uppingham, an English public school, and Cambridge University. He was picked to keep wicket for England while still an undergraduate, played eight Tests, and later captained Middlesex at Lords for a number of years. His practice as a stockbroker spared him, it seems, from pseudo-amateurism. His relatively early death was not due to drink or suicide, the nemesis of numerous noted professionals of the era, but to a heart condition. The worst alleged against him (in our eyes) was that, rooming at Cambridge in luxury with Sammy Woods, the rich son of an Australian merchant, he exhibited all the moneyed loutism which persisted amongst toffs and sporting 'hearties' when I was at the university in the 1960s, and perhaps echoes there even now. On one occasion the young MacGregor, bear-fighting with Woods, was pushed by the latter right through a window. Despite badly cut hands, the story runs, the Scot kept wicket as superbly as ever next morning (Meredith, 27).

Which brings me to the reasons why MacGregor is in this book. Firstly, while a very great deal of cricket has been played in Lowland Scotland for a couple of centuries, we have produced damn few top-class heroes, and amongst these only MacGregor could be classed as 'legendary'. Furthermore, I kept wicket for years myself, at 'good club' second eleven level, and had my days of success. The courage of MacGregor fascinates me – *because, perhaps even with cut hands, he 'stood up' to Sammy Woods' bowling*.

An obituary by a former team-mate tells us that MacGregor and Woods operated with 'machine-like precision'. Woods, a big man, was undoubtedly fast. 'The faster Sam bowled, the nearer the sticks stood Mac, and he took the five and a half ounces of leather, cork and string, as if it were a ping-pong ball! He took it on the off- or on the on-side with equal facility, and he would throw the ball back, time in and time out, with the suggestion that he was a little tired at the simplicity of it all' (*Wisden*, 1111).

The wicket-keeper, unlike the goal-keeper in soccer, is not purely defensive. His steady job is to ensure that when the batsman misses the ball it does not pass towards the boundary so that 'byes' can be run. But if the batsman misses and is out of his ground – feet past the crease – the keeper can whip off the bails and stump him. Slow bowlers, operating at around 50 mph, actually aim for stumpings – to draw the batsman forward and beat him. To stand up to a quicker bowler is an act of aggression – 'watch it, mate, if you try moving forward to put the bowler off his length, I'll stump you!' Normally, the keeper standing back to a fast bowler is in no danger of accident. But standing up, where the batsman's body may obscure his view of the ball, he can expect from slow and medium pace bowling the occasional nasty, though not lethal, mishap, as the ball comes suddenly at him, bumping into his face or ribs or thighs. I would regularly come off the field bruised. Like keepers of MacGregor's day, I wore no protection except pads guarding calves and knees and very thick gloves. *But my pads and gloves were superior products compared to those of the 1890s.* I have seen international-class keepers stand up from time to time to medium-fast bowlers operating at 70 mph. But Woods, it is clear, was authentically 'fast'. So we have to imagine speeds from the top seventies up to 85 mph. MacGregor must sometimes have missed balls slipping very wide or rearing over his head. The now obsolete fielding position of 'long stop', whatever people chose to call it – 'sharp leg', say – must have been employed to cut down byes. But the evidence is that MacGregor was a 'tidy' keeper who did the defensive business well, with byes at a minimum. In fact, his personality seems to have settled down, post-Cambridge, to that of the dour, quiet, efficient Edinburgh Scot, never flamboyant on the field, rarely emotional, a 'useful' batsman with no 'beautiful' strokes. 'It is difficult', a writer remarked about his keeping in 1899, 'to realise that so much can be done with so little fuss' (Fry, 68). He was not remembered as a daredevil, but as a steady man.

Now, very fast overarm bowling was, around 1890, an innovation. MacGregor's generation of wicket-keepers was the first to adjust to it. Bill Storer, a professional with Derbyshire, playing for MCC against the touring Australians in 1893, indubitably stood up for a while to the bowling of Charles Kortwright – though on another occasion 'Korty' was angry when Harry Martyn, keeping to him in a Gentlemen v Players fixture, did the same. Despite a warning, 'Martyn stood his ground, gathered the first of Kortright's rockets right-handed outside the off stump, and tossed the ball back to the bowler so swiftly that it hit the poor unprepared fellow in the chest' (Frith, 86).

This is weird stuff. Kortwright was faster than Woods, and, indeed, contemporaries went on believing that he was the fastest of them all decades later, after the chance to watch many challengers. We must assume that he was superfast, perhaps capable of 95 mph. He was also addicted to hurling down short-pitched balls aimed to intimidate the batsman, who had to get out of the way as they reared up, or sustain severe bruising. Straight balls on a full length posed another hazard to anyone behind the wicket when the batsman missed them. On one documented occasion, Kortwright dismissed Johnny Briggs with a delivery which knocked his leg stump out of the ground some seventeen yards, so that it made three complete revolutions. The leg bail flew sixty yards. Yet in this very same match – Gentlemen v Players at Lords, 1893 – MacGregor saw a batsman, Frank Sugg of Lancashire, standing outside his crease as Kortwright bowled. He came right up to the wicket. He took neatly one or two balls which Sugg missed. 'Then Sugg got a thick edge and MacGregor caught him, low down, in his right hand . . . MacGregor was later very modest about it. It was, he said, a great fluke and he had afterwards moved back, having learnt sense.' Yet it seems that next day, for limited periods, he in fact stood up to Kortwright again (Meredith, 69–70).

We are talking about superb reflexes, of course. But perhaps good contemporary wicket-keepers might trust their own reflexes as bravely as MacGregor did.

David Frith, The Fast Men, *1977; C. B. Fry, ed.,* The Book of Cricket, *1899; Anthony Meredith,* The Demon and the Lobster, *1987;* Wisden Anthology 1900–1940, *ed. Benny Green, 1988.*

Madoc (Wales) *fl.*1170?

It seems quite certain that more than 500 years before Columbus, Biarni Heriulfson, a Norse trader, missed Greenland on a voyage there and saw the coast of North America – Labrador and Baffin Island. It is equally clear that in 1001, Leif Ericsson, having bought Biarni's knarr, set forth to explore further these terrains. Baffin Island he called 'Helluland' – Land of Flat Stones – and Labrador 'Markland' – Land of Forests. He placed a settlement on the northern tip of Newfoundland, in an area called Vinland, presumably not on account of grapes found there, so far north, but of a profusion of 'wineberries' – red currants, gooseberries or cranberries. Hostile natives were a problem. The Norsemen abandoned Vinland after a third and final attempt to colonise in 1013.

So even if a Welsh prince called Madoc had made landfall in North America late in the twelfth century CE, he would not have been the first European discoverer.

The Madoc story goes like this: after the death of Owen Gwynedd, king of North Wales, his son Madoc, a skilled seafarer, sickened by the ensuing civil war, resolves to take a contingent of his countrymen to somewhere they can live in peace. He sails west in 1170, strikes suitable land, leaves 120 colonists there, returns to Wales, fills ten ships with more prospective colonists, departs – and is never heard from again.

The presumption that Madoc had discovered, and settled in, America over 300 years before Columbus, on whose voyage of 1492 Spaniards based their claim to the continent, appealed greatly to the court of Queen Elizabeth I when it first saw daylight in 1580. This was the decade when Ralegh planted the first abortive English colony in Roanoke (North Carolina), and of the great Armada of 1588 directed by Philip of Spain against his heretical sister-in-law, Elizabeth I. The tale of Madoc justified challenge to Spain's claims in the New World, granted the conviction that those with precedence in European 'discovery' had a right to seize land occupied already by red aboriginals. Furthermore, it gratified influential Welsh subjects of the Welsh Tudor dynasty installed in London. They liked to emphasise that the Welsh, as Britons, were the autocthonous stock of the island. Dr John Dee, Welshman, 'magician', scientist and geographer at Elizabeth's court, the first man to use the phrase 'British Empire', was the opportunist chiefly responsible for replacing a former claim to priority based on voyages out of Bristol by the Cabots (of Genoese origin, like Columbus), with 'what had evidently been a marginal, perhaps underground story . . .' (Williams, 66).

Sir Humphrey Gilbert was proposing to colonise large tracts of North America. He promised his adviser Dee huge grants of land, with control of the presumed North-West Passage to China. To support formal claims to Elizabeth's Council, Dee produced a lavish map and backed it with brief reference to the story of Madoc. When this surfaced in full, in a proposal by Sir George Peckham in 1583 to settle English Catholics in the New World, it was wonderfully embellished. Madoc in America 'gave to certaine Llandes, Beastes, and Fowles, sundrie Welch names, such as the Lland of Pengwyn, which yet to this day beareth the same.' A bird in the land of Penguin had the same name, meaning white-headed in Welsh 'and in trueth, the sayde Fowles have white heads.' More impressively still, Spanish chronicles recorded a speech by Montezuma, emperor of Mexico, to Hernan Cortes, who would overthrow him, to the effect that his own people had come originally from a far country, to which their 'King and Captaine' had returned. Aztecs thus became the first of many native American peoples supposed to have descended from Madoc's colonists. For his proofs by linguistic survival, Peckham was using the account of one David Ingram who said he had been put ashore in the Gulf of Mexico by Sir John Hawkins in 1568 and had walked all the way north to Maine, where a French ship had picked him up. Beside penguins he had seen, he claimed, elephants, pillars of gold and red sheep. Hakluyt published his tale in the first edition of his epic and immensely influential compilation of the *Principall Navigations* of the English, but had the sense to drop it from the second. Nevertheless, the myth of the Lost Tribe of Wales lingered tenaciously (Williams, 39–43).

Without linguistic proofs, the Madoc story was feeble. Suppose the prince actually had founded a settlement to the West, nothing in the basic story proved that this was in North America. What about Madeira, or the Azores? Following its bizarre exfoliations over following centuries, it is sometimes hard to remember that there may be a core of truth in the legend. A real 'king' of North Wales called Owen Gwynedd died in 1169. Within a few decades, a Flemish poet called Willem, otherwise known as the author of the most successful version of the satire of *Reynard the Fox*, produced a romance, now lost, called *Madoc*, apparently about a seafaring Welsh prince. In the turbulent thirteenth century, when norsemen from Ireland and Iceland roamed through the waters off Wales, it is conceivable that a Welsh leader might have heard of Vinland and had confidence enough to brave the

Atlantic. But what is certain is that no documentary or material trace of a Welsh landfall in America before Columbus has been found.

However, Welsh people did form an important component of the new colony of Pennsylvania after 1681. Some had heard stories of Welsh-speaking Indians. Quite recently, 'one Stedman of Breconshire, sailing in a Dutch ship, had conversed in Welsh with Indians at some point between Virginia and Florida. They told him their ancestors had come from a place called Gwynned in Prydain Fawr. 'Their sachems [the great historian Gwyn A. Williams observes drily] must have been veritable Druids, for the land was not called Prydain Fawr, or Great Britain, until after the accession of James I. At roughly the same time, an English privateer careening his vessel near Florida learned the native tongue, only to find, when he encountered Oliver Humphreys, a Welsh merchant in Surinam . . . that he had learned Welsh' (Williams, 75).

In 1686, Thomas Lloyd, William Penn's deputy in the new Quaker colony, met in New York a discredited Presbyterian pastor, Morgan Jones, who spun him the wondrous yarn that in 1660, while serving as pastor to a colonising expedition in South Carolina, he had been captured by a Tuscarora Indian tribe called the Doeg. When he spoke Welsh, they understood him, spared his life, and entertained him well for four months, during which he conversed freely with them and preached to them in 'the British tongue'. This totally false narrative struck Lloyd so forcibly that he got Jones to sign a statement for him to send home. It provided a model for various eighteenth-century tales of similar purport – 'only it is always a different Indian tribe which speaks Welsh' (Morison, 85).

As the Colonial, then the US, frontier rolled forward without the elusive Welsh tribe materialising, the remote Mandans of what is now North Dakota became the last, best hope. They were an unusual people. They lived in substantial beehive earth lodges ringed with palisades, moats and earthworks, like ancient British homesteads. They built hide-covered wicker boats like the old Welsh coracles. They often had surprisingly fair skin. Mandan girls 'chattered endlessly even while making love . . .' This seemed to one observer further proof of their Welsh descent (Williams, 169–71).

In the epoch of the French Revolution, ardent and discontented radicals imagined free Welsh colonists settling in the region, establishing an autonomous National Home for the Welsh. A young man was found, John Evans, with the daring and tenacity to penetrate the Mandan country. On the turbulent frontier, he met a Scotsman, James McKay, who was working for a trading company established under the Spanish crown in the last spasm of Iberian ambition in North America, not long before the Louisiana Purchase gave all north of Mexico to the USA. McKay's great aim was to find a route to the Pacific via the Rockies. Evans, entrusted with this mission, would meet the Mandans on his way. In the autumn of 1796, he reached the Mandan settlements the first white man to beat an effective blockade by Sioux and Omaha Indians and plant Spanish authority on the Upper Missouri . . .

Most heroic. But the Mandans did not speak Welsh, as Evans, an honest man, felt bound to report.

The Bureau of American Ethnology would eventually state: 'There is not a provable trace of Welsh, Gaelic or any other European language in any native American language' (Morison, 87).

Samuel Eliot Morison, The European Discovery of America: The Northern Voyages 500–1600, *(New York) 1971; Gwyn A. Williams*, Madoc: The Making of a Myth, *(Oxford) 1987*

Ern Malley (Australia) 1918–43

Now that Australia is, triumphantly, a nation with Culture, symbolised by its Sydney Opera House, it is hard to imagine how things were in 1944.

That Australian literature existed at all was a matter of doubt. There was a tradition of frontier balladeering, epitomised by 'Waltzing Matilda'. Poems and novels derived from English models. They seemed 'provincial', not distinctively 'Australian'. The 'Jindyworobak' movement, excoriated by the acerbic A. D. Hope as 'the Boy Scout School of Poetry', had recently transferred the techniques of the Georgian pastoral school of English verse ineffectually, with pseudo-Aboriginal dialect, to the awesome Australian outback. But Australia, with the overwhelming majority of its population concentrated in six sprawling cities, was one of the most urbanised countries on earth. Two forms of philistinism competed. Christian puritanism closed pubs at 6 p.m., in defiance of rambunctious males whose lives were absorbed in sport and gambling.

In this context, if Sydney remained provincial, Adelaide was a province of provinces. Lovely South Australia had never been a convict settlement. Adelaide was most conscious of its high dignity. J.I.M. Stewart, a Scot who arrived there to profess English Literature at the University in the late 1930s, would remark in his memoirs that 'One of the first things I had to grasp in Adelaide was the concept of the Leading Citizen, which was constantly invoked in the local press' (Stewart, 104). It turned out that university academics were rarely if ever Leading Citizens – let alone artists and writers. Yet in this unpropitious environment, a student, Max Harris – oxymoronically a Jewish boy from up-country, where his father was a wholesale butcher – decided to create an Avant-Garde.

Harris, born in 1921, reckoned that the highways of Australian literature must be international. Aged nineteen, he launched a magazine called *Angry Penguins*, its title derived from a line in one of his own poems evoking drunken youths in dinner jackets. It was soon featuring work by innovative painters, including the very notable working-class visionary Sidney Nolan. Nolan lived in a *ménage à trois* in hills outside Melbourne with a rich lawyer with a Cambridge degree, John Reed, and his wife Sunday, the painter's mistress and muse. From 1943, *Angry Penguins* was edited by Harris in Adelaide, designed by Nolan in Melbourne, and financed by the Reeds. It was plush and distinguished, carrying work by well-known British and American avant-gardists. Had Modernism at last arrived in Australia, more than a quarter of a century after its advent in Europe? In particular, could Oz poets catch up with the latest fashion in Britain, the New Apocalypse?

The Apocalyptics had announced themselves not long before the outbreak of war. They were neo-Romantics inspired by the verse of two very young men, Dylan Thomas and George Barker, who rejected the knowing coolness of the dominant Auden school in favour of perfervid imagery close in its application to the wild work of the Continental Surrealists – Freudians and often also Marxists, who believed that exposing free associations derived from the subconscious was therapeutic for mankind and would subvert bourgeois society.

Early in 1944, Harris received a letter from one Ethel Malley. Could he look at some poems by her late brother Ern, found when she was 'going through his things after his death'? She enclosed two samples.

Harris was excited. He asked Ethel to show him the rest, and tell him about her brother. Fifteen more poems arrived, one a faltering unfinished last work. Ethel's tale was very sad. Ern had returned home to Sydney the previous March suffering from Graves' Disease, which made him 'terribly irritable'. That was why he had failed his medical for the army. His full name was Ernest Lalor Malley, born in Liverpool in 1918. His father had died of war wounds in 1920, and his mother had brought her children to Sydney, where she had relations. Ern had not done well at school and after their mother's death in 1933, Ethel could not stop him quitting. He was good with 'mechanical things' and after he got a job in Palmer's Garage on Taverner's Hill, Ethel 'thought he was settled and had got over his wildness'. But then, aged seventeen, he suddenly threw up his job and left for Melbourne. He did not write, but Ethel learnt from someone she knew that he was working for National Mutual selling insurance policies, 'living in a room by himself in South Melbourne. Later, in 1940, I think it was, I did get a letter from him saying that his health was better and that he was making a fair amount of money repairing watches and doing other work on the side.' Early in 1943, Ethel found that he had returned, sick, to Sydney. She persuaded him to come home. 'The weeks before he died were terrible. Sometimes he would be all right and he would talk to me. From things he said I gathered that he had been fond of a girl in Melbourne, but had some sort of difference with her. The crisis came suddenly, and he passed away on Friday the 23rd of July. As he wished, he was cremated at Rookwood' (Malley, 5–6).

Despite the sorrow of this simple tale, Harris was beside himself with joy. These wonderful poems, surrealist in aspect, projected a distinctively Australian urban consciousness, that of a working-class autodidact. (Harris was a member of the Communist Party.) His co-editors were equally moved. Nolan, in particular, found Ern inspirational. He produced a painting, 'The Sole Arabian Tree', derived from one of Ern's incandescent images. This featured on the cover of *Angry Penguins* '1944 Autumn Number – to Commemorate the Australian Poet Ern Malley'. It printed the entire Malley oeuvre, arranged by Ern himself as a very slim volume, 'The Darkening Ecliptic'.

This great event in Australian cultural history would normally have passed unnoticed save by the few hundred people who bought *Angry*

Penguins and handfuls of literati in England and North America who paid attention to the magazine. But cruel fate had fame, or rather notoriety, in store for Harris.

A young journalist in Sydney, Tess Van Sommers, walking in Martin Place in the centre, saw the new *Penguins* on a magazine stand. She remembered something which her friend Harold Stewart had told her at their last meeting. She went straight to the offices of the *Sunday Sun*. She was not allowed, though, to write up her own scoop. Her story was handed to Colin Simpson, editor of the paper's magazine supplement, *Fact*. Meanwhile, Van Sommers spoke on a three-way telephone hook-up to Stewart and their mutual friend James McAuley.

Fact on 25 July revealed all. McAuley and Stewart were old schoolfriends from the depths of the Sydney petty bourgeoisie. Both were poets, but, though older than Harris, had not had his fortune in getting books published. They despised his surrealistic, apocalyptic and modernistic poetics. Both, called up in the army, had been spared risk of death by a remarkable operator called Alf Conlon, who had met them when they were all three Sydney University students. Conlon had sweet-talked his way to the headship of a thinktank in Melbourne which he called the Directorate of Research and Civil Affairs. Here lawyers, scientists, doctors and anthropologists wrote reports on topics ranging from the future administration of Papua New Guinea to the use of pyrethrum as an insecticide.

One afternoon in the spring of 1943, McAuley and Stewart had the Directorate to themselves, with no urgent work on hand. Contrary to later suggestions, they used no alcohol as they set about a task they had been discussing for some time: to fork Harris and beyond him to confound his English idol, the trendy poet, critic and guru of Surrealism and Apocalypse, Herbert Read. Between lunch and nine or ten that night, with maybe an hour off to eat, they concocted the entire Malley oeuvre. His poems, inscribed on an army-issue ruled quarto pad, were deliberately stained with tea as they wrote, to produce a suitably grubby effect. The first poem, 'Durer: Innsbruck, 1495', was an early, rejected work of McAuley himself. It established a standard of technical competence which Ern maintained as his two creators, assisted by dictionaries and a Collected Shakespeare, interrupted each others' free associations so that a duped Harris could not later protest that, whatever their intentions, the outflow of subconscious in Ern's poems was, surrealistically speaking, valid. They invented a brilliant saying by Lenin – 'the emotions are not skilled workers' – to titillate Harris's anarcho-Marxist susceptibilities. They sowed the whole oeuvre with clear confessions by the author that he didn't exist.

The hard bit was creating Ethel, conceived as the archetypal Australian suburban philistine, unable to express herself, disgusted by Ern's bohemian ways, but feeling duty-bound to send her brother's poems on to an editor who might understand them, as she couldn't. Her story was carefully made difficult to check – birth certificate in England; no callup – no army record; no address in Melbourne. The big giveaway was Graves' Disease. An enervating problem of the thyroid gland, it causes sleeplessness, irritability, diarrhoea, excessive perspiration and other nasty symptoms. Sufferers go bug-eyed. But it is not a killer, and a clued-up reader of Ethel's numb narrative might have concluded either that Ern committed suicide or that misinformation was being peddled.

McAuley and Stewart informed readers of *Fact* that they bore no malice against Harris, they had been conducting a serious experiment. Serious critics did discuss seriously the implications of Ern. Herbert Read, invited to comment from England, cabled Harris back: I TOO WOULD HAVE BEEN DECEIVED BY ERN MALLEY BUT HOAXER HOIST BY OWN PETARD HAS TOUCHED OFF UNCONSCIOUS SOURCES INSPIRATION WORK TOO SOPHISTICATED BUT HAS ELEMENTS GENUINE POETRY. Ern could be a fine poet despite the intentions of his fabricators (Heywood, 156–8).

This reasonable view buttered no parsnips with the Australian public in general, to whom Picasso was a species of swear-word and poetry a symptom of poofterism. They guffawed because the Bohemians had been bamboozled.

The Leading Citizens of Adelaide felt obliged to adopt a more proactive stance. On 5 September 1944 police charged Harris with having published fourteen 'indecent advertisements' in the latest issue of *Angry Penguins*, seven of them in Ern's poems. With Reed's anxious support, Harris assembled a strong-looking defence, with a leading psychiatrist as one expert witness and J.I.M. Stewart as another. Stewart appeared despite having been 'warned off'. The registrar of the university had summoned him to his office where he found a judge of the South Australian High Court who advised him '"most strongly", in no circumstances willingly to come forward with evidence in Mr Harris's favour. Only if served with a subpoena ought I to have anything to do with the matter' (Stewart, 108).

A detective named Vogelsang was the chief prosecution witness. (His name translates as 'birdsong', but colleagues knew him as 'Dutchie'.) He was distressed by such words as 'rape', 'genitals' and 'incestuous' occurring in Ern's poems. As Harris wrote later, 'The greatest mystery of the trial was the prosecution of "Night Piece" as neither the defence nor anyone present had the faintest idea how this poem could be interpreted in an indecent way. The indecency lay in the fact that the events took place in a park at night. Det. Vogelsang: "They were going there for some disapproved motive."' Referring to Ern's deathless lines:

> . . . on park-gates
> The iron birds looked disapproval
> With rusty invidious beaks . . .

Vogelsang continued: 'Because of the disapproval and the nature of the time they went there and the disapproval of the iron birds make me say it is immoral. I have found that people who go into parks at night go there for immoral purposes' (Malley, 44).

Oddly, Vogelsang might have been onto something. McAuley and Stewart were not on trial. But the latently illicit nature of their relationship intrigues McAuley's astute biographer. Stewart (1916–95) was a gentle, humorous man, already deeply into the obsession with Eastern art, literature and religion which led him to spend the last three decades of his life in Japan. Like McAuley, he flirted with Theosophy, one bond between them. McAuley (1917–76) was the most charismatic Australian intellectual of his generation. Dramatic in appearance, with a flop of fair hair and a prematurely aged, skull-haunted face, he was an equally brilliant improviser of jazz at the piano or rhymes on the spur of the moment, and the exhaustive and exhausting brilliance of his talk never flagged during his habitual heavy drinking. Most obviously, he was a womaniser. Tormented by the sinfulness of his lusts, he was also subject to frequent horrific nightmares. His connection with Conlon's Directorate would take him to New Guinea, where, amongst Stone Age peoples, he met the **Devil** (q.v.). His conversion to Roman Catholicism in 1952 preceded such extreme anti-Communism during the Cold War and the crises which it provoked on the Australian left that he was an embarrassment to his own CIA-funded co-warriors.

Harold Stewart was a homosexual, at a time when even the Bohemian left to which both men still belonged did not discuss the subject in Australia. An enigma in McAuley's early biography is that, despite his then-infidelity, he played the organ in his teens at the Liberal Catholic Church in Sydney established by the late 'Bishop' Leadbeater, paedophile and associate in Theosophy of **Annie Besant** (q.v.). As he was dying of cancer, McAuley reminisced gratuitously about the 'homosexual taint in the air' of that church and about earlier experiences at the Anglican church where he had been chorister and altar boy and the parson was manifestly a paedophile. His biographer sensibly associates ambivalence in McAuley's sexuality with his horrific nightmares – and his very close friendship with Stewart, which 'wore thin after the Ern Malley affair' (Pybus, 258–62). During the helter-skelter composition of Ern's oeuvre, the two young poets may have opened up elements in their own relationship which they could not explictly discuss even with each other.

However, such speculations were beyond the Adelaide court which heard J.I.M. Stewart aver that some writing in *Angry Penguins* was technically crude, but this did not make it indecent. It seemed at times that the court and prosecution were more outraged by the fact that Ern's poems were hard to explain than by any incitement to sex they might provide – Harris was in effect on trial for publishing obscure modern verse. The judge eventually decided that none of the instances complained about were immoral or obscene but that certain passages were indecent. Harris was fined £5 with costs.

The lurid Ern Malley Affair 'discredited poets and poetry in the eyes of the general public but only for the very short time that it remained newsworthy' (Matthews, 314). In literary circles, though, its echoes resounded for decades. There would be people who said, sincerely or provocatively, that Ern's sixteen pieces were better than any poems published by Stewart and McAuley under their own names. The major US poet John Ashbery was wowed by Ern. A Penguin anthology of Modern Australian Poetry published in 1991 included Ern's oeuvre in its entirety.

McAuley and Stewart won their campaign, in so far as Australian Modernism was, in verse, a lost cause, and the very impressive achievements of Australian poetry since Ern have depended on traditional aesthetics and poetics. For that matter, the New Apocalyptics in Britain passed rapidly and utterly out of fashion.

But Ern wasn't really Apocalyptic or thorough-goingly Surrealist. McAuley was early addicted to T. S. Eliot, and Ern largely derives from 'The Love Song of J. Alfred Prufrock', that voyeur uncertain of his own identity. However, Eliot despised Romanticism, whereas Ern is a devoted Keatsian (very acute students of his story might have noticed that his lifespan was exactly that of the little Cockney master, to the day.) Ern is an archetypal poet-as-outsider, haunting in artisan's work-clothes the Melbourne Public Library, physically sickly, psychically bullish, diffident before the wonders of literature yet convinced of his own genius, an Australian 'black swan of trespass' on the 'alien waters' of European Modernism. How brilliantly, Eliot-wise, he seizes upon a report on mosquito control which happened to be around in the Directorate on his triumphant day of creation:

> 'Swamps, marshes, borrow-pits and other
> Areas of stagnant water serve
> As breeding grounds . . .' Now
> Have I found you, my Anopheles!

But how poignantly yet wittily he evokes love lost amidst shabby Melbourne mundanity:

> Princess, you lived in Princess St.,
> Where the urchins pick their nose in the sun
> With the left hand.

Ern was born dead, but long live Ern!

Michael Heywood, The Ern Malley Affair, *1993; Ern Malley*, Poems, *introd. Max Harris, (Melbourne) 1961; Brian Matthews, 'Literature and Conflict', in* The Penguin Literary History of Australia, *(Ringwood, Victoria) 1988; Cassandra Pybus*, The Devil and James McAuley, *(St Lucia, Queensland) 1999; J.I.M. Stewart*, Myself and Michael Innes, *1987; thanks to Cassandra Pybus*

Beryl Markham (Kenya) 1902–86

The opening up of Kenya to white settlers in the early years of the twentieth century involved the building of a railway from the Indian Ocean to Uganda and the theft of many acres of fertile land from African peoples. 'Captain' Charles Clutterbuck, 'Clutt' to his fellow whites, was one of the pioneers, using a thousand native labourers to clear virgin forest and setting up mills to grind maize flour for workers on the railway and saw wood used to build houses by other settlers.

He was a Rutland farmer down on his luck, whose wife Clara had left him to run a tea shop in Melton Mowbray, but agreed to join him on the Equator. His great talent was for riding horses, and it was his related gift for training them which kept him going through an up-and-down life. Daughter Beryl was less than two years old when she arrived in Kenya. Clutt got started as dairyman for Lord Delamere, who was on his way to becoming uncrowned king of the colony, then acquired his own land in the 'White Highlands', 7,000 feet above sea level. Clara didn't stay long. She fell in love with a Major Kilpatrick, and followed him to England. So Beryl was left alone with her father, the horses he trained for Lord Delamere, and a great many Africans.

She adored her father. She christened the first horse she helped deliver 'Pegasus' when her father gave it to her. Swahili was her first language, her best friend was a Kipsigis boy, Kibii, who came to share her love of horses, as she did his skill in hurling a spear and shooting arrows – and his father *arap* Maina let her go hunting with himself and other grown men, as their own womenfolk weren't permitted to do. She picked up Kipsigis fleetness of foot – later to produce several great Olympic champions – and Kipsigis reticence and stoicism during pain. The habit of going barefoot whenever feasible would remain with her. She lasted less than three terms at the Nairobi European School where she was sent to board aged nine. She loved playing cricket, but not lessons, and ran away in order to get herself expelled.

The Great War, when Africans were conscripted to fight the German regime in adjacent Tanganyika, was terrible for Beryl – *arap* Maina was a casualty. However, Clutt did well supplying *posho*, wood-fuel and remounts for the army. His mistress Emma Orchardson nursed convalescent officers. One of these, Captain 'Jock' Purves, fell for Beryl when she was only thirteen. He was a big, strong twenty-nine-year-old who had been capped ten times for Scotland at rugby. A deal was struck: . . . 'Beryl was bartered for, in much the same way as *arap* Maina would have acquired another wife. The only difference was that instead of exchanging several hundred goats as Beryl's bride-price, Purves offered to pay for her schooling in return for her marriage' (Trzebinski, 50–51).

At Miss Seccombe's School in Nairobi, Beryl dazzled boys with her prowess at cricket and her outstanding beauty. She grew to be 5' 8'' tall, with a willowy build, slim hips, blue eyes, fair hair, wide-spaced teeth (traditionally a sign of lechery), a long oval face, and a strong chin. What she called a 'galaxy of scars' (Markham, 91) – including one inflicted on her leg with a Kipsigis sword in a fight with a black boy whom she bashed with a knobkerrie and others where she had been mauled by a settler's pet lion – only increased her egregious allure. In her third term Beryl one day simply couldn't take any more schooling, got on her bicycle and sped away across the Athi Plains. Other children followed, and she was expelled for inciting rebellion.

She was still under seventeen when Jock Purves married her in All Saints Cathedral Nairobi on 15 October 1919. When Jock took her on honeymoon to India, his former stamping ground, it turned out he couldn't face her in bed without lots of whisky, and she soon sickened of him. Then her father's life capsized. At the peak of his fame as a trainer of horses for the races which obsessed settler society, Clutt was bankrupted and had to sell his stable. He left the colony, finding work as a trainer in Peru.

Beryl's life with drunken Jock on the land he had bought degenerated into frequent physical violence. She often rode off on Pegasus to stay with friends and acquaintances, and did not care to disguise her promiscuous infidelities. And she stole from Jock's bed while he snored to be with her friend Kibii, now, after initiation, *arap* Ruta. She left Jock for good in February 1922.

Following in her father's wake, she had become the first woman trainer in the history of the Turf to gain recognition. (Women would not be recognised as trainers in England until 1966.) *Arap* Ruta followed her on foot after Pegasus had carried her, with no possessions save what she had in her saddle roll, to live at Soysambu and look after Lord Delamere's stud. Around this time she entered the legendary terrain of the Scandinavian Baroness and the Happy Valley Set.

The Danish writer who became famous as 'Isak Dinesen' – known to Kenyan friends as Tania – had married her Swedish cousin Baron Bror von Blixen, and they had settled near Nairobi in 1914. Karen Blixen's book *Out of Africa* (1937) would communicate to generations of gullible readers a romantic view of the lives of Kenya's white settlers. While Bror was as promiscuous as Beryl (and sexual congress between this pair was inevitable), Karen/Tania had just one lover, Denys Finch Hatton. 'He would have cut a figure in any age,' she wrote, 'for he was an athlete, a musician, a lover of art and a fine sportsman' (Blixen, 224). Second son of an Earl, educated at Eton and Oxford, regarded as very handsome despite or because of being prematurely bald, he was thought to be an intellectual and also a mighty white hunter. Basically, Finch Hatton traded on his aristocratic and sexual mystique to relieve exceptionally rich men of as much of their wealth as possible while they pursued, under his guidance, their lust for shooting large animals. Meanwhile, African bearers and trackers did the hard work.

This man became, very publicly, Tania Blixen's lover. Her second biographer believes that Beryl fell romantically for Finch Hatton as soon as she was introduced to him aged twenty, and never ceased to pursue him before and after their first bonk. But with Beryl it is a matter of which old settler gossip you choose to believe. What is clear is that she was not drawn into the worst *niasieries* of the 'Happy Valley Set' – aristocrats and ex-Army officers arriving to settle in Kenya after the Great War, who fuddled themselves with alcohol and rarer drugs while rotating wives and partners as in Musical Chairs. Divorced from Jock, she set about finding a rich husband. In 1927 she married Mansfield Markham, whose father, a baronet, was Liberal MP and coalowner in the North of England. He was very wealthy, but thoroughly civilised – bookish even – a strange, almost wise choice. On their honeymoon in Europe, he dressed her in Parisian gowns. In London, he took her for beauty treatment to Elizabeth Arden. The barbaric African girl was transformed. For the rest of her life she would be conspicuously stylish.

Markham bought property in the Elburgon district, where Beryl and Ruta carried on training horses. But almost at once the Colony was convulsed by news of a forthcoming Royal Visit. Edward, Prince of Wales, and his younger brother Prince Henry of Gloucester had decided to shoot large animals. Finch Hatton, of course, was to run their safari. When they arrived in October, the Markhams were staying at the Muthaiga Club waiting, like every white in Kenya, to meet them. Beryl, of course, slept with both of them, although she was well advanced in pregnancy. The diminutive Prince, 'Edward P.', fitted in well with the gross social *mores* of the club. A band played there, but only on Saturday nights, so the gramophone had to fill in. Sir Derek Erskine, a settler, would recall, 'one night Edward P was dancing with my wife and he suddenly lost his temper with the records which he said were the wrong kind, and I very much regret to say that aided and assisted by my wife, they picked up all the gramophone records and threw them through the windows of the old ballroom . . . Well, I had to pay the bill . . .' (Fox, 27). The Duke of Gloucester, an uncomplicated 'professional' soldier, was not noted for anything much except good horsemanship and heavy drinking. He was taller than his brother, the right height for Beryl. A cheerful chap with a whinnying laugh, he clearly found such an outdoor girl as her a refreshing change from the settler blondes he was otherwise bonking.

Clutt had been summoned by Mansfield from Peru to look after Beryl's horses during her adventure into maternity. She went to have her child in London. Gervase was born on on 25 February 1928. While her sickly son remained in medical care for months, Beryl was soon out carrying on with Prince Henry, who installed her in a suite in the Grosvenor Hotel, near Buckingham Palace. Since she was openly his mistress, many thought that her child must be his. The dates didn't justify this, but after Markham discovered Prince Henry's love letters and threated to cite the Duke as co-respondent in a divorce suit, Queen Mary stepped in to settle things. Beryl was given a capital sum of £15,000 from Henry's funds, enough to provide an annuity of £500 for life. Gervase was entrusted to his grandmother and Beryl hardly ever saw him again.

Back in Kenya, Denys was breaking up with Baroness Blixen and in 1931 Beryl had him to herself for several weeks. This did not alter the pattern whereby all her relationships with men which were more than casual were hard-headedly instrumental. Beryl had decided to learn to fly, and Denys had acquired a Gypsy Moth biplane. On 14 May Finch Hatton crashed his plane near Voi and that was the end of him. Beryl now took up with Tom Campbell Black, Managing Director of Wilson Airways, and her very able flying instructor. He fell out with Mrs Wilson and took a job in England. Beryl, just qualified, flew there solo in the spring of 1932, and startled even the world press by getting there in just seven days. Her affair with Black proved to be finito, but back in the suite the Duke paid for at the Grosvenor, she dallied with her Gloucester again. Then, in Kenya, she worked very hard at her flying, till in September 1933 she got her 'B' Licence which qualified her to take on commercial work. A nauseatingly unpleasant settler peer, Lord Carberry, dared her to fly the Atlantic from Britain against the wind.

She mulled this over while operating as a commercial pilot out of Nairobi – delivering medical supplies to doctors, carrying patients, providing an air taxi service, and acting as a relief mail pilot for East African Airways. The faithful Ruta now helped her with planes rather than horses. She offered hunters on safari an elephant-spotting service from the air, a new way of stacking the odds against big game which Tom Black had devised for the Prince of Wales (Cameron, 85–86).

In 1935, she prepared to act on Carberry's challenge. This was an era when daring solo pilots were celebrities. Transatlantic crossing by air, 'the Waterjump', had become an international fad. A duo, Alcock and Brown, had first done it in 1919. Charles Lindbergh's solo flight from America to France in 1927 had made him a hero. Amelia Earhart next year had become the first woman to achieve this west–east crossing. Jim Mollison, in 1932, had been the first to pull off the more difficult east–west flight, starting in Ireland and landing in New Brunswick. Out of dozens of would-be transatlantic aviators, fifteen had been women, of whom five had vanished without trace. No woman had crossed the ocean east–west.

Her Royal Duke was now married and out of bounds. Beryl got employment ferrying a rich Frenchman about while work proceeded on the Percival Vega Gull which Carbery was lending her. *The Messenger* was specially adapted to carry extra fuel, giving it a range of 3,800 miles at a speed of 150 mph. Beryl first sat at its controls in August 1936. Newspapers were curious. The *Express* sponsored Beryl. Its front page blazoned her rejection of the SOCIETY WOMAN label pinned on her. 'The phrase "Society" is repugnant to me . . . I may be "just another blonde"; but as a professional pilot accustomed to working for my living, and as this flight could not even in my wildest dreams be described as pleasure, I look on it as another job of work' (Lovell, 287–88).

Mollison, now her friend, and Tom Black tried to dissuade her from flying as unfavourable weather conditions set in. After several days of frustration, clad in a white flying suit, with no radio and no life-jacket, five flasks of coffee, a hip-flask of brandy, and iron rations, muttering in Swahili *Twende tu* – 'I am going' – she ignored all advice and flew out of Abingdon airfield near Oxford into powerful headwinds, 'an icy gale'. With her fuel apparently running out, barely 300 feet from the edge of the Atlantic, she landed in a bog near Louisburg, Cape Breton Island. Despite a badly gashed forehead she trudged three miles through fog and mire till she met two fishermen. A lucky local journalist scooped the world. Her flight, of twenty-one hours and twenty-five minutes, was acclaimed as greater than Lindbergh's, because of the headwind. She hadn't made New York, her intended destination, but then, neither had Mollison.

Mayor La Guardia of New York invited her to go there anyway. Her welcome, official and unofficial, was starry. The media couldn't leave her alone. On the liner back to Britain, Jack Cohen, vice-president of Columbia Pictures, signed her up to appear in a movie about her flight.

And the rest of her long life would seem pure anticlimax had she not produced, some years later, a book. When she abandoned Mollison for a heavyweight boxer named Jack Doyle, this was hardly a step up. She went to Hollywood, but failed her screen test. She took up with a journalist and scriptwriter, Raoul Schumacher, who was five years her junior. Together they worked on her memoirs, which Hemingway, who had met her in Kenya, acclaimed as a masterpiece, believing her to be the book's sole author. It seems, however, that the prose, flowery and literary at times, otherwise vivid and jocular, must be Raoul's. The book entered a niche market dominated by the French writer Saint-Exupéry, a poet-pilot who between the wars had purveyed, for international admiration, the mystique of the lone flier above the clouds. It also followed on the success of Blixen's *Out of Africa*. It expressed devotion to old Clutt, Beryl's father, was warm about the legendary hunters Finch Hatton and Baron Blix, and dealt intriguingly with her relations with Kipsigis, whom she now called 'Nandi', since that warlike people were more famous for being picturesque. She did not mention her two husbands, let alone Schumacher, whom she married in 1942 after the book was published as *West with the Night*. It was a bestseller in the USA.

The new marriage didn't work. In California, Raoul drank heavily while Beryl promiscuated. Her most notable conquest was the folk-singer Burl Ives. She returned to Kenya in 1950 in poor health. A difficult menopause made her atrociously bad-tempered. But after a hysterectomy, she found a Danish farm manager, Jorgen Thrane, still in his twenties, who helped her run a property she bought, and resumed her first career as horse trainer, with great success. The war correspondent Martha Gellhorn, former wife of Hemingway, met her, in her sixties, at her base by Lake Naivasha, and 'took her to be a striking woman of forty', dressed as she was in the latest European casual fashion, acquired on credit from a boutique in Nairobi (Gellhorn, viii–ix).

But in the 1980s, with her licence to train revoked, she was subsiding into alcoholic decrepitude – then *West with the Night* was reprinted to fresh acclaim. Flying had lost its mystique in the postwar years, when so many people began to travel by air, but Kenya retained some, signalled by Hollywood's filming of Blixen's *Out of Africa*, and now the women's movement was rediscovering writers. Documentary film-makers tracked Beryl down in a bungalow on the Nairobi racecourse. Due to vodka, little footage of her could be used. But in four years, *West with the Night* sold 140,000 more copies. Battered by accidents, stricken by thrombosis, but still bearing pain stoically, Beryl went cursing and swearing, far from gently, into her good night.

Theo Aaronson, The Royal Family at War, *1993; Karen Blixen*, Out of Africa *and* Shadows on the Grass, *(New York) 1985; Kenneth M. Cameron*, Into Africa: The Story of the East African Safari, *1990;* DNB *1986–90; James Fox*, White Mischief, *(Harmondsworth) 1984 edn; Martha Gellhorn, 'Introduction' to Markham*, West with the Night, *1984 Virago edn; Mary S. Lovell*, Straight on Till Morning: The Life of Beryl Markham, *(Leicester) 1988 edn; Beryl Markham*, West with the Night, *1988 edn; Errol Trzebinski*, The Lives of Beryl Markham, *1993*

Masiin (Inuit) *d.*1958

Masiin was the last recognised shaman of Tikigaq, pronounced *Ti*-keh-ruk, called by Caucasians 'Point Hope', a village on the northwest coast of Alaska which is across the Chukchi Sea and the Bering Strait from Siberia. It seems that Masiin may finally have disposed of the evil Georgian dictator of the Soviet Union, Joseph Vissarionovich Djugashvili, a.k.a. Stalin.

Tikigaq was settled more than 2,000 years ago. Around 1800, before contact with whites, it had a population of about 1,300. A century later, after European demand for whalebone corsets had lured white sailors north, barely a hundred lived there. Russians colonised Alaska for decades, but in 1867, the huge, sparsely populated peninsula was sold to the USA for $7,200,000. During the twentieth century, 'Point Hope' people ceased to be monolingual Inuit of the Inupiaq group, clad in skins and eating raw meat, and became US citizens, combining traditional lifeways with those of modern mainstream America.

A hundred and thirty miles above the Arctic Circle, Tikigaq, on the tip of a peninsula surrounded on three sides by sea, enjoys mild summer temperatures between forty and sixty degrees Fahrenheit. Even butterflies appear. The winter average is minus thirty degrees, made more extreme by ferocious winds. In the dark days of winter, men hunt seal. But the centre of Tikigaq culture is the great whale hunt, which begins in April, when the ice splits to open a channel for bowheads to pass through to their summer feeding grounds.

Before Europeans arrived amongst them, Tikigaq people lived in semi-subterranean houses partly made of whalebone, eating the whale's flesh, blubber and skin. People believed that the Point itself, the land they trod, had once been a huge whale-like being. While men hunted the bowheads, their wives, who still co-own family skinboats, conducted ceremonials. 'The female *umialik*'s visit to the butchering site to give the whale a drink from her ritual waterpot, or *quattaq*, was one of the high points in the ceremonial year.' The soul of the whale was placated.

She pours water in the whale's mouth.
She pours water in the blowhole . . .
She talks to the whale's soul.

'You died at sea!
Your soul must be thirsty!
Thank you for joining us!
Here is water!'

(Lowenstein, *Ancient Land*, 170)

The whale's head was rolled back into the sea, to return to its own 'country' and tell the other bowheads how kind the hunters had been.

All creatures of that terrain had souls. Providing they were given due honour, animals would gladly lend people their meat and skins. After the whalehunt, people dispersed through the bird-flocked, insect-thronged summer. Some fished with nets extended from the shore for trout and salmon. Others hunted caribou and marmots for their meat and skins. Some went to barter sea-mammal goods with inland people for the meat of black bears and the furs of muskrat, wolverine and fox. To the south, at Sisualik, there was a great fair where North-Western Alaskan communities converged, sometimes joined by visitors from Siberia across the water. Beside trading and gossip, there were athletic contests. Spouses were swapped. And shamanistic seances were held.

The spirit of the moon presided over all beings. 'Originally a Tikigaq man and his sister's lover, the moon spirit was keeper of the game and the object of umialik women's supplication.' Women talked to the moon. But the true shamans – including a female minority – went further. While all Tikigaq people owned at least one animal amulet, shamans could assume the shapes of their animal protectors. Shamans had actually *entered* the spirit world. 'Initiation took many forms. Some apprenticed themselves to older anatkuqs, who put them through ascetic ordeals where they waited for spirits to appear with songs and arcane instructions. Other candidates were dismembered and eaten by animal spirits or abducted by tuungaqs and held prisoner until they had absorbed the power to return to themselves whole. Some anatkuqs, waylaid by a talking caribou or seal, caught a glimpse of its inua (the animal's part-human spirit, visible as a human face beneath the skin) or learned to speak animal languages' (Lowenstein, *Things*, xxxiv).

Since narcotics and alcohol were unknown, it was the two-beat rhythm of the drum, repetitive songs, and exhausting dances which sent shamans into trance. Then they could fly to non-human worlds, to the moon, to the seabed, and bargain for animals or for human souls held captive by the spirits. Successful shamans were handsomely paid for their services. But as Christianity ate into the Tikigaq belief-system, people came to think of the shamans as frightening persons, like witches.

Tom Lowenstein, whose books I have been quoting, visited Tikigaq numerous times, from the early 1970s, and lived there for long periods. During the winter and spring of 1976, he recorded stories of old days. The last tales in his collection bring the sequence to the death, in 1931, in a clinic in the town of Kotzebue to the south, of the shaman Pisiktagaaq, who renounced his shamanic powers after converting to Christianity. A young friend, Aviq, then with him, recalled how on his deathbed the shaman repented. '. . . He starts to cry. And while he's crying, he tells us: All over! Barrow, Wainwright, Point Hope, all through the Kobuk River, Diomede, Nome and other villages! Through my power I killed them! *I . . . killed* lots of people through my power. And he cried and cried. "I confess. After you baptize me I will vomit up my power. You will see it."' He asked who Aviq's parents had been. '. . . And he started to cry more: cri-i-i-ed *loud*. "Yes, I tried to kill your mother once – two times. Your mother's legs swelled all over, I made your mother's legs swell and go rotten. I did this through my power."' And Aviq remembered how a woman friend had cured his mother's swollen legs . . . After confessing, Pisiktagaaq began to vomit. Aviq called for paper for him to vomit on. He vomited a two-inch long stone arrowhead. He said, 'It was used for killing people everywhere, in all the villages. Be sure you burn it.' At last, thanking the Christian God, he died smiling. As Tom points out, palming the arrowhead into his vomit was a last 'grisly act of conjuring' (Lowenstein, *Things*, 188–94).

But Masiin, who kept on being a shaman, retained great respect in Tikigaq. Alec Millik told Tom a story about him:

> It was 1953, wintertime. My wife invited Masiin to supper. And after we had eaten, the old man told stories. Then he called me by name and told us he'd been traveling last night. He'd been to Russia. And when he'd flown round for a while, he saw the Russian boss. 'That's a bad man,' said Masiin, 'so I killed him.' Next day, at three o'clock – we had a battery radio – I listened at my coffee break. The news announcer said Stalin was dead.
>
> (Lowenstein, *Things*, 196–97)

Masiin did not listen to American radio. Till the day he died, he knew no English.

Tom Lowenstein, Ancient Land: Sacred Whale – The Inuit Hunt and its Rituals, *1993; Tom Lowenstein,* The Things That Were Said of Them: Shaman Stories and Oral Histories of the Tikigaq People, Told by Asatchag, *(Berkeley) 1992; thanks to Tom Lowenstein*

Alice Duer Miller (USA) 1874–1942

Alice Maude Duer was born in New York into the moneyed elite of WASP North-Eastern USA. Her forebears, English and Scots, had taken part in the Revolution of 1776, but they maintained their links with Britain and orientated themselves towards Europe. Her father was a banker. A blip in the 1890s saw his bank fail. Alice responded by getting some education. At Barnard College, attached to Columbia University, she specialised in maths and astronomy, and graduated BA in 1899. In the same year she married Henry Wise Miller, after a courtship of only three days. Their devoted marriage would produce one son.

While Henry Miller was looking for sites for rubber plantations in Costa Rica, Alice began writing for magazines. When they got back to New York broke in 1903, she taught in a girls school, and maths at Barnard. But Henry was on his way to wealth as a stock trader, and from 1907 Alice wrote full time. Rather unfairly, not needing the money, she made it. Her stories and serialised novels appeared in such esteemed journals as *Colliers*, *Saturday Evening Post* and *New Republic*. Some were adapted for staging on Broadway. *Gowns for Roberta* (1931) became a musical. Though the score was by Jerome Kern, it ran for nearly 300 performances on the strength of one song only – 'Smoke Gets in your Eyes'. The film (*Roberta*, 1935) was equally undistinguished except for an early appearance by Fred Astaire. Other stories were filmed, and Alice herself, inevitably, did stints in Hollywood, as a film editor (for D. W. Griffith), scriptwriter, and even, in one very bad movie, as bit-part actor. But, true to the traditions of her class, she crossed the Atlantic in the summer, living at different times in Scotland, in London and on the French Riviera.

She kept up her family's radical tradition too. She wrote for *The Masses*, edited by Max Eastman, who would be internationally famous as the translator of Trotsky's *History of the Russian Revolution*. She was a trenchantly witty writer in the cause of Women's Suffrage, contributing a column 'Are Women People?' to the *New York Tribune*, reprinted in book form in 1915. She enjoyed demonstrating the absurdity of typical attitudes of males opposed to suffrage, as in:

Why We Oppose Votes for Men

1. BECAUSE man's place is in the armory.
2. Because no really manly man wants to settle any question otherwise than by fighting about it.
3. Because if men should adopt peaceable methods, women would no longer look up to them.
4. Because men will lose their charm if they step out of their natural sphere and interest themselves in other matters than feats of arms, uniforms and drums.
5. Because men are too emotional to vote. Their conduct at baseball games and political conventions shows this, while their innate tendency to appeal to force renders them peculiarly unfit for the task of government.

Her wit qualified her well to assume a place at the notoriously malicious Algonquin Round Table founded in 1919 at the hotel of that name by friends, acquaintances and rivals of the theatre critic Alexander

Woolcott. Here, though much older than most, she would foregather with the likes of the now-underrated comic writer Robert Benchley, Dorothy Parker, mistress of the one-liner, the writers Sherwood Anderson and Ring Lardner, and Harpo Marx, who was dragged into the group after Woolcott, smitten with the Marx Brothers' first show on Broadway in 1924, had barged into his dressing room and told him he was a true artist. Harpo alleged much later that he was the only 'full-time listener' in the group, but he took to Alice, though, as she 'was the most dignified and cultivated lady I had ever met. I thought it would be impossible for me ever to get to know her.' One day he discovered that she shared his interest in baseball. '. . . I found out that the greatest single passion in Alice Miller's life was not writing or literature but the New York Giants . . . From that moment on, we were very special friends. We shared the faith, a bond that could only exist between Giant fans' (Marx, 166–71, 175–76).

Another odd person out in the Round Table group was Harold Ross (1892–1951), a non-intellectual and not obviously witty immigrant's son from Colorado, a gawky man with coarse features and a strange tall pompadour haircut, who had met Woolcott in France during WWI, as a contributor to *Stars and Stripes*, the GI's weekly which Ross had edited. Ross wanted to set up his own magazine. He saw that New York, with nine million people, the centre of US theatre and US publishing, could support a magazine of its own, in which the city's rich shops and restaurants could advertise. Though Ross cared a great deal about grammar and correct usage, and had an instinct for picking writers and draughtsmen in tune with his own droll, quiet sense of humour, he read little except dictionaries and true-crime magazines. Highbrow literature, music and fine art meant nothing to him. He proposed a magazine which would offer humour, cartoons, and gossip for a sophisticated readership. His idea was good. But he needed a backer. Here Alice and her husband were both invaluable.

Henry Wise Miller loved gambling for high stakes. So did those of the Woolcott circle who played poker at the Algonquin or in Ross's home – a combination of commune and salon at 412 West 47th Street – calling themselves the 'Thanatopsis Club'. (The Greek word meant 'contemplation of death'.) The other businessman frequenting these games was Raoul Fleischmann, who was bored with the baking concern from which his family had made its millions. He got on with 'Harry' Miller and admired Alice as a representative of the obsolescent but prestigious old upper class of New York – 'the 400' (Yagoda, 27). Ross told Fleischmann about his pet scheme, asked for his backing, and offered as bait a list of distinguished persons on his alleged 'Advisory Board' – 'at best a fanciful one, at worst plain dishonest' (Kunkel, 92). Alice was on the list. Fleischmann fell for it, and in 1925 the *New Yorker* was born. Instantly successful, it would become, way beyond Ross's initial plans, not only a vehicle for brilliant humour and drawings, but a benchmark of fine writing in fiction and reportage and an arbiter of serious taste and liberal conscience. After his magazine's birth, Ross himself drew away from the drunken fooleries of the Algonquin circle. But Alice Duer Miller did do some 'advising', pushing valuable new writers in Ross's direction.

Her own moment of history came in 1941. Among all her many novels and stories, her collections of poetry, her scripts, the greatest success was a story in verse, *The White Cliffs*. Alice wrote sturdy poetry in a style which would not have seemed in the least old-fashioned in her youth – it was metrically deft, easily rhymed and clear of cliché – though highbrow younger readers in 1941, accustomed to the modernist innovations of Eliot and Auden, must have found her fustily aunt-like. In *The White Cliffs*, using a very wide range of metres, she tells in the first person the story of Susan Dunne, a North-Eastern US citizen like herself, who marries into an upper-class English family in 1914, is widowed by the war, and confronts in 1939 the prospect of her only son serving and dying like his father. Domiciled in Devon, county of 'crumpets and marmalade, toast and cake', but once home to Drake and his seadogs, she expresses the belief that while the British are a strange people with snobbish ways, their cause – freedom – is inherited from Hampden, Cromwell and the founders of Massachusetts, and Americans should support them. Published at a time when Franklin D. Roosevelt was attempting to rally US opinion behind entering the war against Hitler on Britain's side, it was astonishingly successful. Her son, introducing her posthumous *Selected Poems* in 1949, claimed that it had sold half a million copies in the United States alone, and nearly as many in Britain and the Commonwealth. It was possibly the best-selling book of verse in English of all time. Alice read it aloud in many places in the US and Canada, it moved many to tears, it was broadcast on radio, recorded on disc and made the basis of a Hollywood movie, which came out in 1944, after Miller had died, showing great courage through her long last illness.

Her poem picked up themes of Britain's 'People's War' and wrote itself instantly into myth, along with reports by famous US journalists of dogfights over Dover during the 'Battle of Britain' and the ever-popular wartime song which promised 'There'll be seagulls over/ The White Cliffs of Dover/ Tomorrow, just you wait and see'. Miller composed her sequence not as a hired propagandist, but wholly unprompted, out of her own sincere feelings about the values of the American Revolution, the attractive and repulsive aspects of aristocratic British culture, and the need to defy Hitler. It can be read as a last testament of the best WASP values, now overidden by the materialist excesses of the USA during Prohibition, which so repel Susan Dunne on a trip home that

> . . . it seemed like heaven
> To get back, dull and secure, to Devon.

American National Biography, *vol. 15, (New York) 1999; Thomas Kunkel,* Genius in Disguise: Harold Ross of the New Yorker, *(New York) 1990; Harpo Marx with Rowland Barber,* Harpo Speaks, *1978; Alice Duer Miller,* Selected Poems, *1949; Alice Duer Miller,* The White Cliffs, 1941; *Ben Yagoda,* About Town: The New Yorker and the World It Made, *2000; thanks to Helena Nelson, for much material*

Lee Miller (USA) 1907–77

Lee Miller was born Elizabeth in Poughkeepsie, New York State, where her father Theodore was an engineer and top man at the Delaval Separator Company. Her Canadian mother, Florence, had been a nurse. Her elder brother John would become an aviation pioneer, her younger Erik would be chief photographer of the Lockheed Corporation. Elizabeth shared their interest in practical things. Encouraged by Theodore they built a cable car and a railway and catapults which fired snowballs hundreds of feet. Tomboy Elizabeth was expelled from three schools.

But an interior Elizabeth was in formation. On a visit to family friends aged seven she was raped and infected with gonorrhoea, for which she received treatment for two years. Her father, a passionate amateur photographer, took his first nude shot of her in 1915 and thereafter filled album after album with pictures of her. He experimented with stereoscopic techniques, and Lee found in the camera a meeting ground of science and art. She became interested in acting and dancing – but also in stage lighting, costume and design. She was destined to be artists' prey and a predator herself, also the director of her own performances.

Walking in New York early in 1927, now renamed by herself Lee, she was snatched from the path of an oncoming car by Condé Nast, who published the magazines *Vogue* and *Vanity Fair*. He saw her at once as the icon of her era – bobbed hair, boyish appearance, the 'free' woman. She was tall, strong-looking, with soft blonde hair and blue eyes. Her enthralling smile revealed a gap in her front teeth. She soon appeared on the front cover of *Vogue* and modelled for famous photographers whom she persuaded to give her tips on their art. The great Edward Steichen encouraged her and provided her with an introduction to Man Ray.

Ray was the persona created by Emmanuel Radnitsky, the Brooklyn-born son of a Jewish immigrant tailor. He lived in Paris as an artist and photographer at the centre of the Surrealist movement. Lee sought him out and immediately became both his pupil and his lover. Long dedicated to promiscuity, she didn't see why the Surrealists' free-love principles should apply only to men, and he became furiously jealous of her. He visually dismembered her iconic body. In a famous photograph he sheared her head off. Jean Cocteau went further when she starred in his movie, *Le Sang d'un poète*, where she was converted into an armless statue to be destroyed by a mad poet wielding a sledgehammer.

Miller fought back against the control-freakery of the Surrealists. While she was Man Ray's chief inspiration and model, she was also his partner in technical innovation. Together, by accident, they discovered and developed 'solarisation', a process in development which created halo effects around bodies, a notable breakthrough in Surrealism. Back in New York in 1932, Lee set up her own studio, specialising very successfully in portraits and advertising. Then she turned her back on the world of *Vogue* to marry Aziz Eloui Bey, a rich and highly cultivated Egyptian businessman. Travelling out from Cairo, she explored new subject matter for her camera, the landscape and people of Egypt. After three years with Aziz, her restlessness took her back to Paris, where, at a party, an English Surrealist, Roland Penrose, fell in love with her at first sight. Their relationship would endure, unevenly, for four decades.

Penrose (1900–84) came from a wealthy Quaker family. His father was a conventional portrait painter. At Cambridge, active in what was then an all-male student theatre, he had had a homosexual love affair with George ('Dadie') Rylands, a handsome Etonian who later became a revered authority on Shakespeare. But this was the prelude, as it turned out, to a life marked by many heterosexual affairs and random promiscuity. His first wife, Valentine Boué, was a highly strung poet with a strangely beautiful face who came to him with two drawbacks, a horrible temper and a vagina so tiny that penetration was impossible. In the strange world of the Surrealists, the men dressed in respectable suits but projected in various arts bizarre, often cruel, images derived, they said, from the subconscious. Penrose became a lifelong friend of Picasso, on the fringe of the movement, and of the poet Paul Eluard and the painter Max Ernst who were at its centre. He himself was an interesting rather than great painter – to say that he was the best of the British Surrealists is rather like applauding the finest Congolese skier – but he was charming and had lots of money, with which he acquired many works by his friends. When he met Lee in 1937, he had just returned to France from helping to mount a notorious Surrealist Exhibition at the New Burlington Galleries in London, where the painter Dali nearly suffocated attempting to give a lecture in a deepsea diver's costume.

Lee was penetrated by Penrose. In June, 1939, she left Aziz (on friendly terms) and sailed to England to join Roland.

The Second World War saw the apotheosis and collapse of Surrealism. In ruined cities and transformed mundanity it threw up images for the camera more disturbing, perverse and bizarre than Surrealists had imagined. Lee photographed the London Blitz, then, encouraged by a *Life* photographer, David E. Scherman, who came to share her favours with Penrose, she won accreditation as a US Forces War Correspondent. After travelling with Scherman in Britain, she went into Europe as a photojournalist after D-Day, and besides time in liberated Paris and Brussels, she witnessed dramas and horrors, reporting for *Vogue*, which made her a 'war heroine' in her own right. After Dachau concentration camp was overrun, just before the German surrender, she photographed inmates who died as she stood there and SS soldiers beaten to death by their captives. A train stood on the edge of the camp. It had left Auschwitz a month earlier. Lee recorded the moment when GIs opened the door of a truck and rotting corpses slumped out. She went on to photograph the horrific aftermath of war in famine-stricken Central Europe.

Traumatised, then marooned back in numbed but complacent England, Miller soon, one might say, lost touch with Lee. Amidst fashion and society assignments, she found she was pregnant by Penrose. Abortions had coped with the like before, but they decided to see this one through and got married in May 1947. Lee hated pregnancy and childbirth and didn't get on with the child, Antony, born in September. Roland was at the centre of what might be called the Modernist Establishment, a key figure in the founding of the Institute of Contemporary Arts in London, but now old-fashioned as an artist himself compared to the fizzing young founders of Pop Art, Richard Hamilton and Eduardo Paolozzi. Acquisition of a handsome country estate in Sussex was fine for him, not so good for Lee. She retreated for some fifteen years into an alcoholic miasma, from which an interest in cooking eventually rescued her. She wrote for *Vogue* again as, forsooth, a gourmet chef. She became Lady Penrose when Roland, against all Quaker, let alone avant-gardiste, principles, accepted a knighthood in 1966. The interwar icon and the frontline war correspondent were forgotten, along with the avant-garde camerawoman. The Surrealists expired one by one in an atmosphere of sentimental reconciliation. Man Ray, who had befriended the Penroses' son, died in 1976 and so did Max Ernst. Lee succumbed to cancer of the pancreas in 1977. Roland found a new partner and hung on till 1984. At last, around the turn of the century/millennium, Lee was retrieved from under the wreckage of country-house England and acclaimed again as a great photographer.

Antony Penrose, The Lives of Lee Miller, *1985; Antony Penrose*, Roland Penrose: The Friendly Surrealist, *(Edinburgh) 2001; Scottish National Gallery of Modern Art*, Roland Penrose and Lee Miller: The Surrealist and the Photographer, *(Edinburgh) 2001*

Esther Hobart Morris (USA) 1814–1902

In our childhoods 'Wyoming' summoned up the liveliest images of the Wild West – wide-ranging cowboys, chin-stubbled gold-diggers. Alas, we were somewhat deluded. The very name was given to an exact rectangle of nearly 100,000 square miles because Representative James M. Ashley of Ohio, chairman of the House Committee on Territories, had grown up in the Wyoming Valley in Pennsylvania (Roberts, 564). Wyoming developed as a great arena of sheep, not cattle ranching, and while there was gold, coal was its outstanding mineral. As the railroad drove west, it created towns in Wyoming and it went on its way burning Wyoming coal.

Fur traders built Fort Laramie in 1834. The US Army bought it in 1849. It became a railroad depot town in the late 1860s, but when 'Wyoming' was chopped away from Dakota in 1868 as a distinct territory, another such town, Cheyenne, became the capital. Here, on 10 December 1869, Governor John A. Campbell signed into law the first suffrage bill anywhere which gave women equal rights to men.

Women had voted before this in North America. Occasional instances had occurred in colonial days, where women, normally widows, had requisite property qualifications. The anomaly became more widespread, after the Revolution, in New Jersey, where the state constititution was amended in 1807 specifically to quench it.

Canada was a more quirky territory. The USA and its States had written constitutions. Britain, famously, did not. British law down the centuries had never expressly ruled out women voting. It was merely understood that it didn't happen. Framing a constitutional act for Canada in 1791, British legislators clearly took it for granted that the same attitude would prevail in British North America. It didn't. Female property owners in Lower Canada (Quebec) frequently resorted to the polls. Of the other provinces, only New Brunswick specifically debarred women from voting. A Reformer rode into Annapolis, Nova Scotia, during an election in 1840 to find the Tories there 'Getting all the old women and old maids and everything in the shape of petticoats to be carried up to the hustings the next and last day to vote'. He rode all night alerting nearby farmers, and 'they harnessed up their horses . . . and each one 10 of the clock, was back with a widow or a fair young fatherless maid, to vote against the Tory women from Annapolis Royal . . . I believe they numbered twenty-six and our party nearly forty' (Garner, 156). The drive to stop women voting, ironically, came from the left. The Great Reform Act passed at Westminster in 1832 specifically reserved to men the new franchises which it created. When the Province of Canada finally barred women in 1849, liberal reformers were inspired by anger over a particular election in which women voters had secured the return of a Tory. The reaction against women's suffrage which by then had set in all over British North America was such that political emancipation was conceded there only long after most US States had granted it.

Why Wyoming? Amongst fewer than 10,000 recorded inhabitants of Wyoming in 1869 were John Morris, formerly a merchant, originally from Poland, and his wife Esther, *née* McQuigg in New York State. Orphaned when still a girl, Esther had started a millinery shop and done pretty well. In 1841 she had married Artemus Slack, a civil engineer with the Erie and Illinois Central railroads. When he died in 1845, she moved with their young son to Illinois, to claim land which he had owned. To her outrage, Esther found that Illinois did not recognise the right of women to own or inherit property . . .

Nevertheless, she lived there for more than twenty years, after marrying Morris. In 1867, gold was found on the Sweetwater River. To Wyoming, as the great 1911 edition of *Encyclopaedia Britannica* would put it, 'The first great invasion of population following the discovery of gold and the opening of the railway brought many desperate characters, who were held in check only by the stern, swift measures of frontier justice.' A touch of 'gold fever' lured the Morrises to South Pass City. Six feet tall and 180 lbs, Esther, arriving in 1869, was at once an outstanding figure in the frontier community. The miners liked her direct way of speaking. She nursed the sick. People listened when she sounded off about votes for women. Elections came up in September. The story goes that Esther invited both candidates from South Pass City – Herman G. Nickerson and William Bright the saloonkeeper – to a tea party in her cabin where they were confronted by a large number of women. Both pledged support for an act giving women the vote. Bright won, and duly introduced a bill conferring full equality, passed into law by the end of the year.

It wasn't as pure and simple as that. Bright was from the South, and seems to have felt that white women such as his dearly beloved wife deserved the vote as much as black men did. Edward M. Lee, the Secretary of the Territory, favoured women's suffrage, and drafted Bright's bill for him. But Esther's statue stands in front of Wyoming's State Capitol.

She became the first woman in the USA to hold judicial office, in 1870, when she sat as Justice of the Peace over seventy cases, and not one of her judgements was appealed or overruled by a higher court. But Morris was a drunk. In 1871 she left him to live in Laramie with her son, a newspaper publisher. Till her death, she was an activist attending suffrage conventions. She was hardly an ultra-radical, supporting as she did the idea of 'separate spheres' for women and men, but she must take some credit for the fact that Wyoming achieved full statehood in 1890 with equality for women still in its constitution. In 1924, Nellie Taylor Ross, in Wyoming, became the first woman Governor of any state.

American National Biography, *(New York) 1999;* Encyclopaedia Britannica, *11th edn, (Cambridge) 1911; John Garner,* The Franchise and Politics in British North America 1755–1867, *(Toronto) 1969; Charles A. Kromkowski, 'Woman's Suffrage' and Philip J. Roberts, 'Wyoming', in Stanley I. Kutler (ed.),* Dictionary of American History, *vol. 8, 3rd edn (New York) 2003; thanks to Rhodri Jeffreys Jones*

Tricky Sam Nanton (USA) 1904–46

By common consent 'Ko Ko' is one of the finest pieces composed by Duke Ellington for, and with, his Orchestra at what many will insist was its greatest peak. When it was recorded in Chicago on 6 March 1940, Ellington had acquired a few months back, on string bass, the supernaturally swinging and fleet Jimmy Blanton, who would die of TB just over two years later, aged only twenty-three. He drives this track as he did numerous others. Cootie Williams was still lead trumpet (didn't leave to join Goodman's band till later that year), and Rex Stewart, playing cornet his own way, cut his personal showcase, 'Morning Glory' in the same session. Ben Webster's strong tenor had just joined in the sax section the classically blue alto of Johnny Hodges and Harry Carney's definitive baritone. But 'Ko Ko' is dominated by Duke's wholly exceptional trombone section.

'Ko Ko', though confined in length to the bare three minutes available on one side of a shellac disc, is a work which catches one differently on every hearing, a harmonically and structurally complex piece, marked by extreme dissonances, of the kind which had led Stravinsky, Milhaud and Percy Grainger, major composers in the 'classical' tradition, to acclaim

Duke as a master of their craft. It can seem boisterous and feisty, very danceable. A friend to whom I played it just now said it made her think of machinery, which would link it, for instance, to 'Pacific 231', a tone poem celebrating railway travel produced in 1923 by the Swiss composer Arthur Honegger . . . (Duke greatly loved the rhythm of the railway himself.) The jazz historian James Lincoln Collier writes of the 'intense, almost satanic drive' of 'Ko Ko' (Collier, 225–27).

But my own response to 'Ko Ko' is always dominated by whatever it is I hear now in the two choruses by Tricky Sam Nanton which form the only solo in the piece. When I first encountered it in my teens, I couldn't believe that there wasn't a human voice producing a bellow, a wail, a keening, a shout. Now that I've known perfectly well for decades that the 'voice' comes from Tricky Sam's trombone, I still find it wholly human. But what is that human voice crying out? Is it lamentation or triumph, despair or defiance? For years I thought of it as the sound of a representative black man shouting over vast flat acres in the Mississippi delta. But Nanton came from Trinidad, not New Orleans.

'Ko Ko' provides a classic, brief example of the brass style developed by the Ellington band which is variously referred to as 'wa-wa', 'growl' or 'jungle'. When Duke got the job of providing the music nightly at Harlem's famous Cotton Club, towards the end of 1927, with a nightly coast-to-coast broadcast from there thrown in, his men had two remits. They provided music for up to 500 customers (all white) who might want to dance. They accompanied a chorus line of maybe twenty girl dancers, clad in very little but feathers, in a floor show which evoked the primitive sexiness attributed to savage Africa. This was the epoch of the so-called 'Harlem Renaissance', when writers including Langston Hughes, Countee Cullen and Claude McKay were asserting the distinctive validity of black culture. But the Cotton Club pandered to white suppositions that negroes, charming though they might be, were instinctual, hypererotic beings naturally unfit to aspire beyond the social status of entertainers.

Nothing could be further from the truth about Duke's trombonists. Juan Tizol, who joined in 1929, was a white from Puerto Rico, 'like a blob of cream', as Rex Stewart put it, 'in the middle of a bowl of black caviare' (Stewart, *Boy Meets Horn*, 153–54). He was a well-trained musician who couldn't play hot improvised solos but was invaluable as a composer of new tunes, and as someone who could write out Duke's compositional ideas on paper and distribute them to the band as parts. He played valve trombone, which was more nimble than slide, so Duke could blend his mellow noise with the sax section. Lawrence Brown, who joined in 1932 and stayed for nearly two decades despite grumbling incessantly about the degradations of jazz-band existence, was the son of a Kansas church minister, who had studied at first to become a doctor. He did not drink, or smoke, or gamble, and dressed like the high-class undertaker he sometimes said he'd prefer to be. He loved the sound of classical cello above all others and recreated it in creamy solos, though he could also play fast, hot and blue.

Joe Nanton was something else again. Rex Stewart first got to know him as a teenager in the rackety New York club scene of the early twenties, when Nanton quit playing at a club called the Green Parrot 'because he got tired of going to jail every Saturday night'. Stewart first saw him perform at Wilkins' 134th St Club, which 'catered strictly to the underworld', working 'with piano man Fat Smitty and a hell of a drummer, known simply as Crip'. Nanton was 'a gingerbread-coloured man, kind of on the squatty side. His facial contours reminded me of a benevolent basset hound, with those big brown eyes that regarded the world so dolefully, framed in a long face with just a hint of dewlaps.' But he was 'always the life of every party', a great trencherman who could put away three orders of corned-beef hash at a sitting and a dedicated drinker, his board-stiff tux shirt liberally sprinkled after hours with the mixture of gin and port wine which was *de rigueur* for young Harlem musicians. However, his first nickname was 'Professor'.

The exceptional upward social mobility of black West Indian immigrants in the USA has been linked to colonial educational traditions which, however flawed, gave folk in the islands the idea that learning was a good thing. Nanton, who owned hundreds of books according to Stewart, was 'proud of being West Indian'. His people, he reckoned, 'particularly appreciated and took advantage of the opportunities that the North [of the USA] gave them. This brought on a heated discussion, until he quoted statistics (which he documented with printed material) showing how many different businesses the West Indians owned and operated' (Stewart, *Jazz Masters*, 104–11).

When the Ellington band was on tour, he was one member who

wouldn't play cards for stakes or shoot crap – he'd be in the corner of bus or train carriage reading a book. Equally well informed about astronomy, politics and the works of Shakespeare, he was a follower of the Jamaican Marcus Garvey, who was prime prophet of Black Nationalism. Duke remarked drily, regarding this, that 'Bop . . . is the Marcus Garvey extension' – in other words the famous assertion by Parker, Gillespie and others in the 1940s of a kind of black Modernism in music arose from that West Indian's appeal for dignity (E. K. Ellington, 109). It may therefore seem paradoxical that Nanton appeared Anglophile – wearing Brooks Brothers suits and British hand-made shoes and presenting the manner of an English gentleman. Stewart offers a delicious vignette of Tricky in Sweden in 1939. The band had gone to tour Europe, where Hitler was rampant, with trepidation. In Malmo, they were 'rudely awakened by several bursts of machine gun fire. This caused all of us to get up, dress, and go from room to room asking each other, "Is this war? And if so, what do we do?" Joe Nanton, perhaps, was the most unperturbed, as he discoursed at length on the beauty of the porcelain stove in the lobby of the hotel' (Stewart, *Boy Meets Horn*, 188).

With his squeaky, high-pitched voice, sometimes fading to a mere whisper, he was the wit of the Ellington band. His most famous joke was about the Duke himself. Whereas white American *aficionados* typically delighted in the drunken, drug-fuelled, anarchic ambience of jazz music, including Ellington's, from his Cotton Club days onwards Duke attracted the reverential admiration of composers, writers, and intellectuals in general, in Britain and Europe. So a French reporter once asked Tricky if his boss was a genius. '"He's a genius, all right," Sam said, and then he happened to remember that Elllington once ate thirty-two sandwiches during an intermission at a dance in Old Orchard Beach, Maine. "He's a genius, all right," he said, "but Jesus how he eats!"' (Richard O. Boyer in Gammond [1958], 23).

What is this highly intelligent, lovably decent man thinking as he sits at the Cotton Club night after night while dusky lovelies jive and writhe in the floor show, waiting to produce his 'jungle' noises? Presented from this angle, it looks like one of the nastier episodes in the history of popular culture. The Colour Bar was in full force. The big mobsters were not far away (and the kindly offices of Al Capone were at least twice successfully solicited to get Ellington out of dangerous corners into which rival gangsters had pushed him).

Tricky gets into the habit of always carrying a bottle of bourbon in his trombone case, along with an assortment of medicines and mutes. With it tucked into an inside pocket, he sucks on it surreptitiously through a straw as the band plays on.

Yet what he plays is an indispensable ingredient of magnificent music. Till his death in 1974, Duke's bands will always return to Cotton Club classics – 'Black and Tan Fantasy', 'Creole Love Call'. Ellington made 'jungle' a trademark. Critics have written about Tricky producing 'primitive moaning' on his 'vaudeville' trombone, while the trumpeter Freddy Jenkins went in for 'comedy routines'. But stunting is not what we hear on 'Ko Ko'. Over a decade, Duke made growling brass one of the key elements in his mature, distinctive, band-sound and exploited every nuance of which it was capable. Billy 'Sweepea' Strayhorn, Duke's personal assistant as arranger and composer from 1939 till his early death in 1967, famously remarked that 'Ellington plays piano, but his real instrument is his band' (Jewell, 87). After free-for-all brainstorming sessions, he incorporated the musical ideas, and also the personalities, of his sidemen into what became more or less set and finished compositions, so that the great 'Harlem Airshaft' recorded in July 1940 gives us a glimpse of Tricky before Stewart's pawky cornet and the New Orleans Creole clarinet of Barney Bigard take over the evocation of a noisy New York night. Duke knew what he was up to with Tricky, manipulating a toilet plunger at the top of his horn.

Before Nanton joined Duke's then-small band in 1926, Ellington was using a wild character called Charlie 'Plug' Irvis who manipulated in the bell of his trombone a broken example of a kind of mute developed to make a trombone sound like a saxophone. 'Plug' happened to be a drinking buddy of Tricky. Rex Stewart claimed that Nanton also learnt something from one Jake 'Gutbucket' Green of Charleston, South Carolina, otherwise unknown to fame. A well-attested story is that Bubber Miley picked up the growling habit from the legendary King Oliver. Miley more than any other musician defined the Ellington sound in its 'jungle' phase. He could play fine open trumpet, but his speciality was tigerish yet lyrical muted work. Like the still more legendary Bix Beiderbecke, Miley was extremely addicted to strong liquor and died very young, in his case of TB. But he had time to stamp his remarkable imagination on the Ellington repertoire. *En route* with the band from New York to Boston, he spotted on an advertising hoarding the name of a cleaner called Lewando. He began singing 'Oh, lee-wan-do, oh lee-wan-do', and this became the first theme of 'East St Louis Toodle-Oo' (Collier, 111–12).

Miley, it seems, set Tricky's feet firmly on the growl path. Tricky in turn passed Miley's techniques on to Cootie Williams, following Bubber as lead trumpet, who had never heard his predecessor play, and then, in 1940, to Ray Nance, who took over from Cootie. He became the high priest of growl. Duke's son Mercer, who by 1940 was himself composing for the band, claimed eruditely:

> . . . There were three basic elements in the growl: the sound of the horn, a guttural gargling in the throat, and the actual note that is hummed. The mouth has to be shaped to make the different vowel sounds, and above the singing from the throat, manipulation of the plunger adds the *wa-wa* accents that give the horn a language. I should add that in the Ellington tradition a straight mute is used *in* the horn beside the plunger outside, and this results in more pressure. Tricky Sam made such a science of distortion that he would sometimes use a soda bottle when he was playing in the dressing room, thereby changing the fundamental positions of the slide. Musicians like Lawrence Brown and Quentin Jackson did very well, too, when they growled on trombone, but they moved their tuning slide, something that Tricky, Cootie, and Ray Nance never did. Where Tricky was unique was in the way he could make his sound so sheer that someone likened it to tearing paper.
>
> (M. Ellington, 25)

Duke himself fully appreciated how *sophisticated* Tricky's technique was. Cootie Williams and up to a point Ray Nance were able to develop Miley's legacy, and high-squealing Cat Anderson added a new trumpet colour to Duke's palette in the 1950s. But Tricky was irreplaceable. Musicians as gifted as Brown, Jackson and Tyree Glenn could never reproduce for Duke the authentic Tricky sound.

Nanton was utterly loyal to Duke, refusing to work for anyone else, not even on a casual club date or recording session. His going was typically peaceable, though sad. He had been warned by a doctor that his drinking would kill him, but just shrugged his shoulders and carried on regardless. In 1945, aged forty-one, he had a stroke. After a time he rejoined the band, but, on tour, was found dead one day in his hotel room in California, having suffered another haemorrhage while sleeping.

His legacy was recordings in which he progressed from the comic and ironic to the awesome. Richard O. Boyer in a famous *New Yorker* essay on Duke gives Tricky justice, where he describes the band on tour playing in a crowded hall, where dancers are jitterbugging wildly and 'serious thinkers', standing aside, are wittering about the music's profundity. 'Every now and then there is a wail from Tricky Sam's trombone, a sad wa-wa melody which sometimes sounds like an infant crying, sometimes like the bubbly, inane laugh of an idiot, and sometimes like someone calling for help. Sam says, "It's a sad tale with a little mirth. When I play it, I think of a man in a dungeon calling out of a cell-window"' (Boyer in Gammond [1958], 33).

So I play 'Ko Ko' yet again, numerous times. Those pistons, as it were, start driving over Blanton's bass. Tizol plays the same knowing little burble seven times on his valve trombone while the rhythm changes. Ellington, as is his wont, pushes forward a little flick of piano. Then Tricky solos for just over half a minute:

(Big Voice)
Arr ya ya ya – ya-yaa-eah
Ya ya ra ya – ya-ya oleah
Ya ya da ya – ya-ya orleah
(Higher, nasal)
He yee he ye-he – he ye-ye ye-yi
He ye ye, he yo-yo – he yo-yo hi-ye
(Fuller, fading)
yaar a-ya – oyeah

Another time, I might set down the vowels and consonants differently. What this exercise has brought home to me is the extraordinary subtlety of Sam's variations. I cannot fix, never will, what that voice seems to be uttering. Is it, after all, Macbeth's tale told by an idiot? Do we hear a saucy, sardonic man laughing through the bars of his cell window, or Tricky day-dreaming on the train with the band heading west?

Barney Bigard, With Louis and the Duke, *1985; Ian Carr et al.*, Jazz: The Rough Guide, *2000 edn; James Lincoln Collier*, Duke Ellington, *1987; Edward Kennedy Ellington*, Music Is My Mistress, *1974; Mercer Ellington, with Stanley Dance*, Duke Ellington in Person: An Intimate Memoir, *1978; Peter Gammond*, Duke Ellington: His Life and Music, *1958; Peter Gammond*, Duke Ellington, *1987; John Edward Hasse*, Beyond Category: The Life and Genius of Duke Ellington, *(New York) 1993; Derek Jewell*, Duke: A Portrait of Duke Ellington, *1978 edn; Stuart Nicholson*, A Portrait of Duke Ellington: Reminiscing in Tempo, *1999; Rex Stewart*, Boy Meets Horn, *(Ann Arbor, MI) 1991; Rex Stewart*, Jazz Masters of the Thirties, *(New York) 1972*

Merle Oberon ('Tasmania'/India/etc.) 1911–79

Reading about the film star Merle Oberon, one is torn between repulsion and deep sympathy. The first is triggered by the dedication with which, exploiting her acclaimed beauty, she seduced her way up to the title of Lady Korda and later the position of millionaire hostess in Mexico to the likes of the Duke of Edinburgh, Frank Sinatra, John Wayne, the Reagans, etc. Sympathy stems from the fact that her true origins could not be admitted in the racist social ambience of her day. Her nasty primadonna behaviour as a star can be related to strains imposed by literal denial of her self, and constant fear of exposure.

Tasmanians were very proud of her birth on their island. Her studio proclaimed that her father was a Major Thompson, whose death before she was born left her gentle, fair-skinned English mother hard up. So she accepted an invitation from Merle's godmother, Lady Monteith, to visit her in Bombay, where Lord Monteith served the Raj. After the Monteiths left India, Merle's mother invested her savings in a business run by a crook who ran off with her money, so the unfortunate pair moved to Calcutta, where Mrs Thompson had lofty connections and Merle grew up, a dazzling beauty, amongst army officers and government officials . . . Her fourth and last husband, Rob Wolders (a Dutch actor twenty-five years younger than she), was distressed by her unhappy reactions when at his urging she went 'back' to Tasmania a year before she died, to be given a civic reception in Hobart, where a theatre was named after her. He found out later that the local Registrar had established that she had not been born there, and that he was the only person present who had not known that fact.

This was the first time she had been to Tasmania.

Her mother, Charlotte, was from Sri Lanka, a dark little woman part-Irish, part-Singhalese and part-Maori. A tea planter named Harry Selby had been forced to marry her, then seek immediate dissolution, when she was pregnant with his daughter. She named the baby Constance and took her to Bombay. Constance eventually married a short-lived Goanese named Soares. Ailing and embittered, she would plague Merle in her days of fame with requests for money. Charlotte had gone to work as a nurse in Poona, where she met a mechanical engineer named Thompson. Pregnant by him, she got him to marry her, and they went to Bombay. There Estelle Merle O'Brien Thompson was born in 1911. Her father enlisted in the army and died of pneumonia on the Somme. Soon after this Charlotte took Merle to Calcutta, where she grew up in a racy neighbourhood with half a dozen cinemas close at hand. She worked in a telephone company and an apartment store and studied dancing, meanwhile captivating men, including a rich American big-game hunter, Colonel Ben Finney, who recoiled as, escorting her gallantly home, he deduced, when a dusky woman opened the door, that this was her mother. To let her off lightly, he promised her that if she could visit him on the Côte d'Azur next spring, he would introduce her to a friend who was a prominent film director . . .

Unbeknownst to Finney, there was rich sugar daddy on hand, probably the distinguished Sephardic Jew Sir Victor Sassoon. He paid for Merle and her mother to sail to Europe, in the summer of 1929. Charlotte went on from Marseilles to London. Finney had moved on, but Merle met his impressive acquaintance Rex Ingram (a friend of Bernard Shaw and the opera singer Mary Garden), had her budding taste for *grande luxe* confirmed, and got a small role in a movie which Ingram was shooting in Nice. Then she followed her mother to London, worked as a dance-hall hostess, attracted the manager of the famous Café de Paris, the city's most fashionable nightspot, was employed as a hostess there, and found daytime work as a movie extra. Without exactly cruising as a prostitute, Merle made herself readily available. She furthered her career prospects by having a fling with the black Grenadan entertainer 'Hutch', Leslie A. Hutchinson, a crooner and stud fabled for his pleasuring of duchesses and countesses. And then she met Alex Korda, a Hungarian director-producer whose ambition was to make films in Britain which would rival the products of Hollywood (Higham and Moseley, 3–22).

Korda (1893–1955) had been born Sandor Kellner on the plains of Hungary. By his mid twenties, having renamed himself, he was the leading director in the nascent Hungarian film industry, so under the short-lived Communist regime of Bela Kun, in 1919, he was put in charge of it. Escaping from the wreckage of the revolution, he had made films in Europe and Hollywood before he arrived in Britain in 1931, where his gifted brothers Zoltan and Vincent joined him in his visionary schemes. It was said that those who met this highly cultured, charming man were divided between those who thought him a confidence trickster and those who thought him a genius. Combining some of the attributes of both, he vitalised the undernourished British film industry so quickly that in 1933 his film *The Private Life of Henry VIII*, broke box-office records in New York after its premiere there, and launched Charles Laughton as a big star.

But a biographer concludes that 'the best single example of Korda's star-making talent' is provided by the story of the rise of Merle Oberon (Kulik, 128). Though she was very intelligent and worked hard on her films, she had minimal acting talent. Taking elocution lessons to purge her of Anglo-Indian vowels left her with direly stiff diction. Korda had taken on Merle as one of a posse of new 'starlets' announced in the British press, each chosen by him to represent particular stereotypes: two typical English young ladies, a 'high-class beetch', as he pronounced it, and Merle, with her brown eyes and olive skin, as his 'exotic'. But it was her brief appearance in *Henry VIII* as the doomed English temptress Anne Boleyn which set Merle on her way to celebrity.

Her mother meanwhile kept house for her. Most guests thought she was a servant. Frustrated with her role as maid, she threatened to go home to India, but died, aged only fifty-five, before she could do so. She was buried in an unmarked grave. Soon after, Merle had a portrait painted of her fictitious blue-eyed English mother which went with her everywhere she stayed.

Miscast as an English aristocrat in Korda's *Scarlet Pimpernel* she had a very lively affair with her co-star Leslie Howard. On film he would seem the essential, decent, pipe-smoking Englishman, schoolteacher-type or minor poet. He was actually another Hungarian emigré, and very, very randy. In 1935, Korda sold half Merle's contract to Samuel Goldwyn. So she went to Hollywood, where she consoled herself for losing Howard with a young actor, David Niven, who tactfully says nothing about their hot relationship in his hilarious memoirs. It was over, without bad feeling, before he joined the cast of her most significant movie, Samuel Goldwyn's *Wuthering Heights*, in 1938.

The story of the filming of this version of what is arguably the greatest novel ever written in English would make a substantial book (or a most diverting movie) in itself. Merle was fondly miscast by Goldwyn *a priori* as Catherine Earnshaw. The producer then had to strongarm the lusty David Niven, who was under contract to him, into playing the wimpish Edgar Linton, 'the most awful part', he said, 'ever written' (Niven, 194–96). Laurence Olivier arrived to play the surly, passionate outsider Heathcliff in a propitiously resentful mood. He was deeply in love with Vivien Leigh, and thought she would make a far better Cathy than Merle. But Vivien was herself hunting for bigger game, the part, which of course she landed, of Scarlett O'Hara in *Gone with the Wind*. Olivier asked a dear friend, the great actor Ralph Richardson, whether he should go to Hollywood. Richardson replied with his lovable terseness, 'Yes. Bit of fame. Good' (Olivier, 83). But Olivier turned up, for money and 'fame', in Goldwyn's weird world, most unwilling to suffer fools gladly. He reacted to Merle, as he put it, as if she were 'a little pickup by Korda, which she was' (Spoto, 112). She never forgave him.

Goldwyn had sent a crew to Yorkshire to film Emily Brontë's moors, then set out to recontruct them at Chatsworth, Ventura Co., north of Los Angeles. Dry-stone walls appeared there and 15,000 tumbleweed plants, on which the art department sprinkled purple-dyed sawdust, so they looked like heather, except that they were four feet tall. For close-ups, 1,000 genuine heather plants were flown in from Scotland. Directing the film was the great William Wyler. He forced actors through take after take. Merle, in December, had to rush out again and again into an artificial rainstorm driven by a wind machine at 70 mph, until she was taken into hospital with a fever. She emerged to demand successfully that heaters must be used to warm wind and rain, as they did until 'at last Wyler got the effects he wanted and obtained something of a look of passion and abandon on her face' (Higham and Moseley, 71).

Merle simply couldn't match her co-star's professionalism. When she complained that his saliva, in a passionate scene, was spattering her, he flew into a rage which drove her from the set – 'Why, you amateur little bitch! What's spit, for Christ's sake, between actors, you bloody little idiot!' (Spoto, 112–13, Holden, 138–39).

Nevertheless, Olivier's remarkable performance made *Wuthering Heights* a powerful movie, which secured several Oscar nominations. Merle's performance did not receive one. Typically, she was too much of a 'lady', and too much of a 'star' to be convincing.

Soon after making *Wuthering Heights*, she married Alex Korda. He loved her deeply. She liked him. She probably knew about the secret work which he did in America, after war broke out, for British Intelligence. Though he had only been a British citizen for six years, a grateful government gave him a knighthood in 1942. Her Ladyship divorced him in 1945, the year in which she somehow got away with playing George Sand in a popular film about Chopin, *A Song To Remember*. After a second marriage to a cinematographer, Lucien Ballard, she captured a very rich Italian industrialist, Bruno Pagliai, with whom she built a dream palace in Acapulco, lavishly mixing architectural styles and stuffing it with *objets d'art*. Here she was queen of parties flocked to by the richest celebrities. It was perhaps to her credit that she ultimately threw this away when she left Pagliai for Wolders.

I think Merle Oberon's finest hour, in which her pleasure in sex (for which, we must assume, she had abandoned the besotted Korda) was combined with her intelligence and her 'good nature', came in 1941, after she met Richard Hillary. Flying a Spitfire in the Battle of Britain, this clever, arrogant, handsome young ladies' man had been shot down and barely survived severe burns. A great surgeon from New Zealand, Archibald McIndoe, had worked out how to treat such cases with skin grafts and hair transplants, but Hillary had emerged from painful months in hospital looking frightful with his lifeless, remade face and claws for hands. When he was sent to America with a view to his encouraging support for the British cause with talks to workers in factories, the Embassy in Washington decided that such appearances would be counter-productive. He lingered in the US writing a memoir, a bestseller when published next year as *The Last Enemy*, and nursing his resentment against life. The publisher he was staying with in New York was a friend of Merle's through Korda and introduced them at a party. She was drawn to him so powerfully that she soon told her PA to cancel all her appointments for a fortnight, during which she made mad, passionate love with the maimed hero in a hideaway apartment in the Ritz Towers.

It is possible that Hillary awakened a maternal instinct (after an operation for suspected cancer, Merle was unable to bear children). It is probably not the case that she selflessly restored Hillary's crushed sexuality – others before her, it seems, had found him perversely alluring in his damaged state. He went back to the RAF and crashed to his death while retraining. Merle was distraught when she heard of this, and could not work for days. He had touched her very deeply.

There was a strong reason why Merle should feel wholehearted affinity for Hillary. Her face was her fortune, but also her curse. Her oily, olive skin reacted badly to heavy makeup designed to whiten it – Olivier could not have known how much he might have hurt her when he had referred sneeringly on set to her 'pockmarked' face. In 1940 she had developed appalling pustules all over her face and neck and opted for a drastic treatment, 'dermabrasion', which involved stripping affected skin off, and horrible discomfort under bandages until it grew back smoothly. After three attempts, it did. It was years, though, before all trace of pitting in her face cleared away. While Hillary's ghastly mask proclaimed a heroism which he was not sure he had shown, Merle's careful cosmetics hid a secret problem connected with the origins she had denied. His book, still in print in the new millennium, owed little or nothing to Merle's intervention in his life, but so long as it finds readers curious about its author, she may have a place in the affections of some which none of her forty-plus starring roles in cinema is likely to earn her.

American National Biography, *vol. 16, (New York) 1999; Michael A. Anderegg,* William Wyler, *(Boston) 1979; Sebastian Faulks,* The Fatal Englishman, *1997; Charles Higham and Roy Moseley,* Merle, *1983; Anthony Holden,* Olivier, *1988; Michael Korda,* Charmed Lives: A Family Romance, *1980; Karol Kulik,* Alexander Korda, *1975; Axel Madsen,* William Wyler, *1974; David Niven,* The Moon's a Balloon, *1994 (orig. pub. 1971); Laurence Olivier,* Confessions of an Actor, *1982; Donald Spoto,* Laurence Olivier, *1991*

Ogun (Yoruba)

Ogun is the most versatile of all the remarkable gods and goddesses of the Yoruba people of West Africa. He is the personal god of Wole Soyinka, whose plays, poetry and fiction won him the Nobel prize for literature, but also the hero of shanty-dwellers in Brazilian cities and a protean presence in the rites of Haitian voodoo. No god of ancient Greece ranged so widely.

The vivid effigy of one manifestation of Ogun, carved in wood by Kasali Akangbe Ogunof, from Osogbo, Nigeria, has been with me for years now. I acquired it in 1994 when the British Council in Edinburgh hosted, during the Festival, an exhibition of Kasali's carvings of Yoruba Gods. Every morning Kasali demonstrated the techniques of *ogbe* carving – he kept on creating throughout the three weeks of his exhibition. He worked, of course, in specially chosen woods. His gods and goddesses grew out of the wood.

My statuette is just under two-and-a-half feet high. The legs, on a little podium, are short and sturdy. His posture might suggest at first sight a footballer in line facing a free kick from just outside the penalty box and protecting his testicles with his hands, but Kasali has simply responded to what his trunk of wood offered him. Both Ogun's arms are very short. While the left hand trails towards his groin, the right holds what seems to be a baton.

I have pondered Ogun's character most days. This appears in a lank head, jutting forward diagonally, which is a foot-and-a-half long. He has short, woolly hair. Eyes and eyelids are prominent and enigmatic, sightless and visionary. The slim cheeks are cicatriced with patterns which must signify, for Kasali, much. The nose is almost flat and immensely long. Nostrils bulge snubly. The mouth jutting beneath them, under a very long lip, has made me think at various times of a dog's muzzle and a pig's snout. Looking carefully at it again just now, it evokes for me pouting human gloom – 'down in the mouth'. Ogun has been observing me, from up there on my best bookcase to the left of the living-room fireplace, for years now. Every day, I construe his expression differently. He can seem kindly, though quizzical. Or his long face expresses utter contempt. Sometime he merely seems tired and sad.

Though Kasali was selling his work internationally, he remained at heart a village craftsman. His father before him had carved images of Ogun. While Kasali sculpted other gods, Ogun was his main man, by streets. And since Ogun has an infinite number of faces, the subject of Ogun is inexhaustible.

As with the Christian gospels, tales of Ogun vary. Here goes . . .

In the beginning, there were only sky and water. And gods. Olorun, king of the Gods, ruled the sky. He told Orishanla (or Obatala), his senior undergod, to climb down and create land on the water. On the way, Obatala (let's settle for that) joins some other gods in a party. While he is sozzled with palm wine, his younger brother Odudua (or Odua) nips down and creates the world. A big feud results, which Olorun settles by permitting Odudua to rule the world which he has made, while giving Obatala licence to create humankind.

Odudua duly becomes the first Yoruba king, ruler of Ife. From Ife his sixteen sons go off to found their own kingdoms and some of their sons do likewise. Hence the proliferation of Yoruba city states.

The Yoruba were in occupation of their present territory – mainly south–west Nigeria, with offshoots in Benin and Togo – maybe 500 years before the Christian era. There was an astonishing efflorescence of Yoruba sculpture in bronze and terracotta between about 900 and 1400 CE. They were an urbanised people, confident and creative. The most obvious thing about Ogun is that he is an Iron Age god, boss of all metals and all work in them. No pastoral flautist he. Tender love is not one of his specialisms.

However, sex does feature early in his story. Odudua, remember, is Godfather of Earth. So when Ogun, the *orisha* (god) who is king of Ilesha, enslaves war captives, he should send them all to Ife. But he takes a fancy to one girl and sleeps with her, before acceding to the demand that he must pass her on. Odudua mates with her in turn.

They are joint fathers of Oranmiyan, who is born half pale-skinned like Odudua, half black as Ogun. This unusual lad becomes founder and first king of Oyo, eventually the most powerful Yoruba state. He is succeeded by his own son Shango, god of thunder and lightning, of whom more later.

Of the hundreds of Yoruba *orisha*, most of whom once lived on the earth as people, Ogun is maybe the hardest to avoid. Ogun owns all the iron in the world. 'Without him', as the American scholar Bascom points out, 'people could not have their hair cut, they could not be circumcised or have facial marks, animals could not be hunted or butchered, farms could not be cleared or hoed, paths to the farms and water holes would be overgrown with weeds . . . The other deities are also dependent on Ogun, because he clears the path for them with his machete, but he is most renowned as a blacksmith and a great warrior' (Bascom, *The Yoruba of Southwestern Nigeria*, 82–83). More could be added. Railway trains and their drivers, pilots and their planes, modern soldiers and their tanks and missiles, even those who make and use computers, are beholden to Ogun. He is the god of cars and lorries, the god of the road – and also, therefore, the god of road accidents. He rules the Internet and is in the offing when your pc crashes.

He is allied to Eshu, Olorun's messenger on earth, who dispenses rewards and punishments. Those who displease Ogun may get shot by a hunter, killed in battle, mashed up in a car, cut with a kitchen knife, stabbed with a needle. Oh, and since Ogun has a special relationship with snakes, cobras and puff adders also may wreak his vengeance. Ogun is *dangerous*.

In his great poem 'Idanre', Soyinka tells how Ogun, most visionary of the *orisha*, retired from the company of other gods and took to the hills, where he applied his blacksmithry, as 'primal mechanic', to creating tools that would clear a path between gods and men. His job was done, but the elders of Ire persuaded him down from his heights to be their king. He led them into battle – and massacred his own army:

> This blade he forged, its progress
> Never falters, rivulets on it so swift
> The blood forgets to clot . . .

Dogs above all have reason to fear Ogun. Though he enjoys he-goats, tortoises, cocks, snails, maize beer, palm wine and boiled corn and beans, his favourite sacrificial food is dog. His devotees eat dogs. Yet as Kasali made clear to me when we met, Ogun can be the kindest of *orishas*. With his forge, he can even be seen as a patron of fertility. Its hearth is a womb through which new things are made. Destructive though he can be, he stands for the creative impulse. Painters and poets, musicians and all craftsmen – sculptors, of course – relate to him as the master artificer. To aspects which remind us of Mars and Prometheus and Hephaistos, Ogun adds one matching him with Apollo, lord of the Muses.

Bascom reports that there are seven kinds of Ogun. Soyinka sees him as a single versatile personality – 'God of War and Creativity, of Metals, of the Road; Restorer of Rights; Explorer – He Who Goes First' (Soyinka, *Ogun Abibiman*, 23). So far as forced African migration to the New World is concerned, the last bit is not strictly true.

Europeans originally sought slaves for their New World colonies in Senegambia. Rounding the westward bump of Africa, they then set up forts on the Gold Coast, now Ghana. By the mid eighteenth century, the sugar industry's mounting demand for servile labour had taken them to the Bight of Benin and the Bight of Biafra – modern Dahomey and Nigeria. So Yoruba featured prominently in consignments of new slaves.

It seemed to suit white planters that new arrivals turned up in mixed batches, with no common language between themselves and revering all manner of different gods. 'Divide and rule . . .' But African resistance militated against mental dictatorship by slaveowners. Runaways established communities of 'maroons' in the forests. These developed their own syntheses of what people had brought with them from Africa. In St Domingue, the island partitioned between Haiti and the Dominican Republic, Fon from Dahomey seem to have offered blacks the basis of a new shared culture.

The Fon had a belief-system called *Vodu*. Its priests, 'masters of the God', were *hungan*. Some priests were amongst the slaves shipped across the Atlantic. Ogun went with them for an interesting reason. The Kingdom of Abomey in Dahomey (now Benin) was embattled against neighbours, including the Yoruba. Its royal family decided to appropriate gods of its enemies and fit them into *Vodu*. So Ogun (Ogoun, Goun, Gon) features very prominently in Haitian *vodou*, known worldwide as 'voodoo'. The cult became notorious as a result of the occupation of Haiti by US Marines between 1915 and 1934. This was a kind of revenge for the humiliation inflicted on white men by the success of the Haitian Revolution launched by Toussaint L'Ouverture in the 1790s, when black slaves had defeated armies sent by France, Spain and Britain. The USA decided that black Haitians could not govern themselves – they were too savage and primitive. Amazing discoveries about 'voodoo' helped them prove the point. 'Zombies' – dead people resurrected and enslaved by priests – played a minor part in voodoo but featured heavily in Hollywood horror films.

Vodu is West African religion modified in new conditions and accommodated to the rituals and beliefs of the Roman Catholic Church to which most Haitians belong. It is monotheistic, in the sense that there is a top God in charge, 'Le Grand Seigneur', equivalent to Olorun, but he is not directly concerned with earthly matters. The very numerous *loa* (or *lwa*), who are, do have spiritual powers, but are like human beings, demanding, selfish, quarrelsome. The door to the Loas is kept by Legba, a figure much like the Yoruba Esho. Humans approach him and them through a *houngan*, priest, or *mambo*, priestess. Loas respond by entering humans and possessing them – sometimes many worshippers at once, sometime select individuals, always encouraged by drums and dances. The loa 'rides' a possessed human. A person in trance may go out to dress up like the loa, returning to act like the loa, so that a man possessed by Erzulie Freda Dahomey, the leading female loa, may enter into a marriage contract with another male worshipper, as a woman.

Voodoo cultists negotiate with the loas over all the accidents of life – over illness and the weather, over the sex of unborn children and business plans. These negotiations are disguised by the identification of loas with Catholic saints. Thus Erzulie the flirt, despite her polyandrous sex life, is equated with the Virgin Mary, Legba with St Peter, keeper of the keys, and Ogun Ferraille with Saint James the Greater, patron saint of Spaniards when they crusaded against the Moors. Ogun Ferraille, while he represents the spirit of iron, is depicted in Haitian art as a white warrior, often seated on horseback, always clad in armour.

Ogun Badagris, on the other hand, so named after his supposed African kingdom, is one of the recognised lovers of Erzulie. A woman possessed by his spirit will dress in red shirt, red jacket, with a red handkerchief and a red cap, and will take up Ogun's baton or machete.

There are numerous other loas called Ogun. Ogun Batal cures illnesses. Ogun Balandyo watches over travellers. But the Ogun who intervened decisively in Haitian history was Ferraille, the iron man of battle. In 1791, Haitian maroons led by Boukman Dutty plotted vengeance against the whites. Voodoo cultists, they launched rebellion. After Boukman was killed, Toussaint L'Ouverture emerged as the brilliant leader of the revolution. He was the grandson of a King of Allada, in Dahomey. Slaves wore the red of Ogun on their sleeves in battle. Erzulie is said to have fought alongside Ogun.

The next revolution in which Ogun was mixed up was Castro's, in Cuba. Researching in Cuba in 1948, William Bascom met people who knew a lot about Yoruba religion and could converse fluently in Yoruba. The *Santeria* he found in Cuba was an African cult like voodoo, but differently adjusted to Catholicism. Bizarrely, a picture might represent Ogun as St John the Baptist – a blond boy holding a lamb – though the story was told of how Shango (*Chango* in Spanish and French-speaking countries), being a great mutton eater, persuaded Ogun to exchange his lamb for a dog.

The African religious cult in Trinidad is named after Shango, a notable example of how someone can improve his social standing by emigration. In Yorubaland, Shango was not even sole, uncontested, god of thunder and lightning. Even in Haiti the thunder god is Sobo and Shango is seen as Ogun's servant. But he emerged as top Yoruba god in Trinidad – where he is equated with St John the Baptist – and in Grenada. He is also big in Brazil.

Brazil drew more slaves over a longer period of time from more parts of Africa than any other New World Territory. In the last days of European slaving in the nineteenth century, after the British had outlawed their own slave trade and taken it upon themselves to police the activities of nationals of other countries, Brazil, like Cuba, continued to import slaves, and Yorubaland, where the kingdoms were at war with each other, was a likely source of supplies. It is not surprising therefore that Shango remained very popular in North-East Brazil, and that Ogun retained old devotees and gathered new ones in Rio de Janeiro.

Slaves everywhere in the New World had lost interest in Ogun's role in agriculture. What was the point of cutting cane with bright new metal implements if the result was merely gain for the master? In islands without large game and amongst the black proletariat in Brazilian cities, Ogun as hunter was out of a job. But Ogun Militant, Warrior Ogun, represented resistance to oppression and vengeance against the oppressor. In his great history of Brazil, Gilberto Freyre describes Ogun's nineteenth-century role. He was conflated with the Catholic St George, even though typical representations of the Saint would show a white man slaying a dusky devil. In Rio the Church of St George became the centre of Ogun's cult. All over the country, images of St George stood in for Ogun. His cultists wore an iron bracelet as emblem. Ogun's colour, here, was yellow. Oppressed blacks killed whites by dagger, club, poison and witchcraft with the help, as they saw it, of St George, *alias* Ogun (Freyre, 315–16).

Twentieth-century Brazil saw a serious attempt by left-wing Catholics to tame Ogun. In the spiritist Umbanda cult, Ogun became a protector against evil spirits and a guardian of liberty – sometimes, bizarrely, identified with Stalin, seen as leader against capitalist oppression. Amongst African cultists in Brazil, where there are many different sects or rites grouped as *Candomble*, there has been a concern from time to time to purge the veneration of Ogun, Shango and other orisha of such impurities. But the general drift is clear. Ogun in the new world deploys only a small part of his stupendous versatility. In Brazil, as the French scholar Roger Bastide curtly put it, his 'persona as a brutal and aggressive warrior and beheader was the one that won out' (Bastide, 254).

Soyinka, no friend of senseless war or vengeful murder, was himself prepared to accept that aspect of his god. In March 1976, President Samora Machel of Mozambique announced that his nation was now at war with the neighbouring white racist regime in Rhodesia. Soyinka saw this as a move towards the ultimate goal of destroying apartheid in South Africa. He dedicated his long poem *Ogun Abibiman* to 'the dead and the maimed of Soweto'. Ogun kindles his forge:

The Blacksmith's forearm lifts
and dances . . .
Its swathes are not of peace.

. . . Ogun is the tail that wags the dog
All dogs, and all have had their day.

Soyinka allies Ogun with the great Zulu hero Shaka, a mighty nation-builder who in the end went mad and decimated his own people, as Ogun once did. But this is a moment when violence is necessary and Shaka's war cry *Sigidi!* must be heard again.

William Bascom, Shango in the New World, *(Austin, Tex.) 1972; William Bascom*, The Yoruba of Southwestern Nigeria, *(New York) 1969; Roger Bastide*, The African Religions of Brazil, *(Baltimore) 1978; Mircea Eliade, ed., 'Sango' and 'West African Religions', in* The Encyclopaedia of World Religion, *vols 13 and 15, ed. (New York) 1987, Gilberto Freyre*, The Mansions and the Shanties: The Making of Modern Brazil, *(New York) 1963; Henry Gilfond*, Voodoo: Its Origins and Practices, *(New York) 1976; Laennec Hurbon*, Voodoo: Truth and Fantasy, *1995; Wole Soyinka*, Idanre and Other Poems, *1967; Wole Soyinka*, Ogun Abibiman, *1976; Sheldon Williams*, Voodoo and the Art of Haiti, *(Oxford) 1970*

Grania O Malley (Ireland) *c.*1530–*c.*1600

If the Irish Gaels had generally been seafarers, the whole of world history since the sixteenth century might have been different. As it was the English 'seadogs' – Gilbert, Ralegh, Drake – who played a notable, indeed genocidal, role in the Tudor conquest of Ireland, had no native counterparts. The O Malleys and O Flaherties of Connacht were unusual, in that they dominated the west coast with their seafaring galleys, much-feared raiders and privateers. Grania ('Grace') O Malley, who married the chief of the O Flaherties and bore him two sons, is picturesquely referred to as a 'pirate queen'.

She had another son by her second husband, Sir Richard Burke, chief of the Mayo Burkes, who died in 1583. While the Burkes were descendants of the Anglo Norman De Burgos who had come over with Strongbow in the late twelfth century, Grania's people were 'pure' Gaelic. Politically this made little or no difference, in the shifting mosaic of little Irish kingdoms which the Tudors sought, with eventual success, to subdue. Speaking Gaelic, complexly interrelated, chiefs allied with each other, with Scottish Gaels, or with the English, as passing advantage seemed to suggest.

In Gaeldom, wives could be divorced at whim, without legal process. Whereas under English law a widow was entitled to at least a third of her husband's estate on his death, under Gaelic law, the dowry she had brought with her into marriage was all she could redeem. By degrees, mortgaging of lands – which husbands could still enjoy in their lifetimes – came in to provide sureties for eventual redemption of dowry. So Grania remained always one of her own people. When in 1576 Connacht was formally 'shired' by Elizabeth I's Lord Deputy, Sir Henry Sidney, the O Malleys submitted to the Crown as inhabitants of the new County Mayo, and Sidney extolled her as 'a most famous feminine sea-captain' (Hughes). But in 1580 the O Malleys rose in support of the Burkes against the English. Many were put to the sword and Grania's Burke husband was starved into submission in the O Malley stronghold of Achill Island. In 1586 her son Owen O Flaherty was killed in a rising against the English and she herself escaped execution only through the last-minute intervention of her Burke stepson. In 1589 Grania and the O Malleys rose again with other Mayo clans – Burkes, Clandonnells and MacGibbons – burning villages and plundering cattle.

Throughout the confused period which ended with the suppression of the Earl of Tyrone's great rebellion in 1603, it is clear that Grania as a leader more than held her own amongst her male contemporaries – indeed, the Governor of Connacht condemned her in 1593 as 'a notable traitress and nurse to all rebellions in this province for forty years' (Hughes).

G. Hayes-McCoy, Scots Mercenary Forces in Ireland (1565–1603), *1937; Ann Hughes, 'Grania O'Malley', in* Europa Biographical Dictionary of British Women, *1983; Colin Lennon,* Sixteenth Century Ireland: The Incomplete Conquest, *(Dublin) 1994*

Liudmila Mikhailovna Pavlichenko (USSR) 1916–74

The war on the Eastern Front between Nazi Germany and the Soviet Union from 1941 to 1945 was incomparably barbaric. Total casualty figures will never be accurately known, but direct and collateral deaths must have amounted to over thirty million. The great preponderance of losses was on the Soviet side. Major Liudmila Pavlichenko did her best to make the balance less inequitable, as a sniper credited with 309 kills, including seventy-eight German snipers.

Elsewhere in Europe women worked in resistance movements. The British and US military brought women to the frontlines as nurses and auxiliaries. But only the Soviet Union unleashed female regulars in combat. Including partisans, some one million Soviet women served, half of them at the front. To be a medic there might involve extraordinary heroism, as when Olga Omelchenko, serving with the 37th Guards Division, crawled, after a big battle in 1943, towards a man whose arm had been completely smashed. 'The arm had to be amputated immediately and bandaged . . . But I didn't have a knife or scissors . . . I gnawed at the flesh with my teeth, gnawed it through and began to bandage the arm.' This was 'caring' womanhood. But many

Soviet women, willingly, went into offensive action. Some who applied for combat and were drafted instead into nursing later managed transfers. Some trained nurses discovered they really wanted to fight. There were numerous female pilots in the Red air force, and notable woman machine-gunners. The most famous woman tank-driver was probably Maria Oktibrskaia. When her husband was killed, she donated her life savings to buy a T-34 tank, went into combat in October 1943 at the age of thirty-eight, and was killed in battle near Vitebsk in 1944 while she was repairing her tank track.

Sniping was seen as suitable work for women. More than 100,000 were trained for the role. You had to crawl long distances in darkness to get, ideally, 500 metres from the enemy lines, dig in, camouflage yourself – and then wait, all day, lying in snow or perched in a tree or on a roof. There were all-female platoons of snipers, and one of these, fifty women commanded by Nina Lobkovskaia, in the 3rd Shock Army, claimed a score of 3,112 German soldiers.

Conscripted in 1941, Liudmila Pavlichenko graduated from her sniper-training course in 1943 and served in the Crimea. After recovering from severe wounds, she was made a master sniper instructor and then sent to the United States to propagandise for the opening of a Second Front in the West. Though she joined the Bolshevik Party in 1945 she failed, as did other woman heroes, to find a due place in the Red Army establishment. Until 1953 she worked as a researcher at the Headquarters of the Red Navy. Then she faded into obscurity.

Reina Pennington, 'Offensive Women: Women in Combat in the Red Army', in P. Addison and A. Calder, eds, Time to Kill, *1997; J. Vronskaya and V. Chuguev, eds,* The Biographical Dictionary of the Former Soviet Union, *1992*

Fernando Pessoa (Portugal) 1888–1935

Pessoa is hardly short of posthumous recognition. In 2002 the Norwegian Book Clubs published the results of their poll of one hundred well-known writers from fifty-four countries from which they drew a list of the hundred greatest works of literary fiction. *Don Quixote* was the runaway winner, but Pessoa's *Book of Disquiet* turned up amongst the ninety-nine also-rans, although it does not present a narrative but chiefly consists of the cogitations of Bernardo Soares, a prose writer, one of Pessoa's heteronyms, never finally set in order by either Soares or Pessoa (*Herald*, 8 May 2002).

So how does the greatest Portuguese poet since Camões and mainstream hero of world literature gain a place in this present collection of oddballs? Even the pretty well known strange fact that he published verse under four different names in four different styles, as from four very different personalities, is not quite so distinctive as one might casually suppose. Major contemporaries writing in English took the use of *personae* – masks – well beyond previous conventions of dramatic monologue to create, as in the cases of Yeats' 'Crazy Jane' and Pound's Sextus Propertius, alternative voices to their regular own ones. Pessoa merely went one step further – though one could argue that this step took him into new territory.

After recounting the story of Fernando António Nogueira Pessoa's life, I shall come to what I consider, though the Portuguese might not, the oddest thing about him.

Pessoa's father was a civil servant who moonlighted as music critic of Lisbon's leading daily newspaper. His mother wrote verse and played the piano. When Pessoa was just five, his father died of tuberculosis. Next year his infant brother Jorge died, and Fernando started inventing 'heteronyms', characters in his own internal theatre. It is estimated that during his whole life Pessoa – whose name means 'person' – would create seventy-two heteronyms. His chief French heteronym, Jean Seul, would write occasional poems throughout his life.

Late in 1895, his dearly beloved mother married Commander Rosa, just appointed consul in Durban, Natal. In South Africa, Pessoa was educated in English, eventually at Durban High School. He took no interest in sport, was brilliant academically, and made no friends. Instead, aged eleven, he invented an important and persistent heteronym, a Scot named Alexander Search. He created a biography for Search, and wrote under his name – this included early poems composed in English. Pessoa remained a lifelong Anglophile, dressing stiffly in the English manner and devoutly re-reading Dickens's *Pickwick Papers*, which he took with him everywhere. 'Mr Pickwick', he would write in an undated fragment, 'belongs to the sacred figures of the world's history. Do not, please, claim that he has never existed: the same thing happens to most of the world's sacred figures and they have been living presences to a vast number of wretches in need of consolation. So, if a mystic can claim a personal acquaintance and a clear vision of the Christ, a human can claim personal acquaintance and a clear vision of Mr Pickwick' (Lisboa, 122–23).

Aged seventeen, Pessoa was sent home to Lisbon for university education. Staying with various relatives of his mother, he was more alone than ever. He continued to write poems, all in English, though in 1909, 'Pessoa' took over from 'Search'. The University did not console him. After a few months, Pessoa decided to quit and study on his own, which he did avidly. From then on, he usually lived by himself, always in Lisbon, and earned a bare living as a 'commercial foreign correspondent', writing and translating letters in English and French for international companies.

The second decade of the century was one of political crisis, war, and 'Modernist' ferment in the arts. This was amply true of Portugal, where the King was assassinated and the monarchy was overthrown, Portuguese battalions fought against Germany on the Western Front, and literary, artistic and political movements sprang up as short-lived as the magazines which represented them. This was the most vivid phase of Pessoa's life, as an active member of café society, writing critical and polemical articles. He even made friends, though these committed suicide or otherwise died young. Meanwhile, on 8 March 1914 the single most important event of his life took place . . .

He felt poetry coming, and took a sheet of paper to the top of a tall chest of drawers upon which he began to write, as was his habit, standing up. Someone occurred to whom he at once gave the name 'Alberto Caeiro': 'my Master had appeared inside me'. Thirty-odd poems by Caeiro – countryman, 'keeper of flocks', neo-pastoralist – ensued in one go. Then at once he wrote six more poems as 'Pessoa'. Two further disciples of Caeiro were soon discovered, Ricardo Reis, a doctor and inhibited classicist, and Alvaro de Campos, an ebullient, Whitmanesque naval engineer who appeared as poet and controversialist in the transient magazines of the day.

War subsided – Portugal remained turbulent, a land of strikes and coups – Pessoa began, in 1920, to write for the London *Times* as A. A. Crosse. Next year, he founded his own publishing house, Olispo, printing and defending, with the help of Alvaro de Campos, works by openly homosexual writers which were duly confiscated by thc police. Yet in 1928 he wrote a pamphlet supporting the military dictatorship of General Carmona. From under the General's wing, Oliviera Salazar emerged as Minister of Finance and began to create a corporate *Estado Novo*, 'new state', a quasi-Fascist, repressive regime which its author would eventually head for decades. Pessoa didn't agree with it, but accepted it as a fact of life. He deepened his interests in Freemasonry and Rosicrucianism and in new 'religions', translating 'The Great Beast' Aleister Crowley and both **Annie Besant** (q.v.) and her dodgy follower in Theosophy, Leadbeater. Pessoa and his heteronyms were particularly productive in the thirties – though Caeiro had died in 1915 and Reis in 1919, their works still appeared posthumously.

But in November 1935, even Alvaro de Campos was silenced. Beside smoking eighty cigarettes a day – the chief outward sign of inner unrest behind his façade of Anglicised gentleman – Pessoa had drunk a great deal. Cirrhosis of the liver was diagnosed and he died two days later.

Intelligent contemporaries had recognised him as Portugal's foremost creative force. But he had only published one book-length collection of verse in Portuguese, *Mensagem*, which appeared in 1934. The 'Message' was inflatedly patriotic. Like Kipling, another lonely child from a far sphere of Empire, Pessoa was ultra-nationalist. The combination of occult interests with a nationalist agenda reminds one also of Yeats. But whereas Yeats' vision of Irish history had some lopsided grounding in what we call 'fact', Pessoa was a 'Sebastianist' who believed in a version of the second coming. The Portuguese would have their Fifth Empire which would at last join all races in international brotherhood.

Sebastian, born a few days after his father's death, had been the only one of King Joao III's nine sons to survive. On his fourteenth birthday, in 1568, he assumed the reins of government. Mad driver, teetering coach . . . Sebastian's imagination was inflamed by the epic of Portuguese exploration and conquest overseas. He yearned to expand the Christian faith to all parts of the world. He dreamed of conquering Morocco, where Portugal had evacuated its coastal strongholds in 1549–50. Some physical ailment made him impotent, and gave him an antipathy to women. But he was crazy about fitness training, hunting, bullfighting, etc. He hated Lisbon, rarely visited his capital, and failed to impress his subjects. In 1578, he launched his long-lusted-for assault on Morocco. After a miserably botched campaign, he was defeated and killed at the battle of El-Kasr el-Kebir (4 August 1578). Though his naked mangled corpse was found, his rich armour was never traced, and no survivor would admit to having seen him killed.

All but one hundred of Sebastian's army of 20,000 were killed or enslaved. Two years later the throne passed to Philip II of Spain and Portugal lost its independence for six decades. Sebastian's subjects, who had disliked the king and his ruthless recruiting methods, now elevated him to heroic status and conjoined mourning their dead with the belief that he himself was not dead, and would return. The myth of the Returning King was already in place in the Arthurian cycle of legends, and various Messianic beliefs and prophecies were already current in Portugal. Prophetic doggerel verses, *Trovas*, penned by a cobbler, known as *Bandarra*, 'the Doodler' (*c.*1500–56), foretold the coming or return of a Redeemer-King who 'would establish a world empire of right and justice – the fifth world-monarchy prophesied in the Book of Daniel, which would be accompanied by the reappearance of the lost tribes of Israel and the conversion of all unbelievers to Christianity'. As the 'Spanish Captivity' continued, the cult of the *Encuberto*, the 'Hidden King', who would release the Chosen Portuguese people, gained popularity at all levels of society (Boxer, 367–70).

Even after the restoration of a Portuguese monarch, belief that Sebastian lurked immortally in some Atlantic island, biding his time, lingered everywhere in the Portuguese Empire. French invasion in 1808 gave the cult a new lease of life. Throughout the nineteenth century and down to at least 1911, in Pessoa's youth, the *Trovas* of Bandarra were frequently reprinted to meet demand among the lower classes, while intellectuals saddened by the decline of Portugal's imperial power found romantic refreshment in the idea of a Fifth Empire. It involved a dream of beneficent world hegemony and mystified the actuality of Portuguese oppression in Africa. For Pessoa and his co-thinkers it transcended even the hopes placed by some on the British Commonwealth of Nations. Neither conquest nor economic dominance would be involved, merely willing minds and spirits. As Pessoa said in 1923, 'We have already conquered the Sea: it remains for us to conquer the Sky, leaving the Earth to others' (Lisboa, 153). But his poem 'Dom Sebastian, King of Portugal' in *Mensagem*, like many poems based by Yeats on his still crazier occult beliefs, provides impressive statement open to wider, or alternative, interpretations. The King says:

> My madness let the others take from me
> And with it all the rest;
> For without madness what can mankind be
> More than a healthy beast,
> A corpse that breeds before its juices waste?

(trans. Keith Bosley in Lisboa, 26)

C. R. Boxer, The Portuguese Seaborne Empire 1425–1825, *1969;* Herald, *8 May 2002; Eugenio Lisboa, ed.*, A Centenary Pessoa, *(Manchester) 1995; Fernando Pessoa*, Selected Poems, *trans. J. Griffin, 1982 edn; Fernando Pessoa*, The Book of Disquiet, *ed. and trans. Richard Zanith, 2001; thanks to Landeg White*

Emily Pfeiffer (Wales) 1824–90

Emily Pfeiffer missed her just posterity by sad, bad luck. Her husband, who was devoted to her talents as a writer, predeceased her by a year and a day. They had no children. So there was nobody to pull together and force into print her 'Collected Poems', eventually to join those of Mrs Hemans and Alice Meynell (1847–1922, sister of **Lady Butler**, q.v.) on the shelves of second-hand bookshops, and to be rediscovered in the late twentieth century as the women's movement gave new momentum to the reputations of neglected female writers. Instead, as we shall see, she was worthily connected to a building in Cardiff which she never saw.

She was born Emily Davis. Her father, formerly an army officer, owned a 'considerable estate' in Oxfordshire. But her mother's father, a Mr Tilsley of Montgomeryshire in Wales, had given the weight of his squirearchical name to support a county bank headed by his son. When this crashed, he felt honour-bound to meet its liabilities and his son-in-law too was drawn into the disaster. Davis accordingly could not afford to educate his daughter as was then thought suitable, though he encouraged her to study privately and practise painting and poetry. As early as 1843 she produced a slim volume of verse with the disclaimer that 'a severe family affliction' had prevented her from bestowing on the manuscript the 'time and attention' she wished (Leighton and Reynolds, 338–39). It seems that the depressiveness which marked her in later life began as she brooded in her youth 'over the woes of others and the evils of life in many forms' (Japp, 556). In 1850 she had the good fortune to marry Jurgen Edward Pfeiffer, a well-to-do German merchant based in London. She did not need to write for a living. Perceiving herself to be ill-educated, she embarked on a methodical programme of study, 'frustrated through such utter and long-continued physical prostration that for some years she was unable even to write her own letters' (Japp, 557).

She published a prose narrative, *Valisneria*, in 1857 and a narrative poem, *Margaret*, in 1861, but she herself seems to have regarded these as false starts, and silence followed until *Gerard's Monument*, a long poem, appeared in 1873. She remained highly strung, but, in her fifties, became prolific. By 1882 she had published five more books of poetry. Then a fire affecting her publishers, Kegan Paul, Trench and Co., destroyed all unsold copies. Poor health prevented her preparing a new edition, so her husband stepped in to do all he could – he collected her much admired sonnets in a volume for a new publisher (1886). The book opened with a barrage of favourable notices from eminent writers, scholars and public men – it was quite something to have on one's side both the sensuous and morally disreputable poet Swinburne and the high-principled Liberal statesman John Bright, who was a Quaker. Later, Oscar Wilde would express his appreciation (Turnbull, 1). Her poetry had long carried obvious feminist messages. Now she produced articles on the social position of women for periodicals, and a book, *Women and Work* (1888).

Her husband died in 1889. Devastated, she wrote and published one more volume of verse, *Flowers of the Night*, but she followed him the next year. According to his wishes, she had devoted a proportion of their property to the establishment of an orphanage, and she herself offered a large sum for the endowment of a school of dramatic art. Her own will left money to be applied by trustees to promoting higher education for women. Her basic case in *Women and Work* was that many women simply had to earn their own living. She countered the argument put forward by esteemed medical scientists and even the famous sociologist Herbert Spencer that higher education for women would make them ill and imperil the future of the race, overheating their brains and incapacitating them for their proper and essential function: bearing children.

The University of Wales was not mentioned in her will, but that is where her trustees decided that some of the Pfeiffer fortune should go, and there is every reason to suppose that she would have approved of their decision. Though her upbringing had been in England and she had lived with her husband in Putney, near London, she clearly remained conscious of her Welsh 'roots' – a full-length play in blank verse, which she tried and failed to get performed, dealt with a modern Welsh family, 'The Wynnes of Wynhavod' (Pfeiffer, *Under the Aspens*, 133–311). She must have been glad that Wales was in the vanguard of higher education for women.

Girton and Newnham Colleges for women had been established in Cambridge in the 1870s. In 1881, their alumni were allowed to sit exams and receive certificates if successful, but women would not be admitted to full membership of the University until 1947. Somerville College and Lady Margaret Hall had been founded at Oxford in 1879, and here women would get the status of normal students from 1919. But in 1878 London University had opened its degrees to women. The federal Victoria University of the North of England followed suit in the 1880s and the four Scottish Universities in 1892.

In the Aberdare Report of 1881, a distinguished Liberal politician had recommended the founding of new university colleges in both North and South Wales, to be secular in basis and open equally to men and women. Furious lobbying got Cardiff the nod over Swansea as the site of the southern college. At Victoria's accession in 1837, Cardiff had been barely more than a fishing village, but a rich Scottish colonialist, the Earl of Bute, who owned 20,000 acres in Cardiff and the valleys, had big plans for it as a port, assisted by the coming of the railways. Coal was ripped from the raped Rhondda Valley, and the first trainload from there, arriving in Cardiff in 1855, marked the rise of a new city. A population of 20,000 in 1851 had increased nine times by 1911, when only half of 182,259 residents had been born within the city boundaries, and a third were emigrants from England, Scotland or overseas (Cunningham and Goodwin, 9–12). So this was a vibrant, up-to-date sort of place, not wholly subject to the dominant popular ethos of Welsh Nonconformist Christianity.

Viriamu Jones, the first Principal of the University College of South Wales, only twenty-seven when it opened in 1883, was also the first Professor of Physics, and in his secular vision he saw women as entirely men's equals. The 'only true democratic idea' for him was a community 'in which every man is a cultivated gentleman and every woman an educated lady'. He firmly believed that women should have the vote. It must have pleased him that in the first year of the new college the highest entrance scholarship (£40) went to a woman, who duly attained, in 1884, the first BA degree, awarded externally by the University of London.

However, Jones's pro-feminism could not prevail in the matter of social mixing of male and female students outside lectures. Women had separate entrances and common rooms. University College Hall, London, was founded as a hostel for women in 1882 – UCSW was the first to follow suit, with 'Aberdare Hall' in 1885. At first, with just nine students, it merely occupied a rented house. Miss Hutchins, retiring as its Principal in 1892, wrote to warn her successor: 'I discouraged intimacy between my students and the male students and disapproved of their being invited to meet each other in society. I do not however think that Mrs Jones and Principal quite agreed with me in this matter.'

The Great Caerphilly Picnic Crisis of 1887 must have confirmed her forebodings. That summer, after a petition from the students, the Aberdare Hall committee approved a mixed 'pic-nic'. What happened can only be guessed – some incident as mysterious as the one at the Marabar Caves in E. M. Forster's *Passage to India*? – but the outcome was that the following year the Hall committee reversed its policy on the grounds that 'the unrestrained intercourse during a long walk makes it difficult for those ladies who act as chaperones to exercise sufficient vigilance'. However, mixed doubles at tennis – where chaperones could survey the whole scene in one glance – might still be played (Cunningham and Goodwin, 70–72).

In 1891 an appeal was launched to provide for the building of a dedicated Aberdare Hall. The trustees of Mrs Emily Pfeiffer put up £2,000 for a library. The Hall, which was opened in 1895 with accommodation for forty students, still stands unassumingly in the university area of Cardiff, but one can't buy Mrs Pfeiffer's books in the city, new or second-hand, for love or money.

In recent years her cause has been championed by the distinguished poet Gael Turnbull, who argues that she published 'about two dozen poems which deserve rescue from obscurity and which can stand comparison with the best writers of her time' (Turnbull, 2). Unfortunately, he can't so far get his article about her into print.

Vanessa Cunningham and John Goodwin, Cardiff University: A Celebration, *(Cardiff) 2001;* Dictionary of National Biography; *Alex. H. Japp, 'Emily Pfeiffer', in Alfred H. Miles, ed.,* The Poets and the Poetry of the Century, *vol. VII, 1898; Gwyn Jones and Michael Quinn, eds,* Fountains of Praise: University College, Cardiff, 1883–1983, *(Cardiff) 1983; Angela Leighton and Margaret Reynolds, eds,* Victorian Women Poets: An Anthology, *(Oxford) 1995; Jane Lewis,* Women in England 1870–1950, *(Brighton) 1984; Emily Pfeiffer,* The Rhyme of the Lady of the Rock and How It Grew, *1880; Emily Pfeiffer,* Sonnets, *1886; Emily Pfeiffer,* Under the Aspens, *1882; Emily Pfeiffer,* Women and Work: An Essay, *1888; Gael Turnbull, 'Remarks on Some Poems by Emily Pfeiffer: A Reconsideration', unpublished [1995]; thanks to Gael Turnbull*

George Edward Pickett (USA) 1825–75

After midnight, when it was already 3 July 1863, General George Gordon Meade, newly appointed to head the Union Army of the Potomac, convened his corps commanders. They were between the proverbial rock and a hard place. Robert E. Lee's Confederate Army of Northern Virginia had entered the North on a roll, with terrific élan, and collided with the lacklustre Army of the Potomac at Gettysburg on 1 July. After two days of bitter bloody fighting, with both sides calling up reinforcements, the Northerners were installed on Cemetery Ridge south-east of the town. Meade had three choices to put. Stay or leave? If they stayed, should they attack or await attack? If they awaited attack, for how long? The vote was to stay and await attack for at least one more day.

To Lee on the opposite Seminary Ridge, the aim seemed obvious – to destroy the Union army by frontal assault, after which the way to Washington would be open. The Southern Confederacy would gain international recognition. The war for Southern 'liberty' would be won. General James Longstreet, odd man out as the only non-Virginian in Lee's high command – he was from South Carolina – thought Lee was wrong. It would be cannier to march the southern force round to place it between Meade's men and Washington. Nevertheless, Longstreet's 1st Corps was to make the frontal assault, and generations of Southerners would blame him for procrastination.

General George Pickett's division had marched in on 2 July, a body of veterans not involved in recent fighting. Two of Pickett's five brigades had been left behind to defend the Southern capital, Richmond. He probably had just over 6,000 men, all Virginians. Now they were to attack the centre of the Northern lines, converging with the men of General Heth's division, under the temporary command of J. J. Pettigrew, and two brigades from Pender's division commanded by Major General Isaac Trimble, all coming from Pickett's left. These men were from Tennessee, Mississippi and North Carolina. Two brigades from Anderson's division were to support Pickett's right flank – Wilcox's Alabamans and Lang's Floridians.

Longstreet had been slow to move men into action the previous day and on 3 July proceedings were not much faster. Pickett, a friend and former comrade in arms in the Mexican War of 1846–48, was in effect his protégé – an undistinguished soldier now given the responsibility of spearheading the South to decisive victory. Pickett was chuffed. He wanted glory. By 9 a.m. his three brigades were on the battlefield.

Longstreet was despondent. The idea was that the South's artillery (maybe 150 cannon, but, as with most features of this fatal day, hard information is not secure) would pummel the Union lines across the valley in the biggest bombardment of the war. Pickett's men would advance upon men dazed and battered. But Longstreet sent to Colonel Alexander, commanding artillery, an ambiguous note suggesting that he 'should not advise General Pickett to make the charge' unless the bombardment had been decisive. Challenged by Alexander, Longstreet reverted to Lee's basic plan.

Just after 1 p.m., the Confederate batteries opened up. Union gunners responded. The din of the duel was heard as far away as

Pittsburgh. The Southern gunners began to run out of ammunition, but the Union fire had slackened. Reluctantly, towards 3 p.m., Longstreet ordered the charge.

A Yankee prisoner, Bernhard Domschke, had spotted Pickett that morning galloping from his tent to the front – 'The archetype of a Virginian slave baron . . . head lifted in arrogance. On horseback he looked like the ruler of a continent. Obviously, he took pains with his appearance – riding boots aglitter, near-shoulder-length hair tonsorially styled – but the colour of his nose and upper cheeks betrayed that he pandered to the inner man. Pleasures of the bottle left indelible tracks. Indeed, the coarse plebeian features in no way matched the efforts at aristocratic airs' (Gordon, 107). Hostile though he necessarily was, this witness reports what more sympathetic people noticed and photographs reveal. He did not smell the perfume (perhaps already mingled with whisky) in Pickett's fancy pointed beard.

Now, about 3 p.m., Pickett, having ridden along the line conveying orders to his brigadiers, stood straight up in his stirrups, waved his cap and shouted. 'Up, men, to your posts! Don't forget that you are from Old Virginia! FORWARD!'

Across three-quarters of a mile of undulating farmland, Union soldiers saw a sight to inspire genuine awe. In a line a mile long, in parade-ground order, the grey infantry under Pickett, Pettigrew and Trimble advanced with destiny in their step. But it was not the destiny which Lee and Pickett had desiderated.

Though frightened by the Confederate artillery, the Pennsylvanians in the Union centre had held their positions as most shells had hurtled harmlessly over their heads. General Hunt, in command of their own guns, had sensibly ordered them to be silent, so as to lure the rebels forward. He had plenty of shot and canister left for them. The Confederate left, marching over open ground under Pettigrew, were a straightforward target as they came within range of Union rifle fire (something over 200 yards). Pickett's division had the advantage of an undulation across the battlefield which screened them part of the way. They performed a drill which amazed and worried Union observers, moving alternately by front and by left flanks, sidling towards a point in the Union lines which would become famous as the Angle, where a stone wall useful in defence took a ninety-degree turn to the east for eighty yards before heading north again.

As cannon fire shredded them, Pickett's men kept reforming in close order. But this did not spare them when they got within range of Union rifles. Exactly how things were will never be clear because it never was clear. To make a simple point, 'In the age of black powder weapons, smoke quickly obscured a battlefield. Soldiers often could see only a few yards ahead even before they started shooting . . . A man might fight all day and never actually see the enemy' (Mitchell, 15). It is certain that a few score of Pickett's Virginians, and a small number of Pettigrew's men, did heroically rush as far as the stone wall, where intense short-range firing and hand-to-hand fighting went on till the ground was slippery with blood. The noise was 'strange and terrible, a sound that came from thousands of human throats, yet this was not a conmingling of shouts and yells, but rather a vast mournful roar' (Holmes, 165). Of Pickett's three brigade commanders, Garnett had been killed twenty-five paces from the wall, Kemper had fallen seriously wounded, but General Lew Armistead actually pierced the Union line. As battles went in that war, this might just have panicked the Union troops into retreat, but General Webb rallied his Pennsylvanian brigade, called in reinforcements, and the irruption was crushed in fierce fighting at the Angle. Armistead went down mortally wounded forty feet away from Webb – to his rear.

Pickett had led his force to within 400 yards of the Union lines and then – as he should have done – stopped to observe and perhaps direct ensuing action. An appeal to Longstreet for support sent Wilcox on his right flank careering disastrously into some tough guys from Vermont. Helplessly, Pickett watched the carnage. To a staff officer he exclaimed, 'Great God. Where, Oh! Where is my division?' Lee rode up and ordered him to gather such men as he could and reform in case of a Union counter-attack. Pickett, head on chest, sobbed bitterly – 'General Lee, I have no division now . . .' Lee's response was immaculate, that of a true hero (so perhaps some scribe saw fit to invent it). 'Come, General Pickett, this has been my fight and upon my shoulders rests the blame' (Gordon, 116).

Nightfall ended the slaughter, and the Battle of Gettysburg. It was not clear at the time that Pickett's Charge, as it soon became known, had been the 'high-water mark of the Confederacy' and that Lee's decision to head homeward next day was the turning point of the war – which still had the larger part of two years to run. Confederate casualties were appalling. Pickett may have lost half his effectives, dead, captured, or wounded (and in the then-state of field medicine, severe wounds were nearly tantamount to death). But muzzle-loaded rifles could not fire fast. The machine gun had not yet been invented. British troops advancing on the Somme in 1916, under an illusion similar to Pickett's, that artillery had mushed up the enemy, suffered greater proportionate losses.

However, the great Confederate charge of 3 July became a necessary myth, like that of the doomed Highland clansmen at Culloden. Postwar it was eventually a basis for North–South reconciliation. Northerners (who mostly had as little respect as Southerners for black people) were pleased to think that the war had been decided in direct confrontation with the 'flower' of the Confederate army, marching with incomparable discipline and courage to its doom. Men of the Old South saw distilled in the Charge all the chivalric gallantry of their tradition.

Integral to the myth was the idea that Pickett Had Been Let Down. Problematically, this might entail the implication that Lee, the nonpareil of Southern heroes, had Let Pickett Down. Longstreet was a more satisfactory target. Pettigrew an unfair but easy one. The fact surely was that Lee's favoured tactic of direct frontal assault was certain to meet its come-uppance sooner or later. The Union had basic advantages in manpower, manufacturing capacity and military technology, and a massed charge such as Lee ordered at Gettysburg was not the way to balance those. Meanwhile, poor Pickett just could not quite be turned into a great hero for the reunited nation.

He was almost archetypally mediocre. Spoilt son of a slave-owning Virginian businessman and planter, he had entered the US Military Academy at West Point in 1842 and passed out four years later last in his class of fifty-nine, with heavy drinking already one of his problems. Good luck, for him, had been the outbreak of war with Mexico in 1846. Attacking Mexico City, in September 1847, Lieutenant Pickett snatched up the US colours from his wounded comrade James Longstreet as their storming party advanced into the walled citadel of Chapultepec, shot his way to the flagstaff, pulled down the Mexican flag, and raised Old Glory.

He resigned from a small command of at most sixty-odd men in San Juan Island, facing Vancouver, to answer the call of the South when the Civil War broke out in 1861. As a Mexican veteran and experienced regular army officer, Pickett was bound to see swift promotion in Lee's army. Within a month, he was a colonel, in less than six a brigadier general, in just over a year, commander of a division (Gordon, 82, 85–86).

However, obvious defects of character attracted scornful attention. His first wife had died in childbirth in 1851. Now he was besotted by LaSalle Corbell, some sixteen or eighteen years younger than he was. While the Confederates were besieging Suffolk, near her home, he defied regulations by riding across night after night to see her. Yet the heavy whisky-drinking and dandyism were symptoms of paranoid insecurity rather than macho self-confidence. He began to develop a grudge against Lee. Why did he have the smallest division in the army?

After Gettysburg, he was outraged when what remained of his division were given the menial task of guarding Union prisoners. Pushed aside into command of the Department of North Carolina, he launched an attack by land and sea on Union-held New Bern which failed ignominiously. In the spring of 1864 he was relieved of his job and reduced to the status of mere district commander in Petersburg. He appealed through his patron Longstreet and got his division back. But looming defeat soon precipitated mass desertions from the Confederate Army, especially profuse in Pickett's division. In March 1865, Lee for some reason chose him to lead two divisions to Five Forks to oppose a Union flanking movement. Pickett's attack was successful, but he foolishly called a halt at the onset of darkness. He was away from the battlefront carousing at a shad bake when news (which he refused to believe at first) came of a Union counterattack. In 'the most one-sided Union victory since the long campaign began eleven months earlier in the Wilderness . . . Pickett's divisions collapsed, half of their men surrendering to the whooping Yankees and the other half running rearward in rout' (McPherson, 845). That was 1 April. On 9 April, at Appomattox Courthouse, Lee surrendered.

Pickett soon perceived a need to flee to Canada with his young bride LaSalle, whom he had married in September 1863. He had heard that the Federal Government was investigating his war crime – the ignominious public hanging in Kinston, NC, of twenty-two captured Union soldiers originally from North Carolina, who had served as Rangers in their home state, then defected to join the Union Army rather than be conscripted for the Confederate one. Technically, since they had not been regulars, they were not deserters and not subject to such a penalty. Technicalities apart, Pickett's decision had been senselessly brutal. Montreal wasn't fun, and the Picketts were actually back in the US when the government ordered his immediate arrest, on 30 December 1865. But his West Point and Mexican War background redeemed him in the eyes of former comrade Union General Ulysses S. Grant, who interceded in his favour, and he wasn't seized. President Andrew Johnson's general amnesty of December 1868 eventually cleared him.

Meanwhile, returning to his family's acres, Pickett found that he was no good at farming. He turned insurance salesman. He also busied himself in the veterans' Association of the Army of Northern Virginia. After a bad war and a shaky start in the peace, Pickett, abetted by the devoted LaSalle, made himself a niche in public life. In 1870, he bumped into Robert E. Lee by chance in a hotel in Richmond. John Mosby witnessed a strained exchange. As Pickett left, he remarked to Mosby, 'He had my division massacred at Gettysburg.' Mosby replied, 'Well, it made you immortal' (Gordon, 163).

He died suddenly of an 'abscess of the liver' in Norfolk, Virginia, in July 1875. It seems the demon whisky claimed him pretty early. An outpouring of public grief in Virginia climaxed when 40,000 spectators saw 1,500 official mourners assist in the transfer of his remains to lie beside those of other Confederate heroes in Richmond's Hollywood Cemetery.

LaSalle, still in her mid thirties, was a resourceful lady with ample chutzpah. When, in 1887, a contingent of survivors from Pickett's Division were 'reunited' at Gettysburg with men from Pennsylvania who had mown their comrades down, LaSalle was courted by both groups as the star of the occasion. In successful writings which followed, she told the Pickett story glowingly. She invented letters from her husband, and romantic but impossible incidents. Mrs Pickett chopped half a dozen years off her age at marriage, so that she became the Southern-Belle 'child bride' of her cavalier hero, set herself and her husband in an antebellum world of paternalistic slave-owners and loyal 'darkies' and did her utmost to glamorise George. But facts are chiels that winna ding. George was 400 yards behind in a state of tearful shock when that true hero General Lew Armistead fell at the Angle. The myth of Pickett's charge could not incorporate personal valour shown by Pickett. It was an epic moment of collective heroism by folk elsewhere dubbed the Poor Bloody Infantry.

American National Biography, *vol. 17, (New York) 1999; Lesley J. Gordon,* General George E. Pickett in Life and Legend, *(Chapel Hill, NC) 1998; Richard Holmes,* Firing Line, *1985; James M. McPherson,* Battle Cry of Freedom: The American Civil War, *1990 edn; Reid Mitchell, 'The Infantryman in Combat',* North and South, *vol. 4 no. 6, (Tollhouse, CA) 2001; Carol Reardon,* Pickett's Charge in History and Memory, *(Chapel Hill, NC) 1997; thanks to Reid Mitchell*

Piero di Cosimo (Florence) ?1461/1462–1522

Giorgio Vasari in his famous *Lives of the Painters* . . . (1550) got the beginning and end of Piero wrong. His father was not a goldsmith, but a maker of small tools. He was not eighty but around sixty when he died, not in 1521 but in 1522. In between, there aren't many documents referring to Piero and they don't contradict Vasari's other assertions.

Piero was the oldest of six known children of Lorenzo di Piero d'Antonio and his wife Alessandra. Two of his brothers became shoemakers. By 1480, Piero was apprenticed to Cosimo Rosselli, his godfather, a leading painter. He took his master's given name as if it were patronymic and went with him to Rome in 1481–82 when Rosselli was summoned there by Pope Sixtus IV. He painted the landscape background to his master's big fresco of the Sermon on the Mount in the Sistine Chapel. Within a few years, Piero was operating as an independent artist of good reputation. He executed altarpieces and other religious paintings. For the private houses of rich Florentines he produced utterly different items, with subjects drawn from classical mythology. Such men commissioned panels to be set at eye level on or above the wooden wainscotting, *spalliera*, which at this time featured on lower sections of walls indoors, including those of bedrooms, where erotic subject matter was appropriate. Thus Piero's *spalliera* of *Mars and Venus*, now in Berlin, probably dating from between 1500 and 1505, shows those deities lying back knackered after successful congress. The God of War has dozed off. Venus is just awake, paying no attention to her son Cupid. That bloated bairn is either calling out, 'Look, Mummy! See that up there!' or registering alarm about the large white rabbit (signifying fertility and lust) which is nuzzling his fingers while pressed warmly against Venus's half-bare haunch.

Approaching two thirds of Piero's surviving pictures, however, are religious. The common factor with his secular works was Piero's uniquely thoughtful and exact approach to landscape, in the depiction of which he was a pioneer. He was aware of the Netherlandish painters, and how they used landscape. He evidently studied meteorology and was technically so skilful that he could convincingly represent the special colour and intensity of light peculiar to a particular time of day. He also had a powerful imagination. He was in demand to devise *trionfi*, visual happenings in the streets of Florence at carnival and other festive times. For the carnival of 1511, at the behest of rich young men, he secretly prepared a Car of Death. It was painted black with white death's-heads and crossbones. It was drawn by black buffaloes. Behind and in front of it a great number of 'dead men' rode on the boniest nags available. Each had four footmen, also dressed as dead men, who sang the *Miserere* psalm of David with trembling voices as they marched. Death himself stood scything on top of the car. Around it were tombs with gravestones. When it stopped, these opened and out popped men in black with complete skeletons painted on their draperies, who proceeded to chant a mournful canzone. This spectacle, Vasari tells us, 'at once amazed and terrified the whole city'. It was later thought to have alluded to the subsequent return of the powerful Medici family to Florence, 'from the dead'.

If we are to believe Vasari, Piero was extremely eccentric. Unmarried, so it seems, 'he lived the life of a brute rather than a man'. He kept himself shut up, let no one see him work. He wouldn't let persons who tried to help him sweep his rooms or prune the fruit trees in his garden – 'he loved to see everything wild, saying that nature ought to be allowed to look after itself. He would often go to see [unusual] animals, herbs, or any freaks of nature . . .' He 'was endowed with a subtlety for investigating curious matters in nature, and executed [pictures of] them without a thought for the time or labour, but solely for his delight and pleasure in art'. He had a neurotic aversion to common noises – people coughing, bells ringing, church singing. Thunderstorms terrified him, though when it rained hard he loved to see water spouting off the roofs and splashing on to the ground.

He needed lots of glue, which he made himself. Mixed with gypsum, as gesso, and spread over wooden panelling, it provided a white surface on which to paint. While boiling glue, to economise on firewood, Piero also boiled eggs, fifty at a time, which he kept in a basket and gobbled one by one. According to Vasari, they formed his main, perhaps sole, diet.

In conversation, he ranged widely, and made his hearers burst into laughter. But advancing age made him unbearable. He spurned his apprentices. Half-paralysed, but determined to work, 'he doddered about and the brush and maul-stick fell from his grasp . . .' As he was dying, he kept putting off making his peace with God, abused physicians and apothecaries, and went into a macabre discourse about how public execution was the best way to exit – a big crowd to see you go, then, whoosh, straight to heaven. But he was found pitifully perished at the foot of stairs in his house. Terrified of the dark, enraged by the buzzing of flies, he had died alone (Vasari, 176–183).

In 1960, just finished school, I was registered as a student for a summer course in Italian at the Università per Stranieri in Perugia. I learnt virtually no Italian, except from shopkeepers and lorry drivers. I hitch-hiked about. Dizzied by sleeplessness in all-night cafés, I was bowled over by the other Piero, della Francesca, in Arezzo and by Simone Martini in Siena. What one learnt on one's travels was that, while some artists of the Middle Ages and Renaissance were startling, most operated within conventions which, after a time, got boring. For instance, Perugino, teacher of Raphael, had a repetitious line in fair, somewhat bovine Virgins presented with pretty bambini in front of nice, calm, Umbrian landscapes. So, in Perugia's own gallery, Piero di Cosimo's *Pietà* struck me, bang.

It actually echoes in its composition a *Pietà* by Perugino, painted around 1485, a quarter of a century before (Bacci, 95). In the distant background there is Calvary, with three crosses. Up in the air, there are three angels. In the foreground, the Virgin, flanked by St John and Mary Magdalene, cradles and contemplates the corpse of Christ. What grabbed me was the verisimilitude of the faces of the holy figures. The Virgin is a weary woman of the people, John a man palpably in grief. Piero's humans are usually like that – 'real'. His madonnas are rather sparky.

My next startlement by Piero came a year or two later, in the Ashmolean Museum in Oxford. The *Forest Fire* there is Piero's most remarkable picture. In central middle distance, a wood is on fire. Behind and in front of it birds and animals flee. The foreground is a hilltop where creatures have retreated from the fire. At left, a bear which has scrambled up with two cubs growls at a lion with his back to us. On the right a lioness marches along in profile, also growling, but just off her path a crane stands completely unconcerned by her or the fire. Birds of numerous species fly overhead. Right in the centre an ox stands, roaring. No painting has ever more strongly suggested noise.

But what on earth is this picture about? Art historians want every detail in such a composition to mean something, intellectual or moral. The Roman philosopher-poet Lucretius (*c.*99–55 BCE) was popular among advanced thinkers in Florence. His long poem *De Rerum Natura* adopts the atomic theory of Epictetus and tries to show that no divine interventions are needed to explain the course of the world. He has a powerful conception of primitive man evolving from a natural state of fear and savage individualism, obsessed with mere survival, into civilisation and community through the taming of fire. A puzzling detail in *The Forest Fire* – a small, perhaps manmade, fire behind a tree in left foreground – might allude to the early development of metallurgy in which the taming of fire was crucial. But a pastoralist herding cattle in right middle distance is dressed like a man of the European late Middle Ages, so that the scene is made to seem contemporary. Almost in the foreground, two deer are seen looking up into trees, for no apparent reason. One of them has a human face in profile. A little further back, a pig turns an inexpressive, perhaps melancholy, human face towards us. Infrared reflectography shows that Piero inserted – improvised – these weird faces at a late stage when he worked over his drawings on gesso with pigments mixed in linseed oil. It seems to me that Piero that connoisseur of natural freaks, actually liked satyrs and centaurs – mythical monsters non-existent according to Lucretius – whom he painted with great sympathy, and had some instinct, long before Darwin, prompting him to think of man as related to beasts.

There are other impressively strange pictures by Piero. A wonderful *spalliera* in the London National Gallery has been known as *The Death of Procris*, though that subject, out of Ovid, is disputed. A hairy sharp-faced faun is inspecting, tenderly, a prostrate, dead, nymph or maiden, on a grassy level, amidst carefully, minutely painted flowers. A large dog sits on his haunches to the right, in imposingly deep grief. Behind, three other dogs, and birds, are seen on a seashore.

Piero naturally appealed to intellectuals in the Romantic era, and got another boost in the second quarter of the twentieth century, when Surrealists could hail him as a precursor. In between, George Eliot wrote him into her historical novel *Romola* (1863) as a 'Bohemian' artist surrounding himself in his studio with toads, lizards and other animals and insects. I think he might deserve another reincarnation, as a hero of the Green movement.

Sharon Fermor, in a fine monograph, sums up his handling of 'nature' thus: 'Piero is . . . conspicuous among contemporary artists . . . in the extent to which he focuses on the prosaic and the accidental, in his refusal always to select the pleasing in nature, and in his efforts to preserve rather than eliminate the irregularities of its structure . . . He tried to preserve the imperfections of the natural world and the asymmetry of its shapes, and in building his compositions appeared to follow and extend the contours of the landscape rather than to suppress or impose order on them' (Fermor, 192). Back to Vasari. By his standards, Piero was not only a 'beast' in his habits, but an imperfect figure in the transition in painting which threw up the works of Raphael, Andrea Del Sarto (said to be Piero's pupil) and Vasari himself, in which, following Michelangelo, large, idealised human figures dominate everything. The Renaissance, as Victorians would hail it, involved escape from medieval superstition, rediscovery of ancient pagan learning, realism about secular power, and the triumph of European Man, busy conquering the New World, over beastly old Nature. An abstracted version of the dominant Male engaged in heroic action is the pre-eminent subject for painting.

Of course, the development of Dutch genre painting, and the rise of landscape as an independent genre, undercut such domineering rhetoric. People liked to see real people, and things as they 'really' appeared, represented in art they purchased. I suspect that when patrician pro-Medici Strozzi and the arriviste wool merchant del Pugliese (a republican eventually exiled for his anti-Medici views) bought stuff from Piero, they enjoyed his exact rendering of visible and imaginary things, irrespective of any high-falutin' classical or Christian meaning which might be held to excuse the effort. Piero's attention was absorbed by nature as it was, not as ambitious humans thought it ideally should be. More – like Leonardo, whom Vasari excused, Piero was fascinated, as children are, by the appearance of wonderful things within or behind random phenomena. Vasari tells us, 'He stopped to examine a wall where sick persons had used to spit, imagining that he saw there combats of horses and the most fantastic cities and extraordinary landscapes ever beheld. He cherished the same fancies of clouds' (Vasari, 177).

In *The Far Journey of Oudin*, the present-day novelist Wilson Harris has Rajah, an Indian farmer in Guyana, doze off for half an hour while at work on a hot and dusty day and wake to find a change 'from noon to night. A great black cow was swimming across the sun followed by a blacker flock still, and by a shepherd with his crook heralding the storm of a lifetime.' The storm comes and Rajah is struck dead by lightning (Harris, 194–95). Piero seems to have had a sensible honest fear of terrible latencies in the natural world which he loved to depict – to have been hypersensitive both to beauty and to danger.

Mina Bacci, L'Opera Completa di Piero di Cosimo, *'Milan' 1976; Sharon Fermor*, Piero di Cosimo: Fiction, Invention and Fantasia, *1993; William Griswold, 'Piero di Cosimo', in Jane Turner, ed.*, The Dictionary of Art [Grove], *(New York) 1996; Wilson Harris*, The Guyana Quartet, *1985; Giorgio Vasari*, The Lives of the Painters, Sculptors and Architects, *vol. 2, trans. A. B. Hinds, 1963 edn; Catherine Whistler and David Bomford*, The Forest Fire by Piero di Cosimo, *(Oxford) 1999;* *thanks to Kenneth Richards*

Beatrix Potter (England) 1866–1943

For perfection in English prose, we have Edward Gibbon. We have Jane Austen. And we have Beatrix Potter, supreme mistress of laconic irony.

She was born in West London into the suffocating and sterile milieu of the Victorian *rentier*. Both father and mother had inherited fortunes made by enterprising Dissenters in the Lancashire cotton industry. They themselves toiled not neither did they spin. Father, a barrister who did not practise, frequented his London club, took some interest in fine art, and was an expert amateur photographer. Mother maintained her unvarying social round. For three months in the summer, a house would be rented in Scotland or the Lake District where Mr Potter and his friends might shoot and fish. Here, at least, Beatrix and her brother Bertram, five years younger, could develop and sustain their interest in vegetation and animals. Back in London, with Bertram away at boarding school, Beatrix, completely alone except when governesses came to instruct her, did not pine in her old nursery, which was still her base. She kept snails in a plant pot, drew and painted pressed flowers, and attended to her pets – mice and a bat, a rabbit, a hedgehog called Tiggy.

His parents permitted Bertram to select the career of artist. He eventually became a farmer in the Scottish Borders. He married a shop-keeper's daughter, and did not tell his parents he had done so. Though rich, and snobbish, the Unitarian Potters were not of the upper 'Society' class. Beatrix was never launched into the London Season to catch the eye of a future husband. A shy, silent woman in her twenties, dowdily dressed, she haunted the museums and drew what she saw there. She became an expert on fungi. Her scientific paper on the spores of moulds was read to the august Linnaean Society – being female, she could not deliver it herself.

She might have lived and died a mildly eccentric 'old maid' had she not kept up with a lively governess brought in when she was seventeen to teach her German. Miss Carter had married Mr Moore and produced a string of babies. As they grew, Miss Potter told them stories and drew pictures for them. When little Noel Moore aged five was ill, she wrote down for him the tale of a naughty rabbit called Peter (like her own current pet), who invaded the garden of Mr McGregor and barely escaped with his life. Further tales sent to other children delighted them. Aware of their success, Beatrix at last thought she might produce a little book, and asked Noel's mother to retrieve Peter Rabbit. The publishers Frederick Warne & Co. turned it down, but she had 250 copies privately printed, disposed of them quickly and soon printed 200 more. And Warne told her they would publish her if she did coloured illustrations instead of black and white.

Few if any first books have triumphed more completely and enduringly than *The Tale of Peter Rabbit*, first seen in shops in 1902. Over the next eleven years Miss Potter followed up with eighteen more little books, an *oeuvre* largely composed of masterpieces. There was vast success in the USA. There were translations into foreign languages. Beatrix had inherited the business shrewdness of her cotton-making forebears, as she showed when she moved willy-nilly into what we now call 'exploitation'. Outrage when she observed pirated German Peter Rabbit toys invading British shops prompted her single foray into politics, in the 1910 General Election. The Tories opposed a Liberal government committed to Free Trade with a call for Tariff Reform to check foreign imports. Beatrix, at her own expense, printed a pamphlet in that cause. 'A few years ago I invented a rabbit doll which was in demand. I tried in vain to get it made in England . . . My doll is now made by scores in Frau H-'s factory in Germany.' She produced by hand posters showing a British-made doll in poor shape. 'Poor Camberwell Dolly is Dying, Killed by Free Trade . . .' (Lane, 104–06).

She had better luck in the matter of friezes. Hearing from a lady of her acquaintance that the latter had made a frieze for her nursery out of Peter Rabbit and would like to submit it to a manufacturer, she stepped in, designed one herself, and got royalties for it. Suddenly in her late thirties she had become formidable. Of the three brothers who ran the Warne business, she became very close to gentle Norman. When, in 1905, he proposed, she defied her parents – in whose eyes publishing was 'trade', not 'profession' – and accepted. Alas, Norman suddenly fell ill, an advanced state of leukaemia was diagnosed, and within weeks of their engagement he was dead.

That summer, Beatrix stayed with her parents in the Lake District, as often before. This time, with independent means, she bought Hill Top Farm near the village of Sawrey, which became the terrain of the little books which followed. Miss Potter was still trapped in London with her parents mostly, but in 1913 she made the decisive break. She married William Heelis, a Cumbrian solicitor who had assisted her in the purchase of another farm adjacent to Hill Top. Her brief career as a lady of letters was over. There were more little books for children to come, including the imposing *Johnny Town-Mouse* (1918), but she was drawing on her stock of old ideas. Now Mrs Heelis was a dedicated farmer, who went to great lengths to prevent the admirers of Beatrix Potter from tracking her down, succeeding to the point where many thought she must be dead. For the remaining thirty years of her life she stomped the muddy streets and rainy fells, wearing up to three layers of tweed skirt, with sack rather than shawl slung over her shoulders, overcoming local mistrust of incomers and integrating with the life of homespun, stone-dyke Cumbria.

She saw all too clearly what fate awaited the Lakeland of her love. A resort for travellers in search of 'the picturesque' since the eighteenth century, it must surely now succumb in the era of charabanc and motor car to an inexorable tide of 'tourists' seeking out the peace and quiet of its dales and thereby destroying both. Aged sixteen, she had met by Lake Windermere a charismatic local clergyman, Canon Rawnsley, who was crusading for the creation of a National Trust to buy and preserve sites of natural beauty and historical interest against property developers and commercial blight. The Trust had come into being in 1895. Mrs Heelis knew she would have no children. With her own resources, and what she inherited from her parents as they died, she not only supported the Trust directly, but bought up property after property with a view to bequeathing them to the nation. She left the Trust over 4,000 acres of land and fifteen farms.

In 1923 she bought Troutbeck Park, a remote fell farm estate of 2,000 acres, with a stock of hundreds of little aboriginal sheep, archaic creatures prancing nimbly on the heights – the Herdwick breed capable of surviving for three weeks under a snowdrift, nibbling moss and their own wool . . . The National Trust has a problem with these beasts now. Once their extremely rough smoky-blue fleeces were in some demand from carpet makers, and it is hoped that this use may be revived. Meanwhile, their exceptionally lean flesh should, in our health-conscious days, be in demand, but carcasses sell by weight, so theirs seem of lesser worth. Mrs Heelis became president-elect of the Herdwick Breeders Association. She would climb up and watch her tough little sheep for hours.

It's her own toughness which makes her finest Tales so wonderful. The diurnal familial rounds of cooking and shopping and washing are strongly present, but greed and fear dominate her most imposing fables. The entire Rabbit cycle, which includes *Benjamin Bunny* and *The Flopsy Bunnies*, is overhung by the entombment of Peter Rabbit's father in one of Mrs McGregor's pies. The great story where Jemima Puddle-duck brings her quasi-seducer the Foxy Gentleman the means of stuffing her when he roasts her has archetypal tragic pathos. Poor Mrs Tittlemouse, endlessly engaged in keeping her burrow clean, but besieged by intruders with dirty feet and habits, has counterparts in every suburb today. I would pick above all the rest the terrifying *Tale of Samuel Whiskers*, in which naughty Tom Kitten, exploring up the chimney, falls into the clutches of the huge old rat Samuel and his vicious wife Anna Maria, who prepare to cook him in a rolypoly pudding, but are surprised in the act by carpenter-dog John Joiner. The conclusion of this tale is supreme Potter. Tom's mother Tabitha Twitchit is sensibly frugal in the Cumbrian tradition:

> The dumpling had been peeled off Tom Kitten and made separately into a bag pudding, with currants in it to hide the smuts [from the chimney].
>
> They had been obliged to put Tom Kitten into a hot bath to get the butter off. John Joiner smelt the pudding; but he regretted that he had no time to stay to dinner, because he had just finished making a wheel-barrow for Miss Potter, and she had ordered two hen-coops.
>
> And when I was going to the post late in the afternoon – I looked up the lane from the corner, and I saw Mr Samuel Whiskers and his wife on the run, with big bundles on a little wheel-barrow, which looked very like mine.
>
> (Potter, 192–93)

The Whiskers's establish themselves in the barn of Farmer Potatoes, who is thereafter plagued by their children and grandchildren and great-great-grandchildren. So the wicked are not punished, but thrive. Miss Potter liked rats. As proprietor of Hill Top she necessarily waged war against them. But in London she had kept one as a pet.

Margaret Lane, The Tale of Beatrix Potter, *1985 edn; Beatrix Potter,* The Complete Tales of Beatrix Potter, *1989*

Jack Purvis (USA) 1906–62

Someone must write a novel about Jack Purvis. It will have to be picaresque, in the eighteenth-century mode. He is described as the most eccentric jazz musician of all, which is saying something, but should properly be seen as a picaro who strayed in and out of music while pursuing other *métiers* as aircraft pilot, soldier, criminal and chef.

The son of an estate agent in Kokomo, Indiana, he got musical tuition in the institution for boys where he was sent as a child after his mother died. Aged fifteen he was back in his home town playing trumpet and trombone in various bands. A longish spell with the Original Kentucky Night Hawks in Lexington followed, during which he somehow qualified as a pilot and studied music in Chicago. In 1928 he sailed to Europe with George Carhart's band, but played for it only on the first night aboard the *Île de France*, transferring thereafter to the first-class lounge with his fellow aviators Levine and Acosta. Rejoining the band in France, he abandoned it in a hurry via the roof of its Paris hotel. Back in the USA he gadded and gigged about. The Okeh company, in 1929, let him record a direct pastiche of the great Louis Armstrong, then at the astronomic height of his powers. The chutzpah of this white man challenging the black genius did not bar him from sitting in as fourth trumpet with the starry black Fletcher Henderson band, or deter such black greats as Coleman Hawkins and J. C. Higginbotham from joining his orchestra to record his own accomplished compositions.

But 1933 found him playing an obscure gig in Kilgore, Texas, where he met Charlie Barnet, a wealthy but talented white saxophonist: He joined Barnet's band in New York, but then set off again for California, where he worked as a chef and yet, amazingly, was hired to write for Warner Bros studio orchestras – one of his pieces, 'Legends of Haiti', was composed for 110 musicians. In 1935, he drove his baby Austin to New York, where he led his own quartet in nightclubs, then toured for two weeks with Joe Haymes's band – then disappeared again. It was perhaps at this time that he organised an unsuccessful School of

Grecian Dancing for young ladies in Miami. During 1937, he gigged in California, served briefly in the US Army, and then began a prison sentence for robbery in El Paso. He was soon broadcasting from jail, playing piano with his Rhythmic Swingsters, who performed his own compositions. Released, he violated his parole and returned to prison until 1947. His later years are obscure. 'It is rumoured that he resumed regular flying in Florida, but in the spring of 1948 a man resembling Purvis's description was seen sitting in a garden in Royal Place, Honolulu, giving renderings of "The Flight of the Bumblebee" alternately on trumpet and trombone' (Chilton). In Baltimore, where his daughter Betty Lou lived, he jobbed as a carpenter then joined an ocean-going ship as chef. Latterly, he lived in San Francisco under various aliases – Mark Haelrigg, J. T. Lowry, Jack Pegler and Wallace Rinehart – and worked as a radio repair man, until his corpse was found in a gas-filled room.

Ian Carr et al., The Rough Guide to Jazz, *2nd edn, 2000; John Chilton*, Who's Who in Jazz, *4th edn, 1985; thanks to Robert Calder (no relation)*

Queen of Sheba (Arabia) Tenth century BCE

The Christian Bible records the arrival of the Arabian goddess and queen of the Rastas in virtually identical terms in 1 Kings 10 and 2 Chronicles 9. 'And when the Queen of Sheba heard of the fame of Solomon, concerning the name of the Lord, she came to prove him with hard questions.' About theology, presumably. Solomon is the notoriously wise King of Israel who has built a magnificent temple to the Lord in Jerusalem. The Queen turns up in that city 'with a very great train'. Camels carry spices and 'very much gold' and precious stones. She 'communes' with Solomon 'of all that is in her heart . . . It was a true report that I heard in mine own land of thy acts and of thy wisdom . . . and behold, the half was not told me; thy wisdom and prosperity exceedeth the fame which I heard.' So she gives him her gold and spices – 'there came no more such abundance of spices as these which the queen of Sheba gave to king Solomon'. He responds by giving her 'all her desire', anything she asks for, before she trots off back with her camels whence she came.

The Queen is clearly mentioned by the chroniclers to show how far the great king's fame and influence stretched. The episode is diplomatic.

Since Solomon is reported as having loved 'many strange women, together with the daughter of the Pharaoh, women of the Moabites, Ammonites, Edomites, Zidonians and Hittites', and to have had 'seven hundred wives, princesses, and three hundred concubines', he hardly needed to take the Queen to bed. Nevertheless, she gets sucked by association into sex. Solomon was credited with authorship of the Song of Solomon, the most erotic item in Judaeo-Christian scripture, which must have provided many wet dreams for zealous Protestant Bible readers. It was smuggled into the Jewish sacred canon after the destruction by the Romans of Jerusalem's Second Temple in 70 CE on the strength of Solomon's revered name, over the protests of some rabbis. It is a collection of lyrics from oral tradition, smacking of Egyptian origins, possibly organised as a unified poem – in the New English Bible it is presented as dialogue between Bride and Bridegroom with chorus – compiled it seems between 450 and 400 BCE. Solomon, as ideal lover, gets mentioned a lot.

Verses 1:5–6 in the great King James translation read: 'I am black, but I am comely . . . Look not [down] upon me because I am black, because the sun has looked upon me . . .' This suggested to readers that the ardent female lover must be African. The Romanised Jewish writer Flavius Josephus (37–*c.* 100) stated that the Queen of Sheba was from Ethiopia, and that she became one of Solomon's wives. The Ethiopian royal house accordingly claimed descent from their son Menelik, 'then, this origin was combined with ideas of the Messiah, the persecution of the Jews and the subjugation of black people (the true Jews) to whites, the web of ideas which created Rastafarianism in the 1930s' (Lane Fox, 364).

The Queen was associated with Meroe, an African realm both historic and fabulous. The bad idea died and still dies, very hard that all human civilisation must have spread by diffusion from the ancient Middle East so that symptoms of fine craftsmanship and complex social organisation in sub-Saharan Africa must derive, if not from Egypt directly, via Meroe. Victorians would push Solomonic connections far south, with the notion that he had obtained gold from Southern Africa and the racist fancy that people from Palestine, perhaps Phoenicians whose king, Hiram, was said in the Bible to have been Solomon's ally, must have been responsible for the spectacular stone ruins of Great

Zimbabwe, since Africans were supposed to be incapable of such architecture. Maybe the plateau between the Zambezi and Limpopo rivers, with its rich goldfields, had been Sheba? South African white supremacists indignantly rejected the conclusion by an experienced archaeologist commissioned by the British Association for the Advancement of Science in 1929, who reported that Great Zimbabwe was 'of African construction and of medieval date'. It is now shown to have been built from the thirteenth to the fifteenth centuries CE, when indigeneous people developed a trade in gold which brought them luxury imports from as far as China. The Great Zimbabwe state, which probably collapsed because it overstrained the fragile ecology of its environment, was succeeded by the Mutapa state known to early European venturers as a power in the interior from the fifteenth to the nineteenth centuries (Shaw, 106–09; Beach, 24–26).

In biblical times, the Sabaeans, from the land which the Romans called Arabia Felix – 'Fortunate Arabia' – including the present-day Yemen, were great traders, the Phoenicians of the East, monopolising commerce with India in the range of useful and luxurious items later lumped together by Europeans as 'spices'. Sabaea itself was, in fable, immensely fertile and wealthy. Greek writers averred that the odour of spicewood was so strong that it caused apoplexy among the inhabitants, and had to be countered with foul smells. The Sabaeans were said to use cinnamon for firewood. Their meanest utensils were gold and silver (Chambers). The narratives in Kings were finalised centuries after Solomon's death, in exile in the mid sixth century BCE when the Jewish kingdom had fallen to the Babylonians, and those in Chronicles probably date to the fourth century BCE, during a later period of milder subjugation under Persia. The aim of the writers was clearly to glorify the great ruler of united Israel, Solomon, with a fiction associating him favourably with the legendary wealth of the Sabaeans, seen, through their Queen, as virtually paying tribute to him.

Wittingly or unwittingly, the Jewish historians presented a diplomatic triumph over a matriarchal polity, with overtones of sexual subjugation of female by male. Shebat was the Mesopotamian Moon-goddess. Shaybah, or Sheba, 'the Old Woman', was the Arabic-Aramaean title of the Great Goddess – Devi in Sanskrit, also assimilated with **Kali** (q.v.). Her spirit dwelt in the sacred stone of the Kaaba in Mecca. Its guardians were originally women. Sheba was 'the land-name and Goddess-name of Arabian queens in the ancient seat of Government, Marib, in southern Arabia'. For more than a thousand years of recorded history, before Islam eventuated in the seventh century CE, Arabia was matriarchal, dominated by female-centred clans. 'Marriages were matrilocal, inheritance matrilineal. Polyandry – several husbands to one wife – was common.' Mohammed's mother may well have been one of the priestesses serving the temple of the Kaaba in Mecca. He lived with her (not the other way round) till she died. But doctrines attributed to him 'simply reversed the ancient system in favour of men'. Within Islam, however, the Shi'ites and the Sufis maintained worship of the feminine principle (Walker, 51–54, 931).

A recent historian of Judaism states that Solomon, builder of the Temple, certainly existed, 'but at the very least the Bible inflates a second-level Near Eastern monarch to one who operates at a very high level of grandeur, power and wealth. This cannot be confirmed, and is highly unlikely' (Cantor, 51).

The story in which the Wise King meets the Queen of Spices is not just 'highly unlikely' but clearly untrue, and there is no basis whatsoever for assimilating the Queen with the dusky female singer of the Song of Solomon. Yet this remains compellingly beautiful, as it asserts equality of passionate desire, if not of social status, between male and female. The New English Bible version isn't bad:

> *Bridegroom* . . . How beautiful are your breasts, my sister, my bride. Your love is more fragrant than wine, and your perfumes sweeter than any spices. Your lips drop sweetness like the honeycomb, my bride, syrup and milk are under your tongue, and your dress has the scent of Lebanon . . .
>
> *Bride* . . . When my beloved slipped his hand through the latch-hole my bowels stirred within me. When I arose to open for my beloved, my hands dripped with myrrh; the liquid myrrh from my fingers ran over the knobs of the bolt . . .

Yeah!

D. M. Beach, Zimbabwe before 1900, *(Gweru) 1984;* Bible, Authorised Version, *1611*, New English Bible, *1970; Norman Cantor*, The Sacred Chain: A History of the Jews, *1995*, Chambers Encyclopaedia, *vol. 8, 1879; Robin Lane Fox*, The Unauthorised Version: Truth and Fiction in the Bible, *1992 edn; Bruce M. Metger and Michael D. Coogan, eds*, The Oxford Companion to the Bible, *(New York) 1993; Thurstan Shaw, 'Africa', in* The Atlas of Archaeology, *1982*, *Barbara C. Walker*, The Woman's Encyclopaedia of Myths and Secrets, *(San Francisco) 1983*

Jeannette Pickering Rankin (USA) 1880–1973

A pacifist witness is often arduous. In Jeannette Rankin's case, her achievement as the first woman to be elected to the US House of Representatives was controverted and clouded by her principled opposition to both World Wars.

She was the daughter of a successful developer and Olive Pickering, a schoolteacher, born near Missoula, Mon., eldest of eleven surviving children. Her future was unclear to her after she graduated from Montana State University, but sight of the slums of Boston in 1904 inspired her to enrol in the New York School of Philanthropy, which later became the Columbia University School of Social Work. A brief experience as a social worker in Spokane did not satisfy her, and she enrolled for a wide range of courses at the University of Washington, Seattle. In 1910 she launched herself into the cause of woman's suffrage, agitating across fifteen States. She became the first woman to address the Montana legislature, on behalf of the Equal Franchise Society. Never married – though she had an abiding close relationship with Katherine Anthony, a writer – she committed the rest of her long life above all to women's rights and world peace. These, along with legislation to protect children, were her platform when she ran for Congress as a Republican in 1916, to be elected despite a near-clean sweep by the Democrats in Montana. First woman in the House, she was famous. She was courted. But she opposed the drive towards war with Germany. Barely arrived in Washington, she was impelled to cast her vote, with fifty-six others, against US intervention.

Co-thinkers in the National American Woman Suffrage Movement were appalled as her intention became plain, and put great pressure on her. They were on the brink of winning votes for women throughout the USA. Jeannette's gesture could set the cause back twenty years. Carrie Chapman Catt, leader of NAWSA, though formerly anti-war herself, expressed only anger and contempt for Rankin after she cast her vote against war, and endorsed her opponent when she ran for the Senate in 1918. Rankin recorded that the 'only support I received from women in my vote' came from Alice Paul, leader of the National Women's Party, who came to see her the night before, told her that her organisation as such could take no stand on the war, but said that she personally was on her side . . . (Lunardini, 113–14).

Actually Jeannette Rankin did more than just vote. She broke with 140 years of precedent when at the roll call she prefaced her vote with an explanation, to make sure that her view was included in the *Congressional Record*. But NAWSA was wrong. In January 1918, Rankin opened the long debate on federal woman's suffrage, when President Woodrow Wilson's Nineteenth Amendment of the Constitution to that effect achieved two-thirds support in the house by just one vote – that of Frederick C. Hicks Jr of New York, who had left his wife's deathbed to be there, at her insistence, then went home to bury her. In 1920, the Amendment at last won through the Senate.

Jeannette Rankin had left Congress in 1919. Between the wars she worked as a lobbyist for social welfare provision and peace. Representing the American Association of University Women at the first Conference on Cause and Cure of War in Washington DC in 1925, she called on American people to 'recognise war as a crime, as the greatest crime against humanity' (Van Voris, 200). In 1940, when her wealthy brother Wellington backed her to run again for Congress in Montana, opposition to new war against Germany was widespread. Jeannette proclaimed that the country's real enemies were hunger, poverty, unemployment and disease. She won comfortably, by more than 9,000 votes. She argued in Congress for continued US neutrality.

Then, on 7 December, 1941, the Japanese attacked Pearl Harbour. After that traumatic shock, only one person voted in Congress against a resolution supporting war. Again, Rankin read her reasons into the record. 'As a woman I can't go to war, and I refuse to send anyone else' (ANB). Then, she had to take refuge in a telephone booth. Press condemnation was nearly universal. Knowing that she would never be re-elected, she spent the rest of her term denouncing wartime fraud and defending free speech.

Thereafter, of pensionable age, she travelled widely abroad, mainly in India. Longevity ensured her an epiphany of vindication. In 1968, having gained a whole new cohort of admirers, she led the Jeannette Rankin Brigade of several thousand marchers through Washington to protest against US involvement in Vietnam.

American National Biography, *(New York) 1999; Christine A. Lunardini,* From Equal Suffrage to Equal Rights: Alice Paul and the National Women's Party, 1910–1928, *(New York) 1986; Jacquelin van Voris,* Carrie Chapman Catt: A Public Life, *(New York) 1987; thanks to Rhodri Jeffreys Jones*

Nancy Riach (Scotland) 1927–47

After the Great Slump of 1929–31, while south-east and midlands England recovered as the new 'light engineering' boomed, western Scotland, home of traditional 'heavy' industries – coalmining, shipbuilding, steel – remained an arena of high unemployment and low hopes. In the 1930s, the steelmaking town of Motherwell acquired a remarkable Superintendent for its Corporation Baths. David Crabb sought to give the town's Swimming Club national, even international, fame. He aimed to catch future swimming stars as early as seven, and so help young people rise above social and economic deprivation. A self-proclaimed Communist, he led singing of 'The Red Flag' in the club coach and lent his young protégés left-wing books.

After war broke out in 1939, he persuaded the local council not only to maintain its swimming facility, but to let him train swimmers there till midnight and open it on Sundays for practice sessions. So he sustained a water-polo team which beat all opposition in Scotland, then in England, and he created, in Nancy Riach, a sporting icon.

Competing against older girls, she had won her first championship in 1938. She broke her first Scottish record at fifteen and within two years held twenty-eight records – Scottish, native, allcomers and British. She was top in freestyle, breast-stroke and backstroke.

She wasn't like Crabb's working-class stars. Her dad was a policeman who rose in the Motherwell force to become an inspector, her mother was a primary-school teacher, they were members of the Orange Order and voted Conservative. They could afford to support their daughter as she qualified as a teacher herself. She sang in the church choir and refused to compete in swimming tournaments on Sundays.

But she wasn't snooty. In wartime, with young males called up to the armed services, football, Scotland's passion, was not the great spectator sport it had been. Beating the English at swimming filled a niche. Crabb's young Motherwell swimming stars, Riach pre-eminent, performed for capacity crowds in club galas, and in England prices for such events went as high as thirty shillings for a seat and 3s 6d just to stand. Their show included 'Rhythmic Swimming' by a dozen comely young people accompanied by pipe and drums. Nancy agreed to model swimwear, still regarded as rather saucy – and went along with the efforts of Rex Kingsley, a journalist on the Glasgow tabloid *Sunday Mail*, to build her up as a 'Forces Sweetheart', so that her pin-up decorated the quarters of Scottish soldiers as far away as Burma, and she received heavy fanmail.

Swimmers peak early. Crabb turned his attention away from Nancy to Cathie Gibson, and this new Motherwell star set twelve new British records in 1946, when she was just fifteen, and went on to win a bronze medal in the London Olympics of 1948.

Nancy – who still held seven records – had her sights on those Olympics when she went to Monte Carlo in September 1947 with a British team competing in the European Championships. Polio had become a 'summer plague' in Europe and America, disabling and even killing young people, until Jonas Salk's vaccine was successfully introduced in 1955. Nancy brought polio with her from an outbreak in Britain. After her symptoms developed, she insisted on competing in heats against doctor's orders. The flight of her parents to be at her bedside made front-page news in Scotland, but she died before they reached her. Thousands lined the route of her last journey to Airdrie Cemetery, where she was buried in her swimming costume. But by now football was back in full stride. Swimming never regained the high profile in Scotland which it had had in Nancy Riach's heyday.

Graham Walker, 'Nancy Riach and the Motherwell Swimming Phenomenon', G. Jarvie and G. Walker, eds, Scottish Sport in the Making of the Nation, *1994*

Jeannie Robertson (Scotland) 1908–75

Regina Christina Stewart, known as 'Jeannie', was the youngest of five children of Donald Robertson and Maria Stewart, who were probably not married, but passed as such. Two elder brothers were registered at birth as 'Robertson', another brother and sister before her as 'Stewart'. When she herself was about to be married, aged nineteen, in 1927, to Donald Higgins, a very fine piper who was her mother's grandnephew, she decided to call herself 'Christina Jane Robertson'. They had eloped. Both Donald's parents and hers opposed the match. Donald's widowed father had recently married Jeannie's elder sister, so Donald's own father would become his brother-in-law . . .

Such complex patterns of interrelationship were common amongst the travelling people of Scotland – the Whytes and Williamsons, MacGregors, Robertsons and Stewarts, a few characteristic surnames spread across several hundred family units. Travellers did not like being called 'tinkers' or 'tinks', but accepted the designations 'summer walkers' and 'ga'en-aboot people'. They hibernated in towns, then took to the roads in spring. While the men worked as blacksmiths, farrowers, tinsmiths and vets, the women peddled cloth, yarn, thread, baskets and knicknacks to people in remote farmhouses. They provided cheap seasonal labour as berry-pickers and potato-lifters. In their camps they shared fiddle and pipe music, and traditional songs, with each other. The twentieth century bore down hard on their old way of life, but the Second World War perversely recharged it. Jeannie and Donald fled the bombs falling on Aberdeen, where they had settled, bought a splendid new caravan, complete with Queen Anne fireplace, and toured the hinterland finding work. They gathered with other refugee travellers in cheerful reunions. Their daughter Lizzie Higgins was growing up a fine singer, in a style more influenced by Donald's piping than by the grave ballad manner which Jeannie had learnt from her own mother, Maria.

Jeannie reminisced, in 1953, that when Maria was dying she told her, 'Sing my songs tae everybody. I want the *warld* to hear them.' How could this come about, Jeannie had asked her. 'I'm askit t'sing at nae place but the hoose here or maybe amang wir ain people' (Porter, 130). But when this was recorded, fate had ensured that Jeannie, now forty-five, could fulfil her mother's wish.

Hamish Henderson, a Perthshire man and Cambridge-educated scholar, had written and adapted many songs while serving as an Intelligence Officer in the British Eighth Army in North Africa and Italy. When Alan Lomax, the great US folklorist, came to Britain after the war looking to record traditional music, Henderson was one of the helpers he conscripted. And when Henderson was talking to travellers in Aberdeen market in 1953, he was told that Jeannie was the best and directed to her house in the Gallowgate. Henderson told the story as if Jeannie had glowered at this large, posh, embarrassed man on her doorstep, regarding him like an unwelcome vacuum-cleaner salesman until, in desperation, he began to sing a ballad and she said, 'No, no, that's not right. Come in and I'll sing it to you properly.' Jeannie's own mellower account, as recorded later, had her worn out looking after two lively young nephews. Impressed by Henderson's 'beautiful Highland dress' and military bearing, she nevertheless insisted that she was too tired to sing, but Henderson contrived to stay for tea, 'an' then I sang for him steady till two o'clock in the morning' (Porter, 41).

Thanks to Henderson's persistence, and to that novelty the portable tape recorder, Jeannie was soon singing to the world. Taped songs were broadcast on the BBC Scottish Home Service. Henderson got Jeannie down to Edinburgh to take part in the People's Festival organised as an anti-élitist riposte on the Fringe of the famous International Festival. Before long Jeannie was singing in the EIF itself and in other festivals, and in clubs which burgeoned with the Scottish Folksong Revival. Her repertoire of well over a hundred songs fed into that revival and young non-travelling musicians came to stay with Jeannie and learn from her. She got as far as London, but she refused offers of engagements in the USA and the USSR and had no aspirations to the life of a star. She didn't earn much from her concerts and from the long-playing records made of her singing, but it helped provide comforts for her ailing husband. In 1968 she became the first traveller ever to receive an honour from the monarch, when she was made MBE, 'Member of the British Empire'.

The Folksong Revival uncovered several very powerful traditional singers, but Jeannie was undoubtedly the finest. Alan Lomax himself described her as 'a monumental figure in the world's folk song' (Munro, 32). When I was in my first year at Cambridge University, 1960–61, my tutor was a great scholar from Aberdeen, Helena Mennie Shire. One day she announced to her group of eight students from King's College that we were to have a great treat. She had got Jeannie down to sing to the Saltire Society formed by exiled Scots, and she would perform also, especially for us, in Helena's front room. This happened. Afterwards, we went to the pub with Jeannie. She went on singing, talking in easy familiar terms about the people she sang about. 'When James V walked the roads as a gaberlunzie man, long ago – not so very long ago – they sang this about him . . .' With every great ballad, she knew people who had known the family in question. She believed that every word she sang was true. An American who came to know her well later, Herschel Gower, has confirmed what I picked up that day. 'She could have had little sense of "historic" time,' he writes, 'so that "long ago" could mean half a century and five centuries, without distinction' (Porter, 59–61).

She habitually sang unaccompanied – instruments put her off. Her great tragic rendition of the classic ballad 'Son David' could take three-and-a-quarter minutes or six-and-a-half, but was always delivered with enormous emphasis. She gave weight even to her lighter, bawdy songs:

> Fin I was cook aboot the hoose,
> Fin he was bit a laddie,
> I gied him a' my breid and milk
> Tae tickle up ma baggie.

No one who heard her deliver that could imagine a slim person performing the song. There was much substance to Jeannie. With her black eyes and raven hair and sharp mind she maintained her dignity in any company.

Hamish Henderson, Alias McAlias: Writings on Songs, Folk and Literature, *(Edinburgh) 1992; Ailie Munro,* The Democratic Muse: Folk Song Revival in Scotland, *(Edinburgh) 1996; James Porter, with Herschel Gower,* Jeannie Robertson: Emergent Singer Transformative Voice, *(East Linton) 1995*

Babe Ruth (USA) 1895–1948

George Herman Ruth, the 'Babe', was the most legendary of baseball players, and the most famous legend about him concerns his alleged called-shot home run in the 1932 World Series between his New York Yankees and the Chicago Cubs.

The Yankees had won the first two games in New York, then they repaired to Chicago. At Wrigley's Field Ruth faced a redoubtable pitcher named Charlie Root in the fifth innings. After each of two 'strikes', when he did not hit the ball, Ruth held up his hand. Before the third, as newsreel would confirm, he pointed with his bat. Was he pointing towards Root? Gesturing at the Cubs dugout, who were getting heavy with him? Indicating that he had one strike remaining? Or did he gesture towards the bleachers – cheap uncovered seating behind the centre field – 'calling' the home-run shot which he then promptly deposited there, a mighty 440 feet from the centre plate? Anyway, he put the Yankees in the lead and another homer from his longtime partner-in-destruction Lou Gehrig gave the Yankees a win and the Series – the last in which Ruth appeared, as it happened (McNeil, 53–54).

Months after, the press and Ruth, always buddies, decided between them that he had indeed picked his spot in the bleachers and pointed to it. Root was furious and said that if he'd thought Ruth had done that, he'd have knocked him down. Hollywood, in the second movie about him (Ruth played himself in *Pride of the Yankees*, 1941), improved the legend of the called shot – according to *The Babe Ruth Story*, that homer had been promised to a very sick boy, who, of course, recovered.

In the years when America fell into catastrophic depression, when Prohibition spawned organised crime on an epic scale, when cynicism about the American Dream was endemic, Babe Ruth was a surrogate for hope. He had come into the big-time game when its reputation was dirt. Gambling around the sport had always been heavy, and much sleaze had come to light, but nothing so bad as the 'Black Sox' scandal. Eight Chicago White Sox players were indicted by a grand jury for throwing the 1919 World Series at the behest of gamblers. Ghastly revelations preceded and followed this. Baseball was reorganised, with a noted trust-busting judge presiding as Commissioner with investigative and punitive powers over the affairs of the National, American and minor leagues. This may have been the first time the word 'Czar' was used in the sense that Judge Landis was called the 'Baseball Czar'. (It was an odd coinage, since the Empire of All the Russias had been notorious for despotism and bureaucratic corruption.) When the 'Black Sox' players, to the disgust of the press, were acquitted by a jury in August 1921, Judge Landis nevertheless barred them from the sport (Seymour, 294–339).

Baseball had been extolled as a pure expression of the spirit of the USA, teaching the will to win fairly, perseverance, grit and athleticism. Nine out of ten boys were said to play it. Their idols were national role models. So the nation needed a redeemer, and Ruth was at hand.

Babe was born in a Baltimore slum where his German-American parents ran a combined grocery store and saloon. Conditions were so bad that only one of his seven siblings survived to adulthood. By seven, Babe was a hardened delinquent and his parents committed him to St Mary's Industrial School for Boys, operated by Xavierian brothers as a combination of training school and reformatory. Brother Matthew, in charge of discipline, which was savage, became a substitute for the boy's own father, who would be killed in a brawl outside his bar in 1918. The priest saw that Babe was a naturally gifted left-handed baseball player and encouraged his progress in the sport. Six feet two inches tall, Babe was a star pitcher and catcher in school games. In 1914, he was signed for the Baltimore Orioles who promptly, to stave off bankruptcy, sold him on to the Boston Red Sox, who played in the American League. So Babe became a major league pitcher, and a very successful one. In 1915, 1916 and 1918 he helped the Red Sox win the league pennant and the World Series. His record of scoreless innings pitched in World Series lasted until 1961. But his promise as a hitter was such that he was more and more diverted to the outfield, and in 1919 he batted .322, set a major league record of twenty-nine homers and led the American League outfields in fielding average and assists. Then he was sold to the New York Yankees for a record fee.

The Yankees didn't have a ground of their own, but rented a share of the Polo Fields (on which polo had never been played) from their New York rivals, the Giants. When their new Yankee Stadium opened in all its magnificence in 1923, with an astonishing attendance of 74,000, which exceeded by more than 30,000 the previous baseball record, it was nicknamed 'The House that Babe Built' and our hero duly hit the first homer in the new ballpark (Spatz, 90). He had been packing the fans into the Polo Fields with his prodigious hitting and had set the Yankees on their way to decades of dominance in the sport.

Changes in baseball had converged to favour a great left-handed hitter. As major league teams had built or rebuilt stadiums, while distances to centre field and left-field fences had shortened, right-field distances were shorter still. A sudden surge of big hitting in the early 1920s was associated with the arrival of a 'lively' ball filled with yarn from Australia, which was tougher than US yarn and could be wound tighter, producing a harder projectile. Also, various 'trick' balls deployed to effect by pitchers – 'spit ball', 'emery ball' and so on – were now banned (McNeil, 10–11, 28, 33).

Babe had reached his full-grown fighting weight of 210 Ibs. He had modelled his swing on 'Shoeless Joe' Jackson, who had begun as an illiterate millhand in South Carolina and risen to attain the prodigious average of .356, as 'perhaps the greatest natural hitter in baseball' (Seymour, 86). But Ruth kept his feet closer than Jackson had, so that he could stride into the ball, achieving both vicious power and supreme grace at the moment of contact. (And he looked good even when he made no contact.)

With Ruth's arrival, total attendance at Yankee home matches rose from 619,000 in 1919 to about 1,300,000 in 1920. In that year, he rewarded his new fans with fifty-four homers. In 1921, he hit fifty-nine, and led the Yankees to the first of three consecutive American League championships. He was not the shining-pure Galahad the game needed in theory – he was, in practice, uniquely Babe Ruth. He got into punch-ups on the field and arguments with management off it. His nickname 'the Sultan of Swat' applied as much to his prodigious appetite for women as it did to his imperious swing. He drank illicit liquor in large quantities, often in company with admiring pressmen. In 1925 he went right off his game, hitting 'only' twenty-nine homers in a season when he was out of action for seven weeks under treatment for an intestinal abscess – 'the stomach-ache that was heard around the world' – after which he resumed heavy drinking and was fined and suspended by the Yankees' manager after staying out all night for several nights running. The Yankees slumped to near-bottom in the league. But he not only revived the public's zest for baseball after the Black Sox affair, he took it to new heights, with a rumbustious personality with which little people could identify. Spendthrift, sunny Ruth, a soft touch for charities, was generosity personified, as in the tale that once in St Louis during a hot spell he wore twenty-two silk shirts in three days – and left them all behind for the chambermaid, who was, presumably, black (Seymour, 431).

Though no black man would play in the major leagues till 1946, baseball was otherwise a 'melting pot'. It had native-American heroes, Jewish heroes, Hispanic heroes. In the 1920s, it spawned Italian and Slavic heroes. The Babe, otherwise 'Bambino', stood as an example for all kinds of impecunious ethnicities. They loved to see a slum kid living it up. In 1926, when his earnings reached an amazing $200,000, he regained his lead in the American League home-run table and he held it for six consecutive seasons. His record of sixty in 1927 stood for thirty-four years. In that year, there were 2,240,000 paid attendances at the Yankee Stadium (ANB). In 1935, after his departure, to hit his last few homers in a brief career with Boston Braves, Yankee home attendances slumped to only 657,508 (Spatz, 145–46).

His record of 714 homers stood till 1974. Other records endured longer – his home-run percentage of 8.5 and his total of 2,058 bases on balls. Diverse people have towered thus over particular sports – Matthews and Pele, Nicklaus and Tiger Woods, Bradman and Sobers, **Tilden** (q.v.) and Navratilova – but perhaps no such hero has ever been so wholeheartedly well-loved as the Babe, who made his last non-playing public appearance at the Yankee Stadium in June 1948, just two months before he died of throat cancer. While his body lay in state in the stadium, 200,000 people filed past it (*ANB*).

American National Biography, *vol. 19 (New York) 1999; William F. McNeil,* Ruth, Maris, McGwire and Sosa: Baseball's Single Season Home Run Champions, *(Jefferson, NC) 1999; Harold Seymour,* Baseball: The Golden Age, *(New York) 1971; Lyle Spatz,* New York Yankee Openers . . . 1903–1996, *(Jefferson, NC) 1997; thanks to William Rubinstein*

Kurt Schwitters (Germany) 1887–1948

In May 1940, after Hitler's *Wehrmacht* had struck triumphantly into France through the Low Countries, Churchill's new Coalition Government came under pressure from hysterical newspapers obsessed with the idea that 'aliens' resident in Britain might be spies and fifth columnists. 'Intern the lot' was the slogan, and over the summer this happened. Numbers of the genial Italians who ran restaurants and ice-cream parlours in Britain were actually sympathetic towards Mussolini, and there were a few 'alien' supporters of Nazism, but of scores of thousands of refugees from Germany, Austria and Czechoslovakia, the great majority were Jewish and others were left-wing and conservative opponents of Hitler. Such 'aliens' were rounded up, then mostly decanted upon the Isle of Man, in peacetime a holiday resort, now given over to prison camps.

There were two camps for women on the island, two for Italians, one for pro-Fascist British subjects and six, later seven, for Germans and Austrians. No sooner were these occupied than liberals in and out of Parliament were shouting out for the release of harmless people with useful skills. Amongst those who got out pretty quickly was a circus employee who had served in the British Army as a valiant Company Sergeant Major in the First World War but had never taken out citizenship. But astonishing reserves of talent lingered on the Isle of Man, and helped to make Hutchinson's Camp in particular a byword for learning and artistic achievement.

To create Hutchinson's, the government had requisitioned a swathe of terraced boarding houses and surrounded them with a barbed-wire palisade. Landladies had been cleared out and with them all furnishings bar bare essentials. Each boarding house elected a 'house father', under an overall 'camp father' to deal with the Commandant. Men perforce cooked and sewed for themselves, to the subsequent delight of surprised spouses. Meanwhile, a 'University' was set up to engross those not immobilised by anger or slumped in depression. Over thirty professors had been interned in Hutchinson's, and lectures were delivered incessantly on almost all standard disciplines. A technical school flourished, and a debating society modelled on the Oxford Union. Musicians gave concerts. An 'Artist's Café' was established in one of the houses where painters and sculptors foregathered each afternoon.

The giant in this circle was Kurt Schwitters. Anathema to the Nazis as a 'degenerate' modernist, he had exiled himself in Norway before the war, then come to Britain when Germans invaded that country. As a middle-aged German Gentile whose gifts were of no obvious value to the war effort, he would be detained on the island longer than most. But he seems to have enjoyed himself, at least according to fellow detainees. One of these, Ronald Stent, would write with affection of 'recitals of his own poems; one which sticks out in memory was written to be read by stammerers . . . In the camp he had a captive audience, he was in his element . . . For reasons unknown he preferred to sleep on the floor in a makeshift dog basket into which he crawled at night; he always barked before he went to sleep.' One night, he was answered by a bark from the foot of the stairs. An elderly Viennese businessman had yearned all his life to bark like a dog, but 'inhibition had always prevented him from giving nightly voice to his cravings. Now at last he could indulge in a nightly duet with Schwitters.' While Schwitters sounded like a dachshund, his interlocutor was more like a mastiff (Stent, 169–71).

Schwitters freely indulged his long-term artistic habit of creating collages from bric-a-brac. And he pioneered in a new medium – 'sculptures fashioned out of stale remnants of porridge, which he assiduously collected from breakfast tables. They had the colour of Danish blue cheese and emitted a faintly sickly smell. Alas, they did not survive long; the mice soon got at them' (Stent, 171).

Schwitters had been born into bourgeois comfort in Hannover, studied at the Dresden *Kunstakademie* and begun as a naturalistic, then impressionistic, representational painter. But after service as a clerical officer and mechanical draughtsman in the Great War, he entered the orbit of Expressionism through the magazine *Der Sturm*, which published his modernistic poetry. He also liaised with the Dada movement. Launched in Zurich with the 'Cabaret Voltaire' in 1916 by a group including the poet Tzara and the artist Arp, Dada mocked bourgeois aesthetics so thoroughly that recent controversial Turner Prize winners merely echo faintly its splendid bangs. As Dada spread to New York, Marcel Duchamp exhibited there its most famous provocation – a urinal entitled 'Fountain' and signed 'R. Mutt'.

The Berlin Dada group, in the bloody aftermath of German defeat, included the savage left-wing satirists Heartfield and Grosz. Schwitters was not 'political' enough to participate. It has been said that in his poem *An Anna Blume*, which made him famous in 1919, 'petty-bourgeois sentimentality is made fun of – but in petty-bourgeois language . . . Thus the poem could become a real love poem . . .' (Werner Schmalenbach, quoted in Elderfield, 39) –

> Blue is the colour of your yellow hair,
> Red is the whirl of your green wheels,
> Thou simple maiden in everyday dress,
> Thou small green animal,
> I love thine!
>
> (trans. by the poet, Elderfield, 38)

Denied official membership of any Dadaist circle, Schwitters came up with his own concept of Merz. The term originated from a chance fragment cut from the phrase *Commerz und Privatbank* and incorporated into one of Schwitters' collages, but he later played with various possible meanings, referring the term to Mercury, god of messages and commerce, so that his art might be seen as a special kind of product, or deriving it from *ausmerzen* – to reject – since he used what others had thrown away. He wrote in 1919, 'A perambulator wheel, wire-netting, string and cotton wool are factors having equal rights with paint' (Humphreys, 196). Just as his poems incorporated overheard snatches of everyday conversation and phrases from newspapers, so his collages, *Merzbilder*, used what he picked up in streets and parks.

A success in public performances as an experimenter in the 'concrete poetry' and 'sound poetry' which became fashionable in the 1960s, Schwitters had friendly links with Russian Constructivists and with the austere De Stijl group of the Netherlands. But he was his own man, more earthy than conceptual. Friends remembered in his home a distinctive Schwitters pong, composed of cooking smells, his pet guinea pigs and the pots of glue and paste he used in his collages. While intermittently publishing his own magazine, *Merz*, Schwitters converted part of his Hannover studio-home into his *Merzbau*, in which he collected refuse and 'found objects' in suitcases and specially made wooden boxes, creating what the Surealist Max Ernst called a 'huge abstract grotto', made around and within a basic structure of wire, wood and plastered struts. Pieces of friends' clothing, scraps of hair and even Schwitters' own bottled urine were stored in compartments and behind secret panels. This was presumably the artist's masterpiece. Begun in 1923, it was 'finished' when he left Germany for Norway in December 1936. An Allied bomb destroyed it completely in 1943.

Schwitters meanwhile had traded successfully. His design agency had been 'guiding light' for an association of modernist advertising agents, and he had acquired a 'reputation as an eccentric and brilliant businessman' (Humphreys, 197). But in Norwegian exile the romantic in him resurfaced. He painted naturalistic landscapes and incorporated natural forms, such as bits of stone and wood, in his *Merzbilder*.

So his last years were not quite so sad nor so perversely out of character as they might seem. Released from detention in October 1941, he lived in London with his son (his wife died in Hannover in 1944) and acquired a devoted female friend, Edith Thomas. In 1945, he moved to the English Lake District, to live near Ambleside, in 'Wordsworth Country'. To make a living he painted portraits. Some collages continued to incorporate natural objects, but others, using glossy magazine images, chimed curiously together with experiments at the same time by Eduardo Paolozzi which fed into 'Pop Art'. He had created a second *Merzbau* in Norway – it would burn down in 1951. Now the Museum of Modern Art in New York granted him funds, in 1947, to commence a *Merzbarn* in an old straw barn in the Langdale Valley. This was left unfinished when he died, but one surviving wall shows him working with abstracted forms derived from natural sources. In Wordsworth Country, Schwitters' art now reflected the special qualities of a remarkable landscape. It is pleasant to think him in death, like Wordsworth's Lucy, 'Rolled round in earth's diurnal course,/ With rocks, and stones, and trees.'

John Elderfield, Kurt Schwitters, *1985; Richard Humphreys, 'Kurt Schwitters', in Jane Turner, ed.*, The Dictionary of Art, *vol. 28, 1996; Ronald Stent*, A Bespattered Page? The Internment of His Majesty's 'most loyal enemy aliens', *1980*

Lady John Scott (Scotland) 1810–1900

Alicia Anne Spottiswoode, always published as 'Lady John Scott', was one of numerous artist-ocratic ladies who made signal contributions to the remarkable Scottish tradition of folksong. Jean Elliott (1727–1805), daughter of a High Court Judge, produced the standard version of the lament for the King of Scotland's defeat at Flodden, 'The Flowers of the Forest'. 'Auld Robin Gray' by Lady Anne Lindsay (1750–1826) and 'The Land o' the Leal' by Lady Nairne (1766–1845) also became standards. But Lady John's 'Annie Laurie' remains the best-known song of the lot.

Alicia was the eldest child of John Spottiswoode of Spottiswoode, East Lothian, an 'improving' landlord in the Lammermuir Hills, in the world-famous heyday of 'Lothian husbandry', who reclaimed moorland and planted many trees. Her two brothers became soldiers, her sister married Sir Hugh Campbell of Marchmont.

Her feminine accomplishments were lavishly cultivated. She read Italian fluently and wrote verse in French. The prominent watercolourist Peter De Wint taught her painting. Her music teacher was Manuel Garcia, brother of the great *diva* **Pauline Viardot** (q.v.). She sang as a well-modulated contralto and played the harp to considerable effect.

Her great-niece recalled that 'She was always making tunes, or recalling the old ones with which her memory was stored; and she would sing to herself for hours during those interminable drives of which, in later life, she was so fond' (Scott, *Songs and Verses*, xvi). As a child, she collected the songs and stories she heard in the Spottiswoode cottages.

Song-collecting had been a Scottish passion for generations. Following Ramsay, William Thomson and Herd, Burns had contributed scores of songs reworked to old Scottish airs to collections published by James Johnson and George Thomson. Walter Scott had first made his name by collecting *The Minstrelsy of the Scottish Border*. Latterly, Allan Cunningham, a Dumfriesshire stonemason who had moved south to become a prominent member of the Scottish literary colony in London, had published, in 1825, four volumes of *Songs of Scotland, Ancient and Modern*. He reprinted a song of two stanzas, 'Annie Laurie', from a little collection of ballads edited by Walter Scott's eccentric antiquarian friend, Charles Kirkpatrick Sharpe, who had taken down the words from the recitation of Miss Margaret Laurie of Maxwelton, his father's first cousin. The ardent author of the lyric was supposed to be William Douglas of Fingland (*b.*1672) who had been attracted by Anna (1682–1764), the ninth and last child of Sir Robert Laurie, first Baronet of Maxwelton in Dumfriesshire. Unromantically, William had gone on to marry the daughter of an Edinburgh merchant, and Anna a nearby landowner.

Soon after her sister married in 1834, Alicia was staying with her at Marchmont and found Cunningham's collection there. She had in her head the tune she had made to 'an absurd ballad, originally Norwegian, I believe, called Kempie Kaye'. She saw that the words of 'Annie Laurie' would fit it, but disliked the second stanza, so she altered that, and added a third completely her own. Her sister and brother-in-law admired the result, and accordingly she wrote it down for them (Scott, *Songs and Verses*, xxiii).

A few years before, Thomas Pringle, another Borderer writing in exile in London, had pestered his old friend James Hogg, famous poet and novelist known, from his origins, as 'the Ettrick Shepherd', for a contribution to an annual which he edited, called *Friendship's Offering*. But when Hogg had finally complied, Pringle had rejected his ballad as 'too strange and droll' for the genteel readership of his '"douce" and delicate publications'. Anticipating Dickens's Podsnap by nearly forty years, he told Hogg that he could include nothing 'which would call up a blush in the cheek of the most delicate female if reading aloud to a mixed company' (Pringle to Hogg, 28 May 1828, National Library of Scotland, ms 2245 f 122). 'Victorian' prudery was well-established before the young queen was crowned in 1837. From the 1780s, Evangelical Protestantism had been massing its forces to take hegemonic control of British public life. There is no evidence that Alicia was particularly prudish – on the contrary, her favourite poet was bad Lord Byron, and her conversations with the lower orders and interest in their songs must have exposed her to many indelicate expressions – but like Pringle she knew what would and wouldn't do.

While she hardly changed the first stanza of 'Annie Laurie', in the second, the lines:

She's backit like the peacock,
She's breistit like the swan,
She's jimp [*slender, dainty*] about the middle,
Her waist you may weel span . . .
And she has a rolling eye . . .

– which give her a carnal appeal – are replaced in Alicia's version by vaguer adoration:

Her brow is like the snaw-drift,
Her neck is like the swan,
Her face it is the fairest,
That ever sun shone on . . .
And dark blue is her e'e . . .

Thus rendered unexceptionable, the song passed into general circulation. British soldiers sang it during the Crimean War of 1854–56. Afterwards, the author gave 'Annie Laurie' and several other songs to Lonsdale to publish for a bazaar in aid of the widows and orphans of war casualties. 'Annie Laurie' thereafter travelled all over the world, from the parlours of Europe to the Antipodean outback.

It seems clear enough that, more secretively, Alicia was authoress of 'The Bonny Banks O' Loch Lomond', which became a trademark song, in the twentieth century, of the hugely successful entertainer Harry Lauder. A version was printed in Edinburgh in 1840 'as written by a lady'. This was assumed to be her work, but she came up with another version which she claimed that she and her husband had picked up from the singing of a little boy in the streets of Edinburgh. The great song collector Gavin Grieg surveyed the question around the turn of the century and concluded that these verses, 'clearly literary and modern', were actually by her (Grieg, n.p. Song XCL). It is readily conceivable that, as with 'Annie Laurie', Alicia 'improved on' her source, in this case an actual little boy. In any case, the tale demonstrates that in shared tastes she found the basis for contented marriage.

In 1836, Alicia had married Lord John Scott, brother of the Duke of Buccleuch. He had a public role at that time as MP for Roxburghshire, and after a couple of years their chief residence was a stately home at Cawston in Warwickshire, his property by inheritance. Alicia did her best to make it less stately. 'To reach it from Rugby, you turned off across the fields along a farm road barred with many gates, and eventually you found yourself in the stable-yard, into which the front door opened and the dining-room windows looked. At one time there was a much better way in through the park from the Dunchurch side, but when Lady John enlarged the garden, she took in this road, and as personally she always preferred driving over the grass, she never troubled to make a new approach, with the result that would-be visitors were occasionally found wandering round and round the place, unable to find an entrance' (Scott, *Songs and Verses*, xxv). She went to London as rarely as possible, and the only thing she really enjoyed there was the opera. For all her comeliness and her accomplishments, she was shy in high society.

As for Lord John, he had no wish to be a statesman. Hunting, shooting and fishing were passions to which he added yachting. Lady John enjoyed going out with him on his shorter trips in the sheltered western sea-lochs. He would have been the last person to baulk her preference for an outdoor life in Scotland whenever possible. In other respects, too, he was a soul-mate. He was merciful to poachers and positively approved of gypsies. It is said that while renting the forest at Blair in Perthshire, he once secretly renewed the whole plant of an illicit still which had been destroyed by excisemen.

They had no children, and the landmarks in Alicia's life were mostly bereavements. Her husband died in 1859 – it was thought because of the toll which so many damp, cold nights outdoors had exacted on his system. Her sister died young, both her brothers were dead before her beloved father expired in 1866, and her mother's death in 1870 left her quite alone as chatelaine of Spottiswoode and Cawston.

Her verse – she wrote scores of songs and poems – typically expressed plangent, elegiac melancholy. Unlike **Queen Victoria** (q.v.), she wore her deep griefs lightly. Though she kept her mother's room exactly as if she might return at any moment, she didn't mind if children romped around in it. Her zest for life was unabated. So was her passion for Scotland – 'I would rather live in a pigsty in Scotland than a palace in England.' She took a cold bath every morning, breaking the ice when necessary. Trim-figured, simply dressed, with a red shawl round her shoulders even when she wore black for mourning, her fine skin unblemished despite, or because of, many batterings by raw weather, her eyes still deep blue, the incessantly charitable Lady John went far beyond the calls of *noblesse oblige*. She had a special concern for imbeciles and deformed people – her bailiff had to restrain her from offering a whole house to Merrick, the famous 'Elephant Man'. In the last three decades of her life, she travelled every summer to Thurso, in the far North, and sometimes beyond, to Orkney and Shetland. She bathed in the icy waters of the Pentland Firth, tossed packets of books out of her carriage whenever she saw any unoccupied children, and visited every prehistoric archaeological site she heard of, while sketching the notable cliffs and bays. She became aware of the oppression of the inhabitants of Fair Isle by the Truck system, and bought them a schooner big enough to take their fish catch independently to market at Kirkwall and Lerwick, so that the landlord's tyranny withered away.

Her youngest relatives found her great fun. Her great-niece recalled that 'she had no small fidgets about torn clothes, wet feet, getting into mischief or being late for lessons'. She talked to children as if they were adults, freely quoting Shakespeare and Pope's *Iliad* to them. But she would set up treasure hunts for real 'treasure'.

She was still fit as a flea, and taking a close interest in the South African War, just before influenza swept her away in March 1900. She was buried in a blinding snowstorm in the old kirk at Westruther on the sixty-fourth anniversary of her marriage, in the Lammermuir country which she loved best of all – 'Heaven won't seem heaven if I don't see those benty fields and tufts of rushes there.'

Allan Cunningham, ed., Songs of Scotland, *1825; Gavin Grieg,* Folksong of the North East, *(Hatboro, PA) 1963; Gordon Irving,* Annie Laurie: The Romantic Story of the Song and Its Heroine, *(Dumfries) 1948; Lady John Scott,* Songs and Verses, *with a biographical preface by Margaret Warrender, (Edinburgh) 1904; Reverend Joseph Yair,* A Tribute to the Memory of Lord John Scott, *(Edinburgh) 1860*

Mary Seacole (Jamaica) 1805–84

Mary Seacole was born in Jamaica in 1805, daughter of a free black woman and a Scottish army officer, probably named Grant. Her mother, who kept a boarding house where she cared for invalid officers and their wives, taught her folk medicine and Mary developed a rare gift for handling dread diseases, such as yellow fever, which decimated armies in the Caribbean. She also acquired wanderlust, travelling to Britain aged only twelve. Street urchins jeered at her dusky features – though, typically, she concluded that her 'very dark' companion attracted their derision more than her own 'yellow' skin (Seacole, 4). She stayed in England a year, returned later for another two years, trading initially in West Indian preserves and pickles.

Back in Jamaica, she married an ailing man called Horatio Seacole, and kept him alive with her nursing as long as possible – not very long. Her mother died soon after, and Mary carried on her business of looking after soldiers, always seeking to find out more about medicine from naval and military surgeons who came her way. In 1850, she learnt all too much about cholera, when it hit Jamaica. In the same year, her younger brother Edward headed off for Panama, which prospectors heading for the California Gold Rush used as a short cut, as did lucky miners returning with their gains. Mary followed her brother. She opened hotels, enduring the chaos and squalor of a frontier society. She developed strong anti-American views, based largely on the prejudice shown against her by transients from the Deep South, and approved of the help given by local people to slaves travelling with these bigots who wished to escape.

While Mary was in Panama, word came that Britain had gone to war with Russia. Regiments she had known in Jamaica were headed to the Crimea. Mary, 'Mother Seacole' to them, felt that she must join her 'sons'. Notoriously, Whitehall bungled. The commissariat cocked up. Soldiers were stranded on a barren plateau outside Sevastopol in extremes of cold and heat without adequate equipment, fuel or cooking facilities. Disease scourged the poor bloody infantry – of 20,000 soldiers lost in that war, only 3,000 would die in battle. Mary Seacole turned up in London, offering to help, with good testimonials. The War Office, the army medical department, the quartermaster-general's department and the secretary for war closed ranks in turn against 'this plump, middle-aged West Indian lady in her flamboyant red or yellow dress and blue straw bonnet from which flowed a length of scarlet ribbon' (Fryer, 247). Official position denied to her, she went to the Black Sea anyway. With a distant male connection of her late husband she launched a firm called Seacole and Day.

Before and after she turned up near the British camp in the Crimea, Mary sent letters to her 'sons', including such distinguished persons as General Sir John Campbell. The British Hotel – strictly no gambling, closed at 8 p.m. sharp each day, shut on Sundays – which opened in the early summer of 1855, at 'Spring Hill' between Balaklava and the besieged city of Sevastopol, was built from wreckage floating in the harbour. The whole Army soon knew that at Mother Seacole's establishment a man could find anything he needed, 'from an anchor down to a needle' (Seacole, 114).

Every schoolchild who pays attention has heard of the so-called 'Lady with the Lamp', the remarkable Florence Nightingale, who went out with thirty-eight nurses to reorganise the base hospital in Scutari, Turkey, an effort largely sabotaged by an intrinsically insanitary site. Mary, whose services had been refused by Florence, roamed the battlefields under fire helping the wounded and dying, of all races, including Russians. At her own establishment, as one survivor recalled, 'She had the secret of a recipe for cholera and dysentery; and liberally dispensed the specific, alike to those who could pay and those who could not.' A present-day historian adds, 'Not only did she bring relief to the wounded on the battlefield but her cheerful personality and undaunted refusal to give in to the prevailing bureaucracy helped make life tolerable for those in her care' (Royle, 256–57).

In sub-zero conditions on occasion, she went down to the Balaklava landing stage every day when wounded from the front were embarked *en route* to Miss Nightingale. An admiring army surgeon saw her 'in rain and snow, in storm and tempest . . . in any shelter she could find, brewing tea for all who wanted it, and there were many. Sometimes more than 200 sick would be embarked on one day, but Mrs Seacole was always equal to the occasion' (Fryer, 249). When not performing such prodigies, she would be taking books and papers to men in the local military hospital, or mending soldiers' torn uniforms.

W. H. Russell of the *Times*, the first modern 'war correspondent', gave Mary due attention. 'I saw her at the assaults on the Redan, at the Battle of the Tchernaya, at the fall of Sebastopol, laden . . . with wine, bandages and food for the wounded or the prisoners . . . Her hut was surrounded every morning by the rough navvies and Land Transport men, who had a faith in her proficiency in the healing art . . .' (Fryer, 250). Her stores and livestock were subjected to constant depredations by thieving Greeks and still-worse French Zouaves. 'I depended', she would write, 'chiefly upon two sailors, both of questionable character, two black servants, Jew Johnny' – this was a loyal Greek lad who had attached himself to her in Constantinople – 'and my own reputation for determination and courage' (Seacole, 112–13).

She did, though, have powerful friends. The Pasha commanding the Turkish force was happy to ignore Islamic restrictions and drink Mary's beer, sherry and champagne, while attempting to learn English from her instruction. One day Sir John Campbell was tippling with other officers in front of Mary's premises when a familiar figure rode into view, raffishly garbed as ever. They 'called out "Soyer! Soyer! come here – come this way . . ."'

Alexis Soyer (q.v.), most famous chef of his day, a Frenchman long domiciled in England, was a one-off to match Mary. He had read Russell's Crimean dispatches with horror, and in February 1855 announced that he would go to the Crimea at his own expense to reorganise cooking facilities in the hospitals at Scutari. Friends were reluctant to voyage with him to Hell on the Black Sea, but he somehow persuaded 'T.G.', whom he described as 'a gentleman of colour', to be his companion. Scutari sorted out, Soyer proceeded, as the War Office had requested, to reform army cuisine at the Crimean battlefront. He had brought with him specimens of the 'Soyer Stove', eminently portable, and very economical with fuel. These were successfully tried out, and 400 more, enough for the whole army, were ordered from Britain. The Soyer Stove was still used by British forces in World War II. He had revolutionised battlefield cooking.

Hence that meeting of two philanthropic fodderers at the British Hotel was epic, not least because Mary Seacole fancied her own Jamaican delicacies against Soyer's Frenchified extravagances. As Soyer told the story, he was chatting away with Campbell and other acquaintances when 'an old dame of a jovial appearance but a few shades darker than the white lily, issued from the tent, bawling out, in order to make her voice heard above the noise, "Who is my new son?" to which one of the officers replied, "Monsieur Soyer, to be sure; don't you know him?" "God bless me, my son, are you Monsieur Soyer of whom I heard so much in Jamaica? Well, to be sure! I have sold many and many a score of your Relish and other sauces – God knows how many . . . I had a gross about ten days ago, and they are all gone . . . Come down, my son, and take a glass of champagne with my old friend, Sir John Campbell"' (Soyer, 142–44). Soyer returned often to see her, praised her cooking, refused on grounds of gallantry to accept her challenge of a public contest, and suggested that they should make rivalry impossible after the war, by opening together the best restaurant in Europe . . .

In Britain, thanks to W. H. Russell, Mary was now a household name, overshadowing even Miss Nightingale's reputation. For reasons connected with the general movement towards democracy (the franchise would be extended to working men – some of them – in 1867) there was suddenly a disposition in Britain, from Queen Victoria downwards, to acclaim common soldiers as heroes. As a heroine of the heroes themselves, Mary Seacole was granted an enormous tribute in 1857. She had returned to London bankrupt – the end of the war had left Seacole and Day with expensive, unsaleable stores on their hands. Word of her plight reached the press and *The Times* and *Punch* uttered on her behalf. Two noble army commanders stepped forth to help her. Over 40,000 people attended a benefit festival in her honour, held in the Royal Surrey Gardens over four consecutive nights in July. There were almost 1,000 performers, including nine military bands and an orchestra. Charge for admission was quintupled, and still people flocked there. The music-hall was packed out, so many hundreds stood outside. 'Mrs Seacole sat in state in front of the centre gallery, supported by Lord Rokeby on one side, by Lord George Paget on the other . . . The genial old lady rose from her place, and smiled benignantly on the assembled multitude, amid a tremendous and continuous cheering' (Edwards and Dabydeen, 166).

Mary's autobiography, the second and last book in English by a black woman to be published in Britain in the nineteenth century, came out in the same month, with a preface by Russell, sold well, and was reprinted within a year. It is suffused with Mary's proper satisfaction over her own remarkable exploits. She remained in Britain, is said to have served the Queen's daughter-in-law, the Princess of Wales, as a masseuse, and died very comfortably off, even making bequests to Lord Rokeby and his daughter – a loyal woman of Empire to the last.

Heads are now shaken over her ruling ideas. She was ultra-patriotic, imperialist, and ambivalent about her own colour. She surmised that it was the 'good Scotch blood' in her veins which had spurred her to travel and notable deeds. She referred to herself as 'yellow' or 'brown', whereas she called black people 'niggers' – and Mediterranean peoples were 'cunning' and 'lazy'. In short, she endorsed Victorian British stereotypes.

The irony is that, just as her Crimean victories were recorded shortly before Pasteur's germ theory of disease at last gave Western treatment of illness a truly scientific basis which seemed to make Mary's folk medicine obsolete, her triumph with the British public coincided with a damnable watershed in attitudes. The Indian 'Mutiny' – or War of Independence – of 1857 was presented as the action of dusky subhuman fiends. Atrocious British reprisals required no excuse. Sane men succumbed to the nightmare fantasy of the raping nigger. From the Mutiny on, prejudice against 'niggers' ruled more and more uncontrollably. The obviously 'civilised' qualities of Indians of princely status or manifest learning sometimes conquered it. A Parsee, Dadabhai Naoroji, scholar and businessman, was elected Liberal MP for Central Finsbury in 1892 for three years and was the first Asian to sit in the

House of Commons. But those people of African descent who were not merely deemed lazy and simple-minded were held to display all the despicable shiftiness of 'half-castes' or the unattractive vitality of naturally polygamous would-be cannibals.

Mary Seacole was written out of the history books. A bestselling, authoritative, biography of Florence Nightingale, published in 1950, did not even mention her. She was rediscovered nearly a century after her death, a well-preserved specimen of a loyal, respectable, much-loved Victorian lady. In 1973, her grave in the Roman Catholic section of Kensal Green cemetery was reconsecrated, and the headstone was restored. In the same cemetery her friend Alexis Soyer is buried under his heartfelt monument to his early-dead and adored wife Emma. He had caught 'Crimea Fever', come home a sick man, and died short of fifty in 1858, a martyr to his own good nature.

Ziggi Alexander and Audrey Dewjee, Mary Seacole, *1982; Paul Edwards and David Dabydeen, eds.*, Black Writers in Britain 1760–1890, *(Edinburgh) 1991; Peter Fryer*, Staying Power: The History of Black People in Britain, *1984; Helen Morris*, Portrait of a Chef: The Life of Alexis Soyer*; Trevor Royle*, Crimea, *1999; Mary Seacole*, The Wonderful Adventures of Mary Seacole in Many Lands, *1857 – facsimile reprint (New York) 1988, introd. William L. Andrews; Alexis Soyer*, A Culinary Campaign, *(Lewes) 1995 reprint; Cecil Woodham Smith*, Florence Nightingale, *1950*

Chelita Secunda (Trinidad) 1945–2000

In 1970, T. Rex was riding high in the charts. The moment of Glam Rock was about to dawn, but it awaited a crucial intervention from Chelita Secunda, the band's publicist. She observed that Marc Bolan, the band's bisexual lead singer, was extremely pretty, with his elfin face and corkscrew curls. She took him to clothes shops for women in London, whence he emerged with feather boas and beautifully embroidered jackets. Tony Venturi recalled, 'There was a place in the World's End that sold clothes that were considered kind of kitsch. That famous chartreuse satin jacket with the music notes embroidered on it . . . Marc took it very seriously and started walking around like that.'

More . . . With T. Rex's 'Hot Line' at No. 1 and the band due to appear on BBC TV's *Top of the Pops*, Chelita put glitter under Marc's eyes. 'Marc claimed he'd done it purely for a laugh', Venturi went on, 'and thought no more about it, but at the next T. Rex gig he was greeted by the sight of hundreds of beglittered fans' (Hoskyns, 18).

Glitter had been pioneered in Andy Warhol's New York theatre a few years previously, as a statement of excess. The glam craze of which it became a part raised in public impudent questions about truth and sexuality and can be said to have culminated and expired in 1975 with the great chartbusting 'Bohemian Rhapsody' devised by Freddie Mercury (formerly Farokh Bulsara from Zanzibar) for Queen. Bolan expired in a car crash in 1980, after years of self-parody. But Chelita Secunda, through him, had made some history.

She was born Chelita Salvatori, into a rich family of Corsican origins which owned a department store in Port of Spain, Trinidad. Her father, George, loved racing cars. Her mother, Connie, was English and she was educated at the Lycée in South Kensington, London, from which, not liking the nuns, she ran away. She was eighteen when her father died from burns after his yacht blew up.

A family friend was the photographer Norman Parkinson, who bought land in Tobago in 1964 to pursue what he considered his true vocation, farming. Parkinson (1913–90) had done well during the thirties as a fashion photographer for *Harper's Bazaar*. He looked like a somewhat faded Indian Army colonel – an upright 6' 5'' with conservative values to go with his appearance – but was revered as the top man (*Vogue* during and after the war, now *Queen*) who had, with sometimes anarchic humour, set models in posh gear in 'real life' settings, as when grimy Lancashire coalminers held up a startled beauty in her brand-new dress.

Chelita went back to London and resorted to Parkinson. This was in 1963, remembered by Philip Larkin as 'the year of the Lady Chatterley Trial and the Beatles' first LP' when 'sexual intercourse first began'. It was now that 'the Sixties' really started, and Parkinson was well placed to launch Chelita straight into them. He set her off as a journalist with *Harper's* – she moved on to *Woman*, then to *Nova*. She married, briefly, Tony Secunda, who managed rock bands, and she was soon on phone-number terms with the Beatles and the Stones. She fell in with an avant-garde designer, Ossie Clark, and became his PR. She dyed her hair blue, then went in for rainbow eye makeup with cheeks highlighted in pink. Her angular features made her hard to photograph, so she didn't become an icon, but she had a famous smile and famous wit. Initially she spurned stimulants, even alcohol, but in the seventies she was sucked into excess, making 'drug sorties' for members of the Stones, bingeing on smack herself, and getting busted. In 1979 she retreated to Trinidad, planning to open a small hotel, but was arrested, again, for cocaine possession. Eventually she found strength to kick the habit. She resumed her journalism and in 1988 had a small part in *Caravaggio*, one of the remarkable films of her long-time artist friend Derek Jarman.

Designers adored her tiny distinctive person and gladly gave her hats and clothes to wear. She drove round London in a Bentley with a pair of King Charles Spaniels. But eventually she wearied of fashion and the metropolis and relocated to Marrakesh, where she was working single-handed to open a hotel in the souk when a fatal heart attack felled her. She had told the friend who had lent her money for the building that there were enough diamonds under the floorboards of her flat in Chelsea to recompense him if anything went wrong. This turned out not to be true.

Martin Harrison, ed., Parkinson: Photographs 1935–1990, *1994; Barney Hoskyns*, Glam: Bowie, Bolan and the Glitter Rock Revolution, *1998; Philip Hoare, Obituary*, Independent, *18 March, 2001; Terence Pepper, ed.*, Photographs by Norman Parkinson, *1991; private information*

Sidi Muhammad Ibn Abd Allah (Morocco) reigned 1757–90

Otherwise referred to as Muhammad III. For his virtues and his eccentricities, see **Gloag**. He was a tolerant and, it seems, humane ruler whose bizarre behaviour towards the end of his life echoes that of his 'mad' contemporary George III of Britain. He was a monarch of the Sharifian Alawi dynasty, founded in 1666 and persisting to the present day. It had supplanted the Sharifian Saadi. Both these desert clans were 'Sharifian' because they claimed direct descent from the prophet Mohammed.

Elizabeth Marsh, in her narrative *The Female Captive* (1769), played up her encounters with this potentate. She was the daughter of a British official in Gibraltar, who was seized off the coast of North Africa by

Sale corsairs in August 1756 and held captive in Morocco with her fellow-passengers until late that year because Sidi Muhammad was annoyed by British diplomatic hauteur. She reported two interviews with 'the Prince' – who was 'tall, finely shaped, of a good complexion, and appeared to be about five and twenty . . . His figure, all together, was rather agreeable, and his address polite and easy.' She claimed that he tried to persuade her to join his harem. She pretended to be married already, rode out the prince's anger, refused to convert to Islam and was finally released. Linda Colley, relating this doubtful story, goes on to make the interesting point that Marsh's two volumes were the first *female* narrative of captivity under 'the Moors' of North Africa . . . 'British captivity literature had traditionally been far more concerned to stress the sexual threat to male captives in Barbary.' The Moors were held to be addicted to sodomy, and to asserting their cruel power by raping Christian men. But by 1769, the growth of British power and the waning of the Ottoman Turks had reduced fear of rampant Islam, 'leading to an emphasis instead on the supposed heterosexual lusts of Muslim men and on their harems of docile, scented females. Claiming that Turks, or Moroccans, or Algerians collected and domineered over sexually pliant women, both entrapped Europeans and non-Europeans, was a way also of saying that these peoples were no longer in a position seriously to threaten European males' (Colley, 126–31). *Vide* the comic 'Orients' of Mozart's *Seraglio* and Rossini's *Italian Girl in Algiers*.

Linda Colley, Captives, *2002; Elizabeth Marsh,* The Female Captive, *1769*

Hannah Snell (England) 1723–92

On 9 June 1750, James Gray proceeded with his comrades, Marines just returned from service in India, to collect back pay in Downing Street, London. Naturally, they went on to celebrate. In the pub they met Susannah Gray and her husband, James, a carpenter, who lived in Wapping. This couple corroborated the startling revelation by the man they knew as Jemmy, that 'he' was really Hannah Snell, Susannah's sister . . .

Cross-dressing lassies serving as soldiers or sailors were staple fare in English popular culture. Ballads and chapbooks usually attributed such behaviour to the desire to track down a lost lover, an ingredient in Hannah's tale. She had no trouble agreeing terms with an enterprising publisher, Robert Walker. A third-person account of her alleged adventures in forty-six pages was on sale by 3 July. A much longer illustrated version – 187 pages – soon followed it. Abridgements meanwhile appeared in the *Gentleman's Magazine* and the *Scots Magazine*. A Dutch translation was not long preparing. Chapbook versions for indigent provincial readers would follow . . .

Popular theatre also loved female soldiers. On 29 June, Hannah sang two songs on stage at New Wells, Goodman Fields. Sixty more appearances there followed, and she extended her act to include a demonstration of the 'manual exercises of a soldier' – Marine drill. She shortly appeared for five nights at New Wells Spa, Clerkenwell, and then took her stage act on to Bristol and Bath. This was jam on her bread and butter, since on the strength of wounds suffered at the siege of Pondicherry, she had been admitted as an Out-Pensioner to the Royal Chelsea Hospital for old soldiers, and granted 5d a day for the rest of her life . . . (Stephens, 37–46)

From 1751, there is a gap in her record. She reappears in Newbury, Berkshire, where in 1759 she marries Richard Eyles, a carpenter, and bears him a son, George. Both James and Susannah Gray die of consumption in a workhouse a few years later, but Hannah breezes on. Widowed, now nearly fifty, she marries a Bedfordshire man, Richard Habgood, in 1772. Six years later, a parson diarist, Rev. James Woodforde, encounters her travelling in Norfolk as a pedlar. In April 1780, her son George commences a Clerkship, with a King's Bench Attorney. Assuming that Hannah could not have afforded the education and fee entailed in that, has some 'lady of fortune' become George's patroness?

By 1785, Hannah was so 'infirm' that the Chelsea Hospital increased her pension 'in compassion' to 1s a day. Living now with George and his wife, she broke down at last completely, was admitted to the Bedlam Hospital for crazy people in 1791, and died there early next year.

Such are documented facts. The narrative published by Walker as *The Female Soldier* is something else – adjusted to the taste of a middle-class public which could afford to buy leatherbound books and was in tune with the rising 'sentimental' style. Bits of it must have some truth in them.

We may accept that Hannah was born in Worcester in 1723, one of nine children of a hosier and dyer. And if most of these either became or married soldiers, it is very possible that Hannah in childhood played soldiers with her friends and declared she wished to go to war. Aged seventeen, she went to London to live with sister Susannah and her husband Gray. She married a Dutch sailor, James Summs, who cheated on her and plundered her then fled the country when she was pregnant. The record says that her six-month-old daughter was buried early in 1746. Walker's narrative alleges that Hannah, determined to track down Summs after the death of her infant, enlisted in Guise's Regiment at Coventry in November 1745 and marched north with it to fight the Jacobite Rebellion, deserting from quarters in Carlisle when someone turned up in town who might have recognised her. In fact, Guise's Regiment was in Scotland at that time. And why would she go looking for a Dutch sailor in the northern mountains?

It does seem that Snell/Gray did, as *The Female Soldier* tells us, join Marines in Portsmouth who were sailing with Admiral Boscawen to assist the East India Company in Madras against its aggressive French rivals. In August 1748, they advanced on the French headquarters, Pondicherry. Hannah's account, via Walker, of her doughty part in the siege of that place is plausible enough, but what follows is most striking. Injured by shots in both legs, she had a further shot in the groin which raised the agonising possibility that treatment must lead to the disclosure of her femininity. So in the field hospital she enlisted the help of a 'black' (Indian) woman who gave her healing salves to apply after she had pulled the ball out with finger and thumb. Phew! Then she let surgeons attend to her legs . . .

But documents show that a fit 'James Gray' embarked on the *Eltham* man-of-war after the arduous battle of Pondicherry. The same Gray was involved, in June 1749, in the siege of Devicotta. A month and a half later, he was admitted to the hospital at Cuddelore, where he spent two months. So where did Hannah acquire the wounds which were testified to by Colonel Napier and qualified her for a pension?

Those who eagerly purchased *The Female Soldier* clearly didn't care much if it was true or not. They must have readily enough accepted the poignant scene in Lisbon where 'Gray' and comrades on their way home are in an 'Irish' pub and meet an English sailor who has recently been aboard a Dutch vessel. Hannah asks if this man knows her old friend Summs . . . But of course. Hearing in Genoa that Summs was in gaol for murdering a prominent citizen with his *sneeker-snee*, this sailor and three or four mates went to see him. Summs admitted that he must die for his crime, but said he was more dejected over the wrong he had done a young woman in London, his wife. He would die in peace if he could hope that she could pardon and forgive him. His friends promised to inquire after her, but could not have soothed his conscience, since he was soon after sewn up in a large bag, with enough large stones in it to make him sink, and thrown into the sea . . .

Well, her narrative disposed of Summs decisively enough for Hannah to feel free to marry again. It was important that her readers believed that, living in crowded conditions with rough men, she had preserved her disguise and her virtue. Thomas Seccombe, writing about her in the *Dictionary of National Biography* (1909), clearly found her a shade too tame for his taste. 'Her nautical experiences', he sniffed, 'were probably eclipsed by those of "William Brown" (a negress, so rated on the books of the *Queen Charlotte*) who was proved to have served eleven years when that ship was paid off in 1815 and was conspicuous for her agility as captain of the maintop no less than for her partiality for prize-money and grog.' Point taken.

Dictionary of National Biography; *Dianne Dugaw (introd.)*, The Female Soldier; Or, The Surprising Life and Adventures of Hannah Snell, *reprint, (Los Angeles) 1989; Matthew Stephens*, Hannah Snell: The Secret Life of a Female Marine . . ., *1997*

Flora Solomon (Russia/England) 1895–1984

Grigori Benenson was from Minsk. Sophie Goldberg, whom he married, was from Pinsk. She bore their eldest daughter, Flora, in Pinsk.

Both were towns in the Jewish Pale of Settlement within the Tsarist Empire. Jewish activity was hamstrung by law and confronted by militant anti-Semitism. But Grigori wouldn't be impeded by either.

Benensons descended from a line of 'wonder-rabbis', mystics with direct access to God. Grigori did wonders with money, first of all in the timber business. Then, in the late 1880s, he acquired an oilfield. Flora's early childhood, with a French governess and attending a Christian school, was spent in Baku, in the Caucasus, on the Caspian Sea, where, as she would write in old age, 'the Tatar near-slaves of the oil-fields did not hate their masters a tithe as much as they hated their better-educated Armenian fellow-workers' (Solomon, 26). The Revolution of 1905, which brought Russia a parliament, the Duma, was accompanied by inter-communal butchery in Baku, as well as pogroms against Jews in other parts of Russia. Grigori decided to head for St Petersburg. He was famously rich. But since he was Jewish, members of his family, as Flora found out in practice, were not allowed to sleep anywhere in the city except their own home, and Rasputin, the Tsar's demonic favourite, was able to extort money from Grigori for one of his nefarious projects.

To tolerant Germany Flora was sent to be polished. Under the spartan regime of the school kept by the Wolff sisters in Wiesbaden, she never saw a Russian book for five years. She would say later that she spoke four languages, none of them properly. Back in St Petersburg, in 1910, she continued to idolise her brilliant father, whose magic was now working, by remote control, in Siberia, which he never visited. He attracted British capital for a joint venture exploiting goldfields by the Lena river. In 1912, Flora's faith in her affluent circumstances received an irreversible shock. Lena miners struck against slave conditions. Police fired on a protest march, massacring 200. The Duma sent a bright young lawyer, Alexander Kerensky (1881–1970), a supporter of the Social Revolutionary party, east to investigate what had gone on. The horrors of life in the goldfields were revealed. From then on, Flora felt that she owed a debt to the working classes.

Grigori's mistress, Tamara Kolinskaya, had been pressing him for years to divorce his wife. At what was meant to be a 'final' meeting, in a moving train, on the outskirts of St Petersburg, she offered him a chocolate and, as he bent to inspect the box, withdrew vitriol from her muff and threw it in his face. Only in Germany could surgery save his sight and rebuild his face. Flora accompanied him to Jena, and was at his side when the First World War broke out. His devoted surgeon was called up to head the naval hospital at Hamburg, treatment was incomplete, and Grigori and Flora had to follow him, while mother and sisters were trapped elsewhere in Germany. Fortunately, the Germans were far more anti-British than anti-Russian. A Hamburg banker, Max Warburg, of the to-be-famous family, somehow managed to liberate funds for Grigori from both London and St Petersburg, and nearly a year after the war had started, thanks to Flora's fluency in German, the family got out via neutral Sweden. Grigori took Flora and Manya with him to London. Mother and Fira went back to St Petersburg.

Beside Eastern European Ashkenazim, recent poor immigrants, there was a sparse but distinguished community of wealthy Jews in Britain, some of them Sephardis who were descended from Iberian or Middle-Eastern stock. The rich Benensons, who stayed in Claridge's Hotel, were perfectly welcome. Before long, Flora was driving the natty little Scripps Booth motor car which her father had given her to the door of Herbert Samuel, the first professing Jew to be a member of the British Cabinet. (Disraeli, Victoria's Jewish Prime Minister, had been a Christian convert.) Cocooned by both Judaism and wealth, she could hardly refuse Harold Solomon, ten years her senior, when he proposed to her in the Cavalry Club.

The Solomons had emerged as merchants in Britain's tropical empire, then one had made a fortune in England out of introducing steel pen-nibs. Harold had been educated in a house reserved for Jewish boys in a famous public school, Clifton. Sandhurst and the 18th Hussars had completed the sterotype of the English gentleman, and he had been decorated for his recent work in a British Military Mission to allied Serbia. He was now on his way to chase the Germans out of East Africa, where he would be promoted to Brigadier General, receiving the OBE on his return home. Flora dutifully waited for that.

Meanwhile, Grigori was in more hot water. Back in Russia to look at his assets there, he had bumped into the October Revolution. The family mansion had been seized and he had gone into hiding. But a Commandant in the Bolshevik Department of Foreign Trade remembered the Jew's generosity to him in Monte Carlo before the war, after he had lost all his money at the gaming tables, and smuggled Grigori and family out with a trade delegation to Stockholm. When Flora married Harold in 1919, Grigori made her a settlement in trust and gave her a personal allowance of £1,000 a month.

Her visit to Herbert Samuel had been on Zionist business. She had been drawn into the movement led by Chaim Weizmann, a brilliant immigrant chemist whose work was indispensable to the British war effort. In November 1917, A. J. Balfour's Declaration on behalf of the British Government that Palestine would provide a home for the Jewish people had been a huge boost to Zionism. Herbert Samuel had lost his parliamentary seat but was going to Palestine as High Commissioner in a territory governed by Britain under mandate from the League of Nations. Flora talked Harold into accepting Samuel's offer of a job on his staff.

The result was for Flora an idyll, for Harold a revelation. 'Proudly he brought me the first pound of butter made on a new Jewish farmstead. And a basket of strawberries cultivated in an area where the native people had never seen the fruit. Just then, I was able to break the news to him that I was pregnant . . .' (Solomon, 101).

When Peter was born in London in July 1921, Harold at once put his son down for Eton, but meanwhile it was back to Palestine, where the Solomons observed the first stirrings of the armed Haganah movement among Jewish settlers. Their time in a land moving beyond idyll was cut short when, at a point-to-point in December 1923, Harold was thrown by his bay horse, which kicked his spine. He was soon paralysed from the waist down, and Flora's intimate life with him was over.

Jews in Britain, however wealthy, were commonly ill-at-ease with the Conservative Party, where anti-Semitism was rife. Labour formed its first, short-lived Government around the time of Harold's accident. Flora, back in London, became friendly with 'Red Ellen' Wilkinson, militant and novelist, and Margaret Bondfield, who would become Britain's first woman Cabinet member, as Minister of Labour in the second Labour Government formed in 1929. Flora was impressed to learn of Bondfield's 'earlier shop-assistant existence as a live-in drudge on her feet seventy hours a week for a pittance' and to behold the 'fire of resentment' breathed by Wilkinson as 'she fought and fought to improve the laundry girls' lot' (Solomon, 127). Still employing eleven servants at her home in Kensington, Flora began to consider herself a socialist.

Grigori, meanwhile, was riding high in New York, where he owned the largest docking system in the hemisphere, and the Benenson Building was one of the highest skyscrapers in the city. Visiting in 1927, Flora went with him to hear a voice from the past.

Alexander Kerensky had become Minister of War in the the provisional administration set up after the February revolution in Russia in 1917, then Prime Minister. Lenin had seen him off in October. Now, based in Paris, he dreamed of victorious return. In New York, his was a very hot ticket, retailing at three times its face value. Russians packed the 5,000-seat Century Theatre by Central Park, while thousands more milled outside. Kerensky's Monarchist and Communist opponents were there to jeer him, but most of the audience rose to cheer this striking, manly figure with crew-cut hair. A woman came forward to offer the speaker a lavish bouquet, then slapped him three times in the face. It turned out that she blamed him for the deaths of her brother and fiancé, both young officers, in 1917. She had something in her glove, according to Flora, and Kerensky went on to denounce the Bolsheviks, pressing a handkerchief to his cheek to staunch the flow of blood. Afterwards, they met at a reception, whence Flora, against the rules of her hotel, conveyed him to her room . . . There followed a relationship which Flora termed 'emotionally intricate and geographically wearisome'. They hopped between London and Paris, with bedbusting holidays together in Annecy. 'My love affair was not so much a restoration of my sexuality, but its discovery' (Solomon, 133–36).

Restlessly active, Flora set up Blackamore Press, to publish foreign classics in translation. But her life, in her mid thirties, was fated otherwise. First, Harold died suddenly in 1930, from an infection caught bathing in the Danube when he was on a trip back to his beloved Serbia. Then Grigori, who had sailed through the Wall Street Crash of 1929 with ease, still expanding, was ruined in 1931 when huge loans were called in. His allowance to Flora ceased. She decided to get a job.

She had long known the amiable Simon Marks, who, with his brother-in-law Israel Sieff, ran the successful chain of Marks & Spencer stores, first famous in the North of England as 'Penny Bazaars'. Now, hearing Simon hold forth at a dinner party on the firm's plans for expansion, Flora cut him short by stating that her friend Margaret Bondfield said that it was firms like his that gave Jews a bad name.

On the spot, Simon offered her the job of overseeing the conditions in which his shopgirls worked.

So Flora, on a salary of £5 a week, went round inspecting Simon's stores. She reported back to him. She was appalled that any trader in Britain could hold staff behind counters until late at night while providing no facilities for rest during breaks. She was shocked to find Marks & Spencer's girls getting 17s a week, less if they were under eighteen. But she thought that trade unions had been wrong to press always on wages and working hours. 'Human dignity' was the real issue. Simon endorsed every word.

With the title of 'Staff Superintendent', the chair of the Welfare Committee at Marks' London headquarters at 82 Baker Street, and five assistants, Flora became very busy. She started with subsidised staff canteens in every store. Then pleasant rest rooms with easy chairs. Better loos. Friendly advice and even personal loans for staff in trouble. Holiday camps at seaside resorts all over the country. Doctors, dentists and chiropodists attached to every store, and arrangements with hospitals to admit M&S employees free of charge at short notice. It was a triumph to get the minimum wage raised to £1 a week, a still greater one when Simon allowed her to provide birth-control instruction to his employees. So far from all this undermining capitalism, unions were complaining that Flora's policies made it hard for them to recruit members, and M&S was outstripping all its high-street rivals. It now invaded the West End of London with a flagship store at Oxford Circus which had splendidly designed staff facilities.

Meanwhile, Europe's crisis worsened. Flora worked with Zionist friends to rescue Jews from Germany. The break with Kerensky came with Hitler's infamous anti-Jewish *Kristallnacht* in November 1938. He said shruggingly that such things were happening all the time in Russia. She flared up, he left in anger. He returned with an ultimatum – marry him or separate for ever. 'He could see my answer in my expression' (Solomon, 174–75).

Grigori died in London in March 1939. His magic touch had never deserted him – he had paid all his creditors and a left a tidy fortune. His last request was that grandson Peter should resume the Benenson name. When war broke out, Flora at once deployed the Benenson magic. Simon Marks agreed to her suggestion that the firm should sponsor cheap communal restaurants. She set up the first in a disused community centre in Kensington. Inevitably, it made a profit. Soon Flora was commandeering church halls and suchlike all over the land. Churchill disliked the name,'Communal Restaurants', which smacked of Bolshevism, so they became 'British Restaurants', providing sound food for all in times of social disruption and intense rationing.

When the Luftwaffe set about bombing London in earnest, Flora sped down to the devastated East End. Enter my father. Rescue workers were being served tea. There was none for grieving people rendered homeless.

Flora recorded:

> In the horror of it I found myself talking to three of the most remarkable men it had ever been my good fortune to encounter. One of them, Ritchie Calder, was ostensibly reporting the scene for the *Daily Herald*, but he had shed his journalistic detachment to become a partisan. He angrily proposed organising a march on Whitehall. He was putting this to Father John Groser, a local priest who took his ministry into havoc's maw, recognising that here was a time when a lavatory was more important than an altar. And between them the impelling figure of Mickey Davis, four feet high. His home was not destroyed, for indeed he never owned one. 'Mickey the Midget' as Spitalfields knew him lived as a Spitalfields stray, but in this crisis he was the commander, self-appointed. Joining these three I thought to myself, goodness, another committee.

The next day Flora went straight to the Ministry of Food. The Minister, Lord Woolton, had been a store manager himself. He immediately authorised Flora's demand – support for emergency field kitchens, first in the East End, then anywhere else they were needed. M&S took the lead in providing them. Mickey Davis became commandant of the largest shelter, holding 3,000 people, where Vera Weizmann, Chaim's doctor wife, organised a roster of medics for a sick-bay. Flora borrowed a police car and a Scotland Yard inspector, Arthur Caine, to take her out into the blitz every night. Watching her dishing out soups and sandwiches from one of her mobile canteens a vox pop among the ruins called out, 'There she is, the Lady with the Ladle'. My father,

Ritchie, put that in print at once. 'Ritchie Calder, Arthur Caine, Mickey the Midget, John Groser, we forged a bond never to be severed. Come the day-time and we would often repair to my new flat off Curzon Street for a drink and perhaps a sleep' (Solomon, 181–84).

I think it was Flora who set my father on the path which led him to a fellowship of the Weizmann Institute in Israel, of which he wrote an approved history, and honorary citizenship of Jerusalem, gifted him by Mayor Teddy Kollek. Certainly, he got to know her boss Israel Sieff very well.

Flora's life had its climax during the war, despite a spell back in Palestine, now Israel, helping Golda Meir cope with the influx of immigrants. She was manoeuvred out of her post at Marks & Spencer, though Simon Marks brought her back as a consultant. The highlight of her later years was the foundation in 1962 of Amnesty International by her lawyer son, Peter Benenson. My father's last public appearance was for Amnesty, sitting in a cage to demonstrate the plight of political prisoners. He died in 1982, Flora two years later. I think both of them would have been appalled by the behaviour of Ariel Sharon's government towards Palestinians in the new century – a betrayal of Jewish and socialist ideals which both had cherished, along with an appreciation of the virtues of clean milk and wholesome soup.

Richard Abraham, Alexander Kerensky: The First Love of the Revolution, *(New York) 1987;* Annual Obituary 1984; *Ritchie Calder*, Carry on London, *1941; Flora Solomon with Barney Litvinoff*, From Baku to Baker Street, *1984*

Alexis Soyer (France) 1809–58

Born in 1809 in Brie, home of the famous cheese, youngest son of a small shopkeeper, Soyer achieved precocious success as chef in Paris, but decided to seek fortune in England, where French cooks were in fashion. He worked for various noble and distinguished persons before gaining definitive fame as chef (1838–50) to the great new Reform Club founded by Liberal parliamentarians. On the day when Victoria was crowned queen, 28 June 1838, he prepared breakfast for 2,000 people at Gwydir House, the club's temporary premises. When its handsome permanent building opened in 1841, the Club had the finest kitchens in London.

Soyer was a 'celebrity chef'. He created sensational banquets, and enormously costly dishes (truffles stuffed with ortolans, for instance). He was a wit and notorious practical joker. But he was also famously romantic and warm-hearted, a besotted fan of the ballet and bad poet, devoted to the memory of his English wife, a gifted professional painter who had died in childbirth, and to the needs of the London poor, for whom he set up soup kitchens. One Christmas Day he fed 20,000 down-and-outs. In Dublin, during the terrible Irish Famine, he created a model kitchen capable of dishing out 5,000 meals a day. It served 1,147,279 rations between 6 April and 14 August 1847.

Soyer published bestselling cook books – an expensive one (*The Gastronomic Regulator)* for toffs, a sensible one for the middle classes, and a practical one for the poor. He was also an insatiable inventor – 'patent pots and pans and teapots, an appliance for rescuing the drowning, *entrée* dishes, pantomime illusions, naval kitchens, a device for keeping money in the heels of dress boots . . .' (Morris, 1). He got Messrs Crosse and Blackwell really going by selling them his recipes for sauces, followed by a masterpiece, Soyer's Relish. Another masterpiece was his Magic Stove – a tiny spirit stove such 'that a gentleman may cook his steak on the study table or a lady may have it amongst her crochet'. This could be purchased separately or as part of a 'Magic Kitchen' in a box 14" by 9" by 9" which contained 'everything required to cook and serve a complete meal, including a spice-box, tea-kettle and coffee-pot' (Morris, 60–62).

Working for the War Office to reform Army cooking in the Crimea, Soyer met the legendary 'Mother **Seacole**' (q.v.), and the end of his story is told in her entry.

Helen Morris, Portrait of a Chef: The Life of Alexis Soyer, *1938*

Hans Thurbeer (Switzerland) *fl.* 1940–70s

During the Battle of Britain in 1940, RAF Fighter Command shot down 1,792 aircraft of the German Luftwaffe. Six hundred and ten of these were Messerschmitt Bf 109s, the best German fighters, and 210 were Me Bf 110 twin-engined fighters. The Luftwaffe knocked out 1,142 British fighter planes – more than half of these were Hurricanes, but 403 were superior Spitfires (Green, 75).

The Swiss airforce, Fliegertruppe, in the summer of 1940, had a better record, statistically speaking, against the Luftwaffe. It shot down eleven German planes and lost only three. Most of its victims were Me 110 fighters. Oddly, the Swiss pilots responsible for this splendid kill rate were flying Messerchmitt Me 109 E planes . . .

Switzerland's role in World War II has not attracted much favourable attention. Seventy-two per cent of the 4,200,000 inhabitants of the twenty-two cantons and three half-cantons of the Swiss Federation were German-speakers, amongst whom there was sympathy for Hitler's Germany. (The rest were twenty per cent Francophone, six per cent Italophone, and one per cent speakers of the ancient Romansch language.) Discredit has attached to the key role of Swiss financial institutions in handling wealth looted by the Nazis. Jewish refugees from Vichy France were stopped at the Swiss border. Trade between Germany and Fascist Italy, in coal, steel and agricultural products, went on through the Simplon and St Gotthard tunnels under Switzerland, which depended on German coal and perforce traded with Germany, while overseas imports by sea came via Italy. Switzerland may appear to have been complicit in Axis criminality.

An alternative view, however, is that the Swiss were utterly determined that Nazis should not overrun and control their country as had happened in Austria, Czechoslovakia, and most of the rest of Europe. Nazis had freely advertised before the war their intention to incorporate the German-speaking cantons into Greater Germany. But the Swiss had a tradition of neutrality going back to the late fifteenth century, allied to pride in Swiss military prowess, and special excellence in marksmanship. (The legend of William Tell and the apple is relevant to the exploits of the Fliegertruppe.) Every household had a rifle. During the war, at peak, about one-fifth of the Swiss population were under arms. They were specifically told that no one individual had authority to surrender, and that in the event of invasion, defenders should resort to their bayonets after expending their last bullets. Fifty thousand Jews in Switzerland – natives and refugees – suffered no persecution. Agents of the anti-Nazi allies found Switzerland an invaluable source of information. German spies were efficiently rounded up.

Before dawn on 10 May 1940 when the Nazis hit the Low Countries on their way to France, Swiss anti-aircraft drove away a German bomber flying over Basle. That day, the Luftwaffe accidentally dropped twenty-seven bombs in North Switzerland, where a Swiss squadron engaged its planes and brought down a Heinkel-111 bomber.

The Messerschmitt Bf 109 which accomplished this was one of more than 33,000 manufactured, in numerous variants, between 1935 and 1958 – a record for any combat plane. By 1938 the prestige of this remarkable fighter, which had broken the world speed record for land planes, was so commanding that the Bayerische Flugzeugwerke which manufactured it near Augsburg renamed itself after the designer, Willy Messerschmitt. The Royal Yugoslav Airforce took an interest, and by midsummer 1939 had contracted for 100 Bf 109Es, of which seventy-three were eventually delivered. I have heard Herr Hans-Ekkehard

Bob, who volunteered for the Luftwaffe in 1936 and flew for it right through the war, describe the shock, as his invading German flotilla approached Belgrade in April 1941, of seeing Messerschmitts rise up against them.

Amongst foreign emptors, the sagacious Swiss got the best deal. In 1938 they accepted ten Me 109Ds for familiarisation training pending delivery of the improved 109Es, of which they received a full order of eighty by 27 April 1940. The 109 E was the model which flew in the Battle of Britain, and experts will argue till Armageddon about whether or not it was a better plane than the Spitfire.

Its top speed was similar, but it reached 354 mph at 12,300 feet, whereas the Spitfire, which achieved 365 mph, got there only at 19,000 feet. On the other hand, the British plane was much more tightly manoeuvrable. As the war went on, successive Marks of the Spitfire got faster and faster. The Mark 9 of 1942 reached 416 mph. The Me 109 G had by then yielded supremacy among German fighters to the speedier Fokke-Wulf 190 (426 mph by 1943).

Anyway, the Swiss Fliegertruppe confronted the European crisis the summer of 1940 with fine new state-of-the-art fighter planes. On 16 May one of them shot down a German bomber intruding over Winterthur. On 1 June, thirty-six German bombers straying over Lake Neuchatel were attacked, and two Heinkel He-111 bombers were downed. Orders found aboard read: 'Caution when flying over Swiss territory.' The next day another Heinkel succumbed (Hallbrook, 108).

Because the Germans falsely claimed that the Fliegertruppe attacked Luftwaffe planes over French airspace, Capitaine Hans Thurbeer, of a Squadron, No. 6, drawn from French-speaking Switzerland, would have to face a court martial. But he understood why the Luftwaffe's commander Goering was so angry. 'Just imagine, German-built fighters from a small neutral country, flown for the most part by German-speaking pilots – it was too much . . . He would teach these Swiss a thing or two.' The fourth of June saw more Heinkels over Switzerland, now accompanied for the first time by Me 110 fighters. A dozen Swiss planes, mostly Messerschmitts, attacked them over Chaux-les-Fonds. One Swiss Me 109 fell. Two Bf 110s and another Heinkel were disposed of. Inspecting the downed German planes revealed that orders now read: 'Lure the Swiss fighters into battle and shoot down as many as possible.'

As Thurbeer told the story, 'Goering's temper rose, and for 8 June he ordered the Swiss to be challenged by a complete *Zerstorergruppe* of Bf 110s . . .' Just before noon, three Swiss flying corps rose from Thun. Over the Jura mountains they saw thirty-two Bf 110s. They were disposed at three different altitudes, flying in huge circles, daring the Swiss to come and get them. 'It was a spine-chilling sight,' Thurbeer recalled in the 1970s. By the time Squadron 6 got there, two Me 109s of 15 Squadron had engaged the Germans and one had been shot down. The survivor shot up a Bf 110, which came down near Laufen, then, outnumbered more than thirty to one, decided to skedaddle. With several German planes in pursuit, he dived into the Taubenlochschlucht, a deep ravine into which he knew only a Swiss pilot would dare to follow. The twelve Swiss fighters following up, in a pitched mêlée, brought down three more Me 110s without loss to themselves (Green, 77–78; van Ishoven, 90).

Another formation of Me 110s had attacked and brought down a patrolling Swiss biplane. However, losses were repaired on 25 July 1942, when after navigation error, two Me 109F Luftwaffe fighters – the very latest model – landed in Switzerland, and were impounded. Goering meanwhile turned to sabotage, but the Swiss picked up nine agents in a railway train and interned them for life. A German demand for the return of all Me 109s bought before the war was equally unsuccessful (Hallbrook, 109).

Meanwhile, after France capitulated on 17 June 1940, Goering was distracted from the impertinent Swiss by the recalcitrant British, then by the 'sub-human' Soviets. Adventures over Switzerland should have warned the Luftwaffe that the Me 110 wouldn't be a great success over England either. However, it had virtues as a night fighter over Germany. In this role, on 28 April 1944, an Me 110 G-46 pursued into Swiss air space an RAF Lancaster which had attacked Friedrichshafen. One of its engines failed. Unable to get back to base, it was forced to land near Zurich. It was carrying up-to-date top-secret equipment – the latest radar, Schrage Musik oblique gun installation. The German Ambassador demanded its immediate return to Germany. The Swiss said this would contravene their neutrality. A deal was made. In exchange for burning the plane in the presence of Embassy officials, the Swiss would be allowed to buy twelve Bf 109 G fighters.

German workmanship was faltering. The Swiss were so dissatisfied with the technical problems they had with these new planes that they demanded – and got – reimbursement of half the purchase price.

I.C.B. Deare, ed., Oxford Companion to the Second World War, *(Oxford) 1995; William Green,* The Augsburg Eagle: A Documentary History – Messerschmitt Bf 109; *Bill Gunston and John Batchelor,* Fighters 1939–1945, *1978; Stephen P. Hallbrook,* Target Switzerland: Swiss Armed Neutrality in World War II, *(Rockville Centre, NY) 1998; Armand van Ishoven,* Messerschmitt Bf 109 at War, *(Shepperton) 1977; thanks to Tim Luckhurst*

William Tilden (USA) 1893–1953

Big Bill was not in fact outrageously tall – 6' 1½" – but his major US rival, 'Little Bill' Johnston, was only 5' 8". American crowds preferred gutsy Little Bill to his lankier rival. Big Bill represented the upper-crust past and present of tennis – Little Bill, who had honed his games on courts in public parks, its more democratical future.

Tilden was one of the supreme games-players of all time. In 1950, even after he had served two prison sentences for homosexual interference with minors, an Associated Press poll of US sports correspondents gave him a lead of more than two to one over his nearest rival among such giants as Bobby Jones (golf) and **Babe Ruth** (q.v., baseball), as the greatest sportsman of the past half-century. Tilden, very self-consciously, was an artist. His Spanish opponent of the 1920s, Manuel Alonso, declared of his footwork that 'It was like seeing Njinsky dance' (Deford, 102). His long-time friend the great opera singer Mary Garden said to him once, 'Now you listen to me, Bill, and then don't listen to anyone else. You're a tennis artist, and artists always know better than anyone else when they're right' (Baltzell, 208). She thus expressed the élitist cant of the epoch of High Modernism. The paradox of Tilden (and in this he was similar to another sexually contorted hero of his day, T. E. Lawrence, 'of Arabia') was that he intersected simultaneously with values associated with Stravinsky and T. S. Eliot and with the breenging arenas of mass media and superstardom. It was strangely appropriate that this high-society Philadelphian with a somewhat 'British' accent migrated eventually, like so many Modernist writers and composers, to Los Angeles, where he coached film stars.

'I was born to be a little tennis snob', Tilden wrote – though he claimed to have escaped that fate to become 'a Tennis Bolshevik' instead (Tilden, *Me – The Handicap*, 3–4). His father was a rich wool merchant. They lived near the Germanstown Cricket Club. Few remember now that Philadelphia was a power in the world of cricket before the First World War. In three tours of England with the Philadelphians, J. B. King established himself as one of the great players of the age, easily topping the first-class bowling averages in 1908. Tennis in the USA was nurtured in the bosom of amateur cricket. The Germanstown Club provided the courts where Tilden developed his game.

He was a relatively late developer. But from 1920, when he won Wimbledon and the first of six successive US Championships, he lost only eight out of 322 matches. In 1929, he won the US title again, and 1930 saw his last Wimbledon triumph. Then he turned professional. His income from tennis was enhanced by successful books about the game, but his fiction for boys earned him no glory, and he wasted a lot of money attempting to promote stage plays he wrote himself and his own career as an actor. (He performed the title role in *Dracula* for sixteen weeks on the road. He had two parts on Broadway, and went through a whole season in rep.) This most intellectual of tennis greats, theorist and perfectionist, was said to play not against his opponents but against himself. While he dressed impeccably on (though not off) court, his squeamish refusal to expose his nudity by showering led fellow players to steer clear of his sweaty presence in the changing room. Crowds admired his grace but reacted against his arrogance, which prompted rows with umpires and linesmen.

But he was not without sportsmanship, as he showed in his reactions to his famous Wimbledon defeat by **Henri Cochet** (q.v.).

American National Biography, *vol. 21, 1999; E. Digby Baltzell,* Sporting Gentlemen: Men's Tennis from the Age of Honor to the Cult of the Superstar, *(New York) 1995; Frank Defford,* Big Bill Tilden, *1997; Edward C. Potter,* Kings of the Court, *(New York) 1963; W. T. Tilden,* Aces, Places and Faults, *1938; W. T. Tilden,* Me – The Handicap, *1929*

Tisquantum (Native America) *d.*1622

Exploratory probes by sea to the Americas brought natives back to Queen Elizabeth I's England. For instance, a quondam pirate and jailbird from Yorkshire, Martin Frobisher, went out looking for a Northwest Passage to China in 1576 and came back with a claim that he'd found it (actually, he'd seen a long bay in Baffin Island). He brought some ore which he claimed contained gold, and also a native Inuit. Sir Walter Ralegh sent settlers to Roanoke in what is now North Carolina in 1585, to found a colony which he called 'Virginia' in honour of his allegedly chaste Queen. Though this aborted, it gave scope to the notable scientist Thomas Hariot to provide a full and fair ethnographic account of the Algonquian Indians, accompanying pictures by John White, a very gifted artist who became the colony's Governor.

Fishing, trading and prospecting along the North American coast continued. Soon after James I came to the English throne, two Native Americans gave an exhibition of canoeing on the Thames. Colonising America was a very difficult and risky undertaking, and the fact that prospective settlers made themselves available shows how rotten the prospects were for many in England. Various failed colonies have been forgotten. The first which stuck, also named 'Virginia', was established by an expedition which sailed from London in December 1606 with 144 people, of whom only thirty-eight were alive a year later. Before it began to flourish, on the strength of demand for a new drug, tobacco, which had been found in America, it went through phases of epidemic, starvation, and confrontation with the local Algonquians, led by a tough old customer called Powhatan, who ran an orderly and prosperous domain. One colonist who lived for a time among his people reported that their dancing at feasts was like a Derbyshire hornpipe and that when women and boys played football, 'they make ther Gooles as ours only they never fight nor pull one another doune' – so they clearly would have made little progress in our present-day civilised World Cup (Calder, 133).

Powhatan's young daughter Pocahontas showed an interest in the settlers, brought them food, and seems to have taken a shine to a young planter called John Rolfe, who somehow, in 1611, acquired seeds of tobacco from the West Indies, cultivated them successfully, and secured the colony's future. In 1614, the two were married, after Pocahontas had been captured, held hostage, and instructed in Christianity. They went to London with their infant son two years later. Pocahontas was well received at court. (Anne of Denmark, James I's consort, was certainly not racially prejudiced, and seems to have had a definite taste for black men.) She took part in a spectacular court masque devised by the great dramatist Ben Jonson. Then she died at Gravesend waiting for a ship home.

Meanwhile, other Native Americans, whether persuaded aboard English vessels or kidnapped by nasty captains, penetrated still further into European life. Sakaweston, captured by Captain Edward Harlow, lived for many years in England till he went as a mercenary soldier to 'the wars of Bohemia'. Another American native, described as a 'Pethagorian Indian', also fought in what became the Thirty Years War. He settled in Ireland with the name 'John Fortune', which proved inappropriate when Irish Catholics rose in 1641 and mistook him for an English Protestant (Canny, 161).

Meanwhile, Tisquantum, whom the English called 'Squanto', brokered a peace in one part of what became 'New England' which endured without serious friction for half a century.

The very ordinary English people remembered as the 'Pilgrim Fathers' really do seem to have been as decent as legend has insisted they were. Their impetus for colonisation came ultimately from members of a community of 'Brownists', gentle Puritans in Nottinghamshire who believed that church congregations should govern themselves on the basis of a mutual covenant to forsake ungodly ways. 'Congregationalism', a movement of independent churches, would be a quietly significant leaven in British religious life, more obviously important in North America. It disgusted the minions of the English crown, who fined and imprisoned Brownists. Led by William Brewster, the people from Scrooby fled to Leyden, Holland. But they felt unsettled in that alien place, where making a living in unfamiliar urban conditions was hard. They contracted with a London merchant who had acquired a claim to North American lands. They would work and gather crops, timber and furs for him to sell for his (considerable) profit. The *Mayflower* sailed with 102 'Pilgrims' on 6 September 1620. Only forty-one were Brownists from Leyden, the rest were conforming Anglicans, mostly from London and South-East England. But the 'saints' imposed their kindly will on all, gaining consent to a 'compact' which constituted the group a 'civil body politick', in which all heads of families would have a say. An orphan protégé of Brewster, William Bradford, was elected Governor after the first man chosen had collapsed and died after fieldwork in the place with a harbour where they had chosen to settle in December 1620, which they called 'New Plymouth', south of Massachusetts Bay.

More than half the heads of households had predeceased Govenor Carver. People had come off shipboard sick and the winter had been bitterly cold. Such was the spirit of these good folk that only three out of twenty children perished. But as spring came, there were only half a dozen settlers fit enough to work and tend the sick. Then 'Squanto' showed up.

He was a member of the Patuxet tribe which had lived in the area. It was their farmed plots which the Pilgrims intended to cultivate. His story was even more complicated than theirs. Sir Fernando Gorges had led the 'Plymouth Company' which intended to exploit a grant of land in North America from the English crown. A captain called Waymouth, employed by him to reconnoitre, seems to have uplifted Tisquantum and four other Indians, in 1605, from the coast of what became Maine. He took them to Bristol, where Gorges taught Tisquantum English so that the man could tell him all about the country which Sir Fernando reckoned he owned. In 1614, Gorges sent Captain John Smith, erstwhile Governor of Virginia and pal of Pocahontas, off with two ships to prepare to found a colony in New England. Tisquantum went as interpreter. When Smith had gone home, his second in command kidnapped Tisquantum and other 'Indians', and took them to Malaga in Spain, where he sold them as slaves. After about two years Tisquantum escaped on an English ship. Back in England, he was befriended by John Slany, treasurer of the Newfoundland Company, which was concerned with rich fisheries producing salt cod for the European market. In 1618, Tisquantum went to the fishing settlement at Conception Bay, Newfoundland; in 1619 he crossed the Atlantic again as pilot on a ship commanded by Captain Thomas Dermer. He left the ship at Cape Cod and went back to his Patuxet homeland.

He found that almost all his tribe had perished in a great epidemic which had decimated New England natives in 1616–17. Contact with an unfamiliar European disease was probably the cause. Apprehensively, the sickly English had seen 'Indians' around their encampment. These had rushed away when approached, though one lot had stolen tools left out when settlers had adjourned to eat. On 16 March 1621 Samoset strode boldly in. He spoke only broken English, but enough for the whites to gather that he came from parts East – Maine – where he had picked up some words from visiting fishermen. He told them about 'Squanto', whose English was fluent. He came back later with the stolen tools. After a few days, Massasoit, who was the chief of the most powerful native group thereabouts, arrived with his train, which included 'Squanto'. With 'Squanto's' help a peace treaty was made. The Pilgrims would fight for Massasoit's people if they were unjustly attacked, and vice versa.

Massasoit then returned to his place at Sowams, forty miles away. William Bradford's narrative, compiled in the 1640s, goes on, as is its wont, in the third person – 'but Squanto continued with them, and was their interpreter, and was a spetiall instrument sent of God for their good beyond their expectation. He directed them how to set their corne, wher to take fish, and to procure other comodities, and was also their pilott to bring them to unknowne places for their profitt' (Bradford, 111). Interestingly, the method of using fish as fertiliser for corn which Tisquantum taught the Pilgrims was not an 'Indian' practice – he may have picked it up in Newfoundland. They also sowed English wheat and peas. These did not thrive.

At this stage, colonist and native did have much to offer each other on a mutual basis. The Pilgrims had never heard of the beaver, let alone seen its fur. But this was coming into demand among European hatters. 'Squanto' told them about the ingenious little dam-builder, and they shipped beaver furs, along with timber and otter skins, off to their grasping merchant patron in London, a beginning to the trade which would make a few mercantile fortunes and prompt, decades later, the foundation in London of the Hudson's Bay Company.

Massasoit sent one of his counsellors, Hobomok, down to live with the Pilgrims. He remained 'faithful' to them till he died of old age. Initially, he and Tisquantum, doing business among the natives, fell foul of a malicious chiefling called Corbitant. Hobomok fought his gang off and ran back to New Plymouth. The Pilgrims decided on a punitive expedition which would cut off Corbitant's head if Squanto was found to have been killed. He was alive, and the Pilgrims gave medical treatment to three of Corbitant's people who were wounded in the fray. Peace with local natives thereafter prevailed.

New England now seemed habitable enough. Fish, waterfowl and wild turkeys fattened the Pilgrims. Then came the harvest of 'Squanto's' corn. Massasoit and many followers joined the Pilgrims in a feast in October 1621, on what is now remembered as the first Thanksgiving Day.

However, Tisquantum was playing 'his owne game' deploying his presumed standing with the Pilgrims to operate a kind of protection racket among fellow natives,

> drawing gifts from them to enriche him selfe; making them beleeve he could stur up warr against them when he would, and make peece for whom he would. Yea, he made them beleeve they [the Pilgrims] kept the plague buried in the ground, and could send it amongs whom they would, which did much terrifie the Indeans, and made them depend more on him, and seeke more to him than to Massasoyte . . .

That chief, of whose name Bradford could never settle on a definitive spelling, understandably took a scunner against Tisquantum, and sought his death 'both privatly and openly, which caused him to stick close to the English, and never durst goe from them till he dyed'. And, of course, the English took advantage of the jealousy between 'Squanto' and Hobomuk – divide and rule (Bradford, 128).

In September 1622, Tisquantum, acting as Bradford's guide on a trading expedition, succumbed to what Bradford called an 'Indean feaver, bleeding much at the nose . . .' He died 'desiring', so Bradford had it, 'the Govr. to pray for him, that he might goe to the Englishmens God in heaven, and bequeathed sundrie of his things to sundrie of his English freinds, as remembrances of his love; of which they had a great loss' (Bradford, 141).

Tisquantum's must have been a complex, and perhaps tragic, consciousness. Finding himself bereft of all his kin, after years of perturbing experience in strange lands, it seems likely that he would have cleaved with something like affection to the Pilgrims, as the only family available to him, while he dreamt of making himself their client chief to succeed Massasoit. But even the notably decent and acute

Bradford was not going to transcend Christian English incomprehension of Native American psychology. Reading as best I can between his lines, I think Bradford actually liked Squanto, devious rogue though he might seem, but he didn't have language to say how or why.

American National Biography, *vol. 21 (New York) 1999; William Bradford,* History of Plymouth Plantation 1606–1646, *ed. William T. Davis, (New York) 1908; Angus Calder,* Revolutionary Empire: The Rise of the English-Speaking Empires from the Fifteenth Century to the 1780s, *1981; Nicholas Canny, 'England's New World and the Old, 1480s–1630s', in N. Canny, ed.,* The Oxford History of the British Empire, *vol. I,* The Origins of Empire, *(Oxford) 1998*

B. Traven (?/Mexico) 1882?–1969

In March 1969 an old man died in his home in the centre of Mexico City. Though he had been granted Mexican citizenship in 1951 as Traven Torsvan, it was known to some that he was B. Traven, the world-famous novelist, translated into three dozen languages, with twenty-five million copies of his books in print. He had been married for twelve years to Rosa Elena Lujan, who had worked so successfully as his secretary and agent that in 1963 they had purchased a fine house in Calle Rio Mississippi, making a quiet end to a stormy life. Three weeks after his cremation his ashes were taken to Mexico's southernmost state, Chiapas, to be scattered, at his own request, in the jungle. This area was the scene of his epic series of six novels, published through the 1930s, depicting the oppression of its native peasants and their vicious exploitation in mahogany logging camps, prior to and during the Revolution of 1910–11 which had overthrown the dictator Porfirio Diaz. Any reader of those books would know that Traven, a mordant and irreconcilable critic of Western capitalism, respected with a version of reverence the basic values of the Chiapas Indians and their ancestral ties to their land.

The dichotomy is there in his most famous novel, *The Treasure of the Sierra Madre*, published in German by Buchergilde Gutenberg of Berlin in 1927, in English translation in London in 1934, then filmed by Warner Brothers in a movie directed by John Huston, starring Humphrey Bogart and Huston's father Walter, and released to acclaim and Oscars in 1948. Thanks to this, sales of the book in

America alone passed the million mark by 1955 (Guthke, 351–52).

It is a work of profound simplicity, bringing to mind Leo Tolstoy. In this narrative of three white vagabonds possessed by greed, Traven is supremely good at presenting such elemental matters as hunger, hard travelling, hard labour. His psychology is basic – like Tolstoy he tells us remarkably little about his characters' previous lives – but cumulatively convincing. As with Tolstoy, peasant values are seen as a source of redemption. Without piety, the tale is starkly moral.

These are ample reasons for the novel to have sold millions of copies in many languages. But alas, another has been the Who Was B. Traven? question. The author is notorious as the mystery man from anywhere and nowhere who constantly hid his identity and whereabouts, using a system of pseudonyms. This means that Travenology has attracted the same kind of person as speculates about Japanese pyramids and expects to photograph the Loch Ness Monster.

In Mexico City, the old man in Calle Rio Mississippi was also known as Hal Croves. Huston had tried to meet Traven. Instead, Croves presented himself as Traven's agent, and was hired as consultant during filming on pay of $100 per week. He would not let anyone take a photograph of him, and maintained a deep reserve. In 1959, when UFA was filming Traven's *Das Totenschiff* (The Death Ship) in Berlin, Croves turned up again, and 'phoned up Traven in Mexico' to check some technical detail. In this phase of world fame, scores of notions circulated about who Traven really was. Two old folk in Slovenia named Traven recognised in a photograph of Croves their long-lost brother Frank, who had emigrated to America in 1910. '. . . Traven was rumoured to be a leper in Mexico who was seen only with a bandaged face, or a German ranchero who lived somewhere in the jungle of Chiapas several days' journey from the nearest village in a "house full of books".' Another idea was that Traven was the pseudonym of Aldolfo Lopez Mateos, president of Mexico from 1958 to 1964. His sister Esperanza was undoubtedly Traven's agent and translator until she died in 1951, and at one time the copyright of all his books was in her name. Or did she write them herself? It was asserted that Traven was a plagiarist, or that he was a syndicate – one Travenologist was certain that a collective in Honduras had put the *oeuvre* together, consisting of three Germans, an American called McClean and a

Canadian called Thiel or Theel. One of the Germans, Wollank, had collaborated with Ret Marut in Munich on an anarchist periodical called *The Brickburner*. Marut, living in Honduras under an assumed Spanish name, had also been part of the Traven collective before his death in 1934 (Guthke, 32–43).

Marut was the name, or pseudonym, of a bit-part actor, employed in various German theatres from 1907 onwards. He had emerged in Munich during the First World War as editor of that dissident magazine and author of fiction. In November 1918, revolution swept defeated Germany and King Ludwig of Bavaria fled. In the chaotic left-wing republic which followed, Marut at one point was a leading figure. At the end of April 30,000 right-wing Freikorps marched on Munich. Ten days of terror followed, during which Marut was arrested but escaped. Fleeing a charge of high treason, which entailed imprisonment if not death, he roamed incognito round Austria and Germany with his devoted friend and collaborator Irene Mermet. The last issue of *The Brickburner* appeared from Cologne in December 1921. In the summer of 1923, Marut finally left the Continent. He tried to get into Canada, but was rejected. He turned up in London in August 1923 and was expelled from Britain in April 1924. He attempted unsuccessfully to register himself as a US Citizen, claiming that he had been born in San Francisco. He spent some time in Brixton prison. To the police he claimed to be Otto Feige from Schweibus in eastern Germany. Deported, he did not in fact leave London on the Norwegian ship for which he had signed up as a coal-trimmer, and it will presumably never be known how Marut reached Mexico in the summer of 1924.

Can he be certainly identified with Traven Torsvan, who claimed on an alien registration card in 1930 to be the son of Burton and Dorothy Torsvan, née Croves, born in Chicago in 1890 and resident in Mexico since 1914? As a photographer, Torsvan took part in a scientific expedition to the Chiapas region in 1926. Sometimes Torsvan was Berick Traven Torsvan and sometimes B. Traven. It does indeed seem certain that Marut, concerned to make it impossible for the German authorities to track him down, presented himself as a Norwegian-American, because Irene Mermet, now domiciled in the USA, supplied B. Traven with a much-needed typewriter and actually spent time with him in his southern-Mexican jungle . . . Respectably married later to a professor at Columbia University, she loyally preserved Marut's incognito even from former German comrades.

Anyway, granted that Traven/Thorsvan/Croves was definitely Marut, the question remains, who was Marut? The most likely answer is that even Traven did not know his parentage, which would explain his apparent fascination with the notion, based on strong facial resemblance, that he was the illegitimate son of Kaiser Wilhelm II by an actress. In his study after his death a journalist spotted, not only a photo of the Kaiser, but a picture of the river *Trave* flowing through Lubeck. This is one of many clues associating Marut/Traven's origins, to the point (I think) of virtual certainty, with north-eastern Germany, between Denmark and Poland.

A few years after Traven/Thorsvan's death a BBC TV producer, Will Wyatt, making a documentary about him, thought he had settled the mystery. From Swiebodzin, a town in Poland formerly Schweibus when part of Germany, came word that the birth certificate of Hermann Albert Otto Maksymilian Feige had turned up. He had been born out of wedlock on 23 February 1882 – just two days before the date of birth to which Ret Marut had always admitted. Marut in London had not only used Otto's name, but had also posed as Adolf Rudolf Feige, which was the name of Otto's father, and Albert Otto Max Weinecke: Otto's mother, who married his father three months after his birth, was Hormina Weinecke. Otto's father, a potter to trade, had worked in the brickworks in Schweibus, which could explain the cryptic title of Marut's magazine. Wyatt followed up, met Otto's surviving brother and sister, and acquired details which convinced him that Otto must have been Marut. A bright lad, Otto had wanted to study theology, but his parents, with six other children to support, had him apprenticed to a locksmith. The family moved to Wallensen in Lower Saxony in 1900. Otto emerged from army service a convinced socialist, camping in his parents' front room and drawing attention to himself as a political agitator. After a row, he left, never to be seen by his family again. This was in 1907 – the year that Marut first appears in the annals of German theatre . . . The family heard from Otto once more. He wrote from London after the war to say he was in trouble with the British authorities. Sure enough, the local German police called on his mother – who stoutly denied that she had a son called Otto, so as to avoid any possible trouble (Wyatt, 265–97).

But as Karl S. Guthke pointed out in a thoroughly researched biographical account of Traven published in 1987, seven years after Wyatt's revelations had appeared in book form, all we know about the intricate deviousness with which Traven hid himself, setting up false trails ad lib, suggests an alternative scenario – that Marut had met Feige in left-wing circles, had noted his birth details from some document, and spotted his convenience as an alter ego.

The Feige-was-Marut theory (which I find plausible) complicates the How Did Traven Know? problem. Marut's CV, as communicated to the US Embassy in London in March 1924, had him leaving the US in 1892, aged ten – running away to sea as a kitchen boy on a vessel bound for Australia, thereafter working on ships from Sydney to Singapore, Rio to Rotterdam, until he settled in Germany, where he found employment as actor, theatrical producer and teacher of languages. The advantage of this version is that it explains how Traven, in his first novel, *The Death Ship* (1926), could write in such powerful detail about the lives of merchant seamen.

The Death Ship, which Traven may have begun to write in Brixton jail in 1924, supports two distinct and contradictory notions of Traven's origins. The narrator, Gerard Gales, is an American seaman originally from the Midwest (Thorsvan territory) who loses his papers when his ship sails out of Antwerp without him and is shuttled by police from one European country to another before picking up in Spain a berth on the eponymous 'death ship', the *Yorikke*, a rusty old bucket, engaged on smuggling operations, which is scheduled by its owners to sink, so that they can claim insurance. Gales's dismal experiences with police and in consulates clearly relate closely to Marut's life as a fugitive from 1919 to 1924, and are the basis for wonderful anarchist sermons preached against the bureaucratisation of modern Europe. But the other main character, Stanislav Koslovski, was born in Poznan, formerly Posen when it was the capital of the Prussian province of that name – in which Schweibus (Feige's birthplace) was situated. Now it is in Poland and Koslovski, like Gales, is stateless.

It would be remarkable if the man who wrote *The Death Ship* had had no personal experience at all of the degraded life of exploited merchant seamen such as he describes so vividly. But Marut might have picked that up on his way to Mexico, hungry for detail for a novel he'd already started. Likewise, it is naïve to suggest that the spate of fiction which Traven directed in the middle and late twenties at the Berlin Buchergilde – a left-wing book club the fortunes of which were transformed by the vast popularity of Traven – could not have been produced by someone new to Mexico in 1924, because it is so convincingly circumstantial about the lives of oil-workers, cotton-pickers, ranch hands, Wobbly agitators, Indian labourers and so on. Tolstoy wasn't present at the Battle of Borodino. Zola never worked as a coalminer. Let us agree to disagree about the possible origins of this remarkable man, and conclude with a fascinating point about the texts of his magnificent novels.

Marut/Thorsvan/Traven was concerned always to establish his credentials as a native of the USA, at least until Thorsvan became a Mexican citizen. Furthermore, the writer Traven knew that the biggest market for fiction was in North America. He claimed to be a native English speaker, but his English in surviving documents is dodgy. It may be that he drafted at least some stories and sections of novels in English before in 1925 he sent his first batch of stories, in German, to the left-wing newspaper *Vorwaerts* in Berlin, through which he shortly found his way to Buchergilde and fame. The preponderance of his work thereafter appeared first in German. What strikes me is that like Bertolt Brecht – a contemporary whom he much resembles, both in style and in anti-capitalist views, except that Traven was also severely anti-Communist – his distinctive manner seems indestructible. Traven translates, or translates back, into English, via various hands, unmistakably as Traven. The curt, sardonic, at times pedantic style of *The Death Ship* runs right through to *General from the Jungle* (1940), the last of the epic Chiapas novels. So the paradox is that the writer whose 'real identity' has been so much a puzzle to so many, even perhaps to himself, has ultra-clear identity *as a writer*. As football supporters might chant: 'There's only one B. Traven.'

Karl S. Guthke, B. Traven: The Life Behind the Legends, *(New York) 1991*; *Will Wyatt*, The Man Who Was Traven, *1980*

Walter Tull (England) 1888–1918

Second Lieutenant Walter Tull, of the 23rd Battalion (2nd Football) of the Middlesex Regiment, died in the second battle of the Somme, March-April 1918, shot through the head at the age of twenty-nine. Private T. Billingham, who had played soccer with him for Northampton Town, and another soldier tried to carry his body back to the British lines, but they had to leave it to rot in the mud. Though he would have no known grave, his death was widely reported, in sporting and football newspapers across England. 'The deceased sportsman', an obituary in the *Rushden Echo*, local to Northamptonshire, observed, 'was an officer and a gentleman every inch of him' (Vasili, 51).

Tull was the only black man to be commissioned in the British Army in the First World War. According to official policy, this should not have happened. Blacks had been serving in the Army since at least the seventeenth century, but their recruitment was discouraged and the appointment of black officers who might give orders to white men was officially proscribed.

The history of Tull's family shows it as raised out of misery by Methodism. His grandfather William, born a plantation slave in Barbados, had married another ex-slave, Anna Lashly. Their son Daniel, born about 1850, was educated by Moravian missionaries and became a carpenter. Around 1873 he emigrated to the small island of St Lucia, but in 1876 he moved on to England. He settled in Folkestone, a fashionable seaside resort in Kent, and within five years married a local woman, Alice Palmer, from a family of agricultural labourers. Both were devout Wesleyan Methodists. In 1895 Alice, aged forty-two, died of cancer, leaving Daniel with five children. To help him cope he married his dead wife's cousin Clara. A further child was born to her – then, three months later, in 1897, Daniel died of heart disease.

Clara turned to Grace Hill Methodist Chapel for help. It had given financial assistance to the Children's Home and Orphanage run in Bethnal Green in the East End of London. With subsidy from the Folkestone Poor Law Guardians, two Tull boys, Edward (born in 1886) and Walter (1888) were placed there. The regimen was wholesome though severe. Lads were trained in vocational skills. Walter learnt to be a printer, and seems to have set his sights on a job in the expanding newspaper press. The home aimed to export its orphans to the colonies. But Edward was adopted by a Glasgow dentist, an Ulsterman called Warnock. Meanwhile, Walter was showing exceptional talent at football in the Orphanage team. In 1908, a friend suggested that he join Clapton, a good local amateur club. He became a regular player, at inside left, during a wonderful season in which Clapton won the national Amateur Cup and two other major trophies. He was noticed by Tottenham Hotspur, a rising London professional club, and was rapidly signed up, so that he was with the 'Spurs' first team during a close-season tour of Argentina and Uruguay.

Now that Argentina has long been a major power in world football, it is curious to recall that the game was then in its infancy there, so that accomplished Brits were invited to provide an example of the highest standards. Walter suffered sunstroke, but played well. On return, he performed for Spurs during the club's very first season, 1909–10, in the First Division of the national League (equivalent to the present-day Premiership). In front of a crowd of 32,275 – the largest in the country that day – he was brought down for a penalty in Spurs' first home game, against Manchester United, a 2–2 draw. 'Darkie Tull', though perhaps rather slow for a forward, attracted very favourable attention. It is a mystery that he was dropped to the reserves after just seven games. Possibly the racial abuse – reported as 'a cowardly attack upon him in language lower than Billingsgate' – which he suffered from a section of the crowd when Spurs played in Bristol may have made the club's directors over-sensitive (Porter and Vasili, 63). Black players were an awkward novelty, though in the 1880s a 'gentleman of colour' born in Guyana, Andrew Watson, had captained Scotland, and later Arthur Wharton from the Gold Coast (now Ghana) had followed success as a national champion sprinter by turning football professional.

Next season, Walter played only three first-team games, scoring in one of them. By October 1911 he had joined Northampton Town, winners of the Southern League two years before, for what was then regarded as a big transfer fee. It may be that the social climate in Northampton, notorious for radicalism in the days when its shoemakers kept re-electing as their MP the notorious atheist and

Republican **Charles Bradlaugh** (q.v.), was more congenial for a serious young black man. It is clear that the club's manager, Herbert Chapman, was a genius who later became world-famous as boss of the mighty Arsenal side of the 1930s. Certainly, Walter became a regular star. He converted from forward to wing-half, played 110 first-team games for the club, and scored nine goals. Then, on 21 December 1914, he led his team-mates to war as the first man from the club to enlist in the 17th (1st Football) Battalion of the Middlesex Regiment.

This was part of a mass movement (see **'Grimsby Chums'**, above): 2,000 out of 5,000 professional footballers joined the army early in the war. Walter and his professional 'Pals' continued to play a lot of football in the army, which, later, between the wars, would foreground opportunities for sport in its recruiting posters. While still training in England, Walter guested three times for the Fulham club. He got to France in November 1915. Next year, the 1st Football were thrown into the Battle of the Somme, in which more than a million men died. On 13 November, in one of the last actions of the battle, the battalion was ordered to capture a certain German trench. Out of 400 men, only seventy-nine returned.

Tull survived. In 1916, by now a sergeant, he was invalided out of France with 'trench fever'. On recovery, he was sent to Scotland to train as an officer. While he was there, the intercession of his brother Edward, now a rising young professional man, led to his signing forms for a great Glasgow club, Rangers. But he would never play for it.

As a black man, even his joining the Army had been out of order, when homogeneous white regiments were preferred. It is very hard to understand how he was selected for officer training. He was clearly an excellent soldier, but one suspects that his status as sporting hero induced colour blindness in the authorities, who were desperately trying to make up especially heavy losses amongst commissioned officers. After further heavy casualties, the 1st Football Battalion was disbanded, so it was the 2nd Football to which Walter was posted after he was commissioned as second lieutenant on 30 May 1917. Sent to Italy, he was mentioned in dispatches for his 'gallantry and coolness' in the vanguard during a raid across the river Piave on 1–2 January 1918, but he received neither medal nor promotion before he died in France weeks later.

His brother Edward was desolated by this loss. But his own life proceeded most successfully until his death in 1951. 'Eddie', a fine singer, had visited Glasgow with the accomplished choir of the National Children's Home. He had thus attracted the attention of a childless couple, James and Jean Warnock, who adopted him. He eventually took over his father's practice in St Vincent Street in the centre of Glasgow. Edward Tull-Warnock, as he came to style himself, had met in Aberdeen a Methodist girl, Elizabeth Hutchison, daughter of the head of a large bakery business who was a Bailie of the city. They married and one daughter was born, in 1920. Meanwhile Cissie Tull, elder sister of Edward and Walter, had come north to look after 'Mater', as Edward called old Mrs Warnock. A family photograph shows brothers and sister together with the old lady. To clear up any misapprehension, these people of mixed origin are, in this photo, clearly 'black'. There was no way that Edward 'passed for white' when he became President of the Alan Glen's Former Pupils Club and won, to his jubilation, a golf tournament on the famous Gleneagles course. The fact that he was a Socialist and an admirer of the great left-wing black singer Paul Robeson probably did him less harm in middle-class circles in Glasgow than it would have done elsewhere – the city's politics became in the 1920s dominantly, and famously, 'red'.

His daughter Jean married a Methodist minister, Duncan Finlayson. They had four children, and grandchildren accordingly. Their group photos display a 'normal' white family. But these Finlaysons and Sarjeants know that in their family tree there stands, beside the remarkable Edward, Walter, a singular black hero in both sport and war.

Rev. Duncan Finlayson, 'Story of a Family', ms; 'Scots lay claim to world's first black football player', Herald, *2 February 2002; Andy Porter and Phil Vasili, 'Walter Tull: An Officer and a Gentleman',* Spurs Monthly *(n.d.); Edward Tull, 'The Children's Home', notes for a speech, (n.d.); Phil Vasili, 'Walter Daniel Tull, 1888–1918: soldier, footballer, black', in* Race and Class, *38.2, 1996; thanks to Polly Rewt and Phil Vasili*

Ursula ('Britain') '*fl.*'451

A stone in the church of St Ursula in Cologne carries a Latin inscription probably dating from the latter half of the fourth or the early part of the fifth century CE. A man of high rank, Clematius, we learn, inspired by certain visions, rebuilt a ruined basilica formerly erected on the site where Christian virgins had been martyred. The number of these ladies is not specified, nor are names or circumstances provided. But we may assume that the original place of worship dated from +300 CE.

The feast day of these martyrs was celebrated in Cologne. The earliest written version of their story is found in a *sermo* composed for such a feast day some time in the ninth century CE. The writer admitted that nothing certain was known about them, but relayed the local tradition that their leader was Vinnosa (Pinnosa) and that they had suffered in the persecution of Christians by the Roman Emperor Galerius Valerius Maximianus (*d.*311). 'Ursula''s name first occurs in liturgical sources towards the end of the ninth century, as one of five, eight or eleven martyrs, but in only one source does it come first.

The inflation besetting the Deutschmark after World War I was anticipated by an astonishing upsurge in the tally of martyrs in the tenth century. There had been 11,000 virgins! A wondrous and compelling tale shaped itself around them. Ursula had been the daughter of a Christian king in or of Britain. Her hand was bespoken by the son of a pagan king. Not desiring marriage, she asked for a delay of three years. With ten noble handmaidens, each with a retinue, like hers, of 1,000 more virgins, she set sail in a flotilla of eleven ships (each of which must have been over twice the size of the largest known pre-modern vessels, those of the Chinese admiral **Cheng Ho**, q.v.). As the three-year period was expiring, contrary winds drove them to the mouth of the Rhine. Proceeding up that great river as far as Basle, they alighted, crossed the Alps, and visited Rome. Returning via Cologne, in 451, they were set upon and massacred by the Huns when Ursula refused to marry their leader Attila. Thereupon angels appeared to drive the Huns away, the Christian citizenry of Cologne buried the martyrs, and Clematius built a church in their honour.

In the twelfth century, a common burial ground in Cologne was opened up where huge numbers of bones were discovered. Some of these were of men and children. Noted visionaries – St Elizabeth of Schonau (see **Hildegard**) and the Blessed Herman Joseph – reacted with intricate imaginings. Numerous real and fictitious male dignitaries were stated to have suffered martyrdom with Ursula. Transport of relics out of Cologne to many airts must have boosted the local economy.

The tale of Ursula featured notably in later medieval painting. Among twenty-five cycles portraying it, one may note that of Hans Memlinc (*c.*1430–94), whose version for the Shrine of St Ursula in Bruges depicts up-to-date longbowmen and crossbowmen picking off smug, buxom virgins crammed into tubby little ships with equally serene male companions, and the far more sophisticated sequence executed for the School of St Ursula in Venice by Vittore Carpaccio around 1490. Carpaccio showed Ursula meeting the Pope in Rome, and included a bishop and even a cardinal among her companions in massacre.

In 1544, Pope Paul III approved the Ursuline religious order of nuns founded in Brescia in 1506 by Angela Merici (1470–1540) to educate girls. But despite the respected work of this order, Ursula became an embarrassment to the Church. Under the 'enlightened' Pope Benedict XIV (1740–58) there was a project to oust her from the Calendar, but even when she was generally excluded from it, at last, in 1969, celebration of her feast was still permitted in certain locations.

But how, why, had so many people, not just in Cologne, accepted for so long the intrinsically unbelievable story of the 11,000 virgins? A rationalistic explanation is that someone in the tenth century misread, in good faith, the Latin abbreviation XI M.V. (*undecim martyres virgines*) as *undecim milia virgines*. But why would anyone credit this as factual? And why does Ursula stand out as Top Virgin? The answer must be that she was identified with a pre-Christian deity, known to the Saxons as Ursel or Horsel, the 'She-Bear', 'Mother of Animals', whose constellation still goes by the Latin name of Ursa Major. According to ancient Greeks, as Artemis, the Moon-Goddess, she had ruled all the stars till Zeus usurped her position.

In Cologne, we may suppose that local people continued to venerate the Moon Goddess, with her retinue of myriad stars. So the church, to control their devotion, converted Ursel to Ursula, with her vast train of virgins. As for Angela Merici of Brescia, she had her original vision in an open field under the moon and her initial group of sisters – twenty-eight, the lunar number – made their first devotion in the church of St Aphra, dedicated to another Christianised goddess (Aphrodite, no less). Their project – to educate women – violated long-standing papal policy, but the pressure of their local popularity ensured recognition of the order and eventually (1807) the canonisation of Angela (Walker, 1030–32).

David Farmer, Oxford Dictionary of Saints, *4th edn, (Oxford) 1997; Herbert J. Thurston and Donald Attwater, eds*, Butler's Lives of the Saints, *vol. 4, 1981 edn; Barbara C. Walker*, The Woman's Encyclopaedia of Myths and Secrets, *(San Francisco) 1983*

Pauline Viardot (France) 1821–1910

Our perception of European musical culture in the heyday of the 'classic' bourgeoisie is dominated by big male names – Verdi, Wagner, Brahms. The popularity of the grandiose operas of Meyerbeer, now rarely staged, is noted as historically significant. Chopin gave pianistic creativity a new dimension. Schumann's status as a composer has risen markedly in recent years. International interest in the Russian composer Glinka, founder of what became a great school, has increased. The idiosyncratic genius of Hector Berlioz has transcended the difficulties which it made for itself in his own day, and his mighty opera *The Trojans* sells out.

But Berlioz created the chief female roles in that opera – Cassandra and Dido – with a particular singer very much in his mind. And the period in which the men just named flourished could aptly be named 'The Age of Viardot'. All of them admired, or even revered, the wonderful mezzo-soprano, who worked with some of them on scores produced specially for her, to the point of actual collaboration.

She was born in Paris into an intensely musical Spanish family. Her father, Manuel Garcia, a minor composer and famous operatic tenor who claimed to come from gypsy stock, pioneered a new method of teaching singing. After her father died when she was eleven, her mother kept Pauline at her musical studies. Liszt was one of her piano teachers. She studied composition under the gifted Czech composer, and theorist, Reicha. Her debut as a performer, in Brussels at the age of sixteen, caused a sensation, as she displayed a range of three octaves. In Leipzig, she met Clara Wieck and her future husband Robert Schumann, who would dedicate to Pauline his cycle of songs to lyrics by Heine, Op. 24. Her operatic debut was in London in 1839, singing Desdemona in Rossini's *Otello*.

She was no classical beauty – her features were coarse, her huge eyes were heavily lidded, her long upper lip went down to a big mouth. But her vivacity and intelligence were captivating. The poet Alfred de Musset fell fruitlessly in love with her. She befriended Chopin's partner Aurore Dudevant, 'George Sand', who modelled the singer-heroine of her bestselling novel *Consuelo* (1842) on Pauline. The latter had meanwhile married, in 1840, Sand's friend the writer Louis Viardot, twenty-one years her senior, a steady rather than charismatic personality. From 1843 to 1846, she sang seasons of Italian opera in St Petersburg, adding Russian to the repertory of languages in which she was fluent – beside French and Spanish, she had English, Italian and German, and she composed songs herself in different national styles. She was a uniquely important agent in opening dialogue between Russian and Western musical communities. She also enraptured, to the point of lifelong enslavement, a young Russian – 'bad poet, good shot', they said of him – Ivan Turgenev (1818–83), who would go on to become one of the greatest of all European novelists, and a confirmed semi-exile in Western Europe, where he lived so as to be near Pauline.

Ivan was a very tall, big man with a surprisingly small high voice, in whose fictions dynamic women have their way or sway even over strong males. It seems to have suited him that Pauline was much more famous than he was, at least in Western Europe. It is not clear if he and Pauline ever 'slept together', to use that odd parlance, but he got on well with her husband, whose tastes for talking politics and shooting wildlife he shared, and developed an intermittent *ménage à trois*, introducing into the Viardot household his illegitimate daughter by a seamstress on his mother's estate, renamed 'Paulinette' in his idol's honour.

Meyerbeer created for Pauline the role of Fides in his opera *Le Prophète* (1849), which she sang over 200 times on all the major European opera stages. Berlioz was bowled over – 'one of the greatest artists . . .' Ten years later, seeking to revive the neglected operas of Gluck, he rewrote the castrato lead part of *Orfeo* for Viardot, who had drifted away from the stage. She socked it to 'em in this part some 150 times. Charles Dickens was invited by her to hear *Orfeo* in the Théâtre Lyrique in Paris. When Turgenev, Louis and the director of the theatre, Carvalho, emerged in the foyer after the show, they found Dickens still helplessly in tears, his arms flung desperately across his breast. They insisted that he must pay tribute to Pauline in person. 'Madame, je vous présente une fontaine,' said Carvalho (Waddington 137).

This triumph with Gluck was her last on the stage, from which she virtually retired in 1863, though she appeared in oratorio and in concerts. Her husband being a staunch republican, they preferred not to live under the Empire of Louis Napoleon, and set themselves up (with Turgenev) in the German spa town of Baden-Baden, whither singers flocked from all over the world to learn from her. She created an art gallery in her garden and Turgenev, building a villa nearby, included a small theatre in which she and her children (she had had four) held concerts and performed dramatic works composed by Pauline with libretti by Turgenev. These were admired by fellow-musicians as well as by royalty and other celebrities. She played concert piano duos with Clara Schumann, widow of Robert and object of the platonic devotion of Brahms, whose Alto Rhapsody Pauline sang at a première. After Prussia's defeat of France in 1871, and the revival of the Republic, the Viardots returned to Paris. Louis and Turgenev both died in 1883, but Pauline kept going, a venerated teacher.

Pauline wasn't really a *diva*. From the first, concerned about dramatic continuity in opera, she refused to encore favourite arias. She was an intensely intellectual artist, whose majestic performances in big roles involved managing with superb musicianship a voice which had its technical problems. She was well up to giving Wagner's Isolde her first airing in a private session in Paris in 1860, when the cantankerous composer was hugely impressed by her capacity to sight-read his score. Her own output as a composer was significant. Honoured by the most gifted musicians and writers of her age, she vastly enhanced the status of operatic singers in general. Without her, both European music and the Russian novel would have missed dimensions which now seem essential.

April Fitzlyon, The Price of Genius: A Life of Pauline Viardot, *1964; Stanley Sadie, ed.*, The New Grove Dictionary of Music and Musicians, *2001 edn; Patrick Waddington*, Turgenev and England, *1980*

Victoria (U.K.) 1819–1901

The Queen was tiny, under 5' tall. Once she lamented in despair, 'Everyone grows but me.' Her first Prime Minister, kind Lord Melbourne, replied with a laugh, 'I think you are grown' (Longford 84–85). Her formidable dignity, reinforced, as often happens, by extreme shyness, was in inverse ratio to her lack of inches. No wonder that she became in due course an expert image-builder, for her dead husband, whose talents would have commanded a very high price in today's PR industry.

Victoria was the most iconic of rulers. Caesars and warlords who claimed to be kings had in antiquity been stamped in effigy on coinage. Elizabeth I of England and Louis Quatorze of France had studied couture, cosmetics and ceremony so as to produce resplendent court-icons of themselves. But the postage stamp was a Victorian British invention. Rowland Hill's Penny Post begat in May 1840 the Penny Black, swiftly superseded by the Penny Red (sometimes orange-brown) early in 1841. Both showed the Queen's head in profile, lightly diademmed, glaring firmly to what would have been her right. The stamp, being unique in the first instance, did not need to advertise its country of origin as did those of lesser breeds without the law following suit. This would have taken up a lot of space, since Victoria was Queen of the United Kingdom of Great Britain and Ireland, over all of which the penny rate prevailed. To this day, British stamps use the invariable head of the monarch as a way of evading a statement of what the country is actually called, with Ireland now reduced to 'Northern'.

In Britain the stylised profile, attached to no body, persisted in a series of coarsened designs over six decades to the end of the icon's reign. From the 1850s, some colonies of her Empire used a livelier effigy – a beautiful woman with a more ample crown staring full-face out of the stamp or, more usually, looking upwards, right, as if towards inspiration. The cocky new colony named Victoria went furthest, with a full-length Queen installed on a handsome throne (1852, 1855). In the 1890s through to the Queen's death, some bits of the Empire (British East Africa, Canada, India, Newfoundland, Niger Coast Protectorate, Southern Nigeria, Victoria) had stamps printed with a realistic full-face image of an elderly widow brooding – looking to her right, again (*Gibbon's Priced Catalogue*, *passim)*. Did this imply that Victoria was now loved and revered for whom she actually was, or merely that any iconic display of her signified, amply enough, Empire? In any case her image was daily seen and handled by postmen, officials and businessmen, colonials and expatriates, soldiers and native servants, all over the globe, as omnipresent as Coca-Cola today.

Victoria fully appreciated her own status. She really was as imperialistic – and as prudish – as antipathetic reaction against her during the twentieth century posited. But she hated English high society, didn't like her English courtiers, and spent as little time in London as possible. To sketch the entire life of this remarkable woman is unnecessary. I want merely to point to some interesting facets of her personality and career which are not usually foregrounded.

Though her world-view firmly divided the human race into aristocrats and proles, she had genuine fellow feeling for proles. This played a significant part in a hard-to-explain shift of British public opinion during the Crimean War of the mid 1850s. In most parts of Britain, the licentious soldiery were regarded with contempt and fear. Men so debased as to take the 'queen's shilling' – often, furthermore, Irish or uncouth Scottish Highlanders – found their sufferings in faraway battles were not much mourned. Yet for some reason the British were touched by the heroism and travails of their mercenary troops in the Crimea, and Victoria led the chorus of sympathy.

In May 1855 she presented war medals in person to returned Crimea veterans in Horse Guards Parade. This was at her own suggestion. No reigning British sovereign had ever done this before. Her interest in the army thereafter was constant, epitomised by her institution of the Victoria Cross for valour. She handed out sixty-two crosses in a great review in Hyde Park in June 1857.

It is to her credit that Victoria deplored the British administration's brutal retaliation against the Indian 'Mutineers' of 1857, declaring in a letter to a statesman that 'The Indian people should know that there is no hatred to a brown skin, none; but the greatest wish on their queen's part to see them happy, contented and flourishing.' In her view, Indian subjects were fully equal under the crown (Lee, 1314–15). She certainly became an imperialist, but she wasn't altogether racist.

When her beloved consort Albert passed away in 1861, the Queen was precipitated into many years of deep mourning and seclusion. But her withdrawal from public life was cunningly selective. She hated opening Parliament, and did so only seven times during the rest of her reign. Driving through the London streets to show herself to her people was not a favourite with her either (after all, nutters kept taking pot-shots at her). But in the depth of new grief in 10 January 1862 she sent a message of sympathy, with a gift of £2,000, to the relatives of the victims of a great colliery explosion in Northumberland.

For two years, indeed, her seclusion was extreme. Thereafter, in the years she devoted to promoting the national commemoration of Albert, she seemed to put the institution of monarchy itself at risk by her continued indifference to showing herself in public (see **Bradlaugh**). But she displayed gifts of hard work, imagination and attention to detail which belie the notion of a gloomy depressive trapped in her mourning weeds and perpetual grief. By degrees, as Gladstone put it, statues of Albert 'covered the land' (Lee, 1326), and she would always be pleased to unveil them. If her mausoleum for Albert at Frogmore was a costly near-private indulgence, by 1871 the Albert Hall in London enhanced the cultural life of her nation. Albert, not popular in his lifetime, became a pre-eminent national hero after his death.

Meanwhile, she found solace for her grief in the company of the people of her beloved Scotland, the charm of her favourite Prime Minister, Disraeli, and the poetry and conversation of her Laureate, Tennyson.

Her affection for Scotland has been unfairly judged by recent intellectuals who have deplored the 'Balmoralisation' of the country under her resident influence. Though fake tartans and silly Highland Games were part of the life she constructed there, she was more than a posh tourist. She and Albert had first visited the country in 1842. On their fourth trip in 1848, they stayed at Balmoral House, then little more than a shooting lodge owned by the brother of Lord Aberdeen. They both detested London society. By 1854 they had bought and rebuilt Balmoral as their favourite home. Another retreat, at Osborne on the Isle of Wight, had been purchased in 1844. They paid three or four visits there every year and spent part of each spring and autumn at Balmoral. Totting all her visits up, Victoria spent nine of her eighty-two-plus years in Scotland (and only a few weeks in Ireland – might history have been very different had she and Albert fallen in love with Killarney?).

At Balmoral, Victoria's lifestyle was informal. She liked chatting to the neighbouring cottagers. After Albert's death, she found Scots of all classes, 'but especially of the humbler, readier in the expression of kindly feelings than English men and English women'. Her Scottish chaplain, Dr Norman Macleod, 'gave her more real consolation than any clergyman of the South' (Lee, 1322). John Brown, an outdoor servant at Balmoral since 1849, became her personal retainer, and famously spoke his mind to her in front of toffs, addressing her as 'wumman!' It is important to realise that her undoubted reliance on Brown was not a one-off. She was at ease with other Scots. Seeking even greater seclusion in 1868, she took up residence, with few servants, in a small house, Glassalt Shiel, which she had built for herself on the Balmoral estate. When she grudged opening Parliament she was happy enough, in 1866, to open a waterworks in Aberdeen. And her first venture into authorship, published in 1868, was *Leaves of a Journal of Our Life in the Highlands from 1848 to 1861*.

Routinely 'accomplished' without being 'intellectual', the little Queen seems to have felt genuine awe before the leading literary men of her reign. While she was hiding away from her courtiers, she was very happy to meet Carlyle and Browning over tea at Lady Augusta Stanley's. In 1870 she invited Dickens to Buckingham Palace. But her soul-mates amongst writers were Disraeli and Tennyson.

Neither was the kind of person that Eminent Victorians were later supposed to have been. Disraeli – on top of being Jewish and petty-bourgeois – had been a disreputable Byronic dandy in youth, on the run from creditors, sponging off well-to-do ladies. Writing popular novels hardly improved his claims to respectability, and Victoria had recoiled from him at first in horror. But his flowery eloquence at last won her over completely. Famously, while his Liberal rival Gladstone lectured her pompously, Disraeli could boast that at his own audiences with her when prime minister, he addressed her 'like a woman'. And his master stroke, which restored her fully to public life in a new and spectacular role, was to make her Empress of India in 1876. A note to her in April 1874 had floated the idea almost casually: 'The official intelligence of the contemplated cession of the Fiji islands has not yet arrived and the Cabinet has not yet considered the question, but Mr Disraeli must confess his impression, that your Majesty will feel it necessary to accept the sovereignty of this southern archipelago – as well as the Empire of India' (Moneypenny and Buckle, vol. 2, 797). Gladstone's Liberals hummed and hawed and carped, but it went through. Victoria was delighted, a queen revived.

She dedicated *More Leaves* from her Highland journal (1883) to her 'loyal highlanders, and especially to the memory of my devoted personal attendant and faithful friend, John Brown'. Brown's effectual replacement as her confidant, groom of her chamber, was an Indian whom she called her 'munshi', Abdul Karim, from whom she took lessons in Hindustani. Meanwhile, she inscribed the copy of her book which she gave to Tennyson as from 'a very humble and unpretending author' (Lee, 1351).

Perhaps the most popular poet in English, effectually, ever – allowing that Burns wrote largely in Scots – became in 1884 'Alfred Lord Tennyson'. Yet in early life, from some angles, he had looked like a *poète maudit*. He was a heavy drinker who smoked 'the strongest and most stinking tobacco out of a small blackened clay pipe on an average nine hours every day' (Martin, 239). Well over 6' tall, with swarthy 'gypsy' looks, a massive head and long dark hair, he might have been thought romantically handsome, in his broad-brimmed hat and Spanish cape – but the latter concealed habitually filthy linen, and he took clumsy rustic manners to the point of rudeness, both inadvertent and intentional. As a very old cylinder recording of Tennyson reciting 'The Charge of the Light Brigade' testifies, he spoke with a broad Lincolnshire accent till his dying day. Beside all this he was extremely short-sighted – he once fled in terror from a flock of sheep whom he mistook for autograph-hunters – and the false teeth he wore from 1852 didn't fit, so he couldn't smile.

Yet Alfred (1809–92) was one of the stabler, more normal members of his family. His clergyman father was an epileptic and alcoholic, whose temper got so bad that his eleven children feared for their lives. Four, perhaps five, of Tennyson's six brothers were confined for varying periods in mental asylums. His elder brother Charles, also a gifted poet, was for long spells addicted to opium. A younger brother, whose existence was totally futile, 'once introduced himself to a stranger by rising from the hearth-rug where he had been lying, extending a languid hand, and saying, "I am Septimus, the most morbid of the Tennysons"' (Martin, 138).

As a poet admired by just a few friends who let him sponge on them, Tennyson's life was transformed in 1850 when his long sequence *In Memoriam AHH* was published to national acclaim. Prince Albert admired his great new poem, Wordsworth had just died, the Poet Laureateship was vacant, Albert saw to it that Tennyson got it. When Tennyson in 1853 acquired, on the strength of his astounding sales of poetry, 300 acres at Farringford on the Isle of Wight, he became a neighbour of the Queen when she was at Osborne.

The subject matter of *In Memoriam* made it an especially important poem for Victoria after Albert died. She turned to it repeatedly. Tennyson had marked in it the stages of his grief for his Cambridge fellow-student and best friend Arthur Henry Hallam, suddenly dead in 1833. He had also confronted, years before Darwin's *Origin of Species* (1859) had concentrated debate, the inroads which the sciences of geology and natural history were making on Christian faith. (The earth, it seemed, was heading for annihilation. Man shared his nature with low and savage beasts.) Tennyson's unorthodox but firm Christian faith, and conviction that there was an afterlife, were fine by the grieving Queen, whose own theology was likewise unconventional.

She was further touched by the long poem to Albert's memory with which Tennyson dedicated his *Idylls of the King*, published in 1862. By command, the poet visited her at Osborne in April that year. Presumably he left his pipe behind at home. Victoria's antipathy to smoking was such that Edward her son and heir smoked cigars up the chimney when residing with her. 'Very peculiar-looking . . . oddly dressed, but there is no affectation about him' was her first impression. His eyes filled with tears as he spoke of Albert. Before long,

Tennyson was visiting with his family. But it wasn't until after John Brown died in 1883 that Tennyson and his Queen became intimate friends. It seems that he filled Brown's place, as someone whom she could feel truly understood her. They blethered about the afterlife together. She poured out to him her grief for 'dear faithful Brown . . . he was in my service for 34 years and for 18 never left me for a single day . . . The comfort of my daily life is gone – the void is terrible – the loss is irreparable.' He replied, most intelligently, "I will not say that I am "loyal" or that your Majesty is "gracious" for these are old hackneyed terms used or abused by every courtier, but I *will* say that during our conversation I felt the touch of that true friendship & sympathy which binds human beings together, whether they be Kings or cobblers' (Dyson and Tennyson, 103–05).

She began to sign her letters 'yours affectionately'. Hearing of his death she wrote in her diary, 'He died with his hand on his Shakespeare, and the moon shining full into the window and over him. A worthy end to such a remarkable man' (Dyson and Tennyson, 140).

He had said to her once that funerals should be in white. His own coffin was covered with a white pall. The Queen's minute instructions for her own funeral accordingly laid down that it should be *military* and *white*. For her lying-in-state at Osborne, 'spring flowers were sprinkled on her white dress; her lace wedding veil covered her face and her white widow's cap her hair'. Her coffin eventually arrived in a London from which black hangings had been banished. 'The ominous drum roll of Handel's "Funeral March" was replaced, according to instructions, by Chopin, Beethoven and Highland laments.' After she was laid at last beside her Albert, 'The sleet soon changed to snow and the doors of the Mausoleum closed softly upon a white world. The Queen had had her white funeral' (Longford, 707–10).

Hope Dyson and Charles Tennyson, Dear and Honoured Lady: The Correspondence of Queen Victoria and Alfred Tennyson, *1969;* Gibbons's Priced Catalogue: Part I – Stamps of the British Empire – Jubilee Edition, *1935; Sidney Lee, 'Victoria'*, DNB Supplement, *1909; Elizabeth Longford*, Victoria RI, *1966 edn; Robert Bernard Martin*, Tennyson: The Unquiet Heart, *(Oxford) 1980; W. F. Moneypenny and G. E. Buckle*, The Life of Benjamin Disraeli, *1929 edn; Lynne Truss*, Tennyson and His Circle, *1999*

Robert Wedderburn (Jamaica) *c.*1762–*c.*1835

> Early in 1824, a small pamphlet carrying the melodramatic title *The Horrors of Slavery* appeared in the Holborn and Smithfield bookshops of several leading London ultra-radicals. Its lengthy subtitle explained that this was the exemplary autobiography of a mulatto Jamaican slave offspring, Robert Wedderburn, who had recently been a prisoner in Dorchester gaol 'for conscience-sake'. It did not say that the author was also a ragged Soho tailor and a notorious revolutionary conspirator whose recent imprisonment on a blasphemous libel charge had saved him from certain execution for the more serious charge of high treason
>
> (McCalman, *Horrors*, 1)

So Iain McCalman begins his introduction to a collection of Wedderburn's writings, as ghosted by others, notably the radical lawyer and pornographer George Cannon who used the pseudonym 'Rev. Erasmus Perkins'. Late in life, Robert had emerged as a charismatic leader of the free-thinking, revolutionary, London left.

His paternal grandfather, Sir John (1702–46), had been an

impoverished Perthshire baronet. In 1745 he joined the rebellion of Prince Charles Edward Stuart, and when it foundered in defeat at Culloden next year, he was captured, tried, and executed in London. His title and his estate, ironically called Blackness, were forfeited. His sons, John, born in 1729, and James, a year younger, picked on Jamaica as the place where they could rebuild the family's fortune.

As well they might. This was the largest and wealthiest of Britain's West Indian sugar islands. Since Union with England in 1707, hungry Scots had flocked there, as servants, craftsmen, surveyors and professional people. A local writer in the 1770s reckoned that 'very near one third' of the island's whites were Scots (Calder, 474–75). As the brothers set themselves up as doctors (though neither was qualified), there was no shortage of fellow countrymen to help them prosper. On an island where mortality rates among planters were high, both readily moved on from doctoring to own plantations, and each returned to Scotland with a fortune large enough to buy a country estate.

John featured in an important legal case. In 1772, the Lord Chief Justice of England, Mansfield (himself a man of Perthshire family), had ruled in the case of a slave, James Somerset, brought by his master from America, who had escaped and had been recaptured, that his master had no right to transport him out of the country. This 'Mansfield judgment', hailed by generations of liberal historians as outlawing slavery in England, did no such thing. A judgment by the Scottish Court of Session six years later was much more decisive. John Wedderburn had brought a lad called Joseph Knight back with him from Jamaica as a personal servant. Knight married, left his master's service, and declared himself free. Wedderburn had him arrested, the Sheriff of Perthshire, on Knight's appeal, ruled that 'the state of slavery is not recognised by the laws of this kingdom', and the matter went to the highest court in Edinburgh, which supported the Sheriff's opinion and freed Knight on the grounds that 'The dominion assumed over this Negro, under the law of Jamaica, being unjust, could not be supported in this country to any extent' (Fryer, 120–27).

The law of Jamaica supported one of the most lethal economic systems ever created by so-called humans. In the first three-quarters of the eighteenth century, the island imported close on half a million slaves, but its slave population rose by little more than 15,000 (Calder,

459). It was cheaper to buy fresh grown slaves than go to the expense of rearing slave children. This was because of high mortality rates, actively abetted by plantation owners who drove pregnant and nursing slave women to work regardless. The situation of those female slaves selected to join masters in bed was preferable, though it might have fatal consequences for both parties. Dr James Wedderburn remarked in a letter to his friend the planter Thomas Thistlewood, that of the whites 'who have long been on this island . . . 4/5ths die of the venereal disease, one way or other' (McCalman, *Horrors*, 2).

Dr James eventually took back to Scotland with him a son and a daughter by a free 'Tawny' woman, Esther Trotter, and settled them in his homeland under the name of 'Graham'. Such generosity was not applied to offspring by slave women. According to Robert, after James had made his fortune, he became a 'perfect parish bull' and 'ranged through the whole of his household for his lewd purposes . . .' Visiting a fellow-Scot, Lady Douglas, James's eye fell upon her well-educated black maid, Rosanna. She became his own head servant. After she had borne James two boys – Robert's elder brother James would become a millwright on his father's estate – the free 'Tawny' mentioned above was introduced over her head. Pregnant again, she took this badly, and her rage was such that Dr James eventually agreed to sell her back to Lady Douglas. A condition of the sale was that the child in her belly, who turned out to be Robert, would be free from birth.

Cue for Talkee Amy, whom I regard as the supreme heroine of this entire book. Robert's grandmother was the slave of one Joseph Payne, a merchant, and 'her place was to sell his property – cheese, checks, chintz, milk, gingerbread, &c; in doing which, she trafficked in her own account with the goods of other merchants, having an agency of half-a-crown in the pound allowed her for her trouble'. Beside acting as a fence for illegally imported goods, Talkee Amy was an obeah woman, a practitioner of the sorcerer's arts of Africa which were feared by white and black alike. This formidable businessperson had no qualms about denouncing Dr James as 'mean Scotch rascal' to his face when she took the child Robert to see him and he refused to help support him. However, when Robert was about eleven, her own master was unwise enough to have her 'flogged as a witch'.

Old Joseph Payne had been engaged in a profitable illegal trade, smuggling mahogany out of Honduras in a vessel manned by his own slaves and commanded by a Welshman named Lloyd. Suspecting that Lloyd was cheating him, he went out on such a voyage himself. The ship was captured by Spanish coastguards. His slaves were confiscated and he himself was sentenced to a year's hard labour. After enduring this, he died on the way back to Jamaica. His nephew and heir was persuaded by a sycophantic woman-slave that his poor old uncle had suffered so because Talkee Amy had bewitched his ship, and he had her, aged around seventy, flogged nearly to the point of death. But Amy got her own back, if not through obeah, by Christian forbearance. In a 'judgment of God', the woman who had calumniated her lost her only child soon after. She came to beg Amy to forgive her and to help with the child's funeral. Amy did so. In Kingston marketplace, the woman made public confession of her guilt in telling lies about Amy (McCalman, *Horrors*, 44–50). Robert, baptised in the Church of England, derived from his childhood with Amy a mixture of Christian piety with African conceptions which helps to explain the forms which his religious dissent took later.

Robert's mother Rosanna had inherited Amy's forthright nature. It was her destiny to be owned by Scottish doctors. After Lady Douglas died, her heir sold the talented slave on to Dr Campbell, whose wife found her too much to handle, so she passed into the hands of Dr Boswell. For a minor instance of insubordination, as Robert would report in his *Horrors of Slavery* some half a century later, this man had her stretched out on the ground, tied at hands and feet, and flogged. After this, she passes into total obscurity and Robert's own movements are not too easy to follow.

During the War of the American Revolution, he saw service in the Royal Navy as a gunner, then sailed aboard a privateer. Around 1778 he first reached England. He spliced the surgary tones of Jamaica with the salty voice of the sea, so that during his later career as a radical preacher, spies would notice the below-decks character of his violent and amusing language. But he settled ashore in London and achieved the status of a skilled 'flint' journeyman tailor, self-consciously superior to the 'dung tailors' who accepted sweated conditions and bad wages. Meanwhile, he travelled to Scotland to seek support from his father, now settled at Inveresk, in East Lothian. Dr James acknowledged his parenthood, but called Robert 'a lazy fellow' and sent him away with nothing more than a glass of beer and a dodgy sixpence, both supplied by a servant.

Living among the lower orders in those tumultuous times was precarious. Many, black and white, found hope through conversion by Methodist preachers. This happened to Robert in 1786, in the London slum of Seven Dials. For a time he seems to have displayed Methodistical fervour. But his beliefs shifted. Around 1790, his name first appeared on a pamphlet, in which he rejected the doctrine of the Trinity. He took out a licence as a Unitarian preacher, patrolling the territory between orthodox Christianity and free-thought. His underworld life as a jobbing tailor and petty thief, selling pamphlets from a stall in one of the insalubrious courts off St Martin's Lane, came to a climax in 1813, when he met Thomas Spence nine months before that notable radical leader died.

Spence, a schoolmaster from Newcastle turned ragged street-vendor himself, propagated the view that all privately owned land should be expropriated, and offered publicly for rent by the various parishes, which could redistribute the resulting funds for the benefit of the people at large. One might call this vision of an agrarian utopia either 'socialist' or 'communist'. In any case it had appeal in unsettled times before and after the end of the Napoleonic Wars in 1815, when industrialisation and agricultural reorganisation were bringing changes all over Britain. Spencean 'Free and Easy Clubs' flourished in low taverns and blasphemous chapels, attracting 'immigrants, petty criminals and other members of the outcast poor, along with struggling artisans and a sprinkling of middle-class clerks, surgeons, journalists and lawyers' (McCalman, *Horrors*, 9). In this arena of rowdy debate, Wedderburn, now in his fifties, nicknamed 'the Devil's Engineer', was a star.

After Spence's death in 1814, leadership passed to Thomas Evans, a braces-maker. The movement was named by him the Society of Spencean Philanthropists. In the postwar years, it had 200–300 committed followers and ten times as many regular attenders at meetings – including abundant spies, informers and *agents-provocateurs* (McCalman, *Underworld*, 1). When Evans was imprisoned for a year in 1817–18, after arrest on suspicion of high treason, Wedderburn became the unofficial leader of the Society. After Evans got out of jail, he recast the Spenceans as nonconformist sect of Christian

Philanthropists, using a Haymarket basement which was licensed as a chapel. Here Robert acted as a preacher. But he soon quarrelled with Evans and from April 1819 had his own chapel, a converted hayloft in Hopkins Street, Soho. Soon up to 200 people were paying 6d a head to attend debates there on Monday and Wednesday evenings, and there were 'lectures every Sabbath day on Theology, Morality, Natural Philosophy and Politics, by a Self-Taught West Indian' (Fryer, 223).

At that point, Spenceans favoured non-violent action – a symbolic one-hour general strike was their strategic aim. But a militant wing emerged led by a a minor landowner and ex-militia officer from Lincolnshire, 'Captain' Arthur Thistlewood. (Unbeknownst to Robert, he was the nephew of Dr James Wedderburn's planter friend in Jamaica, Thomas Thistlewood – sugar-and-slavery connections permeated British society.) And the Spenceans associated themselves with the popular Henry 'Orator' Hunt in the organisation of mass meetings for reform. On 16 August 1819, the Manchester Yeomanry Cavalry charged a peaceful demonstration in St Peter's Fields Manchester, killing eleven unarmed people and injuring 500.

Wedderburn and his followers had already started carrying weapons to meetings. The 'Peterloo Massacre' vindicated this development. 'Captain' Wedderburn urged armed revolution, 'haranguing his crowded chapel meetings on the urgent need to arm; wooing soldiers with cash bribes and promises of future land allocations; and practising dawn drills with his comrades on Primrose Hill' (McCalman, *Horrors*, 21). Another black Jamaican now joined Thistlewood. William Davidson (1786–1820) was the son of the island's Scottish attorney-general by a black woman. He was educated in Jamaica, then sent to Edinburgh for further study. He spent some time in a lawyer's office, but ran away to sea and was impressed into the navy. On discharge, he studied mathematics awhile in Aberdeen, but eventually settled down as a cabinet maker in London, married to a white widow. This former Wesleyan Sunday school teacher now emerged as a hot revolutionary. He had no way of knowing that the man who introduced him to Thistlewood was a police spy, egging on the group of two or three dozen ultra radicals till they devised a plan to murder the entire Cabinet as they sat together at dinner, establish a provisional government, and call for general insurrection. 'Black'

Davidson was entrusted with buying muskets and ammunition for the uprising. He was on guard on 23 March 1820 when police stormed the loft where the 'Cato Street Conspirators' were meeting prior to assassinating the Cabinet, put up valiant resistance, but was overpowered and taken away, singing Burns's song against tyranny, 'Scots wha hae wi' Wallace bled'. The public execution of Thistlewood, Davidson and three associates was rather less gruesome than that of Wallace centuries before, but their beheading after they had been hanged was a touch harking back to the Middle Ages.

Robert Wedderburn would presumably have been in Cato Street had the authorities not decided to jail him some weeks previously. His Hopkins Street hayloft had been the scene of joyful uproar. Wedderburn, a hilarious orator, formed a comic team with a dwarf shoemaker, Samuel Waddington. 'The Black Prince' and 'The Black Dwarf' conducted mock worship, switching from burlesque to melodrama. Wedderburn was brought to trial early in 1820 for 'blasphemous' remarks uttered in front of a police spy in his chapel. He had impugned the veracity of the Old Testament. If Jesus said that no man could raise the dead but God, how could the Witch of Endor have raised up the dead Samuel to instruct King Saul? Receiving judgment on 9 May, he elaborated his point before the Court of King's Bench. His own grandmother had been flogged for being a witch – 'now as he, as a child, had frequently picked her pocket of sixpences and shillings, he was well convinced she could not possess the qualities and powers attributed to witches, or she might have detected his petty depredations'. Mr Justice Bailey sent him to Dorchester jail for two years for 'blasphemous and profane words . . . calculated to distress the feelings of those who entertain a reverence for the sacred scriptures' which were so framed as to make anyone reading them, 'more humble, more submissive, and every way a better member of society' (Perkins, *Trial*, 3–4; *Address*, 3–4, 14–15).

In Dorchester prison, Wedderburn, that July, produced a popular pamphlet called *Cast-Iron Parsons*, in which he argued that a metal clergyman should replace the human one in every parish, at a saving of millions of pounds in salaries. While such an officiant 'cannot go about to do good, it is equally incapable of hunting, shooting, horse-racing, card playing, or frequenting balls, routs, and other profane and ungodly amusements' (Wedderburn, 9). His time in Dorchester may have been a pleasant period of reading, reflection and discussion, notably with Richard Carlile, a brave and important freethinker.

Emerging to find the radical movement knocked back, Wedderburn continued his ministry, but eventually changed its name. In March 1828, Carlile's journal *The Lion* published Wedderburn's 'HOLY LITURGY, or DIVINE SERVICE, upon the principles of PURE CHRISTIAN DIABOLISM'. The argument was that God, with his 'omniscience and general perfections' should not be plagued with 'troublesome, complaining and ill-judged prayers', which implicitly 'doubted his goodness and his attention towards us'. Therefore – 'OUR PRAYERS SHALL BE ALL MOST PROPERLY ADDRESSED TO THE *MAJESTY OF HELL*, to the "*GOD OF THIS WORLD*", to that IMPERFECT, that OMNIMALEVOLENT, though POWERFUL BEING, *THE DEVIL . . . a Being to be feared, to be worshipped, to be cajoled*' . . . (McCallum, *Horrors*, 153–54).

In the 1820s Evangelical piety on the one hand, earnest self-improving interest in science and technology on the other, were winning out amongst intelligent plebeians, so that Wedderburn's carnivalesque Christianity – it seems clear that he retained his faith in Christ, whom he saw as a lower-class radical like himself – was now out of fashion. Even infidels and deists were now inclined to be respectable. Wedderburn's Christian Diabolist chapel opened early in 1828 off Chancery Lane, closed in June for want of support. Its aged promoter had one recourse left. He established a brothel in nearby Featherbed Lane. In 1831 he was jailed again, not simply for running such a place, but for brawling in the street outside it. He showed at his trial that he still had his old comic touch, accusing one member of the court of himself frequenting his establishment, in pursuit of one 'Carroty Eliza' normally to be found 'padding the hoof' in Fleet Street . . . (McCalman, *Horrors*, 31–32).

It is common enough for radicals to see causes that formerly got them into trouble achieving success and respectability. By the time Wedderburn died, Parliamentary Reform, in the great Act of 1832, had begun to extend the franchise, and slavery, in 1834, had been abolished throughout the British Empire, after just such a great slave insurrection in Jamaica (1831) as the old Diabolist had hoped for.

Angus Calder, Revolutionary Empire, *1981; 'Sir John Wedderburn',* DNB*; Paul Edwards and David Dabydeen, eds,* Black Writers in Britain 1760–1890, *(Edinburgh) 1991; Peter Fryer,* Staying Power: The History of Black People in *Britain, 1984; Iain McCalman,* Radical Underworld: Prophets, Revolutionaries and Pornographers in London, 1795–1840, *(Cambridge) 1988; Iain McCalman, ed. and introd.,* Robert Wedderburn: The Horrors of Slavery and Other Writings, *(Edinburgh) 1991; 'Erasmus Perkins', ed.,* The Address of the Rev. R. Wedderburn To the Court of King's Bench at Westminster, on appearing to receive Judgement for Blasphemy . . . the 9th of May . . . 1820, *1820; 'Erasmus Perkins', ed.,* The Trial of the Reverend Robert Wedderburn . . . for Blasphemy, *1820; James Robertson,* Joseph Knight, *2003; Rev. R. Wedderburn,* Cast-Iron Parsons: or, Hints to the Public and the Legislature on Political Economy, *1820; thanks to James Robertson*

Major Weir (Scotland) *d.*1670

'Witchcraft' in late medieval and early modern Europe was linked to the survival of pre-Christian beliefs. At the centre of the rites organised by 'covens' of witch-priests (generally thirteen in number) was a figure, always termed **'The Devil'** (q.v.) by Christian reporters, either dressed in black or disguised in animal forms. Witches 'Sabbaths' took place at four times in the year – at Candlemas, 2 February; May-eve; Lammas, 1 August, and November-eve, All Hallow Even. Devotees came from far and wide to dance, sing and feast from evening to dawn. The witch-hunts which occurred in many parts of Europe were the means by which still-superstitious Christians, Catholic and Reformed, demonised and attempted to destroy more ancient superstitions.

Witch-hunts in Scotland peaked in the 1590s, the late 1620s, in 1649 and 1661–62. Nine out of every ten victims were women. Three hundred 'witches' died in 1661–62 alone. They were, Michael Lynch suggests, 'scapegoats for the vagaries of a rural society in which illness struck without warning and animals died mysteriously'. But the lead in witch-hunts was taken by well-off people, lairds and ministers perplexed by theological considerations about good and evil, fearful for the safety of their own souls (Lynch, 185, 295).

James VI of Scotland became obsessed, in 1590, with the idea that witches had confessed to practising magic against him. Along with a coven of witches from East Lothian, a kinsman of the king, the Earl of Bothwell, was tried and convicted. (He escaped.) James interrogated suspects himself, eliciting strange stories of weird doings in the gentle landscape around North Berwick.

Some such reportedly came from the confessions of Dr Fian, alias Cunningham, the young village schoolmaster in Tranent. This would-be warlock, or wizard, fancied a certain lady. When persuasion failed, he turned to magic. The lady was unmarried and had a brother who attended the doctor's school. He took the lad aside and enquired if he and his sister shared a bed. The lad said they did. Fian promised him that he would never beat him again if he would bring him three of the lady's pubic hairs, giving him a magically charmed piece of paper to wrap them in. Unfortunately for Fian, the lady complained to their mother that the boy was keeping her awake by pestering her. Mother, being a witch herself, at once jaloused what was up. She thrashed the boy till he confessed, then decided 'to meete with the Doctor in his owne art'. She went to a virgin heifer and clipped three hairs from its udder, then wrapped them in Dr Fian's magic paper. When they were brought to Fian, he cast spells upon them. So, when he was in church, the heifer burst in and made towards him 'leaping and dauncing'. Thereafter she followed him everywhere, 'to the great admiration of all the townes men of Saltpans, and many other . . .' Suspicion thereby arose that he was a warlock, and when subjected to the boots, a particularly vicious Scottish instrument of torture which involved crushing the legs with wedges of wood inserted into a metal casing, he confessed to this. Then he repented, 'renounced the Devill and all his wicked workes', and vowed to live a Christian life (Yeoman, 150–55).

The story of Major Weir and his tragic sister is not so funny. They were executed in 1670. Their trials fell in a period when the authorities were persecuting, besides witches, zealous Covenanters, of whom Weir was one.

In 1638, the nobility and town leaders of Scotland, followed by many lesser folk, had signed a National Covenant pledging themselves to defend their church against the Anglican, deemed 'Popish', innovations proposed by Charles I. This launched the British Isles into civil war. Calvinist Presbyterians seized control of government in Scotland in the 1640s, to the discomfort of some nobles who had signed the Covenant. A class division opened up, with many of the nobility recoiling from Presbyterianism and many small lairds and commoners favouring it zealously. The restoration of Charles II in 1660 led to the reintroduction of Bishops, execrated by ministers who were debarred from their churches and by their followers who flocked to hear them preach at open-air 'Conventicles'. The latter were the folk subsequently remembered as 'Covenanters'.

I cannot improve, in one most important respect, on the account of Weir given by Robert Chambers in his *Traditions of Edinburgh*, first published in the 1820s, later revised by him in the 1860s. Chambers collected traditions from all sources – from such great antiquaries as Sir Walter Scott himself, from other learned and witty men, from the gossips of the taverns. On the way Weir was remembered, Chambers is definitive.

> In the latter part of the seventeenth century, the inhabitants of the West Bow enjoyed a peculiar fame for their piety and zeal in the Covenanting cause. The wits of the opposite faction are full of allusions to them as 'the Bowhead Saints', 'the godly plants of the Bowhead', and so forth . . .
>
> It must have been a sad scandal to this peculiar community when Major Weir, one of their number, was found to have been so wretched an example of human infirmity . . . His history is obscurely reported; but it appears that he was of a good family in Lanarkshire, and had been one of the ten thousand men sent by the Scottish Covenanting Estates in 1641 to assist in suppressing the Irish Papists. He became distinguished for a life of peculiar sanctity, even in an age when that was the prevailing tone of the public mind. According to a contemporary account: 'His garb was still a cloak, and somewhat dark, and he never went without his staff. He was a tall black man, and ordinarily looked down to the ground; *a grim countenance, and a big nose*. At length he became so notoriously regarded among the Presbyterian strict sect, that if four met together, be sure Major Weir was one. At private meetings he prayed to admiration, which made many of that stamp court his converse. He never married, but lived in a private lodging with his sister, Grizel Weir. Many resorted to his house, to join him and hear him pray; but it was observed that he could not officiate in any holy duty without the black staff, or rod, in his hand, and leaning upon it, which made those who

heard him pray admire his flood in prayer, his ready extemporary expression, his heavenly gesture; so that he was thought more angel than man, and was termed by some of the holy sisters ordinarily *Angelical Thomas*.' Plebeian imaginations have since fructified regarding the staff, and crones will still seriously tell how it could run a message to a shop for any article which its proprietor wanted; how it could answer the door when any one called upon its master; and that it used to be often seen running before him, in the capacity of a link-boy, as he walked down the Lawnmarket.

After a life characterised externally by all the graces of devotion, but polluted in secret by crimes of the most revolting nature, and which little needed the addition of wizardry to excite the horror of living men, Major Weir fell into a severe sickness, which afflicted his mind so much that he made open and voluntary confession of all his wickedness. The tale was at first so incredible that the provost, Sir Andrew Ramsay, refused for some time to take him into custody. At length himself, his sister (partner of one of his crimes), and his staff were secured by the magistrates . . . While the wretched man lay in prison, he made no scruple to disclose the particulars of his guilt, but refused to address himself to the Almighty for pardon. To every request that he would pray, he answered in screams: 'Torment me no more – I am tormented enough already!' Even the offer of a Presbyterian clergyman, instead of an established Episcopal minister of the city, had no effect upon him. He was tried April 9, 1670, and being found guilty, was sentenced to be strangled and burnt between Edinburgh and Leith. His sister, who was tried at the same time, was sentenced to be hanged in the Grassmarket. The execution of the profligate major took place, April 14, at the place indicated by the judge. When the rope was about his neck, to prepare him for the fire, he was bid to say: 'Lord, be merciful to me!' but he answered as before: 'Let me alone – I will not – I have lived as a beast, and I must die as a beast!' After he had dropped lifeless in the flames, his stick was also cast into the fire; and, 'whatever incantation was in it,' says the contemporary writer already quoted [the Rev. Mr Fraser, ms], 'the persons present own that it gave rare turnings, and was long a-burning, as also himself.'

The conclusion to which the humanity of the present age would come regarding Weir – that he was mad – is favoured by some circumstances; for instance, his answering one who asked if he had ever seen the devil, that 'the only feeling he ever had of him was in the dark.' What chiefly countenances the idea is the unequivocal lunacy of the sister. This miserable woman confessed to witchcraft, and related, in a serious manner, many things which could not be true. Many years before, a fiery coach, she said, had come to her brother's door in broad day, and a stranger invited them to enter, and they proceeded to Dalkeith. On the way, another person came and whispered in her brother's ear something which affected him; it proved to be supernatural intelligence of the defeat of the Scotch army at Worcester, which took place that day. Her brother's power, she said, lay in his staff . . . Her mother, she declared, had been also a witch . . . At the place of execution she acted in a furious manner, and with difficulty could be prevented from throwing off her clothes, in order to die, as she said, 'with all the shame she could' . . .

For upwards of a century after Major Weir's death, he continued to be the bugbear of the Bow, and his house remained uninhabited. His apparition was frequently seen at night, flitting, like a black and silent shadow, about the street. His house, though known to be deserted by everything human, was sometimes observed at midnight to be full of lights, and heard to emit strange sounds, as of dancing, howling, and, what is strangest of all, spinning. Some people occasionally saw the major issue from the low close at midnight, mounted on a black horse without a head, and gallop off in a whirlwind of flame. Nay, sometimes the whole of the inhabitants of the Bow would be roused from their sleep at an early hour in the morning by the sound as of a coach and six, first rattling up the Lawnmarket, and then thundering down the Bow, stopping at the head of the terrible close for a few minutes, and then rattling and thundering back again – being neither more nor less than Satan come in one of his best equipages to take home the major and his sister . . . (Chambers, 30–35)

Thus was Major Weir remembered as a *warlock*. But he was not tried or executed as such. Already in the 1820s, the rising tide of

Evangelicalism was swamping any hope of candour about certain matters, even from such a liberal man as Chambers. Weir was tried for adultery, bestiality and incest. His strange remark about feeling the devil in the dark but never seeing him arose at the only moment when the matter was put to him. It was his sister's testimony at her trial which seemed to implicate him in black arts. Even so, she was convicted not of witchcraft but of incest. As David Stevenson observes, 'The horrors related about him in the nineteenth century were bowdlerisations designed to hide the truth while preserving an aura of unparalleled evil' (Stevenson, 65).

Thomas was the son of a small Clydesdale laird, Weir of Kirkton, in the south-west of Scotland where Covenanting zealotry became strongest and endured longest. In 1636 he moved to Edinburgh, where, in 1642, he married Isobel Mein, widow of a merchant, so becoming a burgess. Beside serving for over a year in Ireland, as Chambers mentions, he obtained his title 'Major' as second in command of a regiment raised in 1644 by the Earl of Lanark to assist the Scottish army intervening on Parliament's side in the English Civil War. When he left after a year, it may have been in response to a call from his fellow burgesses, because late in 1645 he was appointed to command the guard raised to police and defend the burgh. Though he lost this position as political times changed and his godly co-thinkers lost control, he retained friends in high places. Hence the reluctance of his acquaintances to believe him when this elderly, substantial, godly man cracked up and began showing terror at every reference to the word 'burn', even when it denoted a small river. It was assumed, when he confessed to vile sins, such as merited hell-fire, that he was mad. But corroborative evidence emerged.

As David Stevenson notes, the 'sad thing' about the incidents exposed 'is that they are all so mundane and plausible'. When she was in her mid teens, his sister Margaret discovered that Jean, his younger sister, was sexually involved with Thomas. The lass was sent away from home. In 1651, when he was going to a 'solemn meeting' in Newmills, a woman saw him committing bestiality. She reported this to the kirk minister. Soldiers were sent to arrest him. His denial was believed and the woman who had clyped on him was whipped through the streets of Lanark. 'Sadly', to make Stevenson's point again, this injustice to her was the one thing about which he seemed explicitly repentant when he was finally convicted (*Satan's Invisible World*, 175–77).

For over two decades, he had an adulterous relationship with a servant, Bessie Wemyss. It further seems that he had committed incest with his step-daughter Margaret. He was said to have married her off (to an Englishman) when she became pregnant. His sister Jean had been keeping a school in Dalkeith. She joined him in Edinburgh after his wife died and they lived together incestuously – until, as she complained, at the age of fifty she was cast aside. The pair of them used some form of contraception to prevent pregnancy but even in the relatively candid seventeenth century, a clergyman could not bring himself to let her describe to him which 'abominable' method they had followed (*Satan's Invisible World*, 180).

James Robertson in his fine novel *The Fanatic* (2000) presents a convincingly sinister picture of the severe Major, but a very sympathetic picture of Jean. This was an era when Quaker women marched naked into churches to expose the nakedness of truth as opposed to the false vestments of formal religion. Robertson gives such a coloration to Jean's final agony. As witnesses reported, 'the hangman struggled with her to keep on her cloaths and she struggled with him to have them off; at last he was forced to throw her over [push her off the ladder] open faced, which afterwards he covered with a cloth' (*Satan's Invisible World*, 183–84). Was she expressing repentance, or defying convention, as she bared her breasts on the scaffold?

It seems fairly clear that we have in Major Weir an extreme case of antinomianism (cf. **Anne Hutchinson**). Calvinist doctrine, such as he undoubtedly accepted, suggests that God has foreknown from the beginning, as it were, of eternity, which of his human creatures will be damned, which 'elect' persons will be saved. If one is saved already, nothing one does can alter God's choice. Indeed, any impulse one feels must be godly . . . What seems to have happened to Weir is that after a life of strenuous self-justification, health and 'sanity' broke down in old age and he confronted the opposite possibility, that he was irrevocably damned. Logically, he could gain nothing by 'repentance' – the ministrations of clergy were irrelevant. His behaviour in prison, therefore, was totally consistent with his former conduct at religious meetings where he had overawed the faithful with his piety, believing himself to be saved for all eternity. The same doctrine now told him that he would burn in hell for ever.

Robert Chambers, Traditions of Edinburgh, *(Edinburgh), 1868; Michael Lynch*, Scotland: A New History, *1991;* Satan's Invisible World Discovered . . . To Which Is Added, That Marvellous History of Major Weir and his Sister by Mr George Sinclair, *(Edinburgh) 1769 edn; David Stevenson*, King or Covenant? Voices from Civil War, *(East Linton), 1996; Louise Yeoman*, Reportage Scotland: History in the Making, *(Edinburgh), 2000; thanks to Sheena Blackhall and James Robertson*

Saint Wilgefortis (Europe, Dark Ages) n.d.

Wilgefortis was one of seven, or nine, children born all at once to the wife of a heathen King of Portugal, or maybe Provence or Sicily. When she was grown, her father wished to marry her to the King of Sicily, or Portugal, but she had taken Christian vows of virginity. She prayed for help. She was rewarded with a fine beard and moustache. The foreign King recoiled. Her father, much enraged, had her crucified.

The man who writes about her in *Butler's Lives of the Saints* is more disgusted than bemused. She is 'a curiosity of hagiology' (fair enough) and her story is 'one of the most obviously false and preposterous of the pseudo-pious romances by which simple Christians have been deceived or regaled' (Butler, 151). Her cult derived authority from a story set down by Pope Gregory the Great (*c.*540–604) – the man who converted the Anglo-Saxons to Christianity. More proximately, it may have stemmed, in the high Middle Ages, from devotion to a certain famous crucifix at Lucca, in Tuscany, which showed Christ on his cross dressed, not in the conventional loincloth, but in a rich robe, crowned, and, of course, bearded. (There is a powerful painting of this image, '*Volto Santo*' *di Lucca*, in a museum in Budapest, attributed to the eccentric Florentine artist **Piero di Cosimo**, q.v.) The name Wilgefortis may come from the Germanic *Hilge varz* – 'holy face'. Or it may derive from *Vierge-Forte* – 'Strong Virgin'. Which brings us to St Isidore of Seville (*c.*560–636).

This learned bishop set much store by etymology. He believed that man, in Latin, was called *vir* because there was greater force, *vis*, in him than in woman. From *vir* came *virtu*, or strength, because men ruled over women by force. *Mulier*, woman, he derived from *molites*, softness. Isidore may have helped determine attitudes in the medieval Church towards transvestism. Cross-dressing by men was seen as wicked and punishable. In women, it was tolerated, and might even be approved of, since it showed a commendable desire in the weaker sex to become stronger and more virtuous – 'more male-like and therefore better persons' (Bullough, 224, 226). **Jhenne Darc** (q.v.) was the only notable medieval European woman to be prosecuted for cross-dressing, but this was a minor factor in the process which led to her execution. Bearded, crucified Wilgefortis, robed like an authoritative male, might be seen as a most acceptable role model.

Anyway, so many pilgrims arrived to kiss the feet of the crucifix in Lucca that it was shod with silver to prevent the wood being worn away by their kisses. 'This also has been turned to the glorification of St Wilgefortis. For it is said that a poor minstrel playing an air before the saint's statue was rewarded by her giving him one of her precious shoes' (Butler's *Lives of the Saints*, 151). A different version of this tale had it that such a fellow was desperate for money. Wilgefortis' father had repented after crucifying her, converted, and built a church in which he set up her golden image. Appealed to by the fiddler, she kicked off one of her gold boots. Of course, he was accused of having stolen it and was condemned to be hanged. He begged to be allowed to play his fiddle in front of Wilgefortis before he died. In view of the king and 'all the people', she responded by kicking off her other boot, and so he was saved from the scaffold (Dunbar, 312).

She was incorporated with Liberata, an Italian lady originally with a different legend. In France she was known as Livrade, in Germany as Ontkommer or Kummernis. The English equivalent was 'Uncumber'. She went by many other local names. In Prague, where her image features in the Chapel of Our Lady of Sorrows in the Loreta by the Castle, she was St Starosta.

She freed people from anxiety and promised them deliverance from troubles and a quiet death. In England, where a shrine to her appeared in the Henry VII Chapel in Westminster Abbey, women afflicted with awkward or detestable husbands were drawn to invoke her aid. The custom was to offer her oats. Thomas More, of *Man For All Seasons* fame, wrote dismissively about this practice, 'Whereof I cannot perceive the reason, but if it be because she should provide a horse for an evil husband to ride to the devil upon . . . Insomuch that women have changed her name and instead of Saint Wilgeforte call her Saint Uncumber, because that they reckon that for a peck of oats she will not fail to uncumber them of their husbands' (Farmer, 437).

At which point we may observe that purportedly 'simple' Christians were not so stupid as modern male priests embarrassed by Wilgefortis may assume. Like folk all over the world, they used legend to explain and justify attitudes and behaviour which might not suit conventional notions of authority. To see Christ as a bearded woman was an unconscious, perhaps sometimes conscious, act of subversion. Might not 'Pray St Uncumber rid me of this lout', or words to that effect, be more acceptable, just, than sticking pins in a wee model of one's spouse?

Mina Bacci, L'Opera Completa di Piero di Cosimo, *(Milan), 1976; V. L. Bullough, 'Cross Dressing and Gender Role Change . . .', in V. L. Bullough and J. A. Brundage, eds,* Handbook of Medieval Sexuality, *(New York) 1996;* Butler's Lives of the Saints, *vol. 3, rev. edn, ed. Herbert J. Thurston, SJ, and Donald Attwater, 1981; Agnes B. C. Dunbar,* A Dictionary of Saintly Women, *vol. 2, 1905; David Hugh Farmer,* The Oxford Dictionary of Saints, *1987 edn, thanks to Dilys Rose and Gary Dickson*

Winkie (Pigeon/Britain) *fl.* 1941

In the magnificent Scottish National War Memorial on Castle Rock, Edinburgh, opened in 1927, Sir Robert Lorimer and his team of craftsmen strove to include not only all fallen soldiers, but also all categories of men, females, and even fauna, who had contributed to victory in the Great War. Thus, there are sculpted effigies of 'the humble beasts' – horse, elephant, ox, camel and dog – who had variously aided the armed forces. 'The Tunnellers' Friends' have their own little memorial – canaries and mice taken underground by sappers to give early warning of gas, to which the birds were fifteen times more sensitive than humans. And the gallant pigeons, too, are remembered.

Hannibal is said to have used homing pigeons to aid his crossing of the Alps. Such birds provided a postal service during the Siege of Paris in 1870 and the British Army employed them during the Boer War. All combatants on the Western Front used them for communication and spying in 1914–18. A valiant French pigeon serving Commandant Raynal at Verdun was mangled by shell fire and dropped dead delivering his message. The grateful French nation awarded it the Légion d'Honneur. The Germans, it is claimed, were so exasperated by British pigeons that they tried to bomb their headquarters in Doughty Street, Bloomsbury, London – but missed.

It is further claimed that of more than 100,000 pigeons serving Britain in the First World War, ninety-five per cent returned successfully (Cooper, 103). Be that as it may, in the Second World War, when the National Pigeon Service conscripted almost twice as many birds, only nine per cent made it back (Le Chene, 145). This was despite the assistance of the Falcon Control Unit formed to protect them from dastardly predators brainwashed by the Nazis, while in the Falcon (Intercepter) Unit, noble Anglo-Saxon hawks were directed to bring down suspicious intruding alien pigeons.

British pigeons, which came in nine distinct varieties, had been trained by civilian 'fanciers' so that they would home unerringly to loft, mate and trainer, even when the loft was moved about. The development of radio during and after the First World War did not make pigeons redundant. The British Special Operations Executive dropped them in containers into occupied Europe for the use of its agents (16,554 birds were sent in but only 1,842 returned – many of the missing must be presumed eaten). Five hundred pigeons served the Allies on D-Day at the Normandy landings. RAF Coastal Command had long supplied them to its crews, which is how the valiant Winkie gained a name resounding to posterity.

In February 1941, a Beaufort bomber trying to return to RAF Leuchars in Fife after suffering severe damage on a mission to Norway plunged into choppy sea more than 120 miles from home. With its radio drowned, the crew found their blue chequered hen pigeon, at this time known to them only as NEHU 40 NSI, pushing her way out of her smashed container. Released in forlorn hope, she flopped into oil slick around the aircraft, but managed, awkwardly, to achieve lift off, into horrendous weather.

Back at Leuchars, the crew had been presumed lost, after fruitless search in the wrong direction. Then a tiny speck in the morning sky proved to be NEHU 40 NSI, who plonked herself in her loft, oily, wet and exhausted, to the surprise of Sgt Donaldson of the Pigeon Service. Somehow, taking into account the time she had flown, the weather, and the drag of oil on her wings, he got an accurate position for the lost aircraft, and very quickly another search found the crew alive and called in air-sea rescue. It was the first time a pigeon had saved RAF personnel in this war. At a dinner in honour of their heroine and her trainers, Ross and Norrie from Angus, it was decided that the bird should be called 'Winkie'. Under that name, towards the end of 1943, she received the 'Animal's VC', the 'Dickin Medal' inaugurated by the People's Dispensary for Sick Animals whose founder was Mrs Maria Dickin. Over sixty years, pigeons would easily outnumber all other species amongst recipients of this award – thirty-two, as compared to eighteen dogs, three horses, and one cat (*Herald*, 6 March 2002).

But nobler honour still came to the long-late Winkie in the 1980s, when the poet Douglas Dunn, himself a major award-winner, spotted her stuffed in a municipal glass case. In his paean to her, which concludes 'FLY WINKIE, FLY!' he describes her exploit and uses it to exemplify the noble, gutsy character of her species, sometimes dismissed by silly humans – who see its representatives pecking abjectly and insatiably at city litter and resent their merry prank of aerial bombardment by excretion – as mere 'rats of the air':

> You are liberty's bird,
> Unstreamlined and civilian . . .
> Olympic bird, love-bird, bird of the peace . . .

(Dunn, 33–36)

Jilly Cooper, Animals in War, *1984; I.C.B. Deare, ed.*, Oxford Companion to the Second World War, *(Oxford) 1995; Douglas Dunn*, Northlight, *1988; 'Briefing: The Dickin Medal'*, Herald, *6 March 2002; Evelyn La Chene*, Silent Heroes: The Bravery and Devotion of Animals in War, *1994*

Ludwig Wittgenstein (Austria) 1889–1951

The funniest of innumerable anecdotes about the tormented philosopher Wittgenstein concerns Bertrand Russell and the rhinoceros.

In the pioneering days of aeronautics – less than five years after Orville and Wilbur Wright had made the first successful flight in a petrol-driven plane – Wittgenstein had gone to Manchester to research the matter, apparently intending to build his own aircraft and fly it.

Attending lectures at the city's university, he had begun to develop an interest in pure mathematics, and a fellow student had introduced him to Russell's book *The Principles of Mathematics*, published in 1903. Russell's view was that mathematics and logic were one and the same thing. Wittgenstein, as he continued to design first an aircraft engine then a propeller (which he patented), was tantalised by an unresolved paradox in Russell's work. At last, after a period of what he described as 'a constant, indescribable, almost pathological state of agitation', he suddenly turned up on 18 October 1911 in Russell's rooms at Trinity College, Cambridge, where the great man was a Fellow. After a tongue-tied self-introduction, he began to haunt the philosopher, dominating discussion at his scantily attended lectures on mathematical logic and following him back to Trinity afterwards to pursue his points till dinner-time. Russell reported to his lover Lady Ottoline Morrell: 'My German engineer very argumentative & tiresome. He wouldn't admit that it was certain that there wasn't a rhinoceros in the room . . . [He] came back and argued all the time I was dressing'. Russell would claim jokingly later in life that he had looked under all the tables and chairs in the lecture room in order to persuade Wittgenstein that there was no rhinoceros present. To no avail: 'My German engineer, I think, is a fool. He thinks nothing empirical is knowable' (Monk, 39–40). What is so charming about this story is that it shows two of the greatest men in the history of Western philosphy deadlocked over such a basic problem. Any clever school student can have fun establishing that we cannot be certain of the existence, or non-existence, of anything. As in the Goon Show catchphrase, 'It's all in the mind, you know.'

The tale of Wittgenstein, Karl Popper and the poker, much debated amongst philosophers over more than a half a century, has much darker overtones and from certain angles isn't funny at all.

Reel forward . . . It is 25 October 1946. Wittgenstein is now established as the dominant figure in Cambridge University's small philosophy department. This is doubly perverse, since Wittgenstein not only hates Cambridge as a place (greatly preferring South Wales, where he finds people warmer) but despises academic philosophers, urging his favourite students to take up something useful instead, such as mindless manual labour. Popper, who gives a short paper that evening to the Cambridge Moral Science Club which brings together dons and students, is also a Jew from Vienna, but he has spent the war years well away from the murderous theatres of conflict, surrounded by sheep in Canterbury, New Zealand. His recently published book, *The Open Society and Its Enemies* (1945), has been well received, and will become very famous and influential. But it is calculated to make enemies for Popper himself – amongst philosophers shocked by his well-merited attack on Plato as a totalitarian, amongst leftists enraged by his assault on Marxism, and amongst followers of Wittgenstein, whose philosophy he thinks trivial because it deals with paradoxes and puzzles arising in language rather than serious problems like those created by the activities of Hitler and Stalin in the 'real world'.

In October 1946 Wittgenstein has no reason to imagine that Popper's reputation will vie with his for supremacy amongst twentieth-century thinkers. This is just another little academic dealing in what Wittgenstein, the great debunker of the pretensions of philosophers, considers to be pointless fiddles with words.

In fact, Popper, forty-four years old (Wittgenstein was fifty-seven), was also a zealot, just then impatient to make up for time away from the epicentre of Western philosophy. And this apostle of liberalism, democracy and free thought was in practice as overbearing and intolerant in argument as Wittgenstein himself. Bryan Magee, who became his (critical) disciple after he first heard him lecture in 1958, recalls 'an intellectual aggressiveness such as I had never encountered before. Everything we argued about he pursued relentlessly, beyond the limits of acceptable aggression in conversation . . . The unremittingly fierce, tight focus, like a flame, put me in mind of a blowtorch . . .' (Magee, 190–91).

So King Kong, as it were, met Godzilla, in a don's room in King's College. There was no central heating to speak of in austerity-clenched postwar Britain, and this room had an open fire beside which sat what would become the most famous poker in the history of Western thought. Wittgenstein's disciples were present, wearing tweed jackets, with shirts open-necked, exactly like their short but imposing Master. So were philosophers critical of Wittgenstein who nevertheless conceded his importance. Chief amongst these was Bertrand Russell, once Wittgenstein's hero, protector and benefactor, now discarded by him as a fissenless populariser. Cambridge people there were used to

Wittgenstein's manner. When he deigned to turn up to the Moral Science Club of which he was, as of right, President, he would dominate discussion (as he always did, for that matter, in cafés, in living rooms and on healthful walks) then leave early to get on with his private thinking. This last point is significant. Did he finally storm out in rage, as Popper thought (never having encountered him before), or merely make his usual abrupt exit, as usual banging the door behind him?

What is perfectly clear is that Popper, recently appointed to a post at the famous London School of Economics, having been invited to 'deliver a short paper, or a few opening remarks, stating some philosophical puzzle', took the chance to attack the notion of 'puzzles', which he associated with Wittgenstein, in the interests of his own concern with 'problems'. Wittgenstein rose to the bait at once. As the man with the haunted eyes slugged it out verbally with the pugnacious upstart with the huge sticky-out ears, the former's hand reached towards the poker . . . 'Someone – was it Russell? – said "Wittgenstein, put the poker down"' (Edmonds and Eidenow, 212–13).

Whoever that someone was, he might well have seen Wittgenstein in action with a poker before. The neo-liberal economist Friedrich Von Hayek was, as it happened, a cousin of Wittgenstein's. Taken to the Moral Science Club as a guest during the war, he would later report thus: 'Suddenly Wittgenstein lept to his feet, poker in hand, indignant in the highest degree, and he proceeded to demonstrate with the implement how simple and obvious "matter" really was. Seeing this rampant man in the middle of the room swinging a poker was certainly rather alarming, and one felt inclined to escape into a safe corner. Frankly, my impression at that time was that he had gone mad' (quoted in Edmonds and Eidenow, 161).

That Wittgenstein was capable of personal violence is unquestionable. He had been twice decorated for his valour as an artillery officer in the Austro-Hungarian army in the 1914–18 war, during which he had written his *Tractatus Logico-Philosophicus*, the only book by him published in his lifetime, if one does not count a dictionary for schoolchildren. The latter arose from his quixotic decision to renounce his vast inherited wealth, train as a schoolteacher and dedicate his intellect to the service of peasant children in a backward part of Austria. He thought the peasants to be 'not human *at all*, but loathsome worms', and they didn't like him much, either. In particular, his habit of hitting pupils who were slow to answer on their heads eventually led to an enquiry after one boy, struck several times, collapsed. Wittgenstein was cleared of misconduct, but the incident triggered his precipitate retreat from schoolteaching (Monk, 212, 232–33).

Our clever school student really enjoys the poker incident. The dons and future professors present cannot thereafter agree on what happened, thus demonstrating two truisms: that all witness-reports of an event, be it a battle or a philosophical argument, are partial in two senses of that word (dependent on physical angle of view, and *parti-pris*) and that memories, even when vivid – or *especially* when vivid – are *even more* untrustworthy than accounts jotted down at the event (minutes) or soon after (diaries, letters). A brilliant book by David Edmonds and John Eidinow, *Wittgenstein's Poker* (2001), makes it seem probable that Popper, interested in exaggerating what he considered to be a triumph over Wittgenstein in their only direct encounter, altered, in memory, the actual sequence of events. According to his account, Wittgenstein asked him to give *one* example of a moral rule, to which Popper, quick as a flash, replied, 'Not to threaten visiting lecturers with pokers.' Upon which Wittgenstein stormed out, presumably beaten . . . It seems more likely that Popper's crack was made after his adversary had left the room (see Watkins).

If there is such a thing as an 'iconic' philosopher, Wittgenstein is that icon. In a book on poetic language published in 1996, one scholar noted eight novels and plays, twelve books of poetry, and some six performance pieces and experimental art works that were directly about or influenced by Wittgenstein. Known to her, that is – the true totals must now be much larger. He appeals to literary artists, and to people sensitive in turn to their art, not only because his prose is epigrammatic and 'poetic' but because he has the characteristics, contingently 'modernist', but in genealogy 'romantic', of the intellectual-as-outsider, the loner anguished because incapable of compromise, the irreconcilable anti-bourgeois . . .

Consider these remarks from his *Tractatus*:

5.621 The world and life are one.

5.63 I am my world. (The microcosm.)

5.631 There is no such thing as the subject that thinks or entertains ideas.

If I wrote a book called *The World as I Found It*, I should have to include a report on my body, and should have to say which parts were subordinate to my will, and which were not, etc., this being a method of isolating the subject, or rather of showing that in an important sense there is no subject; for it alone could *not* be mentioned in that book.

5.632 The subject does not belong to the world: rather it is a limit of the world.

(Wittgenstein, 57)

Philosophers, coming upon this in a work designed to extend Russell's rigorous study of logic, will interpret it as philosophers do. To a non-philosopher, it will seem that Wittgenstein is fraught with a psychological/existential problem which haunted one of his cardinal heroes, Lev Tolstoy. This may irreverently be called 'the poor-little-rich-boy complex'. In Tolstoy's fiction it produces the stock figure of the 'conscience-stricken nobleman', barred by unjustifiable hereditary wealth and position from the 'real' world of toil. As 'subject' this figure is exiguous. But behind his almost-transparent vectors of conscience (Pierre in *War and Peace* is the best-known), one is always aware of the extraordinary ego of Tolstoy, who wishes yet does not wish to abolish the ultimate subject, to dissolve into the nameless peasantry while asserting the pre-eminence of his own lust for virtue.

In so far as he was a political animal (and an Italian Communist exile amongst Cambridge dons, the economist Piero Sraffa, was a close friend who kept him in touch with actual politics) Wittgenstein must be considered a man of the left. In the 1945 General Election, he voted Labour and privately encouraged others to do so. Like many other distinguished Western intellectuals he was prepared, for a time, in the 1930s, to give Stalin's modernising Soviet Union the benefit of various well-merited doubts. However, it seems clear that the bizarre yen which drove him to visit Russia in 1935 with a view to securing employment as manual labourers for himself and his young lover Francis Skinner (he was offered, instead, a chair in philosophy) was inspired by his devotion to

Tolstoy rather than any attraction to 'scientific' Marxism. Apart from anything else, he had come to hate science as the enemy of true cultural values. Above all, he was a 'conscious-stricken bourgeois'.

His father had been one of the richest men in Europe, a steel magnate vying with Krupps. Ludwig grew up in a veritable palace. The great men of music performed here for his family – here Johannes Brahms gave the children piano lessons. Wittgenstein's brother Paul became a pianist, world-famous for performing as a one-handed virtuoso after he lost his right arm in the First World War. Ludwig's relationship with music was intense and, it might be said, reactionary in a proprietorial way. He worshipped what he had grown up with. He could not really see beyond the Viennese classical tradition beginning with Haydn and kept going by Brahms. Mahler, let alone Schoenberg, were not for him. Crushed by an overweening father who wished them to follow him in business, two elder brothers committed suicide (a third would follow suit after what he considered to be disgrace in action during the war). Father died in 1913. Wittgenstein's decision after the war to hand over his share of the vast paternal wealth to his siblings was a second stab at this problem. His first had involved giving money to the great German poets Rilke and Trakl. Now, his path was impeccably Tolstoyan – he went to serve the peasantry, for six ghastly years, as a schoolteacher. But he was not averse to having his sisters help him, when needful, in cash and kind. As with Tolstoy, who retained his great estate while dressing as a peasant and denouncing sex, meat-eating and violence, all pleasures in which he had rather freely indulged, Wittgenstein remained essentially rich enough to think, and try to be moral, as he damn well pleased.

The rich man turned saint (St Martin and the beggarman) is a familiar type. Male saints, historically, have rarely been sweet-natured blokes. Their model has often been the Christ who unpredictably, in Matthew, 21.19, becomes enraged with a certain fig tree – 'he came to it and found nothing thereon, but leaves only, and said unto it, *Let no fruit grow on thee henceforward forever*. And presently the fig-tree withered away.' Jesus then accounts for this gratuitous magic as providing a parable – by faith you can blast fig trees or move mountains. But the story leaves a rather drastic impression on young minds, as did the magnetic personalities of Tolstoy and Wittgenstein, who attracted the worship of uncritical disciples. One difference is that whereas Tolstoy was an insatiably productive published writer, Wittgenstein's literally interminable scribblings, bar the very short *Tractatus* and one article in a learned journal, were left in a welter of not-yet-finalised forms to be edited by disciples after his death. Meanwhile, the leaking-out of his latest ideas as they circulated in a kind of *samizdat* and were presented to the world by others gave much scope to his fig-tree-blasting propensities, since no one, according to Wittgenstein, really understood what he was saying. This applied *a fortiori* to Russell, G. E. Moore, and the philosophers of the famous Vienna Circle, who might have been seen as his equals, but were reacted to by him as especially barren arborescences.

Duly daunted, I am not going to attempt a brief summary of the positions of Wittgenstein No. 1, author of the *Tractatus*, or Wittgenstein No. 2, for whom 'the metaphor of language as a picture is replaced by the metaphor of language as a tool' (Edmonds and Eidenow, 180). I will feebly abstract what seems to be No. 2's useful point that words are defined by use rather than logic, by their role in contingent, maybe muddy, human contexts, rather than their place in some intransigent abstract system. (They *do* things, rather than just formally denoting them.) This has the effect of liberating non-philosophers from the need to study Wittgenstein's first love, logic. A statement in logic such as 'all non-black things are not ravens' becomes as acute and amusing as a line of poetry by Wallace Stevens. As for the iconic sanctity, yes, Wittgenstein's dedication to thinking and indifference to creature-comforts remain deeply impressive, even if some of their symptoms are (endearingly) comic, as when he tells a hostess that he doesn't mind what he eats so long as it is the same every day. He was buried, after his lifelong struggle to make sense out of believing in God, according to Catholic rites, and we may not rule out the possibility that miracles might yet occur at his grave. Indeed, by the autumn of 2001, curious happenings were spotted there. At various times a lemon, a cupcake, a pork pie and a Buddhist prayer wheel were found on it. Then, all unseen, someone visited the grave and began leaving curious combinations of pennies. One set of fifteen neatly underlined the philosopher's name (*Guardian*, 5 September 2001).

Alternatively, we may see him as the Western equivalent of a Zen master, creating instant enlightenment with weird jokes. For some, his posthumous charisma is enhanced by the difficulties which he had with his homosexuality and with the fact that he was three-quarters Jewish 'genetically', though born into a family of Christian converts.

But I wish to conclude with a banal but important point. If he had not been a rich man, he could hardly have afforded to throw up his day job and present himself to Russell as a disciple. If, as a person from the working class or petty bourgeoisie, he had behaved in the anti-social manner attested in many anecdotes, and had advertised such extremes of depression, he would probably have been committed to an asylum. Without the Wittgenstein family wealth, used to bribe the Nazis, his close relatives would have perished in Auschwitz. Philosophers have good reason to be suspicious of any notion that judgement of the validity of ideas may be conditioned by our knowledge of the social origins of those who utter them. But my 'alternative' view of Wittgenstein is that only someone brought up in luxury could have gone so far in dismissing mere 'problems' as unimportant topics for intense thought.

David Edmonds and John Eidinow, Wittgenstein's Poker, *2001; Bryan Magee*, Confessions of a Philosopher, *1997; Ray Monk*, Ludwig Wittgenstein: The Duty of Genius, *1990; John Watkins, 'The Truth Will Out'*, Philosopher's Magazine, *Spring 1999; Ludwig Wittgenstein*, Tractatus Logico-Philosophicus, *trans. D. F. Pears and B. F. McGuinness, 1974 edn; thanks to Gideon Calder*

Iannis Xenakis (Greece) 1922–2001

In the autumn of 1941, Mussolini ordered the invasion, from Italian-held Albania, of Greece, a country so far neutral in the Second World War. The Greeks rallied under their semi-fascist dictator, Metaxas, and actually captured much of Albania. But in April 1941, to secure Hitler's southern flank in his planned invasion of Russia, Germans invaded Greece and quickly overran it. Collaborationist ministers thereafter ruled Greece under the control of Italy till that country accepted defeat in September 1943, whereafter Germans took direct power. The National People's Liberation Army (ELAS) actually dominated much of rural Greece. Its political wing, EAM, was under Communist control.

As the Red Army drove into Eastern Europe, Churchill became obsessed with limiting Communist advance. In October 1944, he did a deal with Stalin whereby the Soviet Union could dominate Romania if the British took charge in Greece. EAM now grudgingly agreed to join the coalition government of the liberal, anti-communist George Papandreou, which was backed by British forces. But demobilisation of ELAS proved an intractable issue. On 2 December, left-wing ministers resigned from the Government. As thousands of pro-EAM demonstrators converged next day in Syntagma Square, Athens, panicking police opened fire and killed fifteen of them. ELAS responded by attacking police stations, and British troops, commanded by General Scobie, who was ordered by Churchill to treat Athens as if it was a conquered enemy city, were soon fighting bloody street battles with their erstwhile guerrilla allies. These hit back so hard that reinforcements were required before right-wing government was established, the prelude to bitter civil war which ended only in 1949.

Fighting in Athens, at the end of 1944, with an ELAS group composed of students, Iannis Xenakis had half his face blown off by a missile from a Sherman tank. Charismatic, an athlete, he had been so handsome that he was nicknamed 'Archangelos'.

His father, Clearchos, had been born in Braila in 1875, part of an exiled Greek community in this small Romanian city near the mouth of the Danube. Drawn to theology, Clearchos nevertheless had to work as an agent for a British import-export firm. Clearchos had a passion for opera, which led to holidays in Bayreuth and Paris. His wife was also devoted to music, and wished that her son Iannis would learn the cello, but she died when he was only five. The boy never learnt to play the flute she had given him, but with friends constructed violins out of cane. After a succession of formidable governesses, he was packed off to a school on the Greek island of Spetze which attracted the children of expatriates. Boys from Britain, France, Germany, the USA and Russia arrived there to be lorded over by native Greeks. The school had two directors – a Greek one for academic matters and (of course) a British director of sport. The lonely Iannis took to the library and soaked himself in the Greek classics, in English and French literature and in such poetry as he could find. The English teacher Noel Paton befriended him and played him music on his gramophone. The school choir, enterprisingly, sang Palestrina and other Italian Renaissance music. Iannis matured to excel in swimming and athletics. In 1938 he went to Athens to study for entrance exams for the Polytechnic. Ensuing events drove this cosmopolitan youth deep into the marrow of Greece itself.

German entry into Romania in the autumn of 1940 prompted Clearchos to take the whole family to Athens. No sooner did Iannis gain entry to the Polytechnic than it closed due to the Italian invasion. It reopened as a wasps' nest of Resistance. Uniquely in Europe. Greeks, with students to the fore, staged huge demonstrations against the Axis conquerors. The first was on the anniversary of the Italian invasion, on 28 October 1941. The winter of 1941–2 was one of famine and merciless cold. EAM organised soup kitchens which were the only source of survival for thousands. Moved by the hardships he saw, Xenakis joined the Communist Party.

As agitation intensified in 1942, Xenakis, the erstwhile outsider, emerged as an inspirational leader, 'running demonstrations, taking risks, courting death with extreme pleasure'. His first love, Aliki, was a comrade also up to her neck in the movement. Xenakis' intensely idealistic Communism was crossbred with Platonism – when the Italians detained him, he carried *The Republic* in his pocket and read Plato in jail (Matoussian, 19–20).

In February 1943, the Nazis announced plans to deport 80,000 young Greeks to forced labour in Germany. Great demonstrations ending in bloody confrontations forced them – uniquely in Occupied Europe – to back down. By the autumn of 1943, after Italian capitulation to the allies, ELAS, standing with British backing directly against Germany, had around two million supporters in a population of seven million. Yet, a year later, Stalin's deal with Churchill hogtied it.

During the anti-British struggle, the increasingly embittered Xenakis turned again to music. With a comrade – a nephew of the Communist Party Secretary-General – he used to knock on the doors of strangers to ask for the use of a piano – and so heard for the first time the music of Debussy, Ravel and Bartok, played by his friend.

ELAS, after erecting barricades to slow down the tanks' advance, withdrew towards the northern suburbs of Athens. The British, with police and national guardsmen, moved in their wake, with mass arrests and summary executions. Xenakis organised the defence of a block of houses. The British turned up with tanks and heavy artillery. Xenakis was indoors with comrades who were killed beside him. He regained consciousness under a white sheet in an improvised First Aid centre, to hear someone say, 'He's only a few hours to live. At least let him die in peace.' He received injections, but no other attention. When he came to again, a female comrade, fellow student, was holding his hand. The next day, the British and their collaborators moved in. He couldn't rail at them, his palate was shattered. His left eye was gone. His own blood was close to choking him. Left for several hours, he was eventually taken to hospital. The woman stayed with him while he underwent an operation, then managed to vanish into the mountains. His father had been searching for him everywhere, and tracked him down with the help of a police agent. At last – this was New Year's Day, 1945 – he was taken away for proper treatment. Three operations were required to reconstruct his face and put his nose back in place. One of these was conducted without anaesthetic.

As EAM's heads gave way to British demands and were amnestied, while their followers were arrested, tortured, murdered, Xenakis emerged from hospital anguished by that betrayal to face the world with half his former face. Yet back at the Polytechnic, he was still active on the left, and was jailed for a third time (Italians . . . Germans . . . British . . .). Crucially, he achieved at last his Diploma in Engineering, in February 1946. He found himself conscripted into the Army. Confronted with a choice between renunciation of his political beliefs and internment in a concentration camp, he refused to sign. Given leave to seek legal advice, he went on the run, now a deserter condemned to death. People extorted bribes from his father to hide him. Eventually, in September 1947, he escaped to Italy with a false passport. Thence, underground, with help from Communist Party comrades, he entered France illegally. He had neither papers nor money. But his Diploma was enough to secure him work in Paris, in the studio of the famous architect Le Corbusier.

As a story of survival, the tale just told would be enough in itself to mark Xenakis out as an extraordinary man. Yet his subsequent reputation – which seemed at times to be in strange contradiction to his passionate early life – came to overlay it so that excavation was required. Xenakis' music derived from such excruciating pressure of experience that it had to be, or to seem, detached from it. He passed into cool realms of modernist architecture, mathematics, avant-garde musical theory with shouting demonstrators, probing searchlights, the cacophony of battle, haunting his wrecked head.

He worked in Corbusier's studio until 1959, first as an engineer, but gradually taking a greater and greater part in design. Thus he contributed parts of the famous government buildings in Chandigarh, India, the rhythmically articulated glass façade of the monastery of St Marie de la Tourette near Lyons, and, most famously, from a sketch by Le Corbusier, the Phillips Pavilion at the 1958 Exposition Universelle in Brussels. Such was the day job. Meanwhile, he developed his passion for music. Attending a course at the Ecole Normale, he was told by the very distinguished composer Honegger that a piano piece he had written was not music. But the analysis course run by Olivier Messiaen at the Conservatoire proved seminal. Messiaen told him he was too old to be bothered with catching up on harmony and counterpoint. 'Build on your grasp of maths and architecture' (Revil).

This advice was as much traditionalist as 'modernist'. From the ancient Greeks through the Renaissance, the interrelationships between mathematics and both music and architecture had seemed plain. The Romantics, emphasising feeling above all, had disavowed such connections. The development of serial music by Schoenberg and his disciples of the Second Viennese School early in the twentieth century had reintroduced mathematical calculation. Its influence was dominant over younger European composers in the aftermath of World War II, producing music which was intellectually fascinating but, for the vast majority of listeners, without direct aesthetic impact. Messiaen stood outside this, in the French tradition inspired by Debussy's experiments, and so did Edgar Varèse (1883–1965), a French-born composer based in America who had pioneered in the use of electronic instruments and pre-recorded interleavings into live performance. In 1956, Xenakis published an essay, 'The Crisis of Serial Music', in which he argued for a new application of mathematics, for 'stochastic' music based on probability theory.

The Greek word 'stokhazomai' means 'to guess at, to aim at a target'. A series of notes selected by tossing a coin, for instance, or generated by a randomly repeating computer programme, would be 'stochastic'. Xenakis, as time went on, also based compositions on game theory, where the introduction of sounds was based on a game-like strategy, and set theory and group theory, by which he treated musical sounds as if they were part of an algebraically symbolic language. From the late 1950s, furthermore, he made increasing use of computers. To complicate matters further, Xenakis always started his music, as with architecture, with graphic sketches. From the 1970s onwards, these increasingly took the form of 'arborescences', with tree-like branching curves drawn on calibrated graph paper. Each branch would blossom, as it were, into a melodic line when translated into musical notation (Halbreich, 16–18, 24).

His first 'mature' work, 'Metastaseis', was premiered at the Festival of Donaueschingen under Hans Rosbaud in 1955. Half the audience jeered, half cheered. The title means 'transformations'. What interested Xenakis was the movement of a mass of sounds made up of many individual sounds. Specifically, he remembered those giant anti-Axis demonstrations in wartime Greece. 'The slogans with their rhythmical patterns and the changes as the procession moved towards the aim, which was the centre of the city, those changing rhythmical patterns were a kind of fantastic sound event filling almost the whole city. And then, when the clash with the Nazis happened, with machine guns, with tanks and the shouts of the wounded, then this kind of rhythmical pattern broke out into a chaotic sound event.' Xenakis made heavy use of glissandi, which correspond to cone-like patterns on a graph and these in turn were used to design the Phillips Pavilion at the 1958 Brussels World Fair. This is described as a 'text-light structure', or, by Xenakis himself, as 'an electronic poem and a vessel containing the poem'. The searchlights and artillery fire of wartime Greece inspired this and later 'polytopes' by Xenakis. The same mathematical shapes were used to determine both the pattern of lights inside the building and the music which Xenakis composed as an interval between performances of Varèse's composition, 'Electronic Poem' (Xenakis Festival programme).

Le Corbusier at first claimed all the credit for the Phillips Pavilion. Xenakis believed that the great architect had grown jealous of him (Varga, 23–25). By 1959 the two could no longer work together. Xenakis moved away into the world of computers, where he got sponsorship from IBM. He founded in 1966 what became a centre for the study of automatic and mathematical music (CEMAMU). Distinguished academic appointments in the USA and France enhanced his status. By 1987, when Glasgow hosted a major festival of his music to celebrate his sixty-fifth birthday, he was a big name in contemporary music circles everywhere in the world.

So far from being mathematically 'difficult', in fact he is an affecting composer. His early ambition was to emulate Bartok's incorporation of folk tradition into modernist music. He retained an ideal of 'untrained "peasant" voices, especially for his musical conception of ancient theatre, in which singers also play bells, gongs, stones and so on' (Hoffmann, 607). Setting the *Oresteia* (1965–66) and other ancient material, he was influenced by the Kabuki and No theatre which he had encountered in Japan. Response to his music validly hovers between a sense of raw emotion (but folk music doesn't express that directly) and the detachment cultivated in No.

The novelist Milan Kundera, formerly a dissident in Communist Czechoslovakia, explores this terrain-between-poles brilliantly in his non-fictional *Testaments Betrayed* (1995). He posits that there is 'an acoustic universe outside the human soul, one that consists not merely of nature sounds but also of human voices speaking, singing, and giving sonic flesh to everyday life as well as to festive occasions . . . The composer can give a great musical form to that "objective" universe.'

Unsurprisingly, Kundera instances Stravinsky's *Les Noces* (The Wedding) of 1914–23. (Edwin Evans recalled taking a cab with Stravinsky through the City of London one Sunday afternoon in 1914. The bells of St Paul's were pealing and Stravinsky stopped the cab and took notes on the back of an envelope. He claimed to hear the most wonderful music in the sequence of 'changes' and Evans believed that at least the percussive element in *Les Noces* was seeded by that 'objective' source [Walsh, 236–37].) Janacek's *The Seventy Thousand* (1909), a piece for men's chorus about the fate of Silesian miners, is a less famous instance. But what Kundera tells us of it – that 'the explosion of shouts from the crowd' in its second half comes 'curiously close' to madrigals in which Clement Janequin turned the street cries of sixteenth-century Paris and London into music – relates to things said above about Xenakis.

Kundera recalls the gloomy years after the Russians occupied Czechoslovakia in 1968. 'I fell in love then with Varèse and Xenakis: those pictures of sound-worlds that were objective but non-existent spoke to me of a life freed from human subjectivity, aggressive and burdensome; they spoke of the sweetly non-human beauty of the world before or after mankind moved through it' (Kundera, 70–71).

Harry Halbreich, notes to Iannis Xenakis: Chamber Music 1955–1990, Montaigne CDs MO 782137, *2000; Peter Hoffmann in Stanley Sadie, ed.*, New Grove Dictionary of Music and Musicians, *vol. 27, (2nd edn), 2001; Milan Kundera*, Testaments Betrayed, *1995; Nouritza Matoussian*, Iannis Xenakis, *(Paris) 1981; Guy Protheroe, notes to* Iannis Xenakis, Wergo CD Wer 6178–2, *1990; David Revill, 'Obituary'*, Independent, *5 February 2001; B. A. Varga*, Conversations with Iannis Xenakis, *1996; Stephen Walsh*, Igor Stravinsky: A Creative Spring . . . 1882–1934, *2000*; Xenakis Festival – A Celebration in Honour of the 65th Birthday of Iannis Xenakis, *programme notes compiled by Donna D. MacDonald, (Glasgow) 1987; thanks to Mark Summers*

Lester Young (USA) 1909–59

Lester was born near New Orleans in 1909. His father was a jazzman who formed a professional band consisting of his children and certain cousins. Lester discovered sax around the age of thirteen – 'just picked the motherfucker up and just started playing it'. But Lester grew up to be a complete contrast to his remarkably normal brother Lee, a success first as a jazz drummer, then on the production side of the record industry. Lester's distinctive broad-brimmed pork-pie hat would emphasise his uniqueness as a man apart.

His subtle style on tenor sax went suitably with his high-pitched speaking voice, his long and wavy hair and his wisp of a moustache. It got him into trouble when he joined the great Fletcher Henderson Band in 1934, replacing Coleman Hawkins, who had gone off to extend his fame in Europe. The Hawk, a.k.a. 'Bean', was the first definitive jazz saxophonist, with a big throaty tone and a romping fast vibrato. His playing was 'heavily ornamental and rhythmically and harmonically complex' (Porter, 10). Lester, by contrast, was light and cool in tone, laid-back and urbane in personality. Henderson's sax section wanted him to play like Hawkins, and even when he bought a burlier tenor, he couldn't. With his 'nancy' ways – he minced up to deliver his solos – some people thought he was gay, though he was married three times, and had two children by his third wife. African-American culture was macho. Whether or not he was actually bisexual, Lester, unspeakably, challenged macho prejudice.

Count Basie rescued him. Colleagues in the Count's new young band relished his good-natured charm. He was the star pitcher in the band's softball team. They got used to his 'gimmick talk', a private language in which the police were 'Bob Crosby' and his response to racism was 'I feel a draft'. He may have invented the usage 'bread' for 'money'. Famously, it was he who called **Billie Holiday** (q.v.) 'Lady Day' and she who nicknamed him 'the President'. Their wholly non-carnal devotion to each other subsisted through shared love of music, though alcohol too was something they had in common.

Lester was always a heavy drinker – his mother insisted that shyness drove him to it – but his ultimate strangulation by alcohol may have been ensured by a traumatic experience in World War II. In the autumn of 1944, he had just completed a short film for Warner Bros, *Jamming the Blues*, good enough to be nominated for an Academy Award, when the FBI tracked him down and he was conscripted. A medical showed that he was not only unfit and alcoholic, but had syphilis and smoked marijuana daily. Nevertheless, he was pitched as 39729502 Private Young into an arena where Jim Crow consorted with Catch-22. In camp in Georgia, he was persecuted by Army psychologists, and court-martialled in February 1945 for possession of marijuana and barbiturates. He was sentenced to forfeiture of pay and dishonourable discharge and served ten months in jail. He emerged profoundly wounded.

Postwar, every tenor sax seemed to be imitating him – and Lester found that the copycats, especially the white ones, were getting more gigs than he did. Melancholy at last drove him to abandon his family and spend his last days drinking non-stop in a New York hotel. Perhaps he knew that he had been great, and thought that his gift was fraying.

When Coleman Hawkins came back from Europe in 1939, fellow saxophonists awaited with awe and trepidation his appearance at an after-hours jam-session where he might compete in a cutting contest with the rivals who had prospered in his absence. According to one account, word went round that he would turn up ready to play at 'Puss' Johnson's tavern in St Nicholas Avenue, Harlem. Chu Berry, Ben Webster and Dick Wilson were mentioned as possible contenders, but the one Hawk himself was gunning for was Pres. They met. They cut. Chilton claims that the bout was 'inconclusive'. Members of the Fats Waller band, present as listeners, thought Hawk had won – Lester said he had had enough after an hour. Their view was reported in *Downbeat*. Billie Holiday saw this and at once contacted the magazine to protest. She insisted that Pres 'really cut the Hawk, and most everyone there who saw them tangle agrees on that' (Chilton, 71–73).

I greatly prefer what may or may not be a version of the same story from Rex Stewart, Ellington's great cornettist, in his wonderful book *Jazz Masters of the Thirties*. According to Stewart, not 'Puss' but 'Nightsy' Johnson, a drummer, had opened an all-night joint for musicians only – 'a basement club, and the pad was always bad'. Lady Day and Pres were there almost every night. The Hawk began to show up nightly too, 'immaculate, sophisticated, and saxophoneless'. When would he play?

One night, later than usual, around 3 a.m., Hawk turned up to find Lady Day singing, 'which rarely happened uptown in those days'. Lester of course was accompanying her. Hawkins 'unpacked his axe and joined them, to everyone's surprise. Then, when Billie finished, she announced to the house that it had been a pleasure to have had the world's greatest tenor saxophonist backing her up – Lester Young! You could have heard a pin drop after that remark.' Hawk's response was to turn to the piano player, request a certain tune, and play, alone, at 'almost unbelievable' fast tempo. 'Then he sauntered to the bar, had a big drink, and waited to see how the cats would follow this avalanche of virtuosity. For some reason, nobody felt like blowing at the moment.' So Hawkins himself went into a ballad, 'finishing up with an incredible cadenza, to thundering applause. He then gallantly started toying with Honeysuckle Rose, motioning for Chu [Berry] and Don Byas to join him, which they did.'

Thoughout this Pres sat aside with Lady Day, drinking – maybe that mixture of port wine and gin which was their trademark tipple. '. . . And I must say,' Stewart remarked, 'that he kept his cool.' As Dick Wilson left, Stewart heard him say to Elmer Williams, 'Well, that's that, Coleman is still the boss' (Stewart, 69–70). But Billie's passionate partisanship was justified. It was Young's style, not Hawkins', which fascinated the young musicians who within a few years were creating bebop, just as it was Billie's singing which marked, as Angela Davis puts it, 'the transition from blues to modern jazz' (Davis, 171).

John Chilton, Billie's Blues, *1975; Donald Clarke*, Wishing on the Moon: The Life and Times of Billie Holiday, *1994; Angela Y. Davis*, Blues Legends and Black Feminism, *(New York) 1998; Dave Gelly*, Lester Young, *(Tunbridge Wells) 1994; Lewis Porter*, Lester Young, *1985; Rex Stewart*, Jazz Masters of the Thirties, *(New York) 1972; thanks to John Lucas and John Pilgrim*

Emil Zapotek (Czechoslovakia) (1922–2000)

Emil Zapotek made endurance running look difficult. Son of a Moravian carpenter, he was an apprentice, during the Nazi occupation of his country, in the famous Bata shoe factory in Blin when one of the directors encouraged him to enter his first race. He came second, in lumpen country style, body leaning forward, shoulders heaving, head rolling. This manner remained with him while he collected eighteen world records, won 261 of his 334 races, and learnt at least eight languages, including English, which he wrote fluently.

When he was twenty-three, a well-built Swedish mile champion, Arne Andersson, visiting Czechoslovakia, put into his mind the notion of intensive training. Without books or coach, he began a daily training regime at which other athletes boggled. The now-common phrase 'interval training' partly sums it up – all-out 400-metre runs interspersed with short breathers, routinely twenty such runs, sometimes up to fifty or sixty on the trot. And he was known to wear Army boots while he was at it, or run through snow and forests. He attached weights on pulleys to his legs while he was exercising, and would jog for hours, knees raised high, on the same spot. But he found ways of making such workouts fun. He would read a book, or listen to the radio. On wash days he would pile all the dirty clothes in the bath and run on them for hours. He loved training. Entering the Army, which gave him time to do it, he pursued his passion even on guard duty, where he experimented with holding his breath for so long that on one embarrassing occasion he fainted. In 1948 he married a javelin thrower, Dana Ingrova. According to a devout fan, the great English distance runner Gordon Pirie, theirs 'was the gayest and merriest house I have ever visited. These two used to romp like children or like beautiful young animals in their perfect fitness of body.' Once, in fun, he threw Dana in a stream. Unfortunately, she broke an ankle. So whilst her leg was in plaster, Zapotek used to run with her on his back through thick snow. They relished a dangerous little game where they hurled a javelin full tilt at each other, aiming to catch it above their heads and return it as fast as possible (Pirie, 50).

Pirie, then seventeen, had seen Zapotek 'scorch through the 10,000-m field' in the 1948 London Olympics. 'He showed runners that what they had been content with up to then was nothing to what could be achieved.' Or, indeed, to what Emil would achieve himself – 1948 was just for starters. His example fired dangerous rivals in Europe, America, the Antipodes. He beat them all. Days before the 1950 European Championships, he was in hospital with food poisoning, forbidden to eat. He lost almost two stone. On Sunday, when there were no doctors around, he sneaked into the canteen and poached some sausages, mustard and beer. Dana had smuggled in his training kit and with the connivance of the nurses, he ran up and down behind the hospital. He overrode furious doctors, caught his plane to Brussels, and won the 10,000 metres by a full lap. It seems that his high temperature, encouraging fast circulation, had replicated some of the effects of training. The Olympics of 1952 were in Helsinki, capital of Finland, whose heroes had dominated distance running between the wars. Zapotek not only retained his 10,000 metres title, he captured the 5,000, in an epic race. Three runners, including Britain's Chataway, later to beat the world record himself in a startling duel with the Russian Kuts, seemed well clear of Zapotek entering the final bend. He went wide round them all and surged home. Poor Chataway, later a Government minister, fell over. Emil went off to rest, missing the victory of Dana in the javelin. Told of his wife's triumph, he said, 'At present the score of the contest in the Zapotek family is 2–1. This result is too close. To restore some prestige, I will try to improve on it in the marathon.'

Even for someone as fit as Zapotek, the distance of twenty-two miles and 1,470 yards was somewhat far. He had never run it before even in training (though by this time his disciple Pirie was *routinely* running twenty or thirty miles a day). There were some difficult rivals to beat, above all the favourite, an Englishman, Jim Peters, who held the world record. One of Zapotek's idiosyncrasies was his habit of chatting to competitors as they ran – in their own languages, of course. Sometimes he encouraged them on, even patted them on the back. On this occasion, finding himself amongst the leaders halfway through, Zapotek asked Peters if the pace was about right. Peters was a wily gamesman. 'I told him I was sure it was too slow. Zatopek thought for a moment – then b-d off up the road and left me.' He entered the stadium with the rest of the field out of sight, to meet a delirious crowd of 70,000 chanting 'Za-to-pek' throughout his final lap. By the time the runner-up arrived Emil had already been chaired round the arena by the great Jamaican relay quartet, and was busy signing autographs.

In 1955, Pirie beat Zatopek over 10,000, then over 5,000 metres. On the second occasion, Zatopek appeared at his shoulder and urged him on – 'Faster, faster – it is getting too slow.' His generosity to rivals was summed up when the Australian Ron Clarke came to Czechoslovakia in 1966. Clarke beat his records at 5,000 and 10,000, scored seventeen world records in all, but never won a major title. Zapotek came out to the plane as Clarke was leaving and pressed something into his hand as they shook goodbye. Assuming that he was smuggling something out for Zatopek, Clarke waited till he was clear of Czech airspace to open the package. It contained one of Zatopek's Olympic Gold medals. Clarke wept.

After he retired in 1958 (with five of his eighteen world records still intact) Zapotek was nominally an Army officer, rising to lieutenant-colonel. In fact, he worked as one of Europe's best athletic coaches. In 1968, when Dubcek defied the Soviet Union in the cause of 'Socialism with a human face', Zatopek signed his manifesto. After Warsaw Pact tanks rolled into Prague, he was stripped of his rank, party membership and title of Merited Master of Sports. He was put to work as a labourer in a uranium mine and a cement factory, driving a truck, even cleaning the streets of Prague. He finally compromised himself with the regime – to his subsequent regret – and was allowed to work as a translator of foreign coaching manuals. He was sometimes allowed to accept invitations to travel abroad, where people still queued for his autograph. The Velvet Revolution of 1989 and Vaclav Havel's ascent to power restored him to his place as honoured citizen. Already, in his running heyday, athletes – and not just in Iron Curtain countries – took performance-enhancing drugs. Zatopek never thought of it. Already, 'amateurs' looked to make money out of their prowess. Zatopek's indifference to lucre was such that when, on a visit to London in 1988, he was offered £50 spending money, he waved it away with an air of embarrassment. Producing an English tenner, he asked if it was genuine. Reassured that it was, he said he would buy a bottle of whisky to take home to Dana. 'We have simple life.'

Obituaries by Norman Harris, Independent, *23 November 2000, and Doug Gillon,* Herald, *25 November 2000; Gordon Pirie,* Running Wild, *1961*

Boris Ilich Zbarsky (USSR) 1885–1954

By 1923, V. I. Lenin was dying. He had atherosclerosis, affecting his arteries. A stroke in March 1923 deprived him of the power of speech. When he paid his last visit to the Kremlin on 18 October, he was very frail indeed. A few days later, the Communist Party secretary, Joseph Stalin, summoned a secret meeting of six out of the eleven members of the Politburo. He put it to them that Lenin, when, as to be shortly expected, defunct, should be embalmed.

This technique, favoured by Egyptian Pharaohs and ancient Peruvians, was hardly in fashion in modern Europe, where, at the other extreme, efficient crematoria now converted the corpses of progressive persons a.s.a.p. into ashes.

Trotsky opposed Stalin. Bukharin argued that to turn Lenin's remains into a kind of religious relic would be 'an insult to his memory' (Zbarsky, 9–12). But Stalin, the quietly evil little Georgian, saw uses for himself in a personality cult of Lenin, and understood the more than residual propensity of the Russian masses to superstition.

Lenin died on 20 January 1924.

Despite a plea from his widow, Nadezhda Krupskaya, in *Pravda*, that there should be no 'personality cult', Petrograd was renamed 'Leningrad' and the Party laid on a grandiose funeral. Felix Dzherzhinsky, a Pole, head of the OGPU political police, took up the idea of embalming. 'A man of the highest idealism and integrity, but a muddle-headed fanatic' (Deutscher, 249), he would have his way.

Lenin's brain had been extracted so that researchers could prove that he was a genius. Otherwise he lay intact in state, visibly decomposing.

A committee of three Bolshevik leaders – Molotov, Yenukidze and Krasin – thought that refrigeration would be the answer. Leonid Krasin, an outstanding industrial technician as well as publicist and propagandist, pursued this idea with scientists. Thus he paid a visit to the biochemist Boris Ilich Zbarsky. Zbarsky told him that freezing wouldn't work, and why. Low temperatures would not eliminate the enzymes causing decomposition. He was brushed aside.

Dzherzhinsky, however, had made contact with Professor Vorobiov, head of anatomy at Kharkhov University, a great expert on embalming. Vorobiov was very reluctant to get drawn in. A failed attempt to save Lenin's cadaver would be fatal to him. During the war, Germans occupying the Ukraine had forced him to sign a paper saying that Bolsheviks had killed most of the people found dead in a certain Kharkhov suburb. He had fled to teach in Bulgaria. He had been allowed back at last with his past hanging above him like a Damoclean sword. He told his friend B. I. Zbarsky, 'I don't want to suffer the fate of the alchemists who undertook to embalm Pope Alexander VI – they had themselves paid a great deal of money, but they were so inept that they destroyed the body and had to flee for their lives' (Zbarsky, 27).

Nevertheless, full of foreboding, he arrived in Moscow on 28 February. On 5 March he advised the Committee for the Immortalisation of Lenin's Memory, presided over by Dzherzhinsky, that the erstwhile leader should be immersed in a 'balsamic' liquid containing glycerine and potassium acetate.

Yet the Central Committee, on 14 March, unanimously agreed on refrigeration.

Here Zbarsky showed himself a master of intrigue, so necessary to survival and prosperity in the new Soviet Union. Before Vorobiov went back to Kharkhov on 12 March, he had persuaded him to sign a letter addressed to Zbarsky himself but actually dictated by him, in which the expert said that he left for home fearing the worst – in a few days Lenin's face would be 'quite black and wizened'. He also got Vorobiov to write in a similar sense to Krasin. Then Zbarsky went to see Dzherzhinsky, showed him Vorobiov's dictated letter to himself, and told him that the pair of them were ready to save Lenin's body. Dzherzhinsky called in Krasin. By now the enthusiast for refrigeration was aware that the cadaver was in crisis. 'The lips were now three millimetres apart; there were more brown patches on the thighs; the left hand was turning a greenish-grey colour; the ears had crumpled up completely' (Zbarsky, 30). Krasin huffed and puffed, but went off to Kharkhov, where he handed Vorobiov a letter from Dzherzhinsky requesting him to do whatever he thought necessary to preserve Lenin's body.

Back in Moscow, Vorobiov was given *carte blanche*. He chose his own assistants, including Zbarsky. The mausoleum was closed for four months. Vorobiov and Zbarsky proceeded most cautiously. The cadaver was now extremely colourful – purplish stains on the head, nose dark-tipped, brown spots on the hands, blue-tinged fingernails. To record this motley exactly in watercolours, so that such ugliness could not subsequently be blamed on the embalmers, Zbarsky called in the architect brother, Alexander, of his friend Boris Pasternak, the writer . . .

As the name just dropped shows, Zbarsky was not a blear-eyed one-track boffin. He was a Jew born in Kamenetz-Podolsk near the Western frontier of the old Tsarist Empire in 1885. His father was a clerk, his mother ran a successful china shop. Hatred of Tsarist anti-Semitism propelled him in his teens into the Revolutionary Socialist Party. Expelled from school because of his political activities, Zbarsky studied chemistry at the University of Geneva. In June 1915 he was working at Moscow University for no salary – as Jew he could not officially occupy a public post – when his advertisement in a newspaper offering private lessons was spotted by the butler of Zinaida Grigorievna Morozova, widow of a very rich businessman. The man hurried round to see him at once. Morozova had told him urgently to find a replacement for the crooked steward of her estate in the Urals, which included two chemical works. Since these were judged vital to national defence, Zbarsky, once he was in charge of them, was exempt from military service.

One day in Moscow he ran into Boris Pasternak, who was fed up with living with his family in crowded conditions. Zbarsky invited the young poet out to Vsevolod-Vilva. Pasternak fell in love with Mrs Zbarsky, and this was reciprocated. But Zbarsky helped him get a job in a chemicals factory, which saved him too from conscription.

Came the October Revolution. By early 1918, the Zbarskys, with young son Ilya, were back in Moscow crowded together in one room, with the Pasternaks on the floor above. Eventually Boris Zbarsky got a job as assistant to a former teacher of his in Geneva, Professor Bach, now Director of a newly founded Institute of Biochemistry. He separated from his wife in the early 1920s. He was a gay dog, with numerous mistresses. A passionate affair with a prima donna helped to draw him on to the Artistic Committee of the Stanislavsk-Nemorovich-Danchenko Musical Theatre where she worked. But from this period also dated his fateful meeting and friendship with Vorobiov.

Vorobiov now removed Lenin's lungs, liver, spleen and other viscera and had his ribcage flushed with distilled water. He immersed the body in a three per cent solution of formaldehyde. He wanted a glass bath, since a metal surface might interact chemically. The best Dzherzhinsky could come up with at this stage was a rubber one, hastily made to order by startled factory workers. But the bath wasn't working. Risking denunciation later for mutilating the Great Leader's body, Vorobiov made incisions. He also added alcohol to the liquid, up to twenty per cent. This improved the colour of the skin and made it more permeable. After six days, the percentage of alcohol was increased to thirty, and twenty per cent of glycerine was added. Two weeks later, the body was put into a mixture of glycerine and water, so that its tissues recovered elasticity. Then came large jars of potassium acetate. By the end of June 1924, the bath contained 240 litres of glycerine, 110 kilograms of potassium acetate, 150 litres of water, and one to two per cent of quinine chloride as a disinfectant. Periodic overhauls at eighteen-month intervals thereafter involved repeating this bath (Zbarsky, 80–83).

Vorobiov tidied up dark blemishes on face and hands with a variety of reagents. Lenin's lips were sewn together. False eyes replaced the originals, so that shape would be maintained, then the eyelids too were sewn together. Krupskaya had opposed the embalming of her husband, but nevertheless handed over a khaki-coloured tunic, like a uniform, worn by him during his last illness. In mid June, nearly six months after Lenin's death, Dzherzhinsky ordered his body to be dressed and placed in a cone-shaped glass coffin. Krupskaya and Lenin's siblings were invited to view it. To Vorobiov's immense relief, Lenin's brother was delighted.

Lenin's mausoleum was a rectangular building in Red Square, surmounted by a low stepped pyramid of six levels, with a small portico at the apex. It was dual-purpose, since there was a viewing stand at front where top Soviet persons could take their position during military parades. In his first sixteen years on display, sixteen million people, it was claimed, came to see Lenin. As treated by Vorobiov, he seemed calm, wise and surprisingly fresh.

Zbarsky told his son he got 25,000 roubles for his work on the embalmment. Still more significant, it made him a member of the inner circle of the ruling elite. Top government and police officials dined at his house. Rybov, Lenin's successor as chairman of the council of commissars, invited him to his country retreat. Zbarsky got on especially well with his patron Dzherzhinsky – naming a new son Felix in his honour. Zbarsky had met his second wife, Eugenie, at the Pasternaks. Vorobiov came up from Kharkhov twice a week to keep an eye on Lenin. He and Zbarsky would smear their 'balsam' on his face and hands to keep them from drying up and wrinkling. Every eighteen months, off came the khaki tunic. Injections of 'balsam' went in under the rubber bandages beneath. Then these too came off and Lenin was immersed in a glass bath with glycerine and potassium acetate.

By 1929, Stalin had achieved uncontested power. The massacre of the kulaks would follow, then the great purges. Zbarsky, scientist-priest officiating at Lenin's tomb, continued to prosper. He inherited the chair of biochemistry at Moscow's First Medical Institute. In October 1937 Vorobiov died. Zbarsky was now clearly Chief Priest, and a booklet which he published in 1944, selling hundreds of thousands of copies, would create the impression that he had always been the prime embalmer.

After the Nazi invasion of Russia in June 1941, one of the Politburo's first decisions was to transfer Lenin's cadaver to Tiumen, a small town in Siberia, well beyond the Urals. Here was a chance for Zbarsky's staff, with no visitors, with peace and quiet, to refine to the uttermost Vorobiov's masterpiece. For excellent work, Boris Zbarsky was awarded the supreme accolade as a Hero of Socialist Labour.

Back in Moscow, from 1945, the mausoleum's laboratory was now greatly expanded. Before the war it had employed four scientists. Afterwards, this rose to thirty-five. More good news . . . Stalin wanted to know what could be done to enable the Soviet Union to match the scientific prowess of the USA. He was advised that higher salaries for scientists would be a good idea. They were quadrupled, so that Boris Zbarsky, as Professor at the First Medical Institute and head of the biochemistry laboratory at the Institute of Oncology, suddenly found himself receiving more than members of the Central Committee of the Communist Party . . .

As the Greek poet said, call no man happy before his death. What felled Zbarsky at last was a simple fact about himself which he may well have tended to forget. He was Jewish. In his last years, Stalin unleashed anti-Jewish purges. Zbarsky was detained in March 1952 and did not see his family for nearly two years.

Under interrogation, Zbarsky's past was presented as a sequence of anti-Soviet actions. He had been a Revolutionary Socialist representative at the Constituent Assembly! He had been a friend of the evil Rybov, purged in the late thirties!! He was a 'Jewish nationalist'. Furthermore, in his booklet about the mausoleum he had added a goatee to the face of one of the guards of Lenin's coffin in a photograph, making him look rather like Trotsky!!! It was in vain for Zbarsky to insist that no such goatee featured in any copy of the booklet which he himself had seen. The judge would not listen (Zbarsky, 168–69). But Zbarsky was finally released, for lack of proof, at the end of 1953, eight months after Stalin's death. A heart attack carried him off in October 1954.

Others had embalmed Stalin, whose body, till 1961, would lie in the mausoleum beside Lenin's. From 1949 – when Zbarsky travelled to Bulgaria to embalm the local Communist leader Dimitrov – the methods pioneered by Vorobiov to embalm Lenin were applied to a succession of leaders of Soviet-bloc countries, from Ho Chi Minh to Agostinho Neto of Angola. In 1970, the centenary of Lenin's birth, the Politburo agreed to the purchase of millions of dollars worth of new equipment for the mausoleum laboratory. Scores more scientists were recruited, till there were nearly a hundred in all.

But the end of the Cold War and the break-up of the Soviet Union brought problems for the laboratory. The state, which had funded it fully, cut its share to twenty per cent in 1991. The directors obeyed the new spirit of free enterprise and created Ritual Service for private customers. The most prominent category of *nouveax riches* attracted by the most expert embalming service in the world were kinsfolk of gangsters in the new criminal mafia. Ritual Service fixed these up, sometimes put their pieces together again, so that they looked good at the funeral. Lenin continued to brood serenely in his mausoleum, now part of a World Heritage site. He was not yet as durable as the Pharaohs, but still on course.

Isaac Deutscher, Stalin, *(Harmondsworth) 1966; Ilya Zbarsky and Samuel Hutchinson,* Lenin's Embalmers, *trans. B. Bray, 1997*

Zwangendaba (Southern Africa) *c.*1780–*c.*1845

The irruption of Shaka, king of the Zulus, in 1818, precipitated the seminal phase of South African history known as the *Mfecane* – 'time of crushing of peoples' – as other groups of pastoralists fled his fierce soldiers. In a time when many families, clans, peoples, moved with their cattle over vast tracts of veldt and river, no one went further than Zwangendaba, whose people, called Ngoni, journeyed from Natal to the verge of Lake Victoria Nyanza and founded mini-states scattered from the now-Zimbabwe to now-Tanzania, from Mozambique to now-Zambia.

The Ngoni began as a section of the Nguni people occupying far south-eastern Africa. Long before the Afrikaner trekboers began to move into country beyond the Orange and Vaal rivers which it suited them to believe had been previously uninhabited, a combination of factors had created a crisis of power among the northern Nguni people densely settled in what is now Natal. They had lived in country ideal for cattle-keeping – central to Nguni culture – but overstocking created an ecological crisis confirmed by severe drought in the first decade of the nineteenth century. White traders, through the Portuguese-controlled harbour at Delagoa Bay, demanded slaves and ivory, then came British and American whalers looking for meat. The prestige goods which whites offered in exchange created fierce rivalry to supply them amongst the region's petty rulers. Centralisation of power must follow. Contests developed between three emerging states – that of the Ndwandwe under Zwide, the Ngwane under Sobhuza, and the Mthethwa led by Dingiswayo, whose area of dominance included the very small chiefdom of the Zulus.

Dingiswayo brought in a new basis of military organisation – 'all young men of the same age group were put together so that warriors from various localities and chiefdoms were intermingled and bound by common discipline and loyalty' (Mostert, 498). One of his conscripts, around 1809, was a very tall and warlike young man called Shaka, illegitimate son of the Zulu chief. When his father died in 1816, Dingiswayo helped Shaka seize the chieftainship. Meanwhile, Zwide had seen off Sobhuza, who retreated with his people into Swaziland, where a descendant of the same name reigns to this day. Dingiswayo now marched against Zwide. He was defeated and killed. Shaka rallied the dead king's subjects and defeated Zwide on the banks of the Mhlatuze River (1818).

For ten years, until reaction against his cruelty provoked his murder, Shaka Zulu (*c.*1787–1828) commanded a mighty military force such as Africa had never seen. To Dingiswayo's age-regiment concept he added ferocious discipline – warriors, forced to be celibate, were executed on the least sign of cowardice – and new military tactics which made the Zulus formidable, even against white troops with rifles, down to their ultimate defeat by the British in 1879. Formerly, Nguni warriors had gone into battle with a supply of assegais which they threw at the enemy till they ran out. Shaka's troops advanced behind shields in close formation, wielding short stabbing spears for close combat. Their formation combined the 'chest', the main marching body, with 'horns' on each flank curving outward and forward to enclose the foe before the 'chest' advanced and destroyed them.

Defeated rivals and over-ambitious underlings naturally sought to put distance between themselves and Shaka. Turmoil followed in the interior, exacerbated by the arrival of Boers to compete for grazing grounds. Mosheshwe (*c.*1786–1870) rallied people who became the Basotho in his mountain fastness and maintained his kingdom (now independent Lesotho) by sage diplomacy, but even the mighty Mzilikazi (*c.*1770–1868), one of Shaka's generals, who moved away after incurring the king's wrath, and dominated the Transvaal with his Ndebele forces had to decamp across the Limpopo after his defeat by Boer Voortrekkers in 1837.

Resettled near what is now Bulawayo in Zimbabwe, Mzilikazi was befriended by Robert Moffat, who headed the London Missionary Society base at Kuruman. He also entertained white hunters and businessmen. So we have vivid accounts of this immensely obese, genial, apparently heartless potentate, whose people in Matabeleland have preserved a language almost the same as Zulu down to our own day. The northern Nguni kings who had allied with Zwide against Shaka are, in contrast, shadowy personages, though Soshangane (*c.*1790–1868) conquered, in Mozambique, an area known as Gaza after one of his ancestors, repelled the last *impi* sent out by Shaka before his assassination, burnt down the Portuguese fort at Delagoa Bay (leaving only one survivor to tell the tale) and destroyed the first Boers to arrive. His realm would vanish though his people, known as 'Shangaans', would remain distinctive.

A garrulous white antiquarian, the Rev. A. T. Bryant, who thought Africans were jolly savage but very amusing, picked up a good story about the young Zwangendaba. Zwide decides to lead an expedition against this underling, the chief of a petty clan 'down seawards'. Zwangendaba defeats and captures him, then generously sends him home with a gift of cattle. The humiliated Zwide resolves on revenge, but on the morning when his army is assembled in the cattle-fold ready to march, his half-mother Nowana rushes into the enclosure, which is strictly taboo to women, and disrobes herself in front of the troops. Dismayed by this terrible omen, Zwide calls his expedition off . . . (Bryant, 162). Be that as it may, Zwangendaba was with Zwide's army when it was defeated by Shaka in 1818. Three years later, he thought it prudent to move north with his followers. By 1823, they were established, as greedy raiders, about 5,000-strong, on the lower Limpopo near Delagoa Bay, where they battered Portuguese troops sent out against them. The commandant of the fort and his soldiers, nevertheless, bought the Ngoni's spoil of cattle and slaves through native traders.

Zwangendaba found himself in contestation with Soshangane in what is now Zimbabwe, moved off to conquer the Rozwi people who lived near present-day Bulawayo, and finally decided to cross the great Zambezi River.

Bryant found this amusing too. He claimed that Zwangendaba got a witch doctor to part the waters for him. But there is actually something awesome about the ageing warlord's crossing. By now his band, ravaged by fighting and disease, perhaps numbered 1,000, a mixture of his surviving original clansmen with Swazis who were fellow-Nguni speakers and residues of numerous unrelated populations they had conquered and intermarried with on their way. In their heads, and perhaps in their order of march, they carried a state organisation ready to put into place wherever they settled. At the top of the hierarchy was the royal family. Beneath them under regional governors and lieutenants, the followers were organised in Royal villages assigned to the king's relatives, and communal villages. The villages, it has been said, were 'like ships of different sizes and importance that preserve a loose formation while the fleet sails from place to place' (Barnes, 196–97).

That the sun was in eclipse on the day when Zwangendaba forded the Zambezi dates the event: 20 November 1835. Still Zwangendaba moved north, to present-day Tanzania. After he died in 1845, some of his followers forayed as far as Lake Victoria Nyanza, long before the Englishman Speke claimed to have 'discovered it'. At this point, following the *Mfecane*, Nguni people with the same clan, praise and family names were scattered over a vast area from this far-north to the Eastern Cape in the south. 'Jele, the clan name of . . . Zwangendaba is also the praise name (in the form Jeli) of the famous Jabavu family, long linked with Fort Hare [in Cape Colony].' Still fighting with 'Zulu' ferocity, the raiding Ngoni were much feared in regions by Lake Tanganyika. As Arab traders told the English traveller Richard Burton (1858) they moved 'in large bodies, with their cattle and baggage placed on bullocks, and their wealth in brass twisted round the horns' (Wilson and Thompson, 99–100).

Before and after Zwangendaba's death, bands peeled off, so that around a dozen small Ngoni kingdoms – all with the same authoritarian, ultra-patriarchal, structure – were ultimately settled in East Central Africa, all destined to succumb to rule by British, Portuguese or Germans by the end of the century. From Zwangendaba's little band, nearly a quarter of a million claimed descent in the Nyasaland (now Malawi) census of 1926, around 60,000 in the Northern Rhodesia (Zambia) census of 1938. Such numbers tended to dwindle in later censuses, as some descendants of people conquered by the Ngoni chose to emphasise their different heredities. Meanwhile, the Nguni language had disappeared except, in some places, for ceremonial purposes. But Zwangendaba, rallying men and women again and again, driving through the belt where Boer trekkers halted because the tsetse fly ruled, fatal to their beasts, driving on, on, on, had transformed the ethnography, history and political geography of one-third of his huge continent.

J. M. Barnes, 'The Fort Jameson Ngoni', in Elizabeth Colson and Max Gluckman, eds, Seven Tribes of Central Africa, *1951; A. T. Bryant,* Olden Times in Zululand and Natal, *1929; W. J. de Kock, ed.,* Dictionary of South African Biography, *(Pretoria) 1968 and on; Noel Mostert,* Frontiers: The Epic of South Africa's Creation . . . *1992; Mary Tew,* Peoples of the Lake Nyasa Region, *1950; Monica Wilson and Leonard Thompson, eds,* The Oxford History of South Africa, *vol. 1 (Oxford) 1969*

INDEX

N.B. Dear Reader: there are a great many proper names in this book. To have indexed all of them would have entailed cutting an entry or two and leaving some of their owners out of the text. When it looked as if there would be less space for an index than there is, Alasdair Gray suggested to me that I should confine it to '-isms'. As it is, I have dropped in some -isms and other abstract and general categories, also some events, amid a selection of names which omits most geographical designations, but includes the human, divine and beastly ones which figure most prominently, as well as unusual ones which take my fancy. I hope that if you are frustrated in some particular search you will nevertheless be intrigued by oddities and interconnections and might pursue them back into the text, where you will, I hope find instruction, amusement, or indeed both at once.

A NOTE ON THE AUTHOR

Angus Calder (*b.*1942) took a first degree in English at Cambridge and D.Phil. in Social Studies at Sussex. He taught in several African universities, but mostly for the Open University in Scotland, from which he retired, as Reader in Cultural Studies, in 1993. He was co-editor of the *Journal of Commonwealth Literature* (1981–87) and amongst numerous journalistic forays collaborated with Alasdair Gray on a series of articles in the *Scotsman*. He is the author of the seminal social history *The People's War: Britain 1939–45* (1969), *Revolutionary Empire* (1981) and the poetry collection *Horace in Tolcross* (2000). His hobbies include cooking, shopping for food, music, cricket, curling and swimming in the sea.

A NOTE ON THE TYPE

The text of this book is set in Linotype Janson. The original types were cut in about 1690 by Nicholas Kis, a Hungarian working in Amsterdam. The face was misnamed after Anton Janson, a Dutchman who worked at the Ehrhardt Foundry in Leipzig, where the original Kis types were kept in the early eighteenth century. Monotype Ehrhardt is based on Janson. The original matrices survived in Germany and were acquired in 1919 by the Stempel Foundry. Herman Zapf used these originals to redesign some of the weights and sizes for Stempel. This Linotype version was designed to follow the original types under the direction of C. H. Griffith.